Snow White with the Red Hair

SORATA AKIDUKI

13

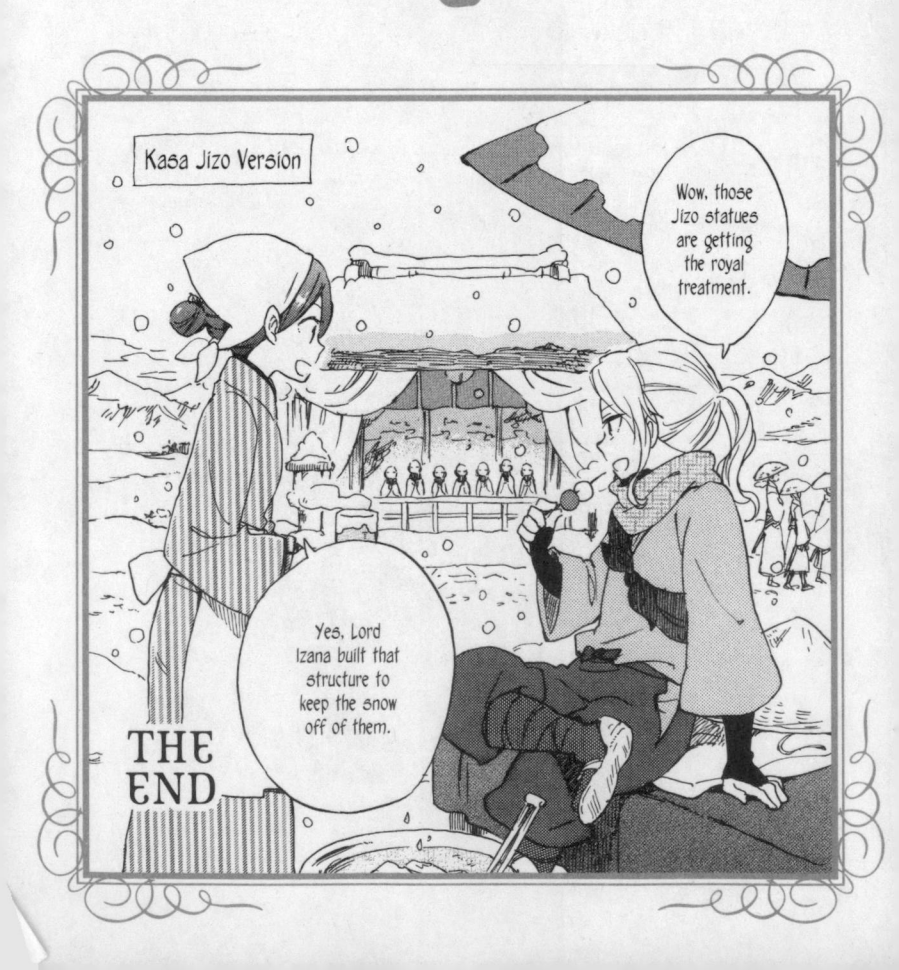

Wow, those Jizo statues are getting the royal treatment.
Kasa Jizo Version
Yes, Lord Izana built that structure to keep the snow off of them.
THE END

VOLUME 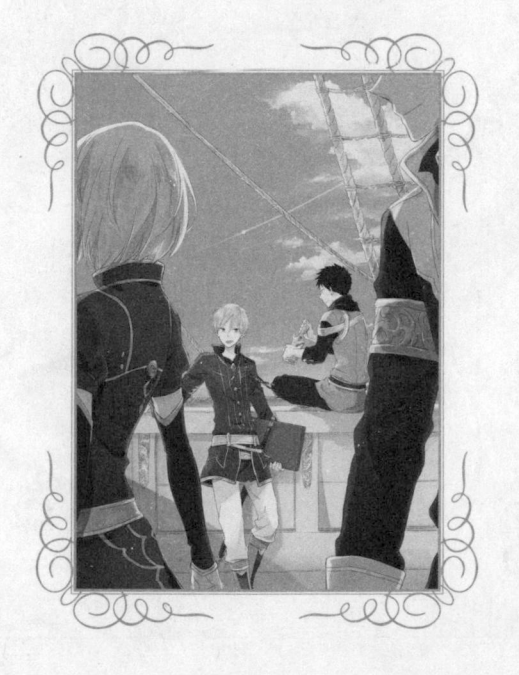13
TABLE of CONTENTS

Chapter 56 ············· 3

Chapter 57 ············· 31

Chapter 58 ············· 61

Chapter 59 ············· 90

Chapter 60 ············· 121

Special One-Shot: ············· 149
Beyond the Drops

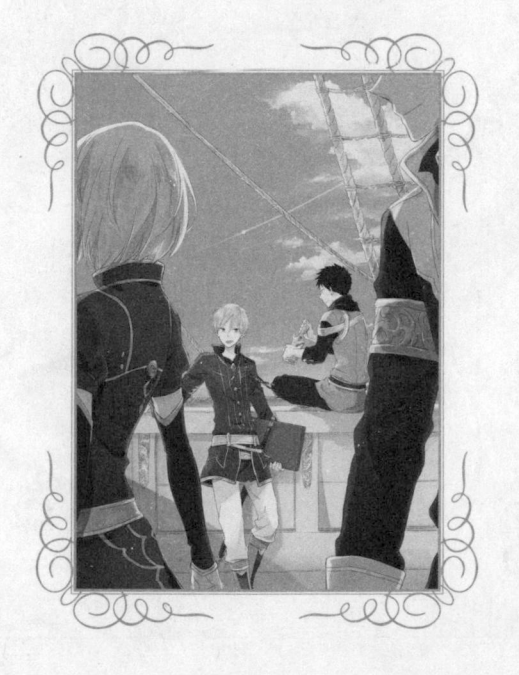

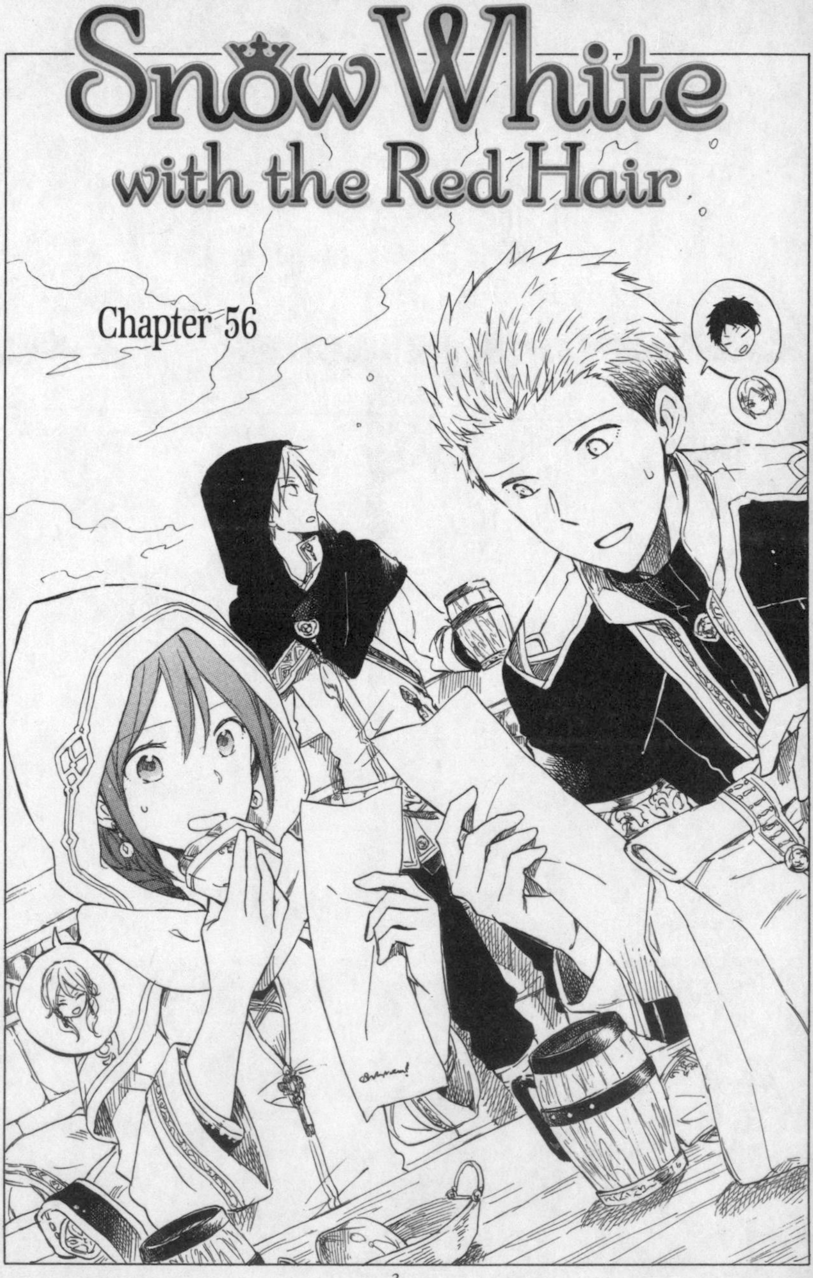
Snow White with the Red Hair
Chapter 56

SHUT

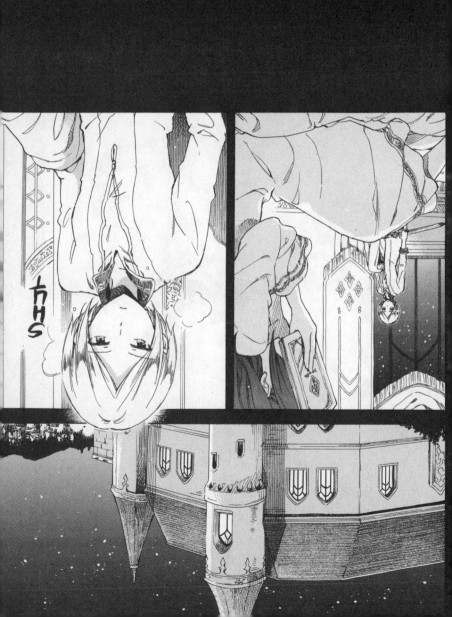

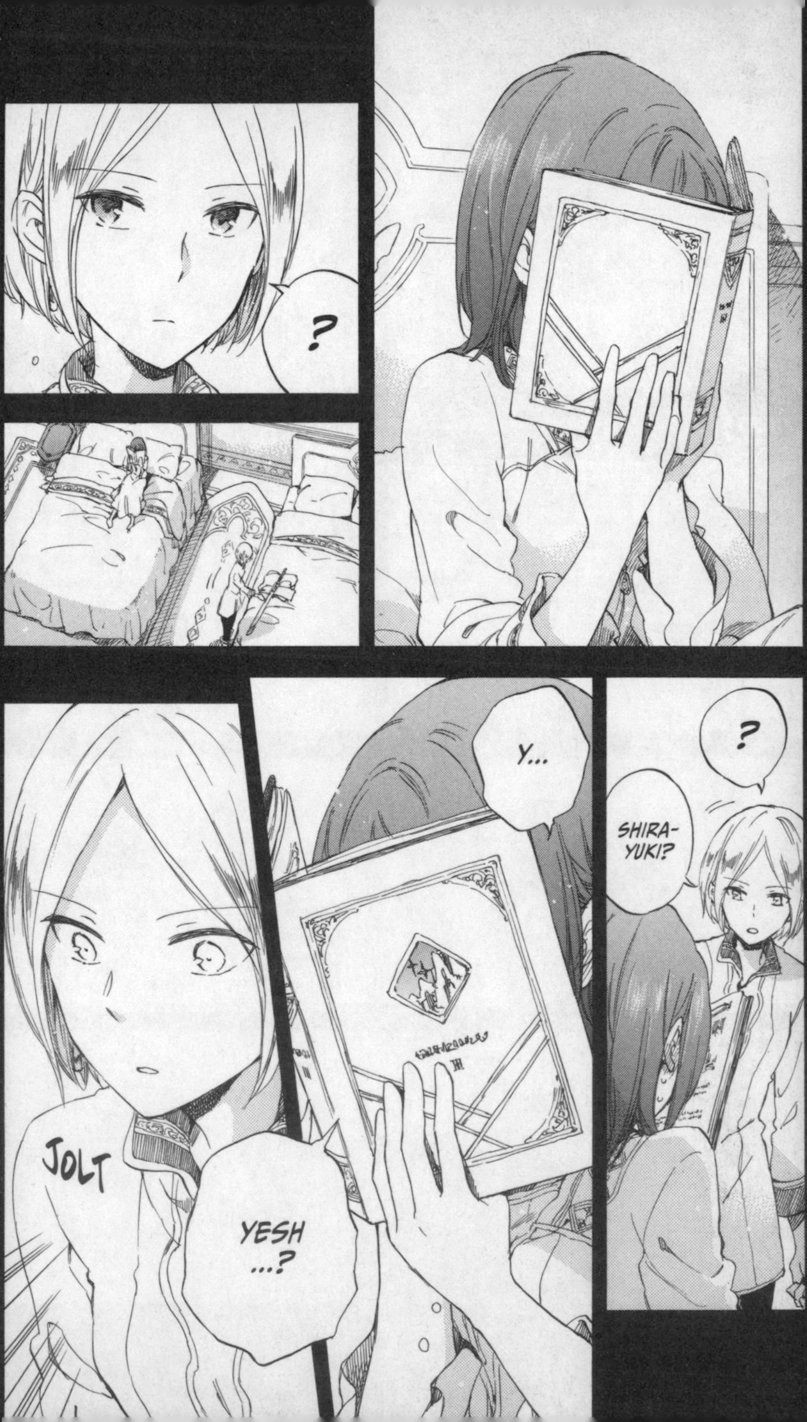
?
?
SHIRA-YUKI?
Y...
JOLT
YESH ...?

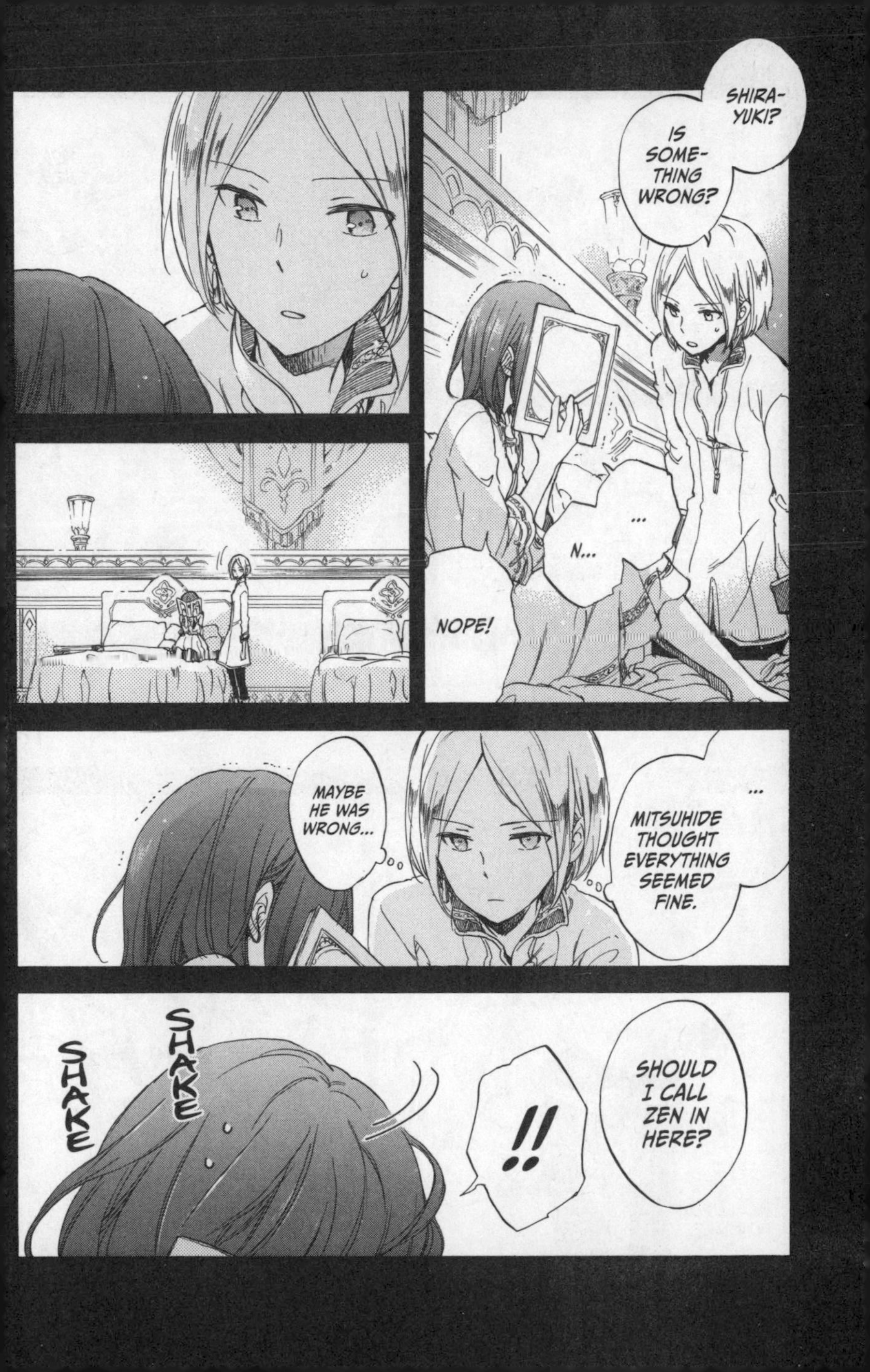
SHIRA-YUKI?
IS SOME-THING WRONG?
...
N...
NOPE!
...
MITSUHIDE THOUGHT EVERYTHING SEEMED FINE.
MAYBE HE WAS WRONG...
SHOULD I CALL ZEN IN HERE?
!!
SHAKE
SHAKE

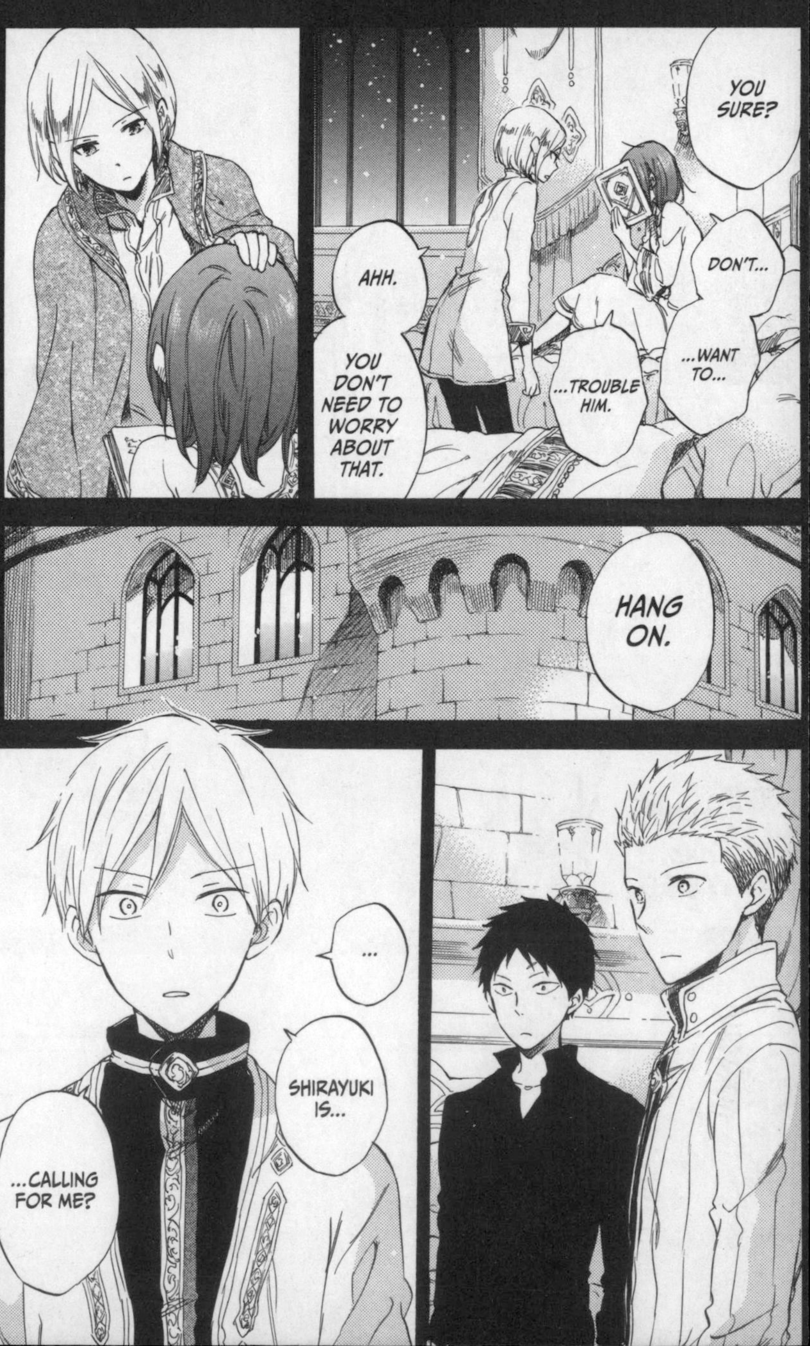
YOU SURE?
DON'T...
...WANT TO...
...TROUBLE HIM.
AHH.
YOU DON'T NEED TO WORRY ABOUT THAT.
HANG ON.
...
SHIRAYUKI IS...
...CALLING FOR ME?

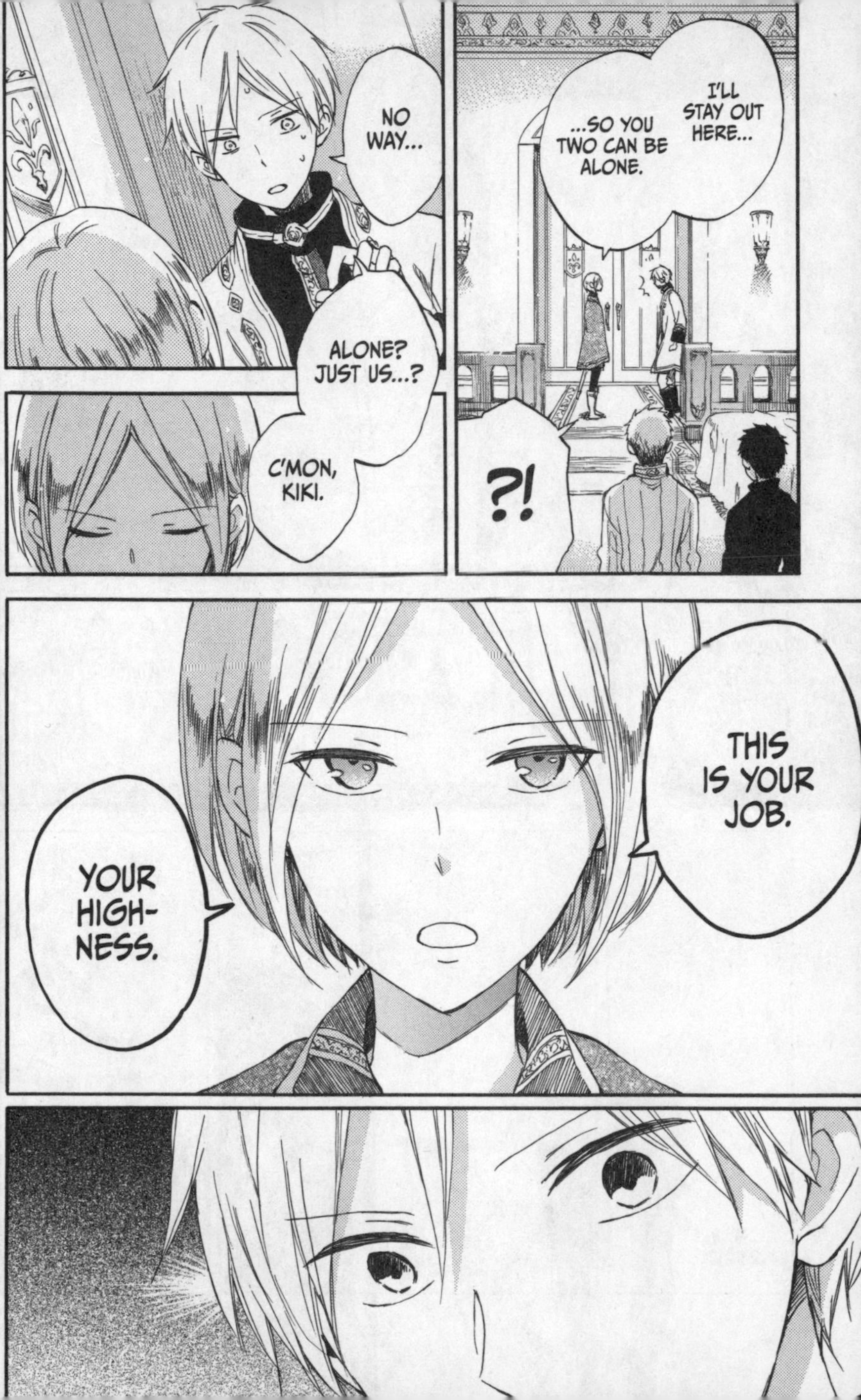
I'LL STAY OUT HERE...
...SO YOU TWO CAN BE ALONE.
?!
NO WAY...
ALONE? JUST US...?
C'MON, KIKI.
THIS IS YOUR JOB.
YOUR HIGHNESS.

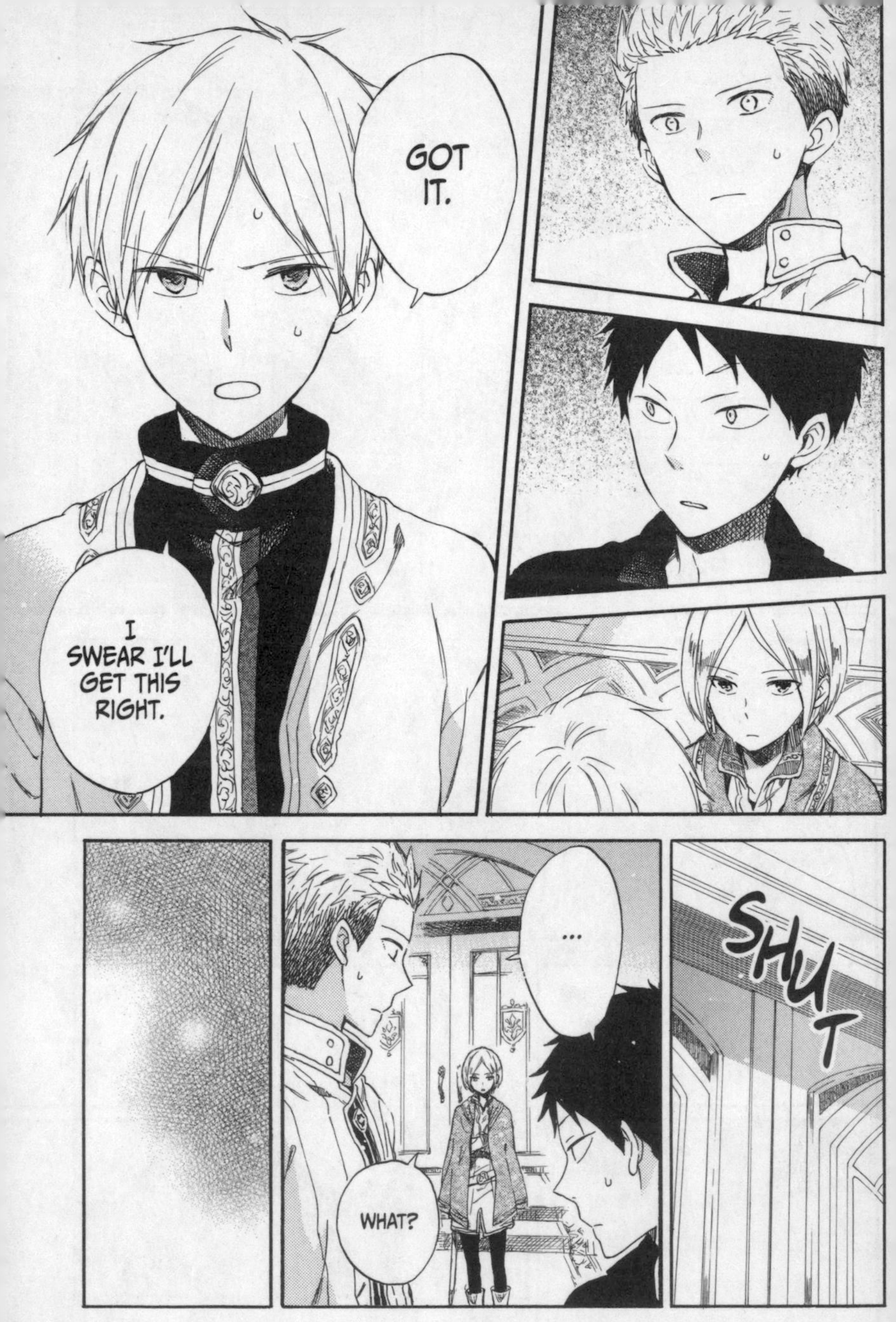
GOT IT.
I SWEAR I'LL GET THIS RIGHT.
SHUT
...
WHAT?

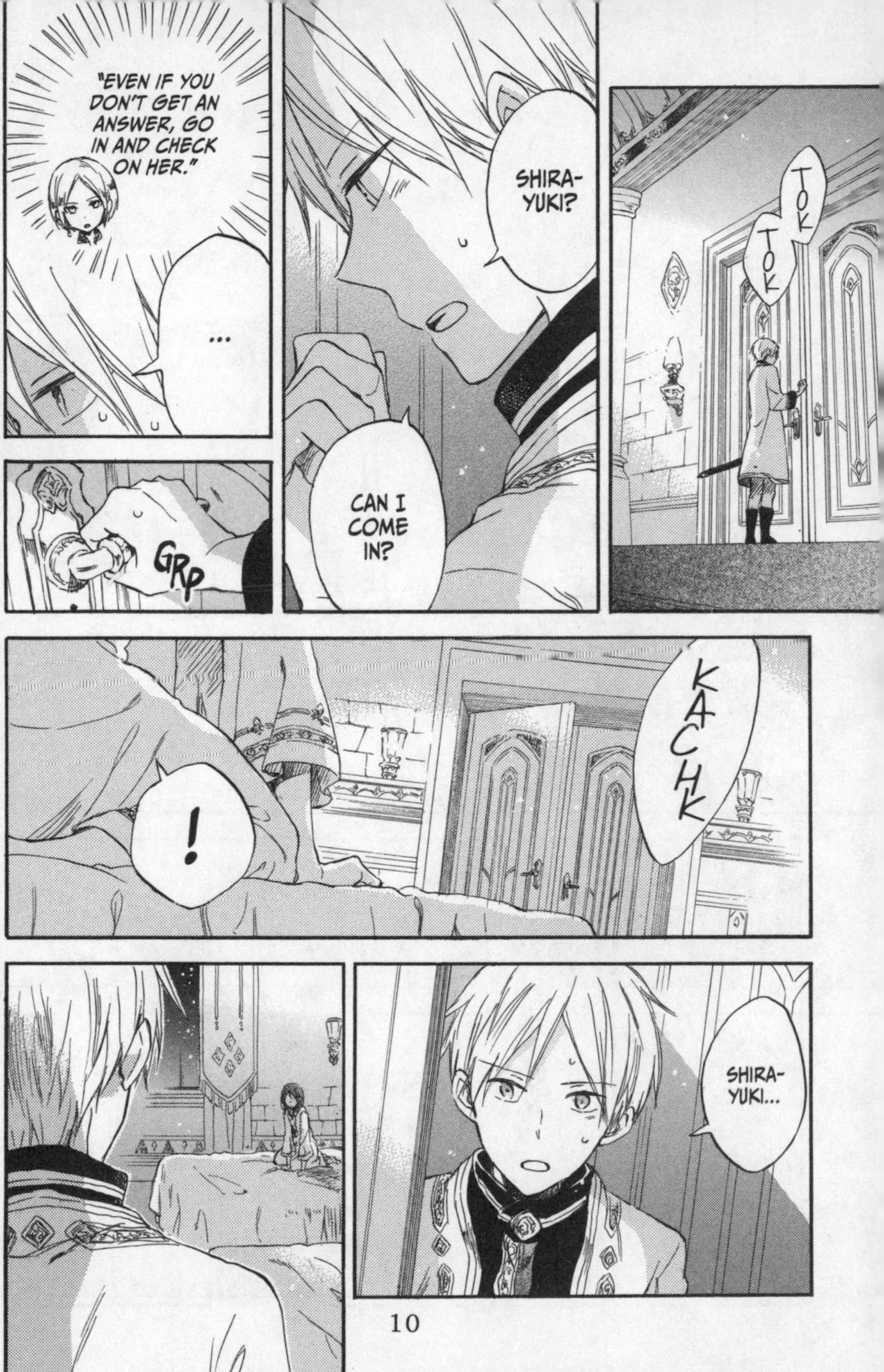
TOK
TOK
SHIRA-YUKI?
CAN I COME IN?
"EVEN IF YOU DON'T GET AN ANSWER, GO IN AND CHECK ON HER."
...
GRP
KACHK
!
SHIRA-YUKI...

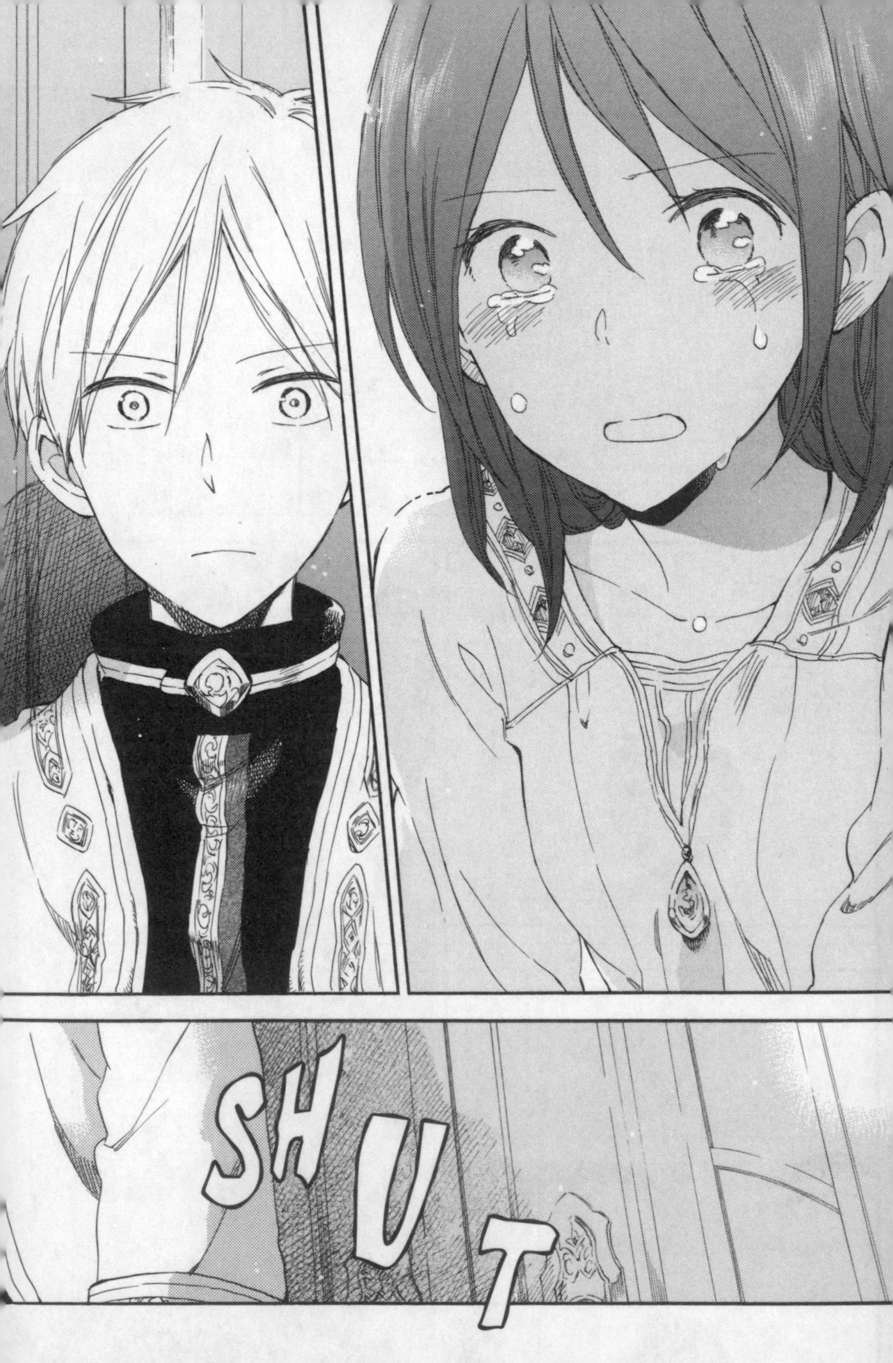
SHUT

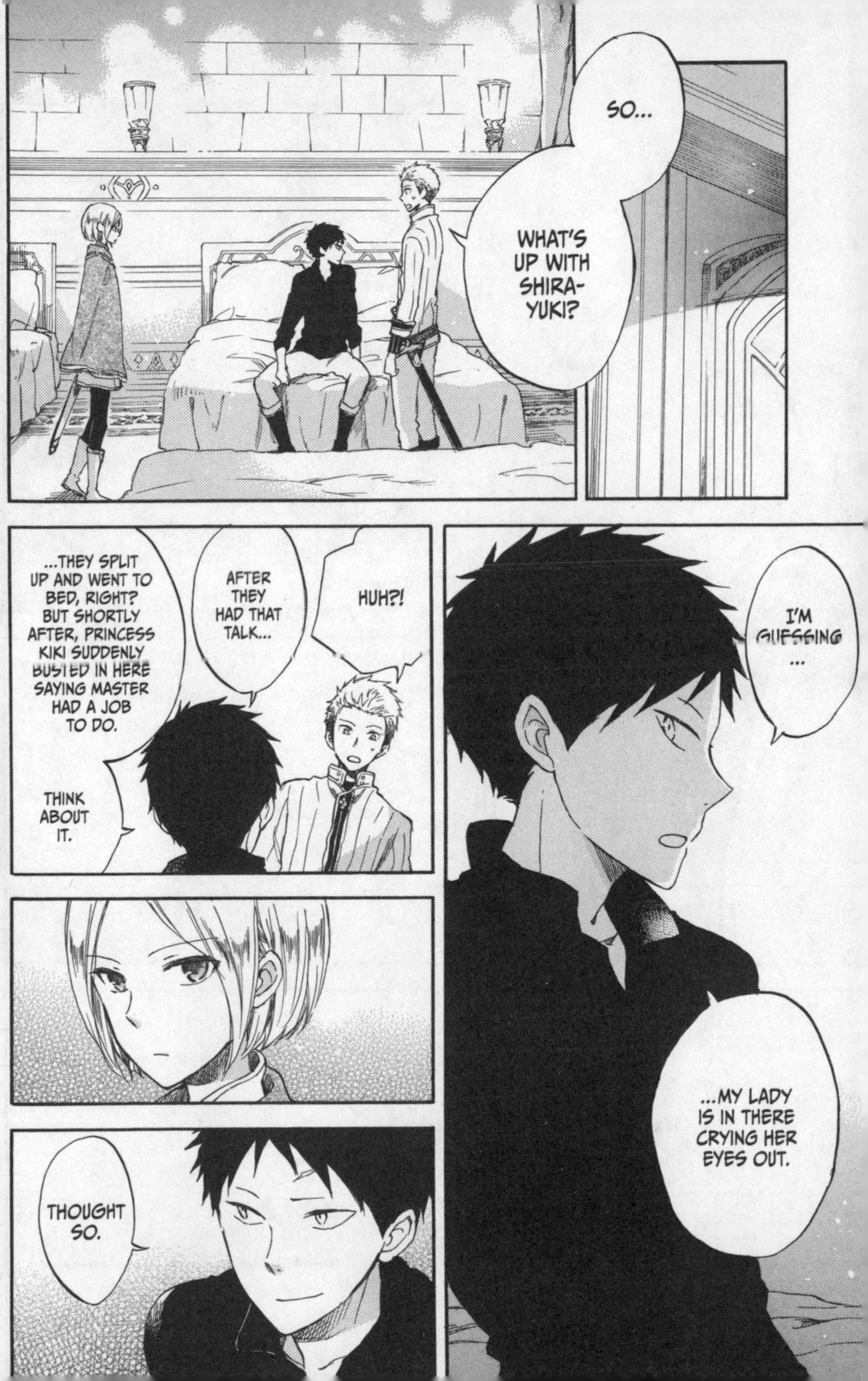
SO...
WHAT'S UP WITH SHIRA-YUKI?
I'M GUESSING ...
...MY LADY IS IN THERE CRYING HER EYES OUT.
HUH?!
AFTER THEY HAD THAT TALK...
...THEY SPLIT UP AND WENT TO BED, RIGHT? BUT SHORTLY AFTER, PRINCESS KIKI SUDDENLY BUSTED IN HERE SAYING MASTER HAD A JOB TO DO.
THINK ABOUT IT.
THOUGHT SO.

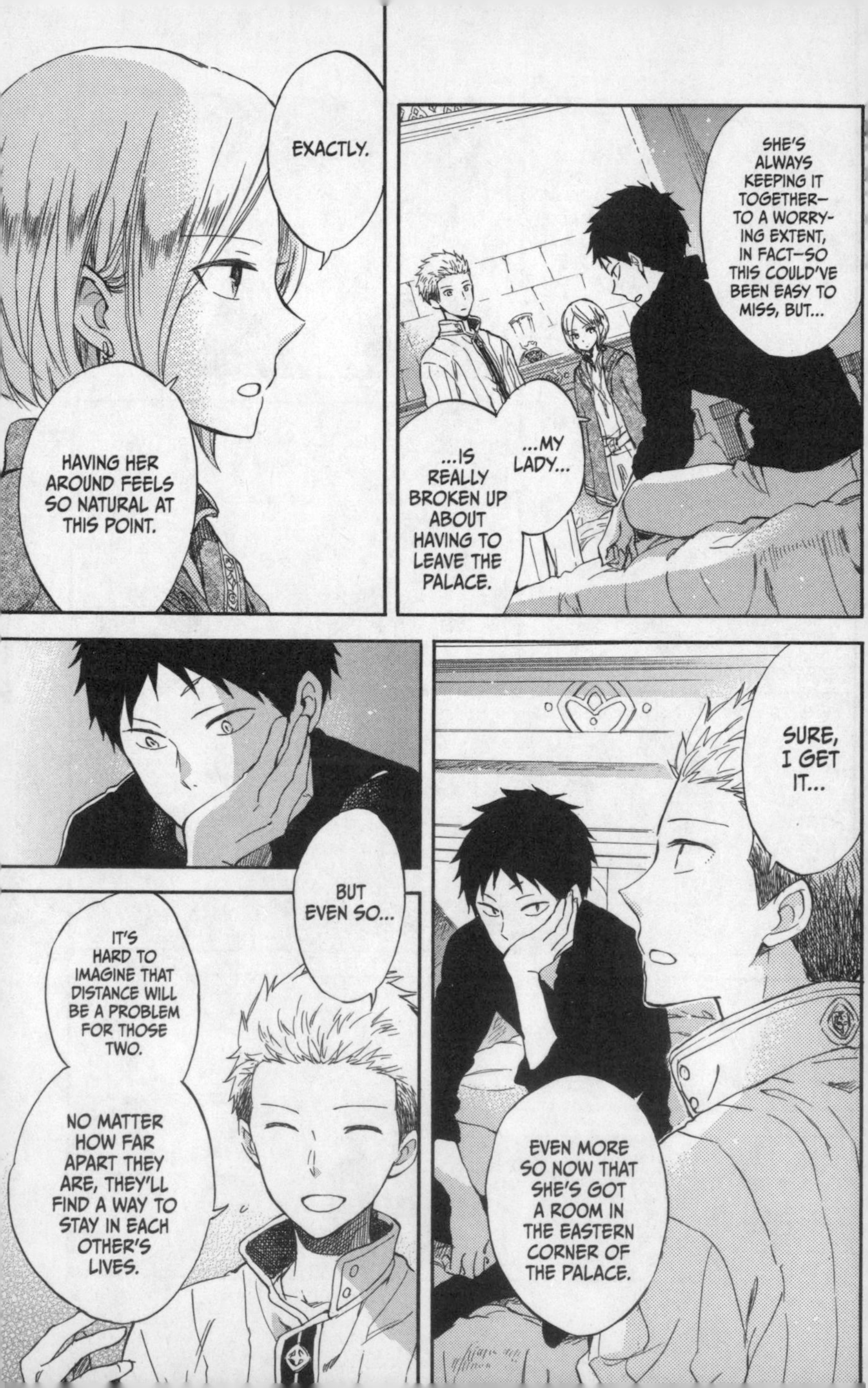
SHE'S ALWAYS KEEPING IT TOGETHER—TO A WORRYING EXTENT, IN FACT—SO THIS COULD'VE BEEN EASY TO MISS, BUT...
...MY LADY...
...IS REALLY BROKEN UP ABOUT HAVING TO LEAVE THE PALACE.
EXACTLY.
HAVING HER AROUND FEELS SO NATURAL AT THIS POINT.
SURE, I GET IT...
EVEN MORE SO NOW THAT SHE'S GOT A ROOM IN THE EASTERN CORNER OF THE PALACE.
BUT EVEN SO...
IT'S HARD TO IMAGINE THAT DISTANCE WILL BE A PROBLEM FOR THOSE TWO.
NO MATTER HOW FAR APART THEY ARE, THEY'LL FIND A WAY TO STAY IN EACH OTHER'S LIVES.

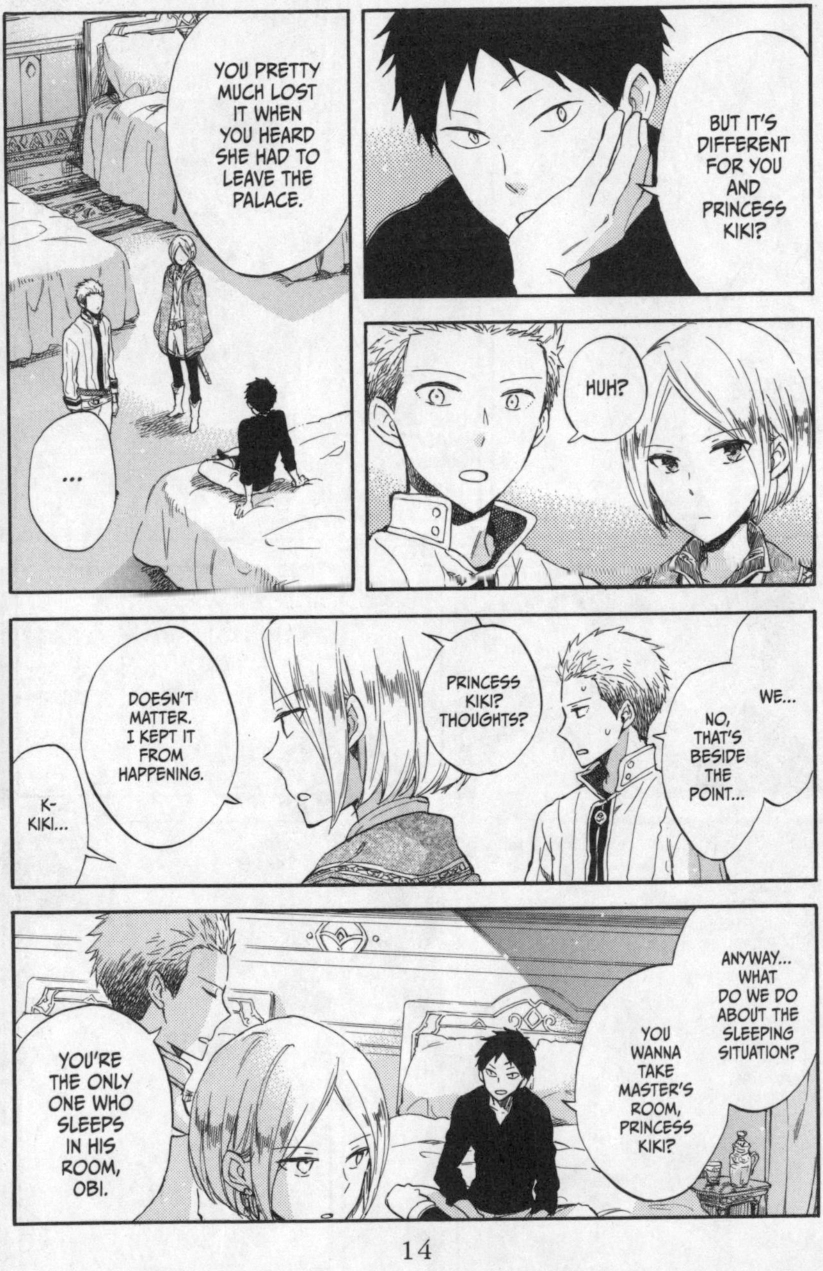
BUT IT'S DIFFERENT FOR YOU AND PRINCESS KIKI?
HUH?
YOU PRETTY MUCH LOST IT WHEN YOU HEARD SHE HAD TO LEAVE THE PALACE.
...
WE...
NO, THAT'S BESIDE THE POINT...
PRINCESS KIKI? THOUGHTS?
DOESN'T MATTER. I KEPT IT FROM HAPPENING.
K-KIKI...
ANYWAY... WHAT DO WE DO ABOUT THE SLEEPING SITUATION?
YOU WANNA TAKE MASTER'S ROOM, PRINCESS KIKI?
YOU'RE THE ONLY ONE WHO SLEEPS IN HIS ROOM, OBI.

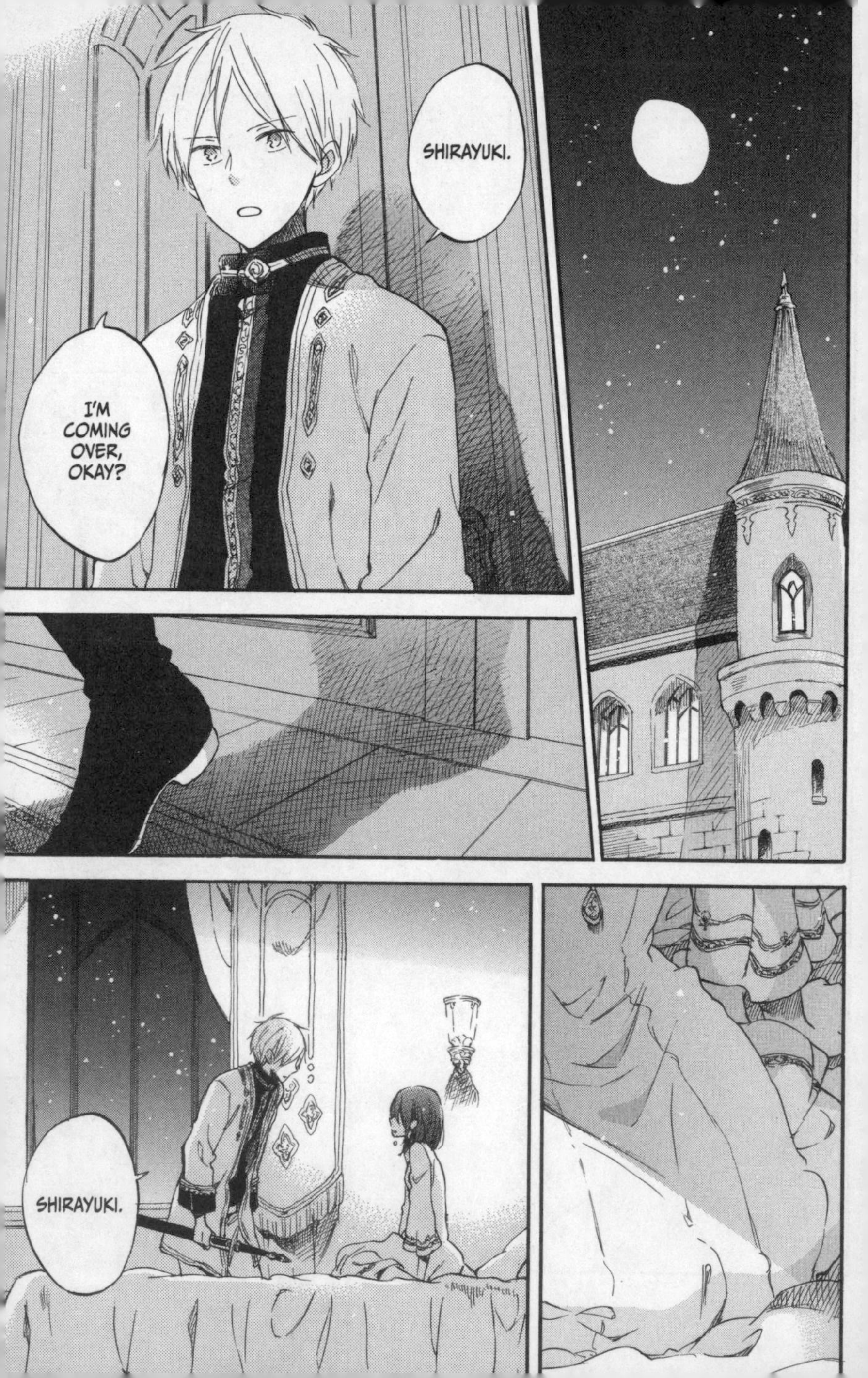
SHIRAYUKI.
I'M COMING OVER, OKAY?
SHIRAYUKI.

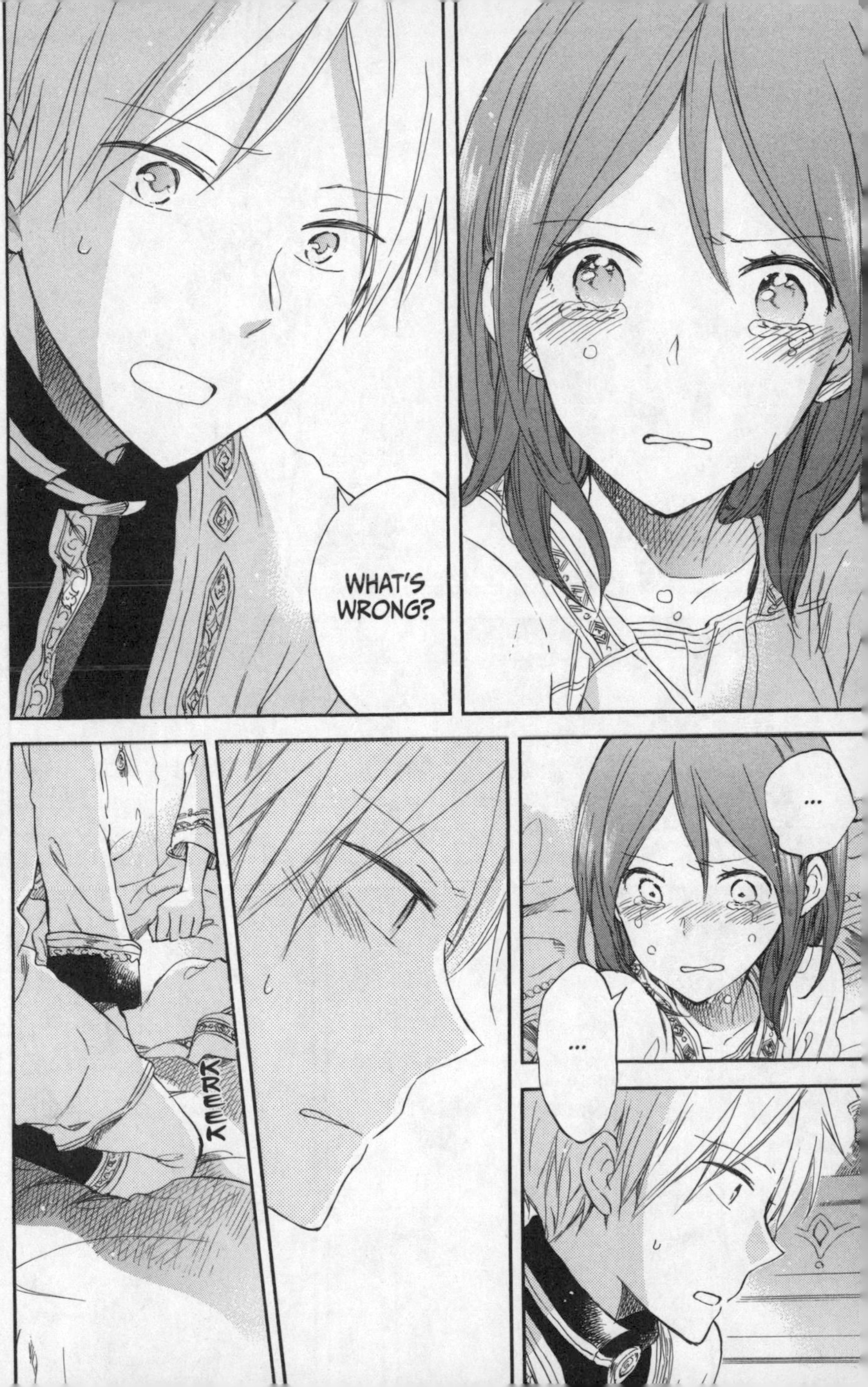
WHAT'S WRONG?
...
...
KREEK

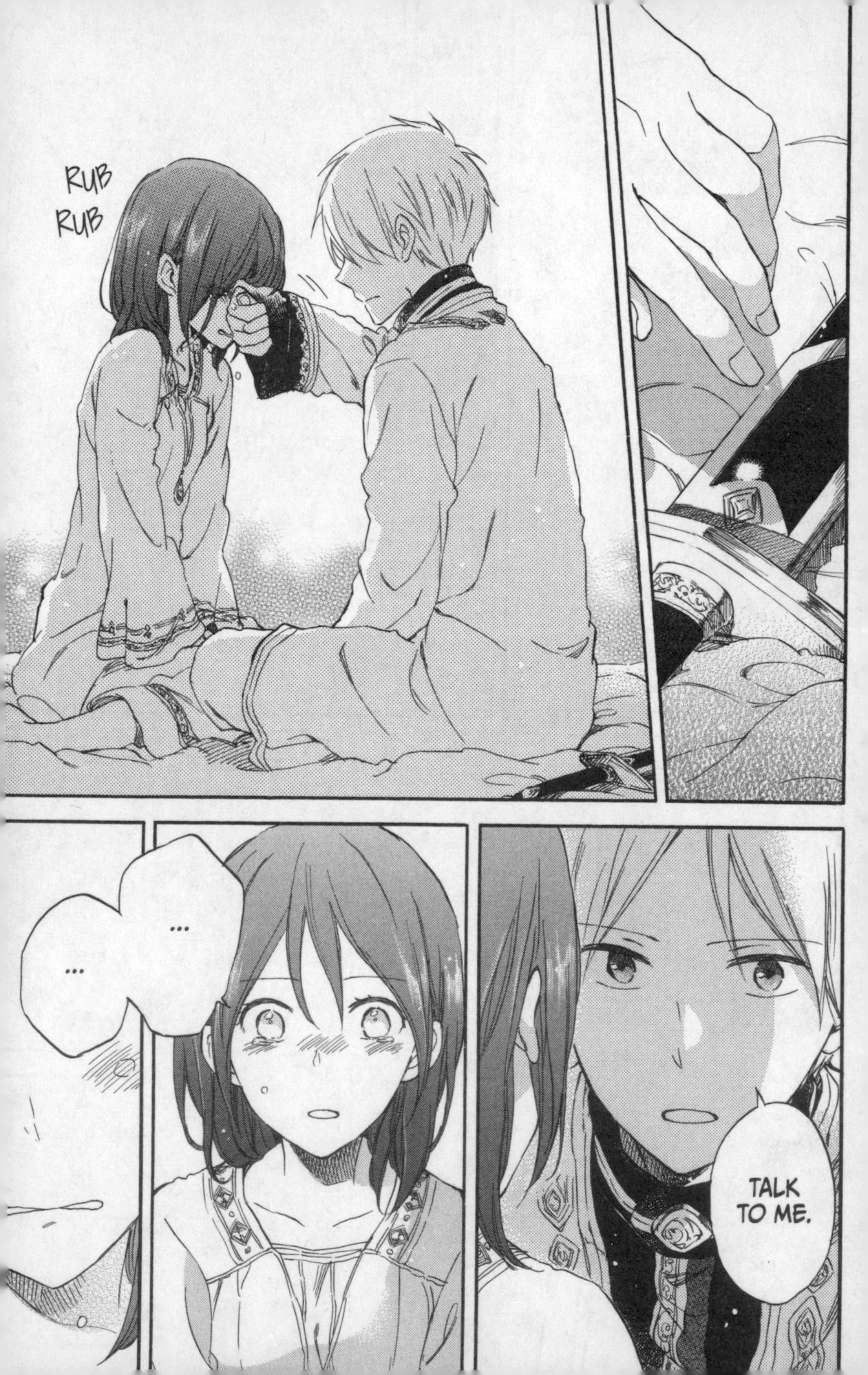
RUB
RUB
TALK TO ME.
...
...

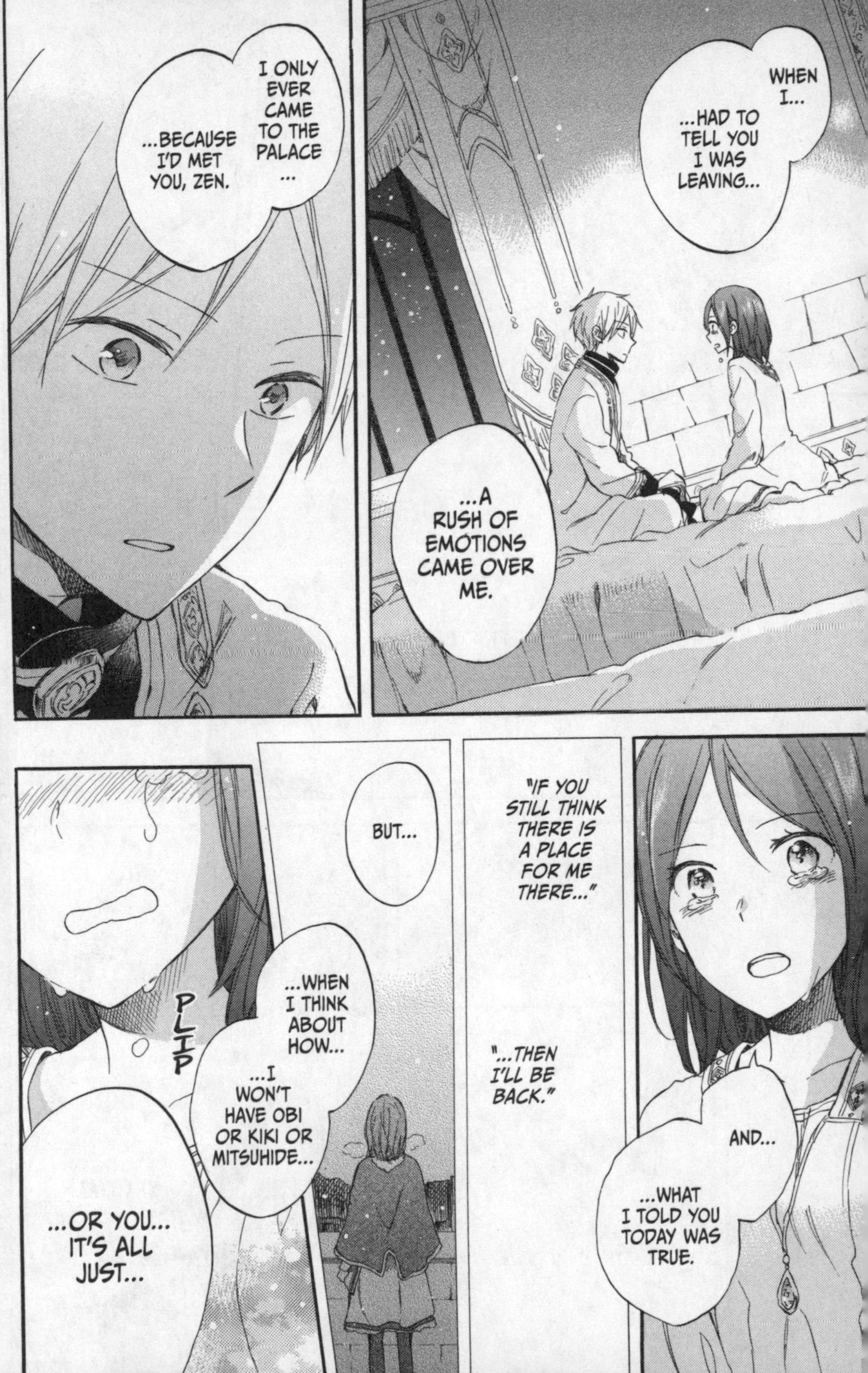
WHEN I...
...HAD TO TELL YOU I WAS LEAVING...
...A RUSH OF EMOTIONS CAME OVER ME.
I ONLY EVER CAME TO THE PALACE ...
...BECAUSE I'D MET YOU, ZEN.
AND...
...WHAT I TOLD YOU TODAY WAS TRUE.
"IF YOU STILL THINK THERE IS A PLACE FOR ME THERE..."
"...THEN I'LL BE BACK."
BUT...
...WHEN I THINK ABOUT HOW...
...I WON'T HAVE OBI OR KIKI OR MITSUHIDE...
PLIP
...OR YOU... IT'S ALL JUST...

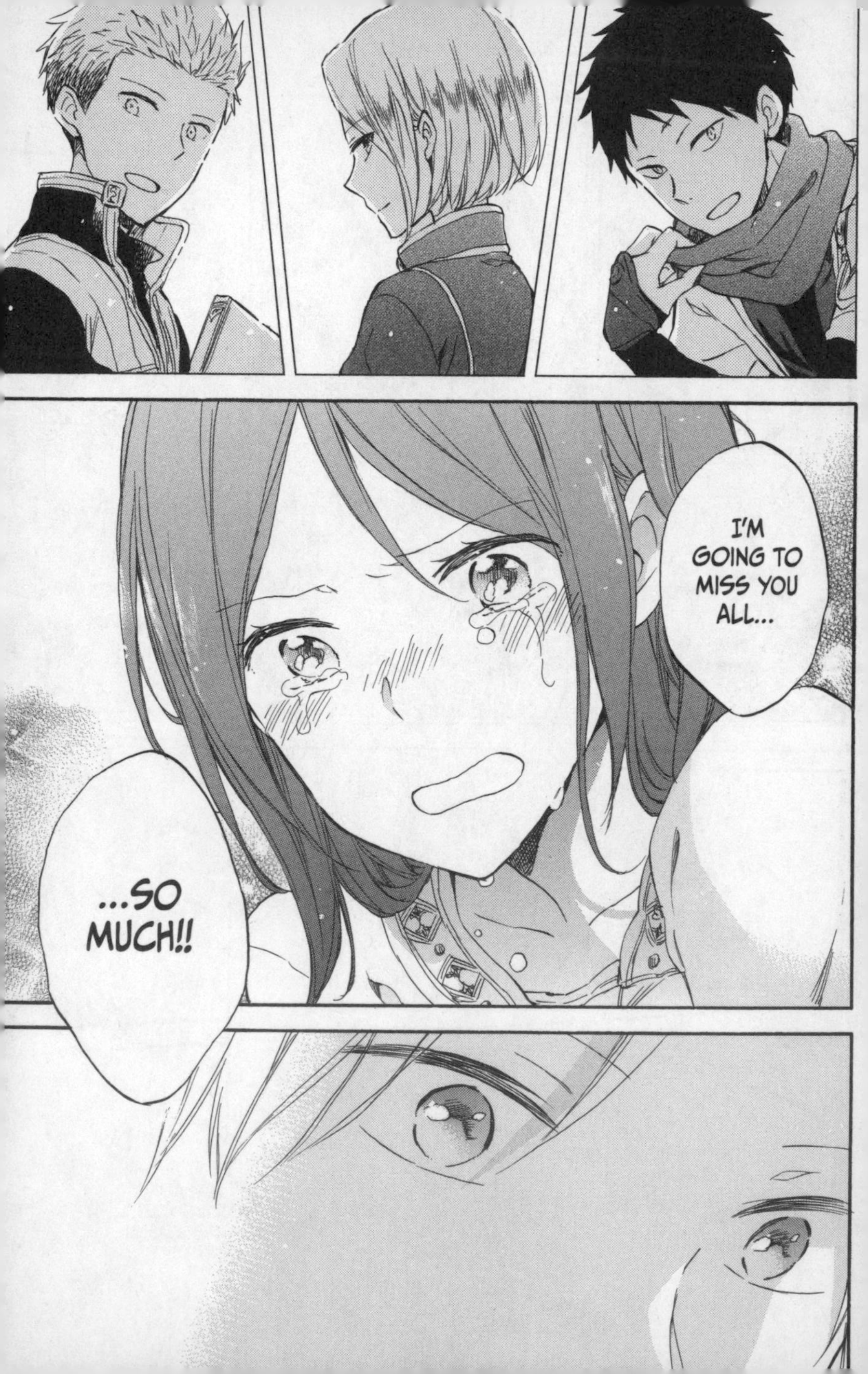
I'M GOING TO MISS YOU ALL...
...SO MUCH!!

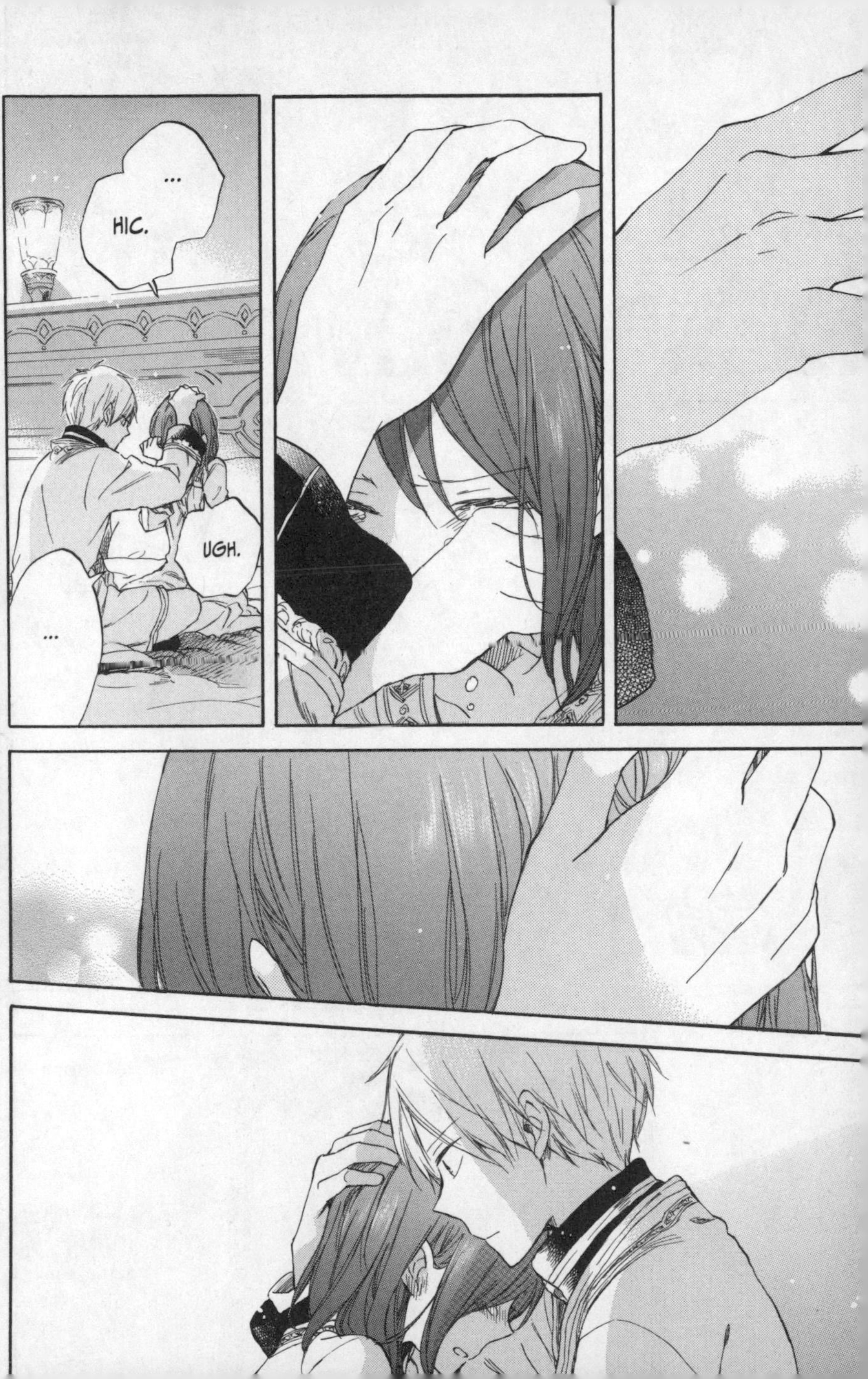
...
HIC.
UGH.
...

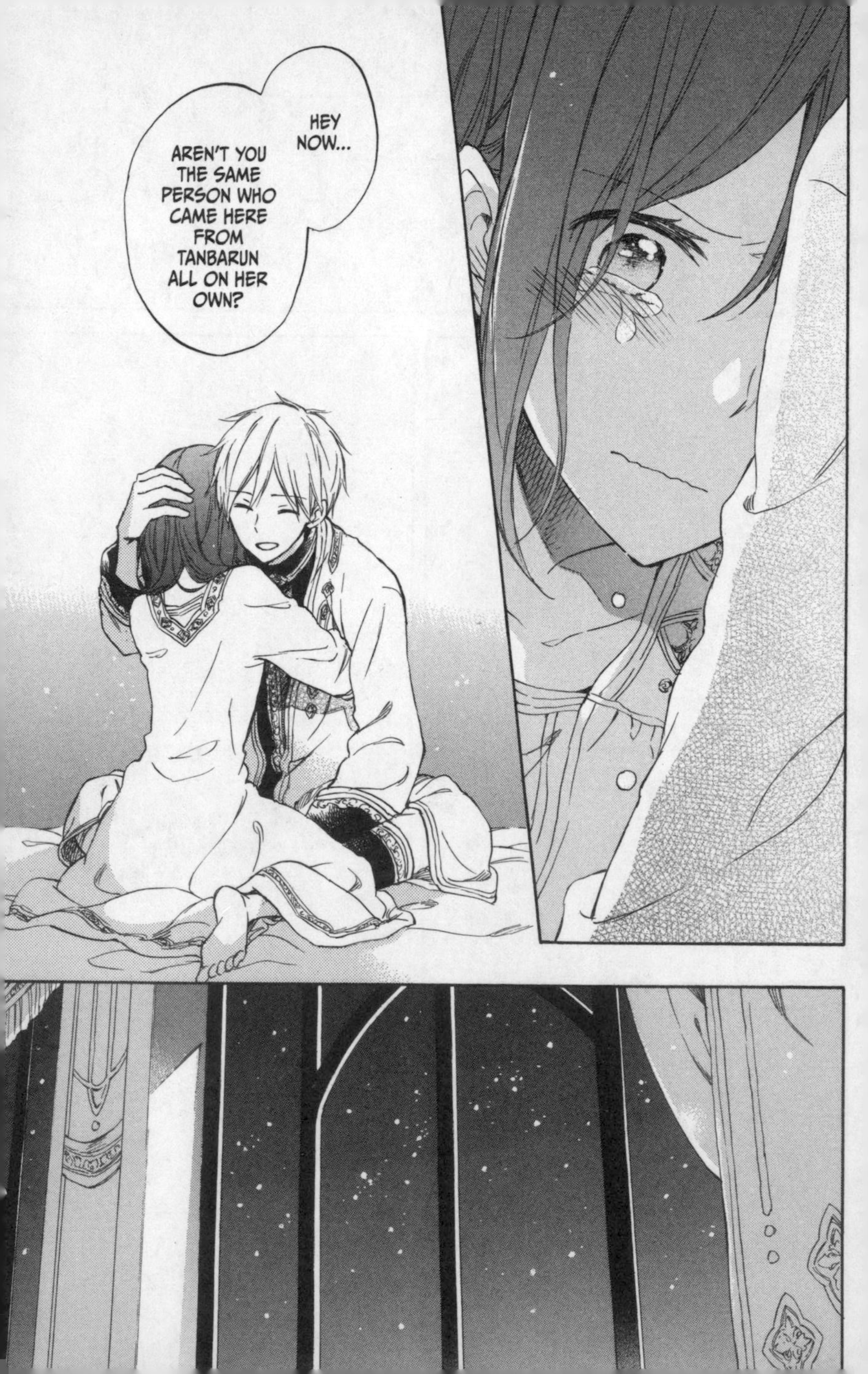
HEY NOW...
AREN'T YOU THE SAME PERSON WHO CAME HERE FROM TANBARUN ALL ON HER OWN?

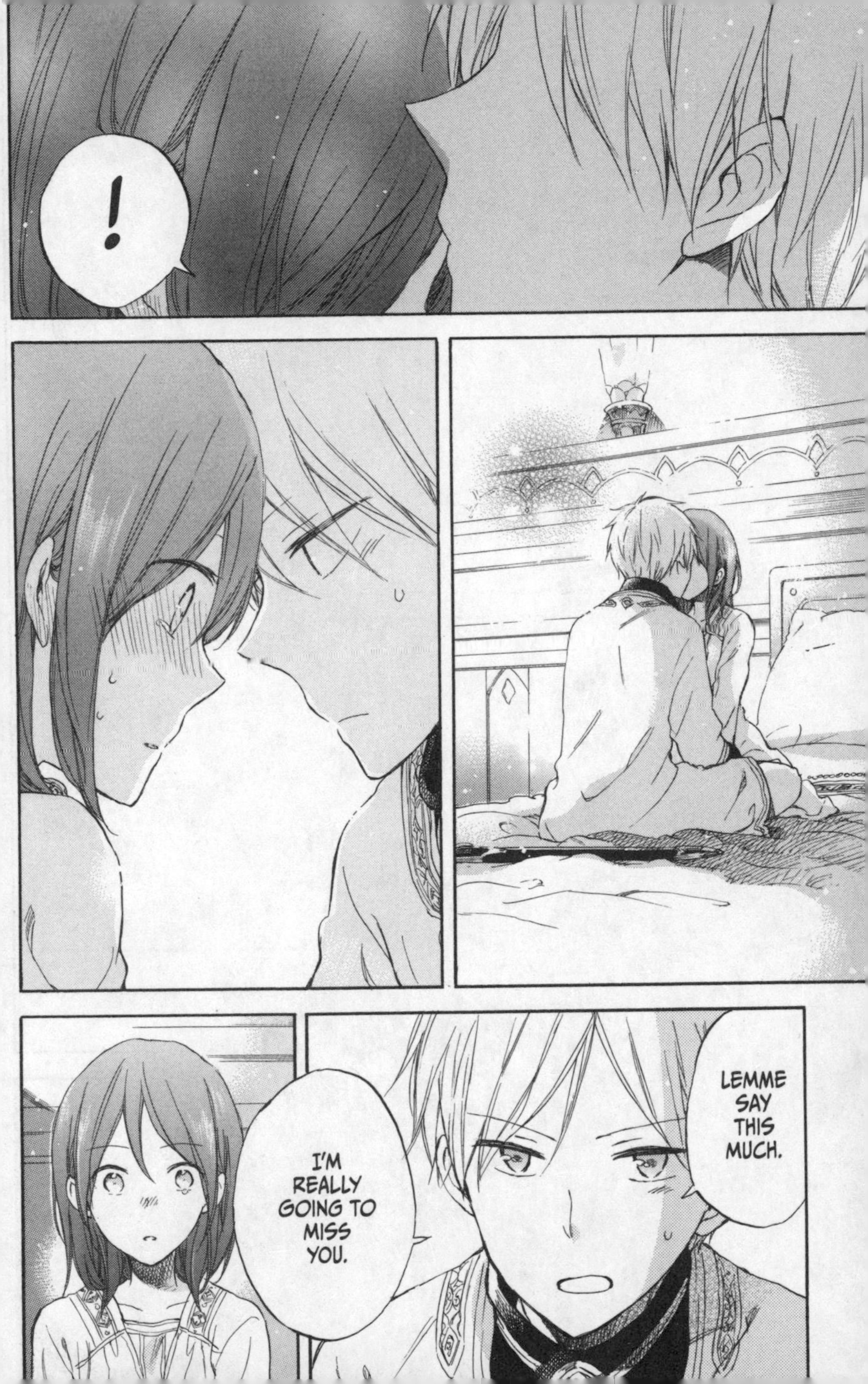
!
LEMME SAY THIS MUCH.
I'M REALLY GOING TO MISS YOU.

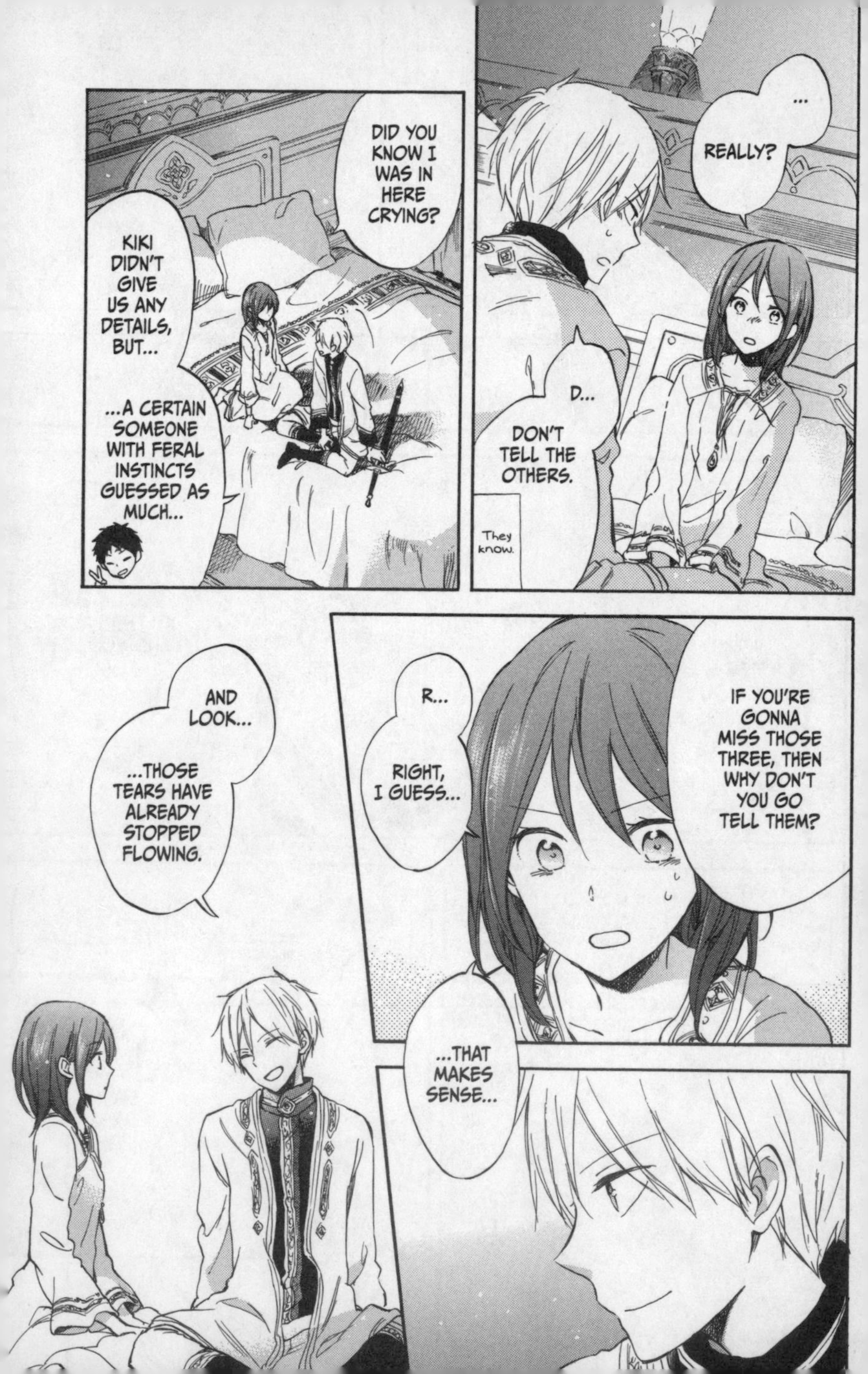
...
REALLY?
D...
DON'T TELL THE OTHERS.
They know.
DID YOU KNOW I WAS IN HERE CRYING?
KIKI DIDN'T GIVE US ANY DETAILS, BUT...
...A CERTAIN SOMEONE WITH FERAL INSTINCTS GUESSED AS MUCH...
IF YOU'RE GONNA MISS THOSE THREE, THEN WHY DON'T YOU GO TELL THEM?
R...
RIGHT, I GUESS...
...THAT MAKES SENSE...
AND LOOK...
...THOSE TEARS HAVE ALREADY STOPPED FLOWING.

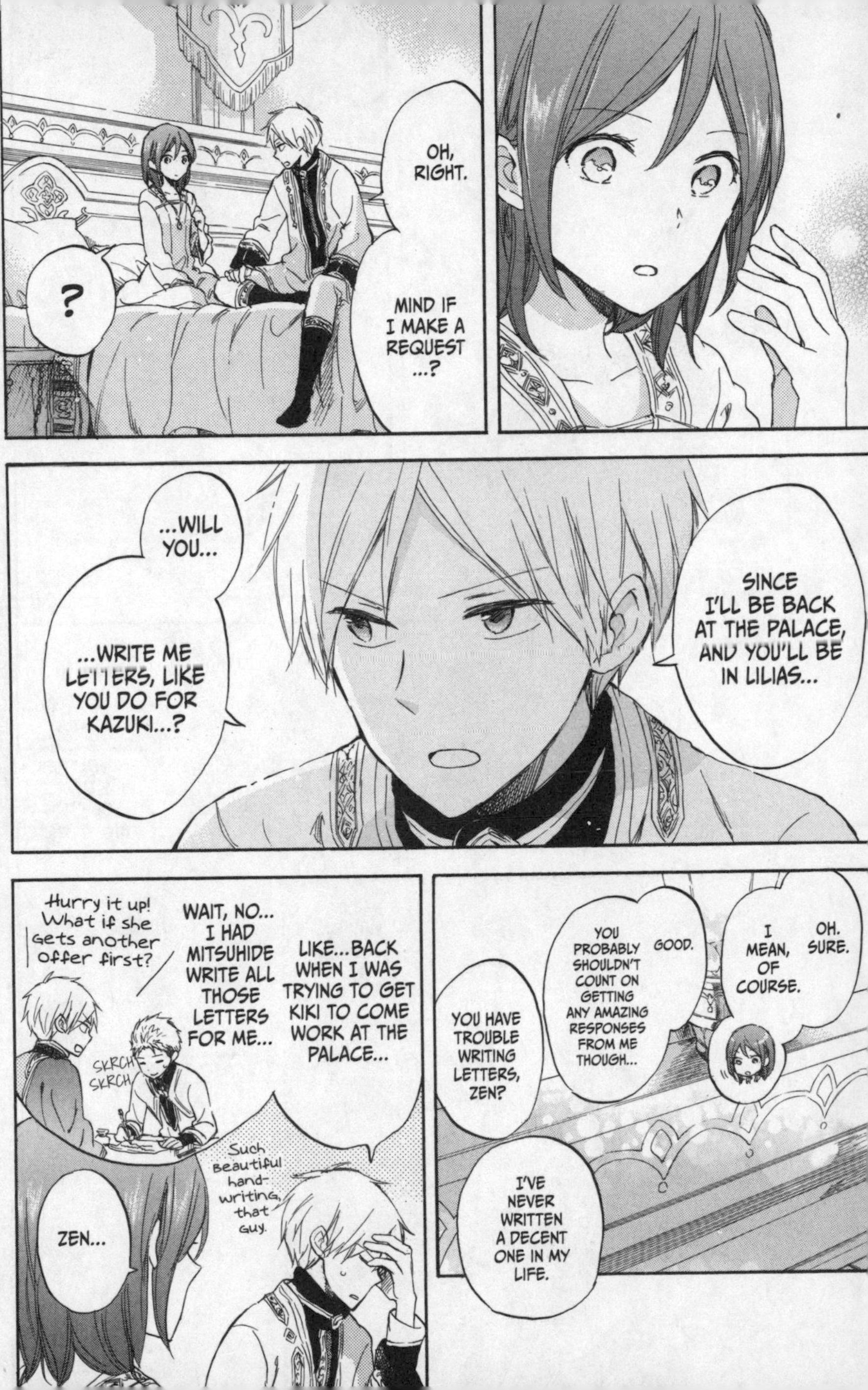
OH, RIGHT.
MIND IF I MAKE A REQUEST ...?
?
SINCE I'LL BE BACK AT THE PALACE, AND YOU'LL BE IN LILIAS...
...WILL YOU...
...WRITE ME LETTERS, LIKE YOU DO FOR KAZUKI...?
OH. SURE.
I MEAN, OF COURSE.
GOOD.
YOU PROBABLY SHOULDN'T COUNT ON GETTING ANY AMAZING RESPONSES FROM ME THOUGH...
YOU HAVE TROUBLE WRITING LETTERS, ZEN?
I'VE NEVER WRITTEN A DECENT ONE IN MY LIFE.
LIKE...BACK WHEN I WAS TRYING TO GET KIKI TO COME WORK AT THE PALACE...
WAIT, NO... I HAD MITSUHIDE WRITE ALL THOSE LETTERS FOR ME...
Hurry it up! What if she gets another offer first?
SKRCH SKRCH
Such beautiful hand-writing, that guy.
ZEN...

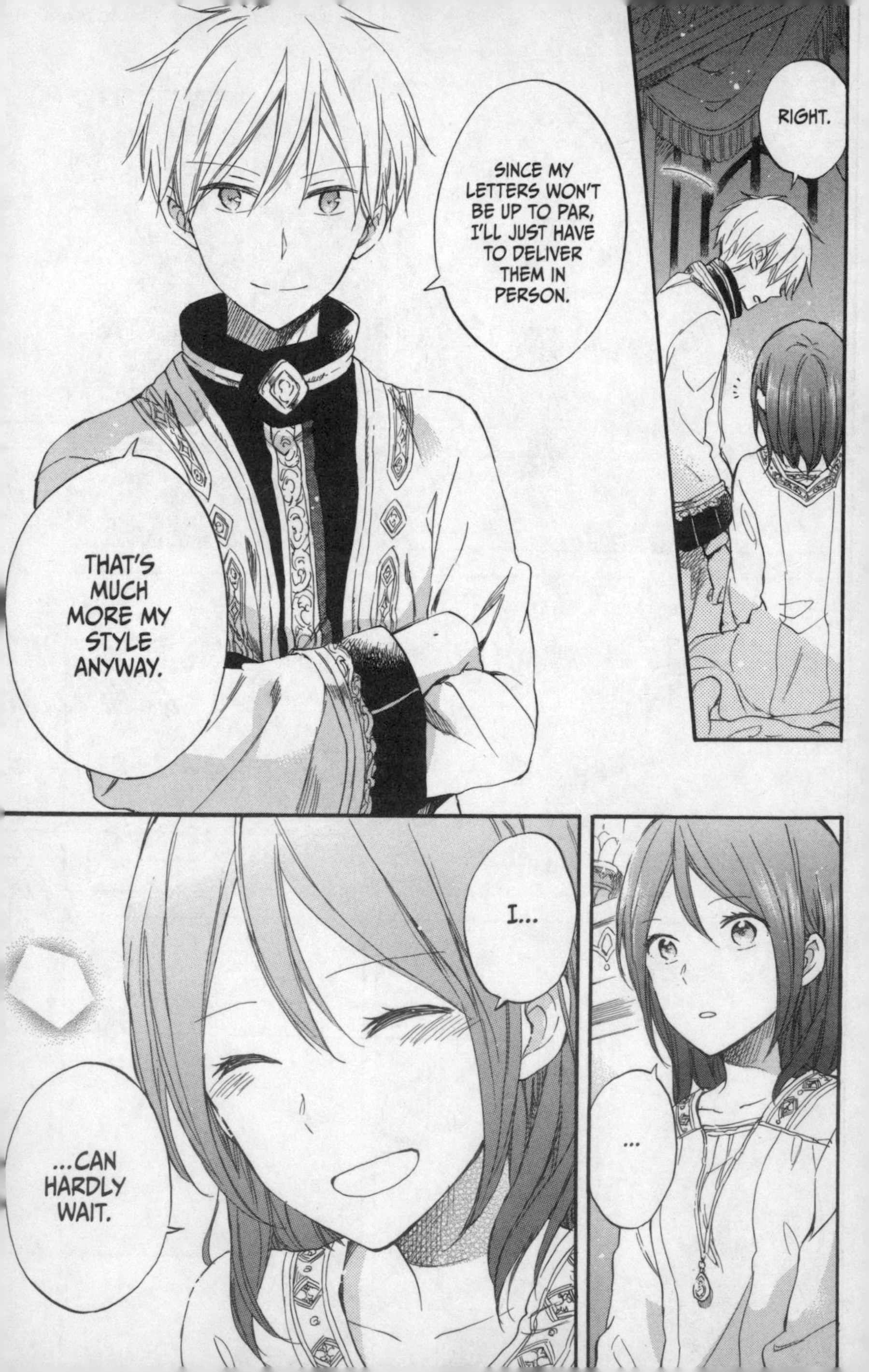
RIGHT.
SINCE MY LETTERS WON'T BE UP TO PAR, I'LL JUST HAVE TO DELIVER THEM IN PERSON.
THAT'S MUCH MORE MY STYLE ANYWAY.
...
I...
...CAN HARDLY WAIT.

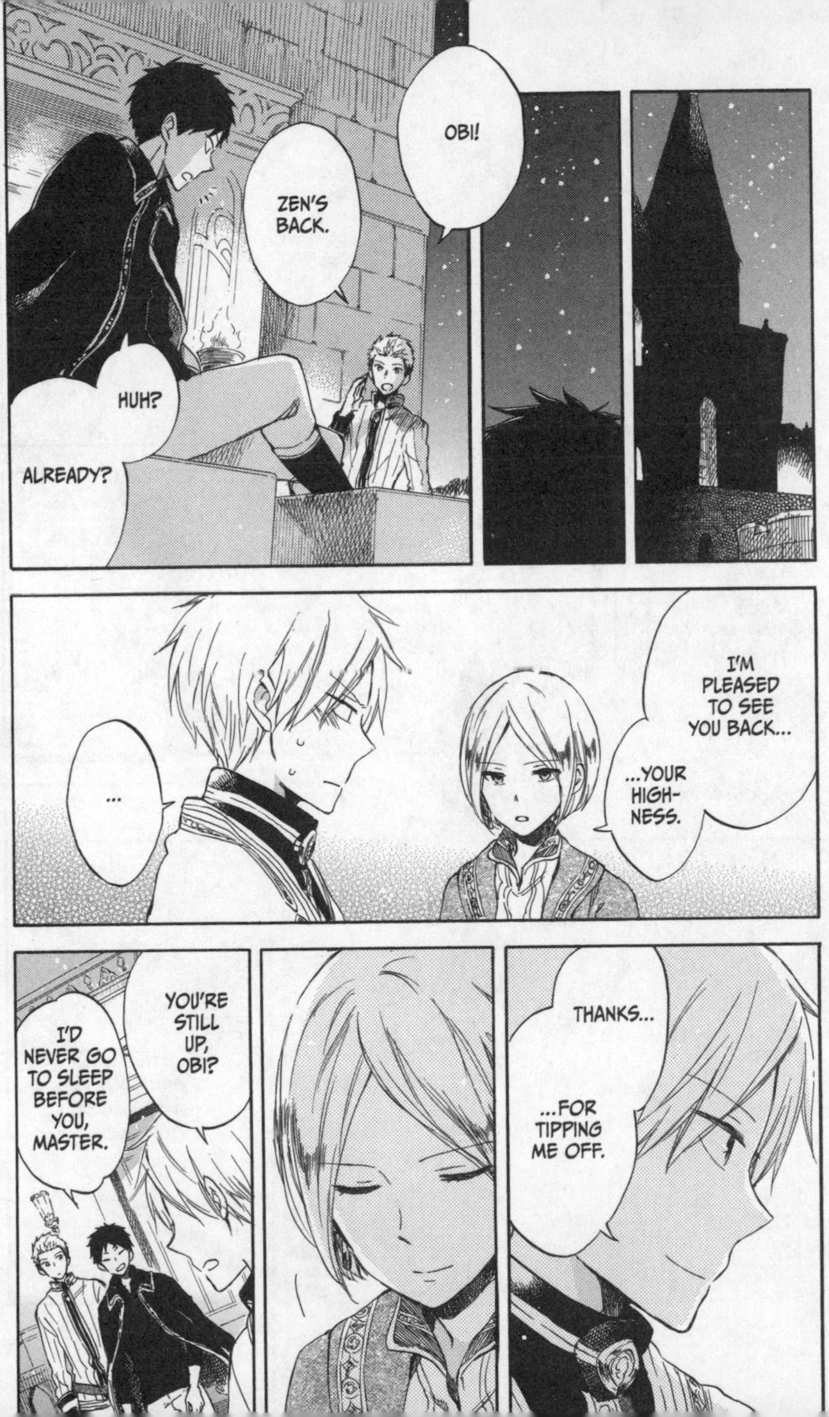
OBI!
ZEN'S BACK.
HUH?
ALREADY?
I'M PLEASED TO SEE YOU BACK...
...YOUR HIGH-NESS.
...
THANKS...
...FOR TIPPING ME OFF.
YOU'RE STILL UP, OBI?
I'D NEVER GO TO SLEEP BEFORE YOU, MASTER.

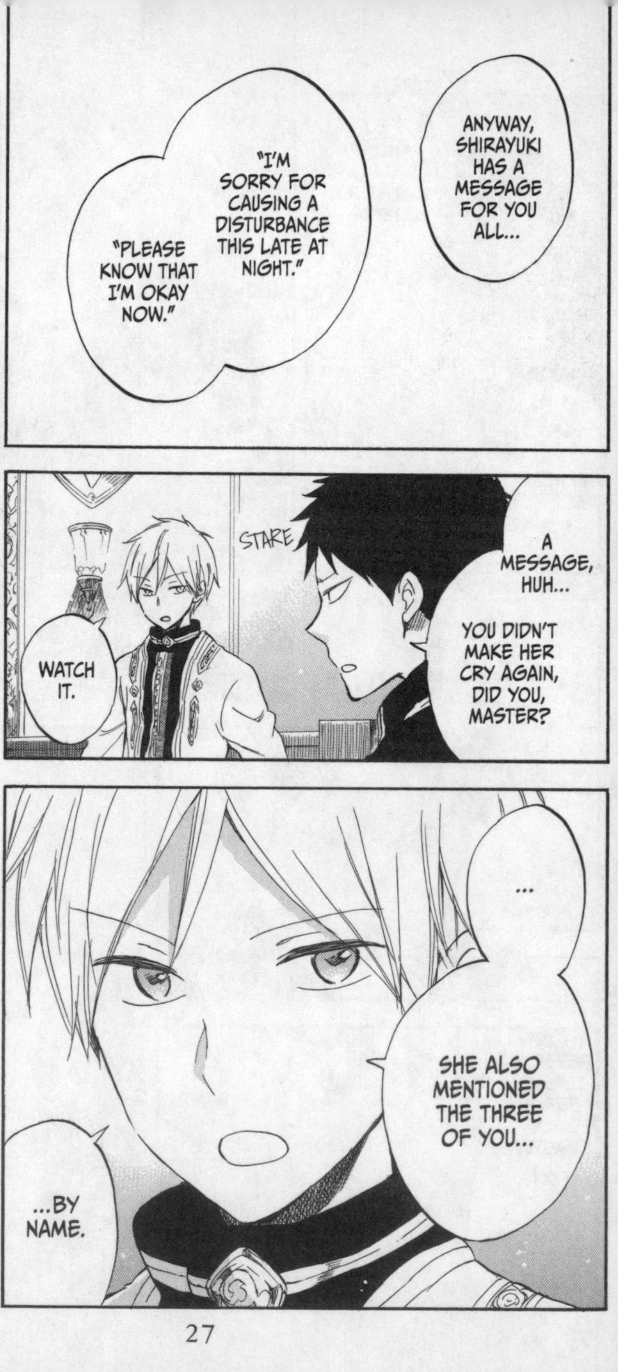
ANYWAY, SHIRAYUKI HAS A MESSAGE FOR YOU ALL...
"I'M SORRY FOR CAUSING A DISTURBANCE THIS LATE AT NIGHT."
"PLEASE KNOW THAT I'M OKAY NOW."
A MESSAGE, HUH...
YOU DIDN'T MAKE HER CRY AGAIN, DID YOU, MASTER?
STARE
WATCH IT.
...
SHE ALSO MENTIONED THE THREE OF YOU...
...BY NAME.

GREETINGS

Hello! This is Sorata Akiduki.

Thank you for purchasing volume 13 of Snow White With the Red Hair!

This volume's cover features Prince Zen and his royal messenger, Obi.

I've got a feeling that Obi's been appearing on a disproportionately high number of covers, though I haven't actually counted.

Whenever I pair Obi and Zen together, I like to make Zen look kind of pompous.

Anyhow, this book picks up right where the last one left off.

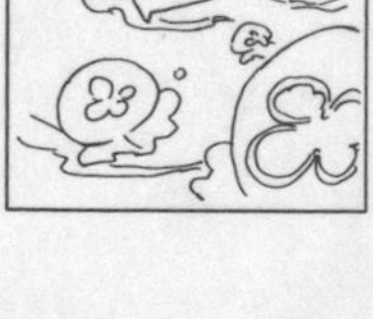

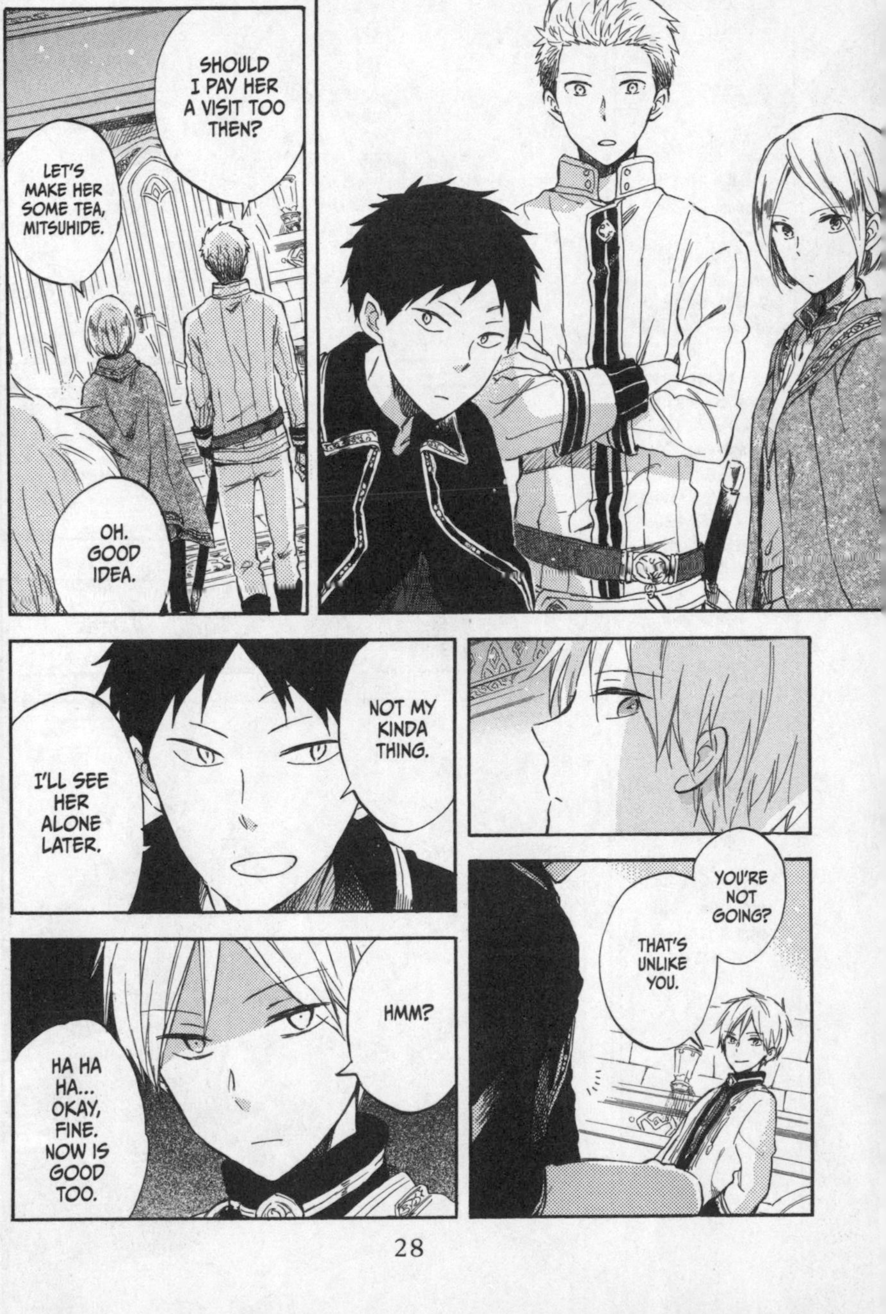
SHOULD I PAY HER A VISIT TOO THEN?
LET'S MAKE HER SOME TEA, MITSUHIDE.
OH. GOOD IDEA.
NOT MY KINDA THING.
I'LL SEE HER ALONE LATER.
YOU'RE NOT GOING?
THAT'S UNLIKE YOU.
HMM?
HA HA HA... OKAY, FINE. NOW IS GOOD TOO.

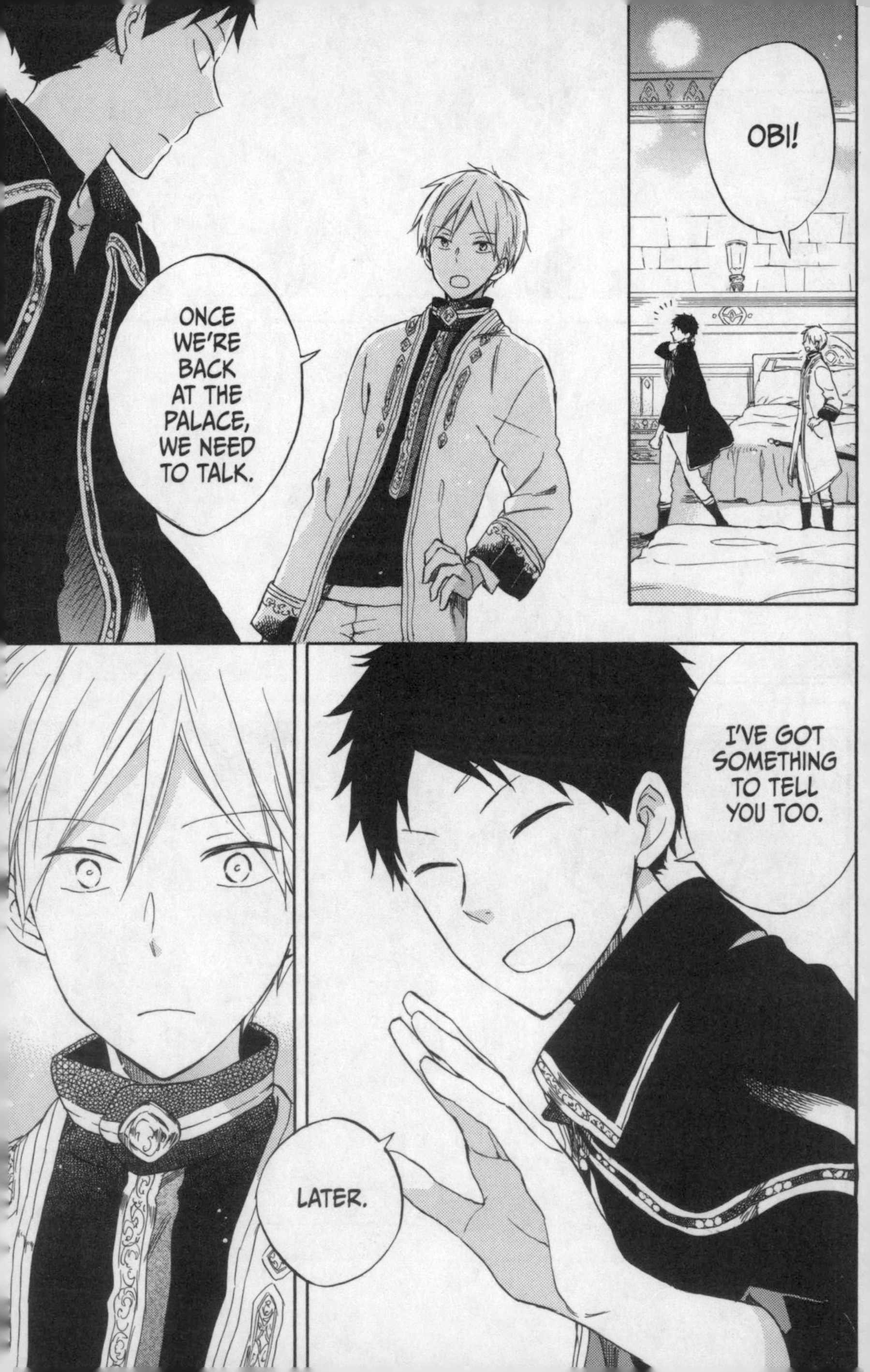
OBI!
ONCE WE'RE BACK AT THE PALACE, WE NEED TO TALK.
I'VE GOT SOMETHING TO TELL YOU TOO.
LATER.

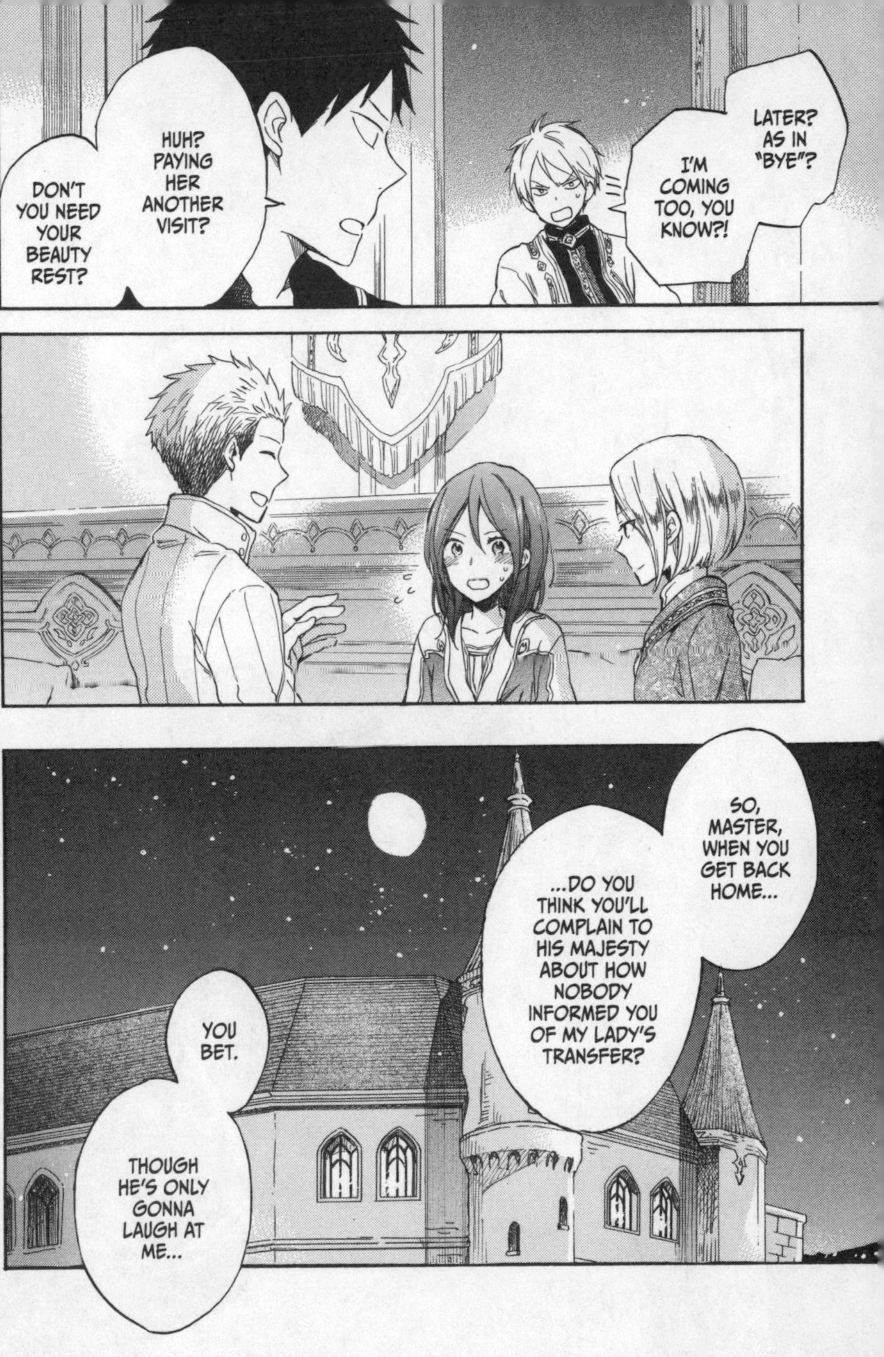
LATER? AS IN "BYE"?
I'M COMING TOO, YOU KNOW?!
HUH? PAYING HER ANOTHER VISIT?
DON'T YOU NEED YOUR BEAUTY REST?
SO, MASTER, WHEN YOU GET BACK HOME...
...DO YOU THINK YOU'LL COMPLAIN TO HIS MAJESTY ABOUT HOW NOBODY INFORMED YOU OF MY LADY'S TRANSFER?
YOU BET.
THOUGH HE'S ONLY GONNA LAUGH AT ME...

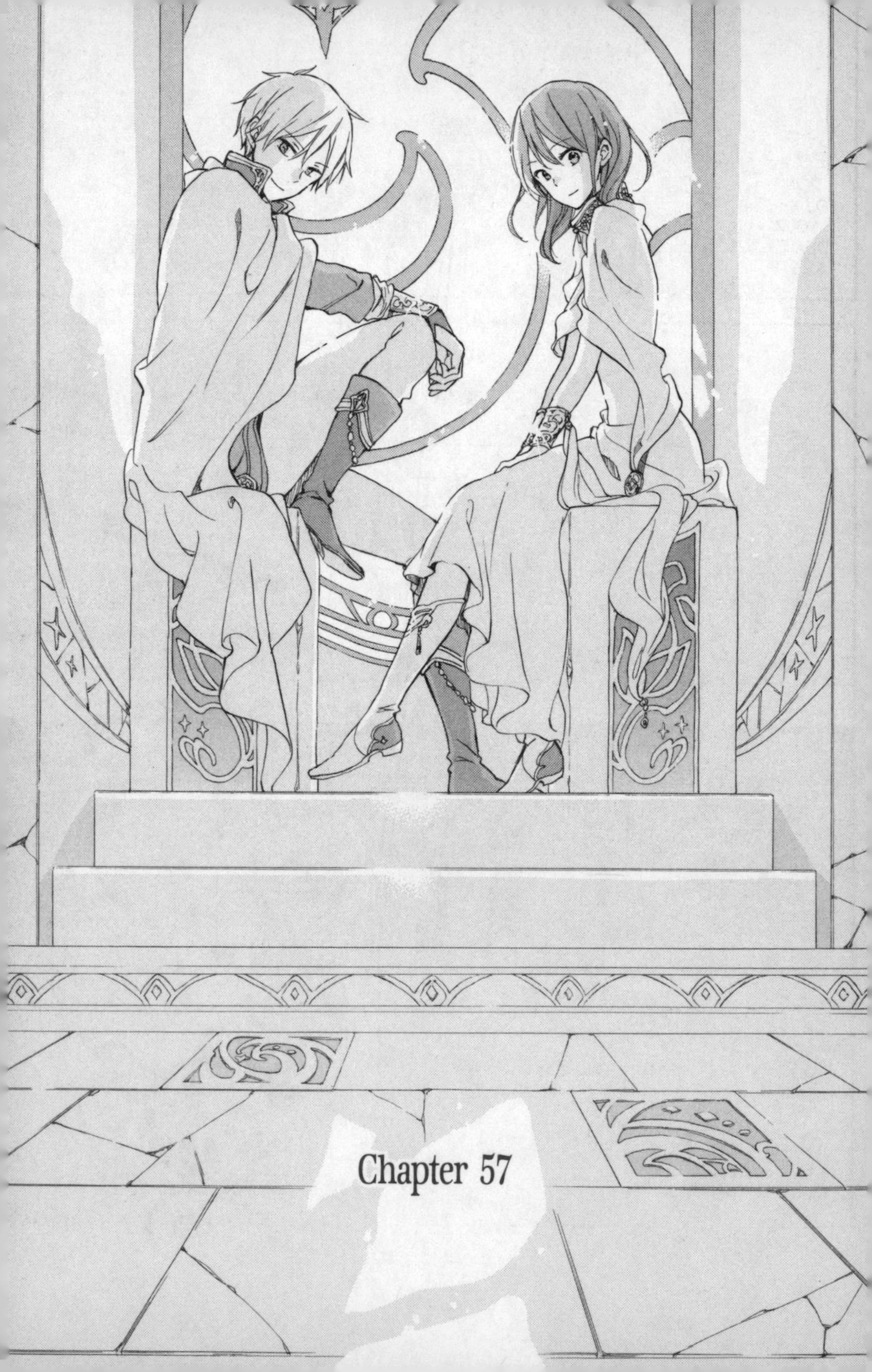
Chapter 57

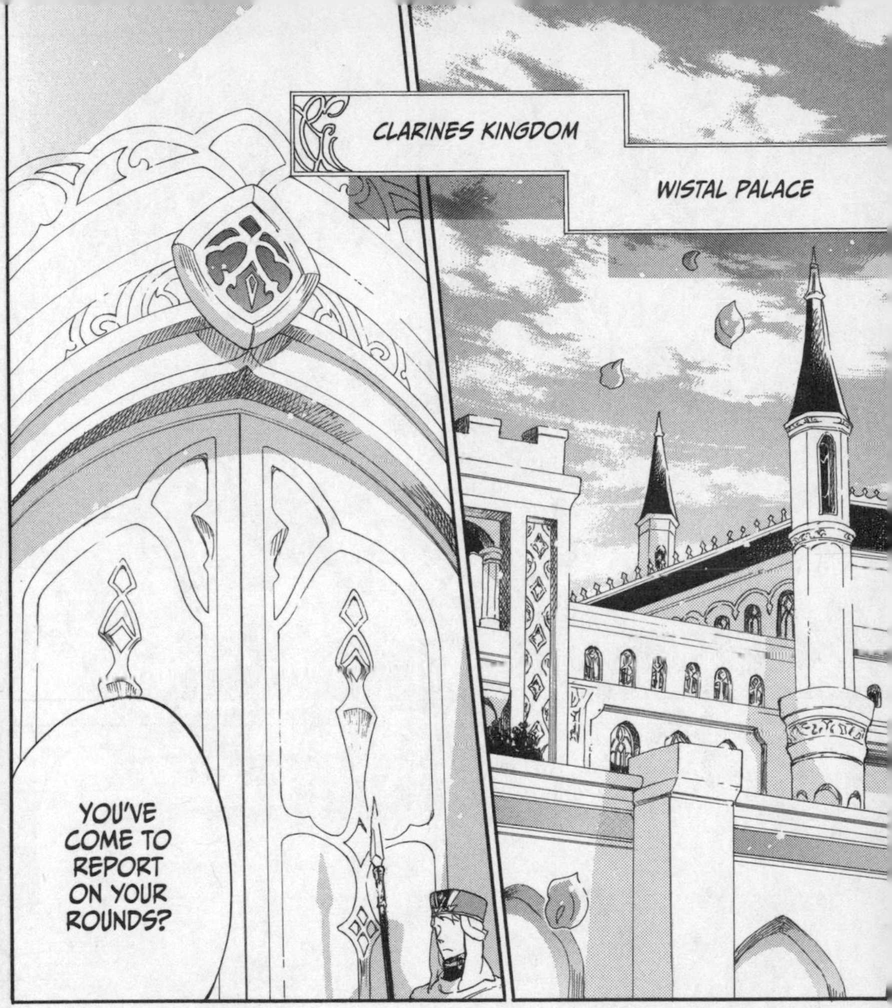
CLARINES KINGDOM
WISTAL PALACE
YOU'VE COME TO REPORT ON YOUR ROUNDS?

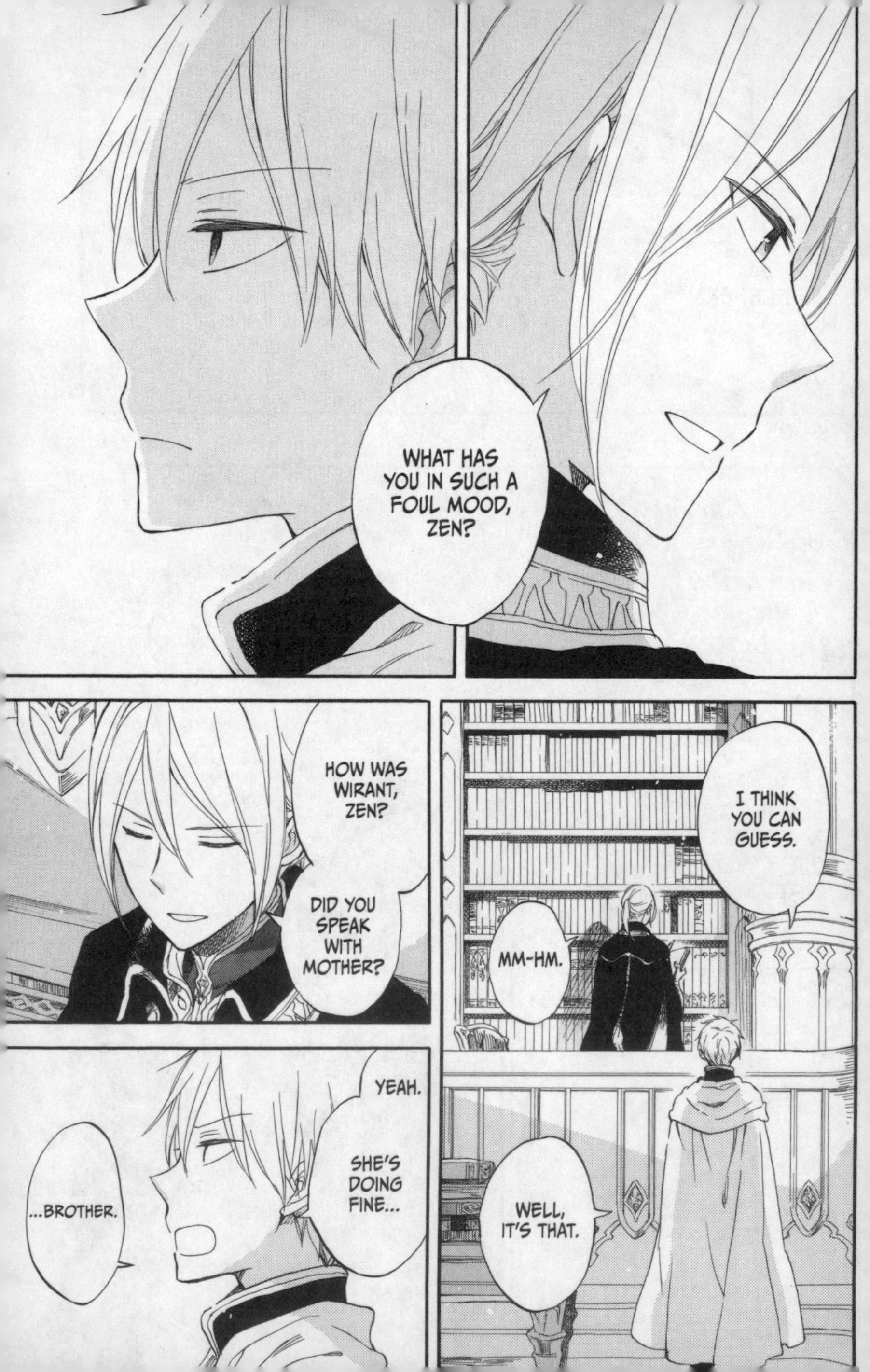
WHAT HAS YOU IN SUCH A FOUL MOOD, ZEN?
I THINK YOU CAN GUESS.
MM-HM.
WELL, IT'S THAT.
HOW WAS WIRANT, ZEN?
DID YOU SPEAK WITH MOTHER?
YEAH.
SHE'S DOING FINE...
...BROTHER.

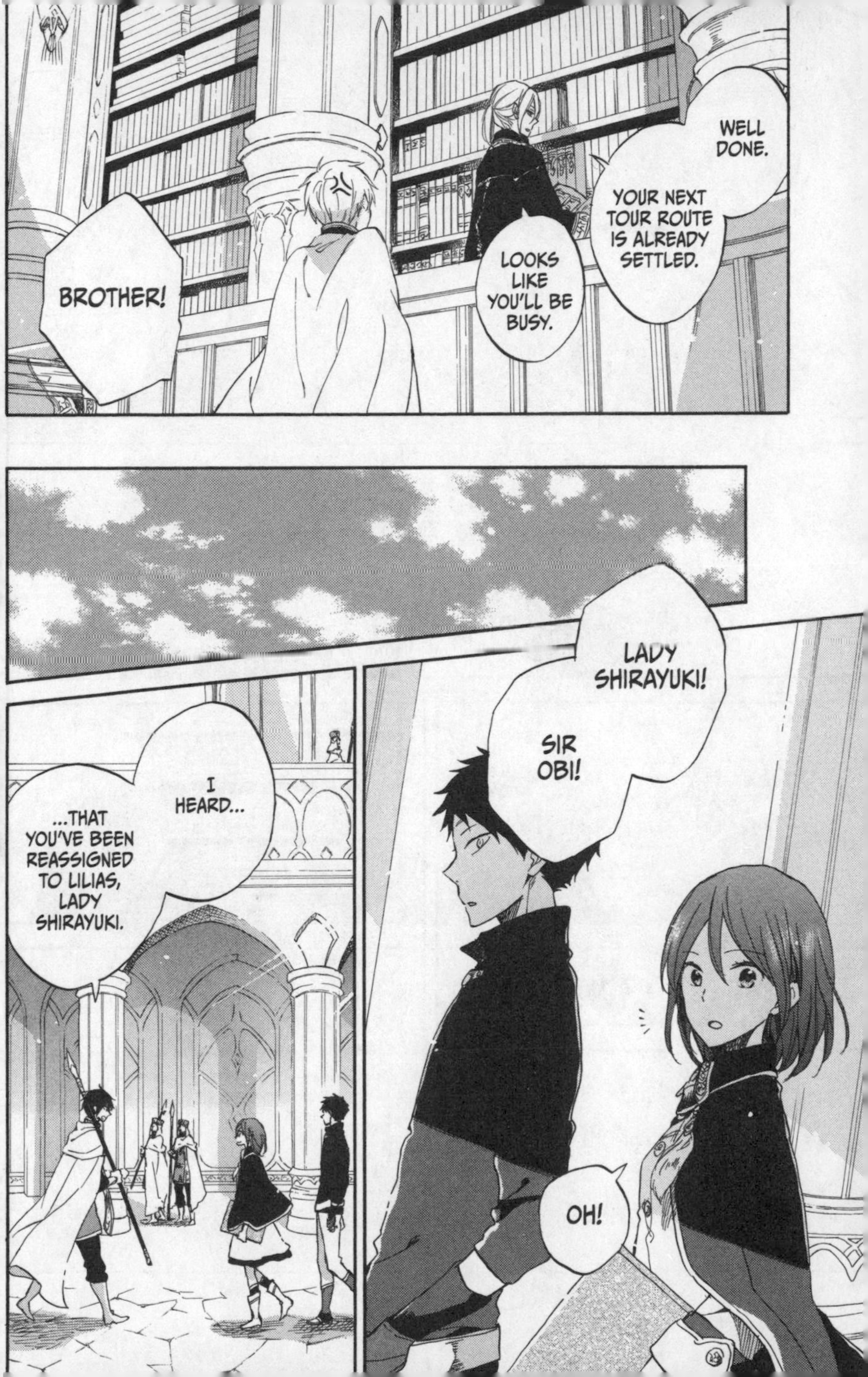
WELL DONE.
YOUR NEXT TOUR ROUTE IS ALREADY SETTLED.
LOOKS LIKE YOU'LL BE BUSY.
BROTHER!
LADY SHIRAYUKI!
SIR OBI!
OH!
I HEARD...
...THAT YOU'VE BEEN REASSIGNED TO LILIAS, LADY SHIRAYUKI.

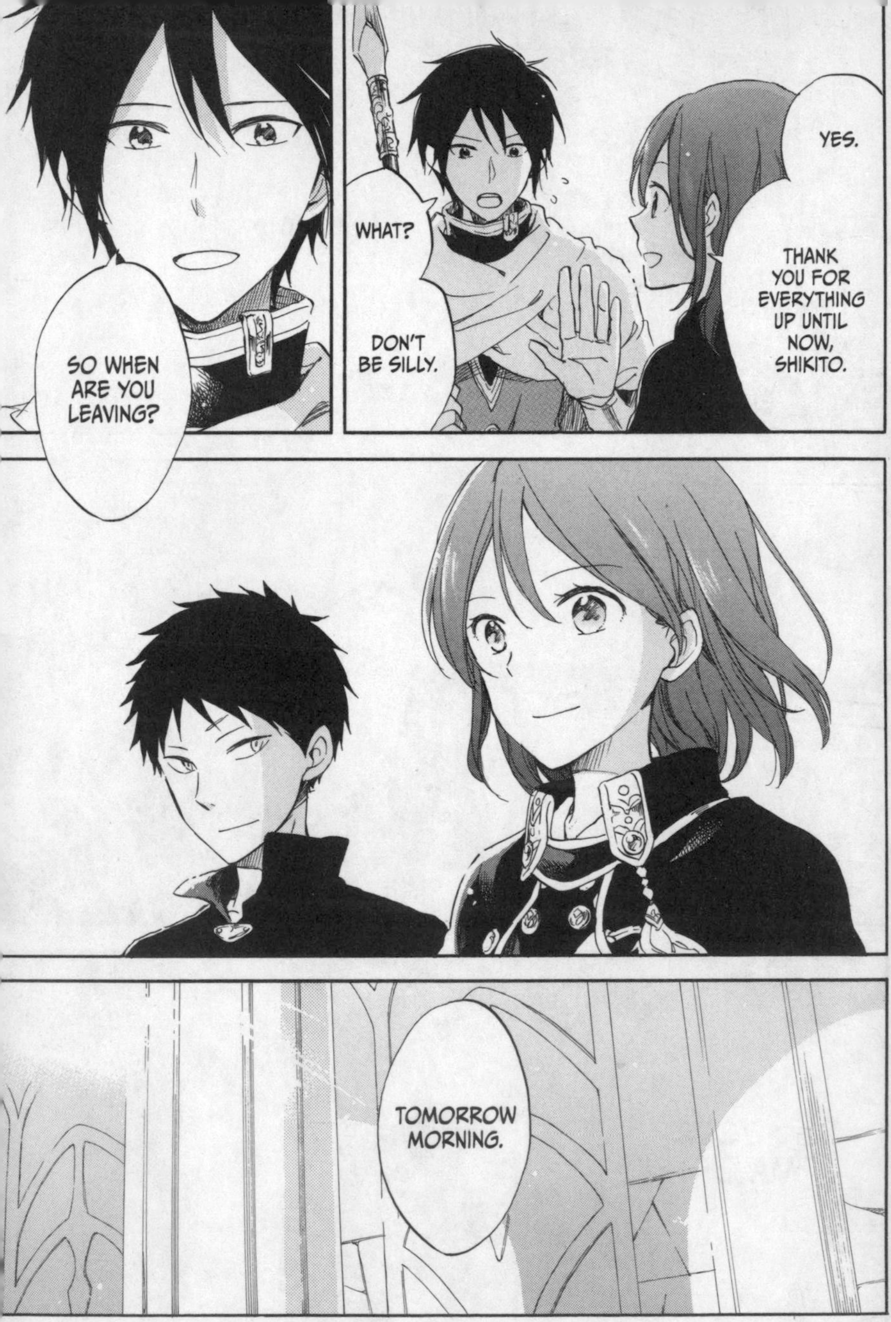
YES.
THANK YOU FOR EVERYTHING UP UNTIL NOW, SHIKITO.
WHAT?
DON'T BE SILLY.
SO WHEN ARE YOU LEAVING?
TOMORROW MORNING.

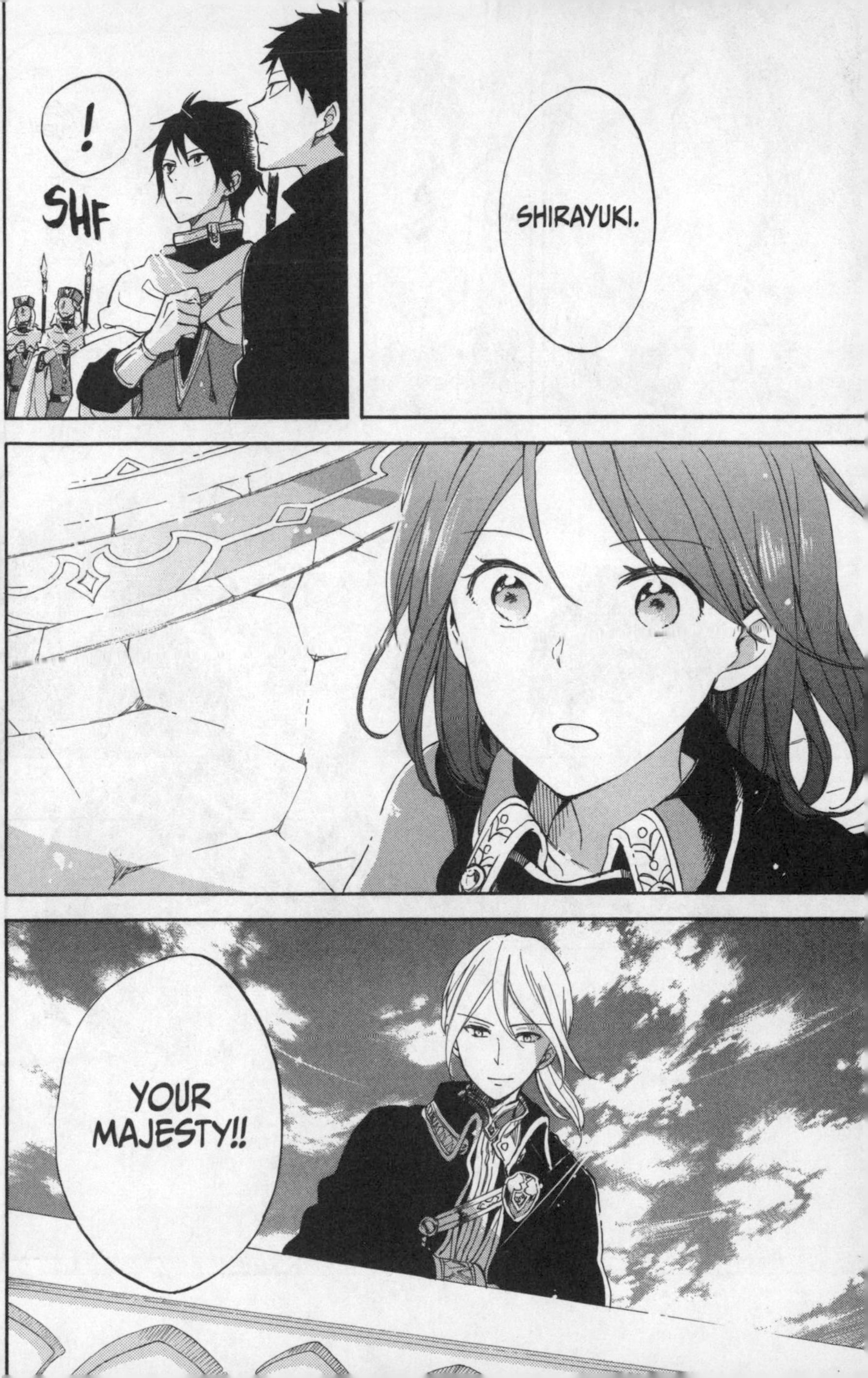
SHIRAYUKI.
!
SHF
YOUR MAJESTY!!

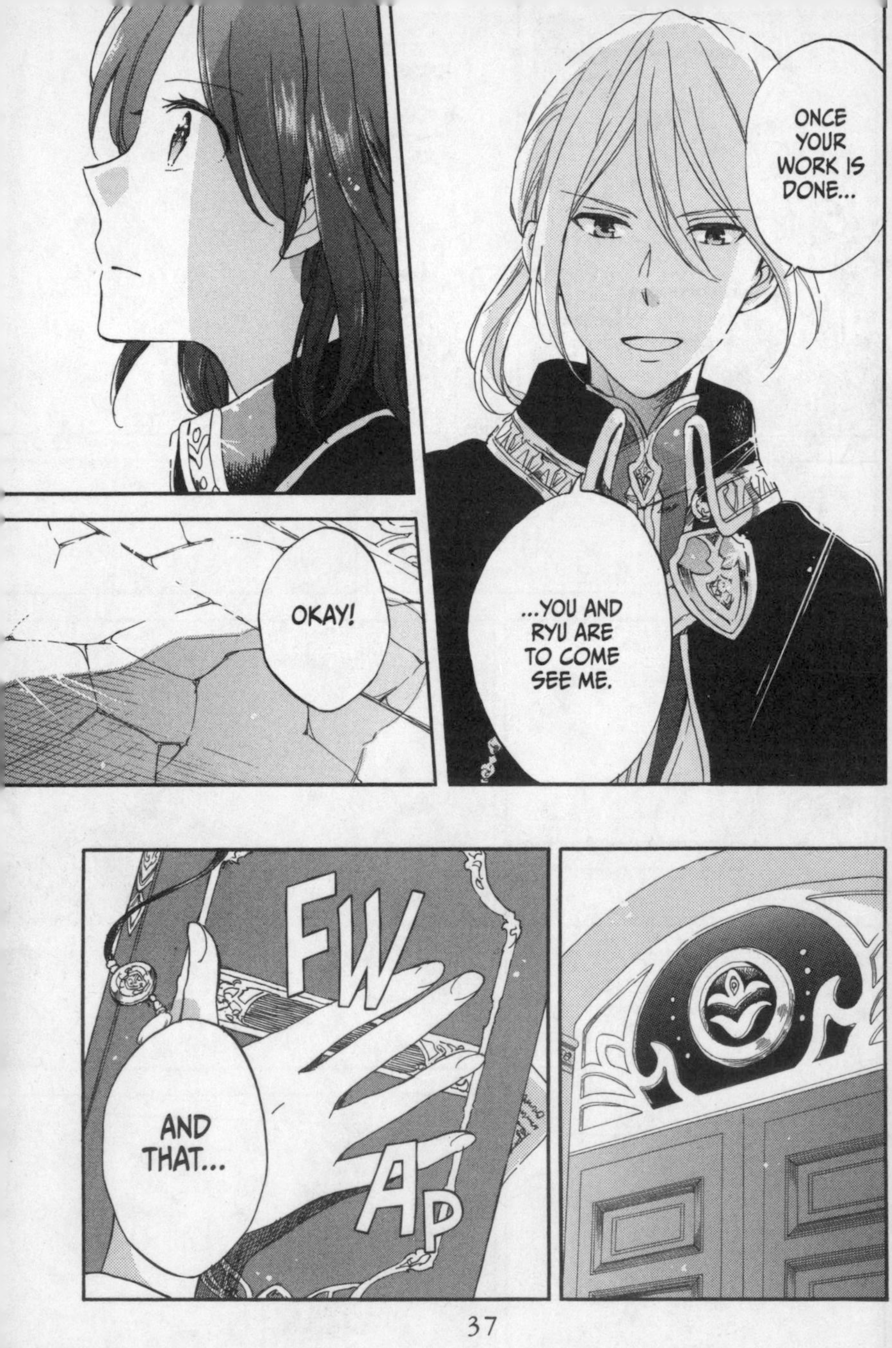
ONCE YOUR WORK IS DONE...
...YOU AND RYU ARE TO COME SEE ME.
OKAY!
AND THAT...
FWAP

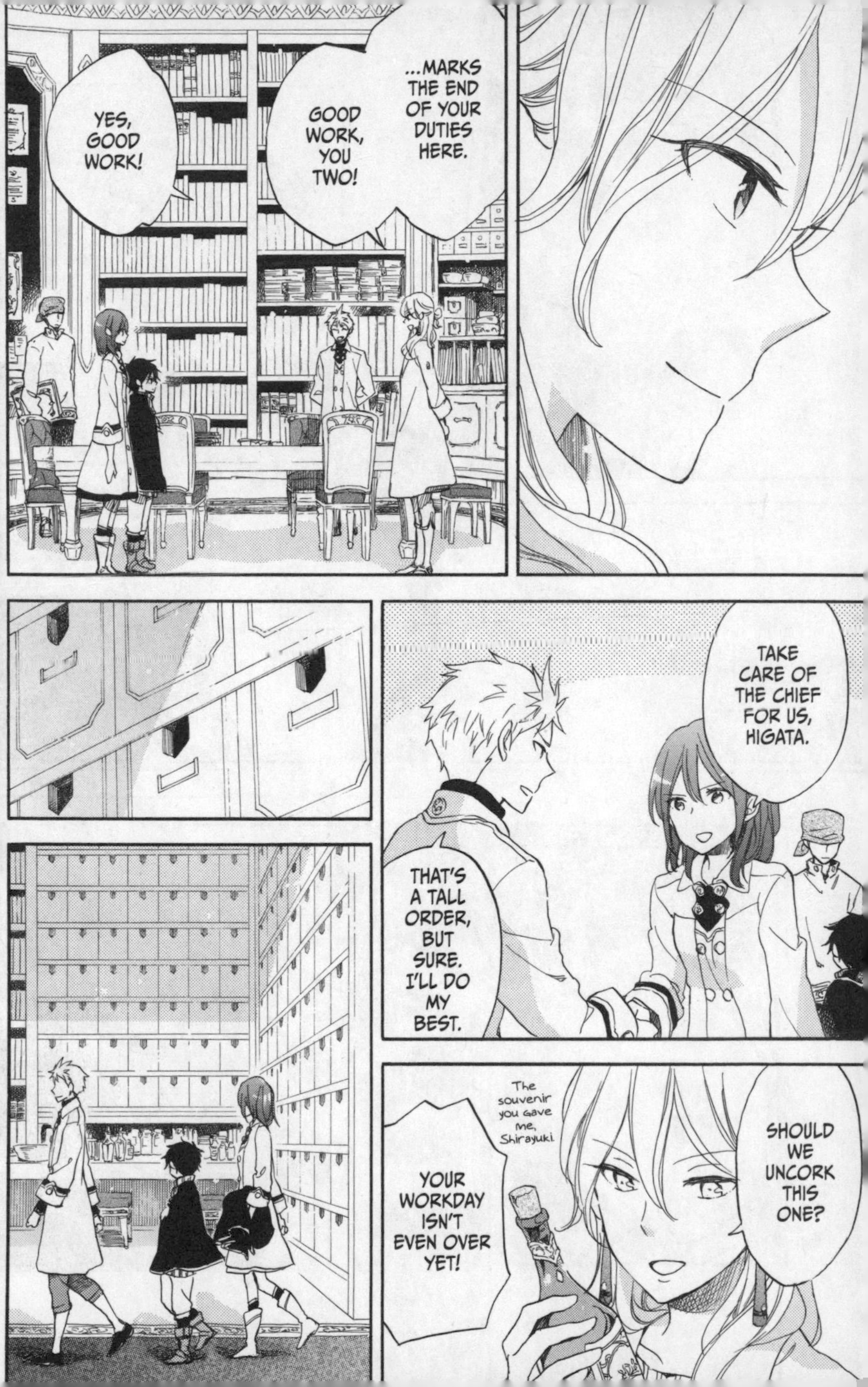
...MARKS THE END OF YOUR DUTIES HERE.
GOOD WORK, YOU TWO!
YES, GOOD WORK!
TAKE CARE OF THE CHIEF FOR US, HIGATA.
THAT'S A TALL ORDER, BUT SURE. I'LL DO MY BEST.
SHOULD WE UNCORK THIS ONE?
The souvenir you gave me, Shirayuki.
YOUR WORKDAY ISN'T EVEN OVER YET!

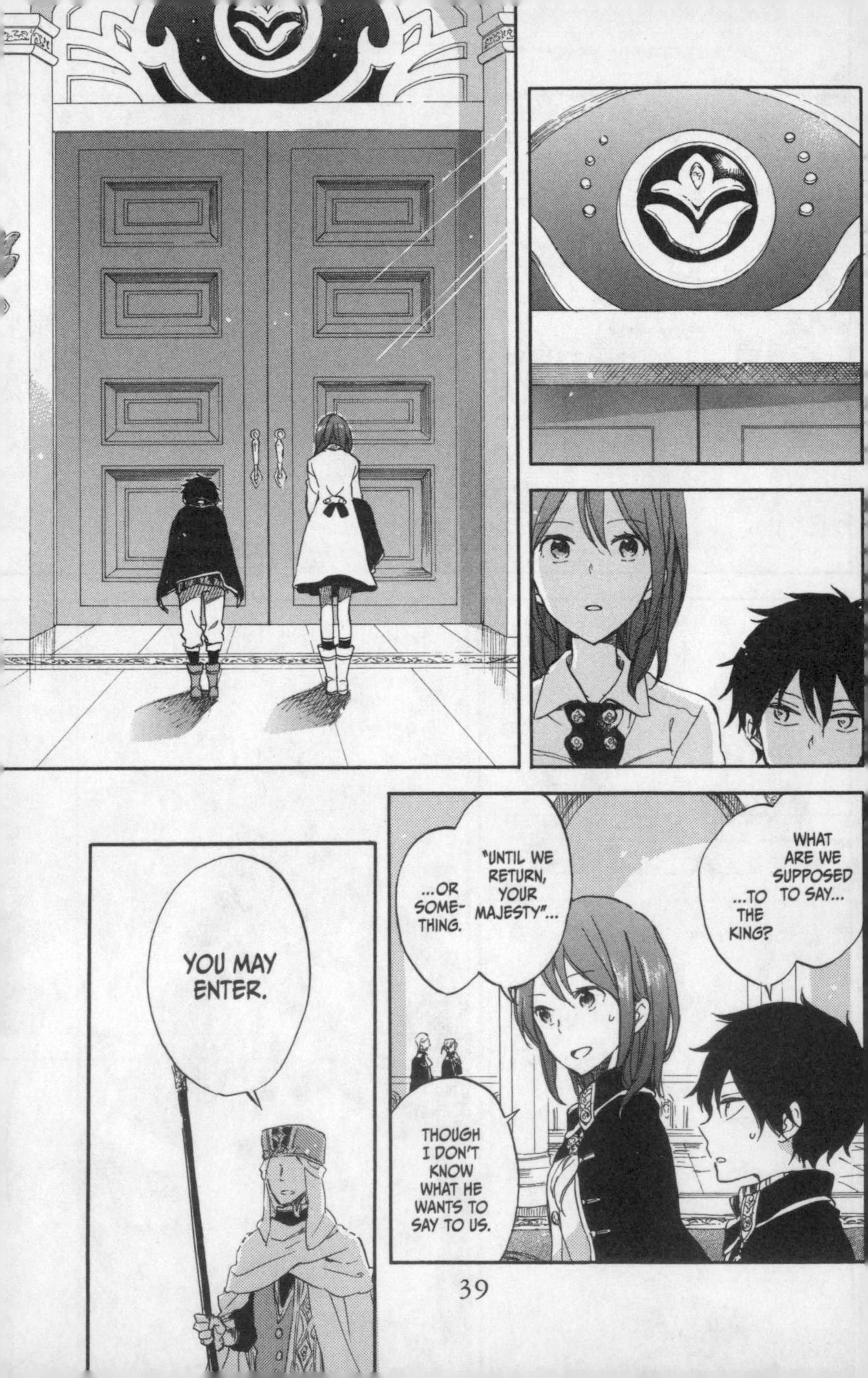
WHAT ARE WE SUPPOSED TO SAY...
...TO THE KING?
"UNTIL WE RETURN, YOUR MAJESTY"...
...OR SOME-THING.
THOUGH I DON'T KNOW WHAT HE WANTS TO SAY TO US.
YOU MAY ENTER.

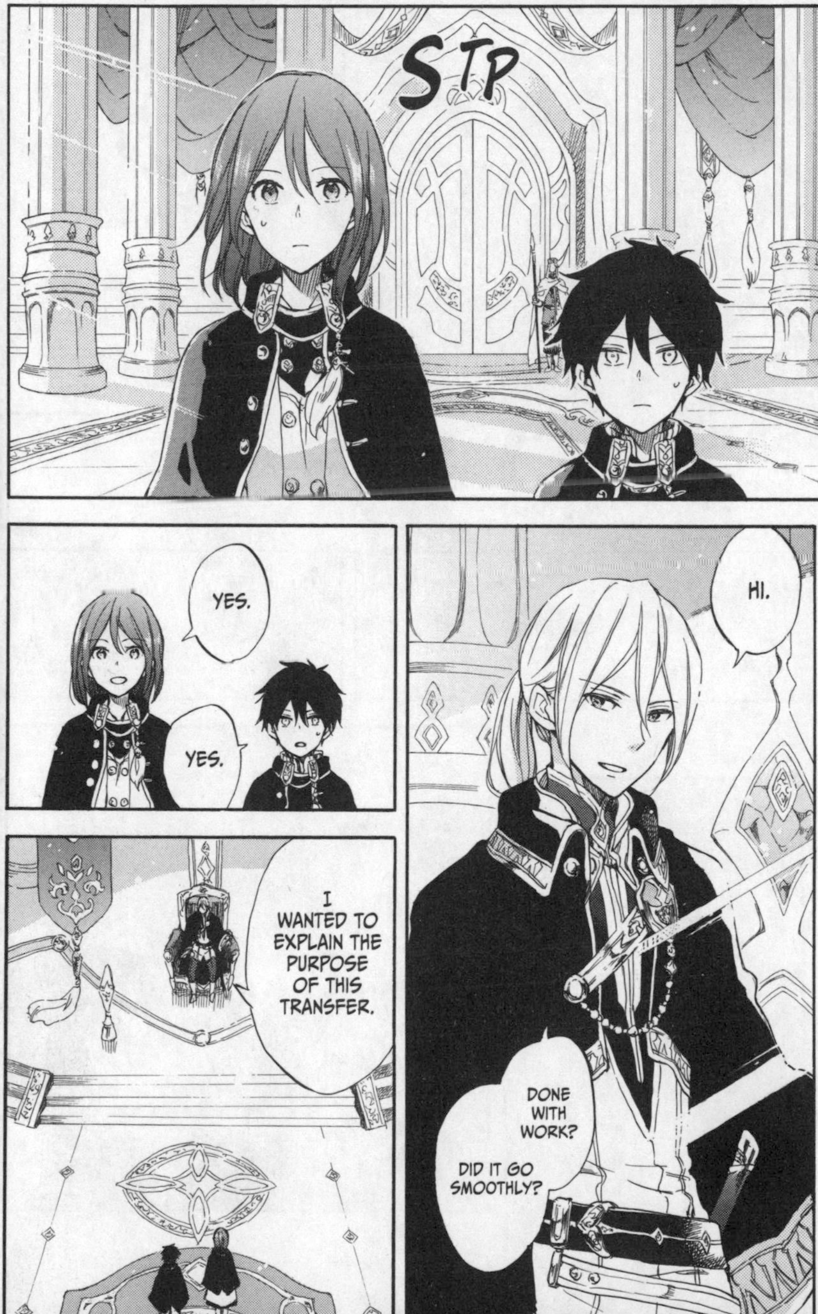
STP
HI.
DONE WITH WORK?
DID IT GO SMOOTHLY?
YES.
YES.
I WANTED TO EXPLAIN THE PURPOSE OF THIS TRANSFER.

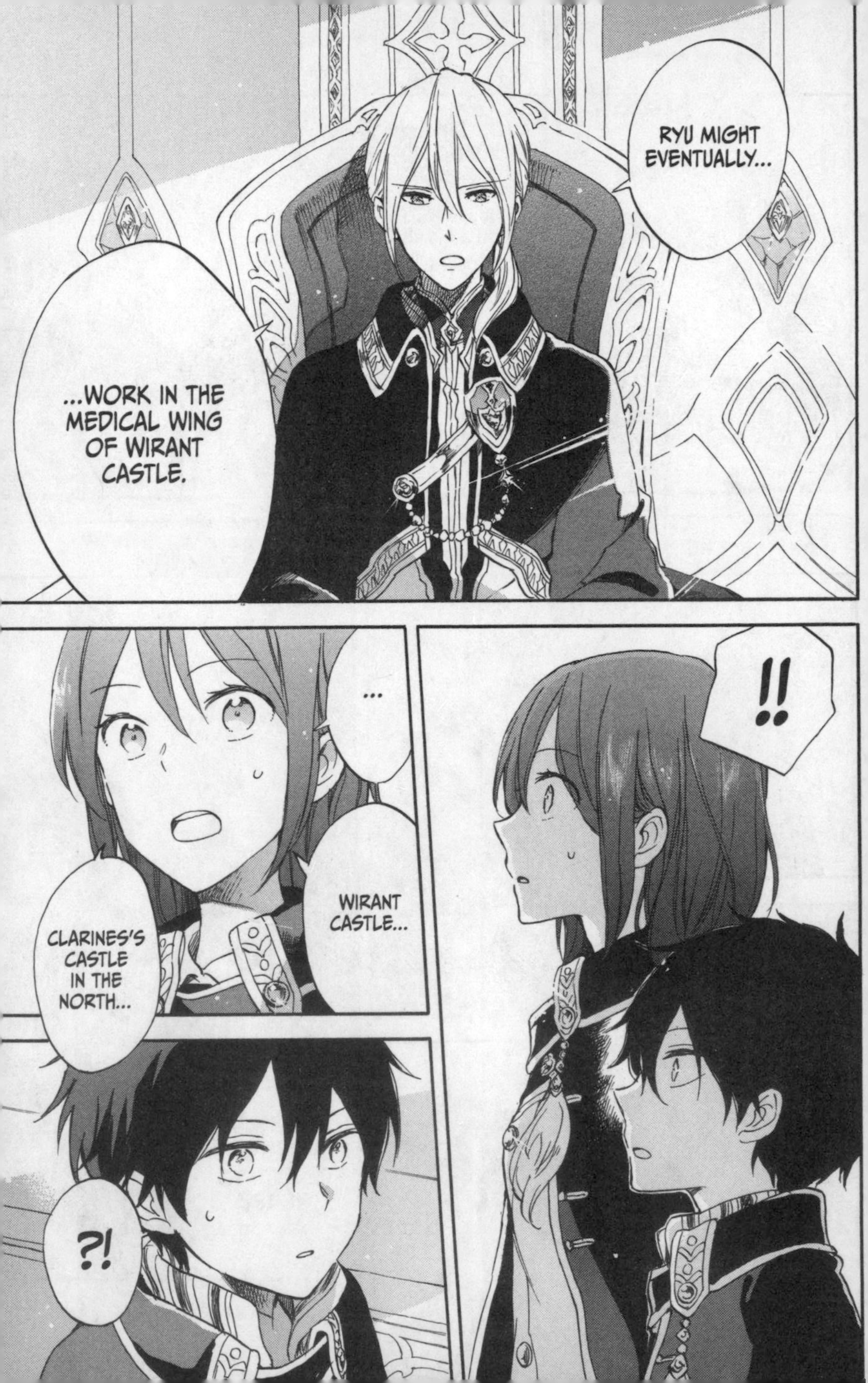
RYU MIGHT EVENTUALLY...
...WORK IN THE MEDICAL WING OF WIRANT CASTLE.
!!
...
WIRANT CASTLE...
CLARINES'S CASTLE IN THE NORTH...
?!

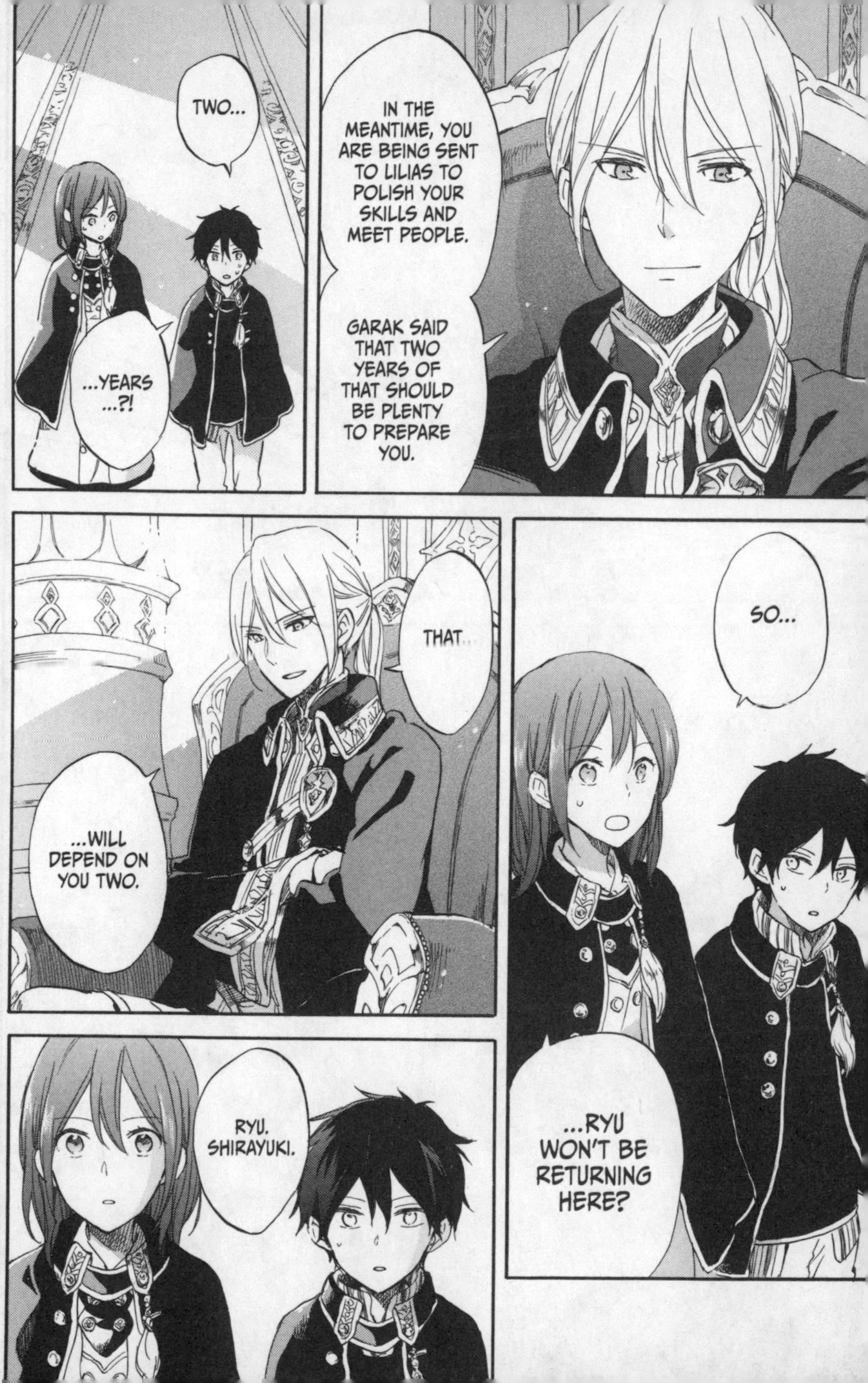
IN THE MEANTIME, YOU ARE BEING SENT TO LILIAS TO POLISH YOUR SKILLS AND MEET PEOPLE.
GARAK SAID THAT TWO YEARS OF THAT SHOULD BE PLENTY TO PREPARE YOU.
TWO...
...YEARS ...?!
SO...
...RYU WON'T BE RETURNING HERE?
THAT...
...WILL DEPEND ON YOU TWO.
RYU. SHIRAYUKI.

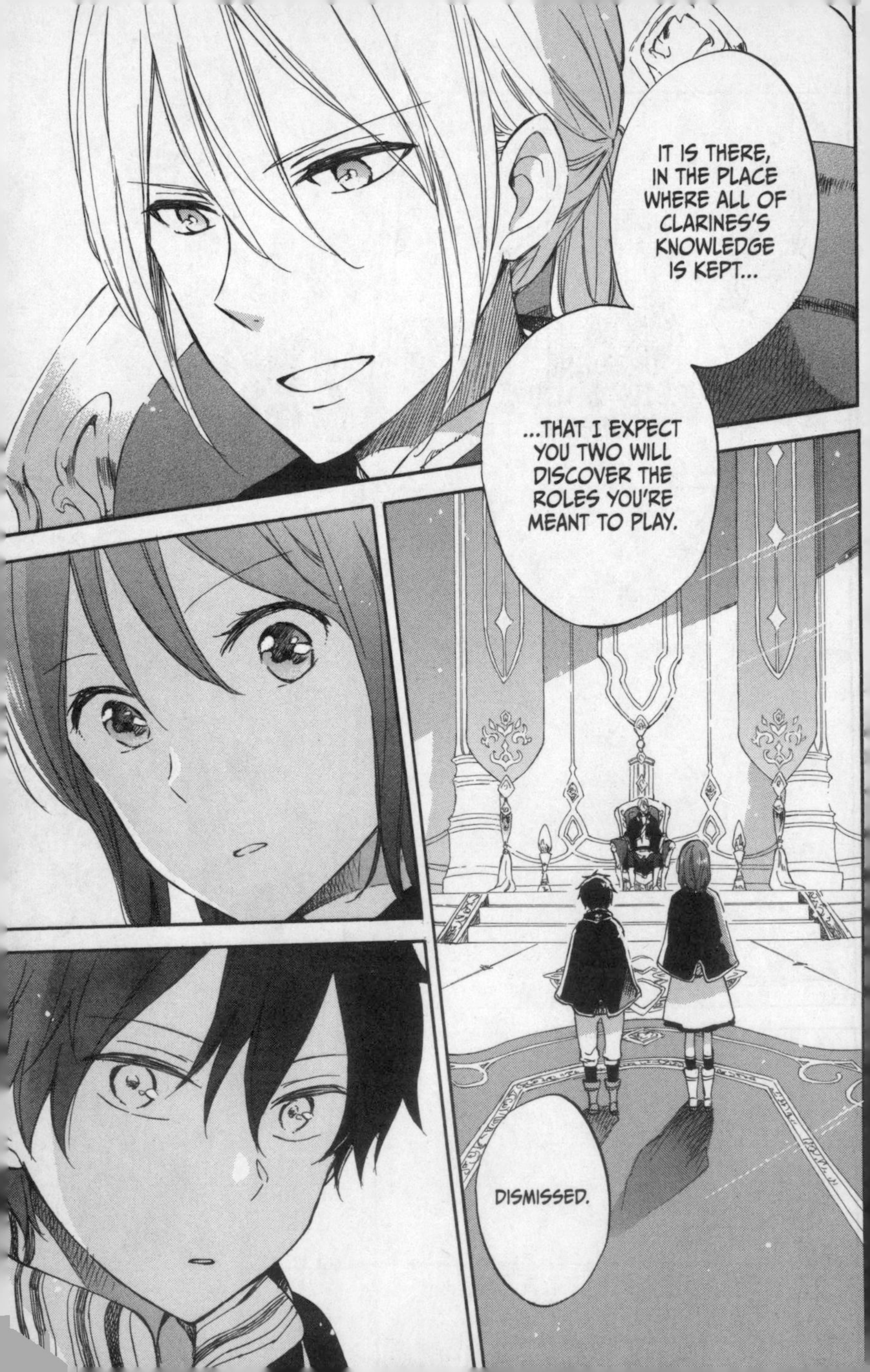
IT IS THERE, IN THE PLACE WHERE ALL OF CLARINES'S KNOWLEDGE IS KEPT...
...THAT I EXPECT YOU TWO WILL DISCOVER THE ROLES YOU'RE MEANT TO PLAY.
DISMISSED.

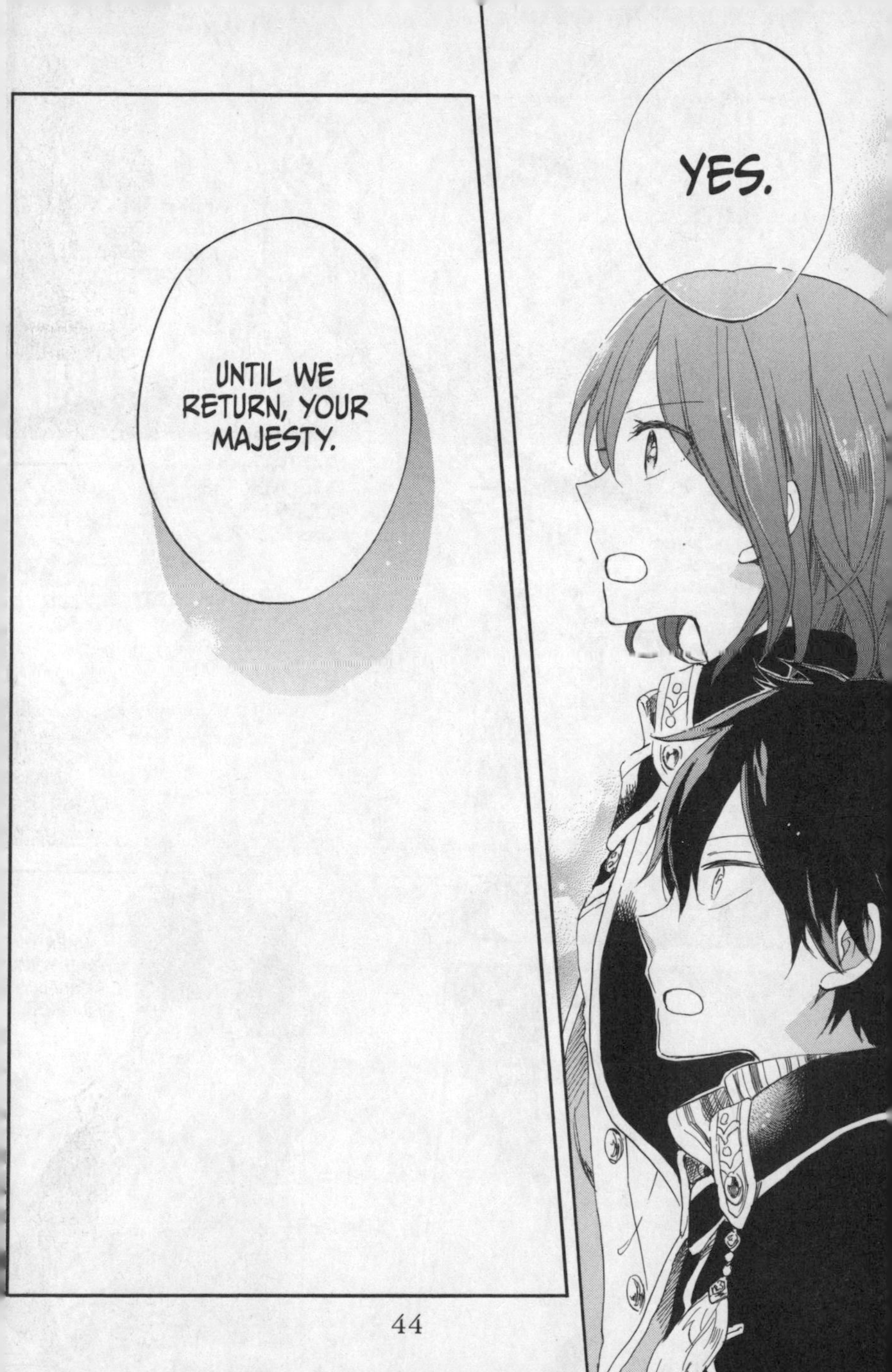
YES.
UNTIL WE RETURN, YOUR MAJESTY.

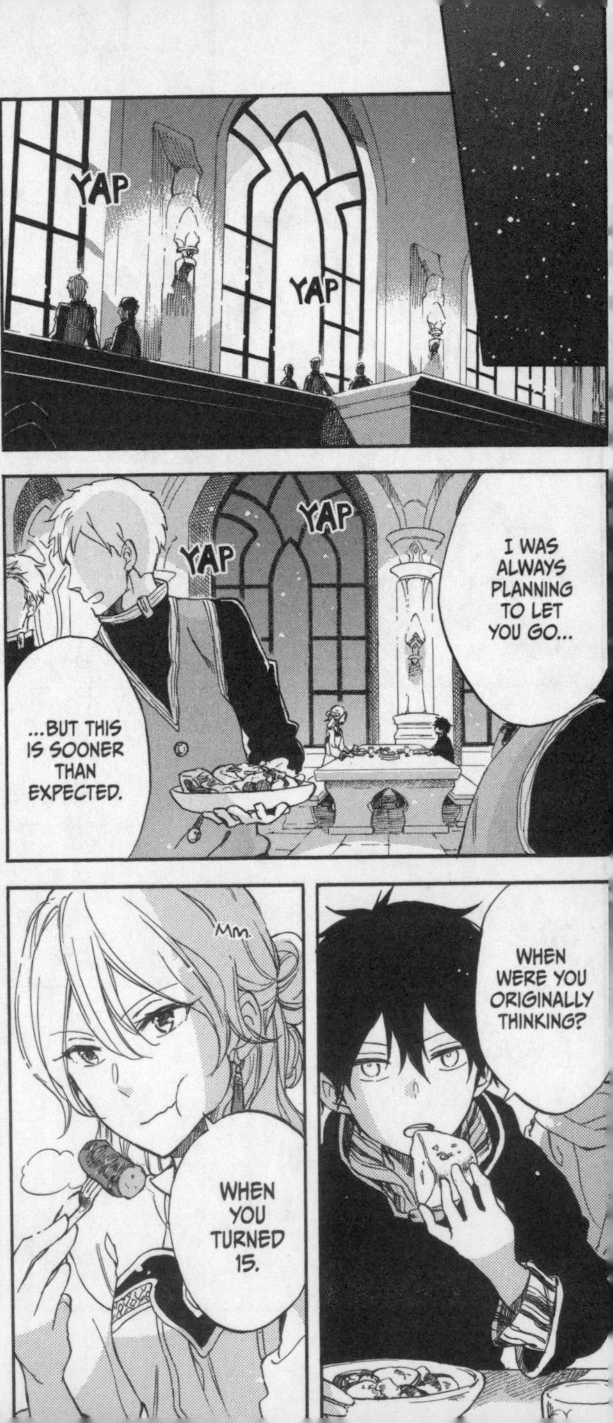
YAP
YAP
YAP
YAP
I WAS ALWAYS PLANNING TO LET YOU GO...
...BUT THIS IS SOONER THAN EXPECTED.
WHEN WERE YOU ORIGINALLY THINKING?
MM.
WHEN YOU TURNED 15.

2

TRIP (PART 1)

Here's a diary entry about my trip to Taiwan!

It was the end of summer 2014. A two-day, three-night weekend trip with Toki Yajima and Wataru Hibiki.

It was brutally hot. Unbelievably so. Whether we were sightseeing or eating meals, it was a constant battle against the heat.

When they served us hot tea with dinner, I almost had a breakdown. So...hot! And they kept giving us refills!

But the food was amazing. Like the potatoes, the shrimp, the potatoes!
↑
Sweet and delicious

We were trying to figure out what our final tourist attraction should be and decided on dinner in Jiufen.

The red lanterns on the second-floor terrace were lovely, and when we took a picture, Hachi and Hibiki wound up looking bright red.

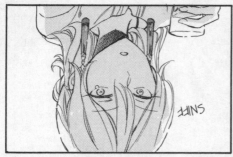

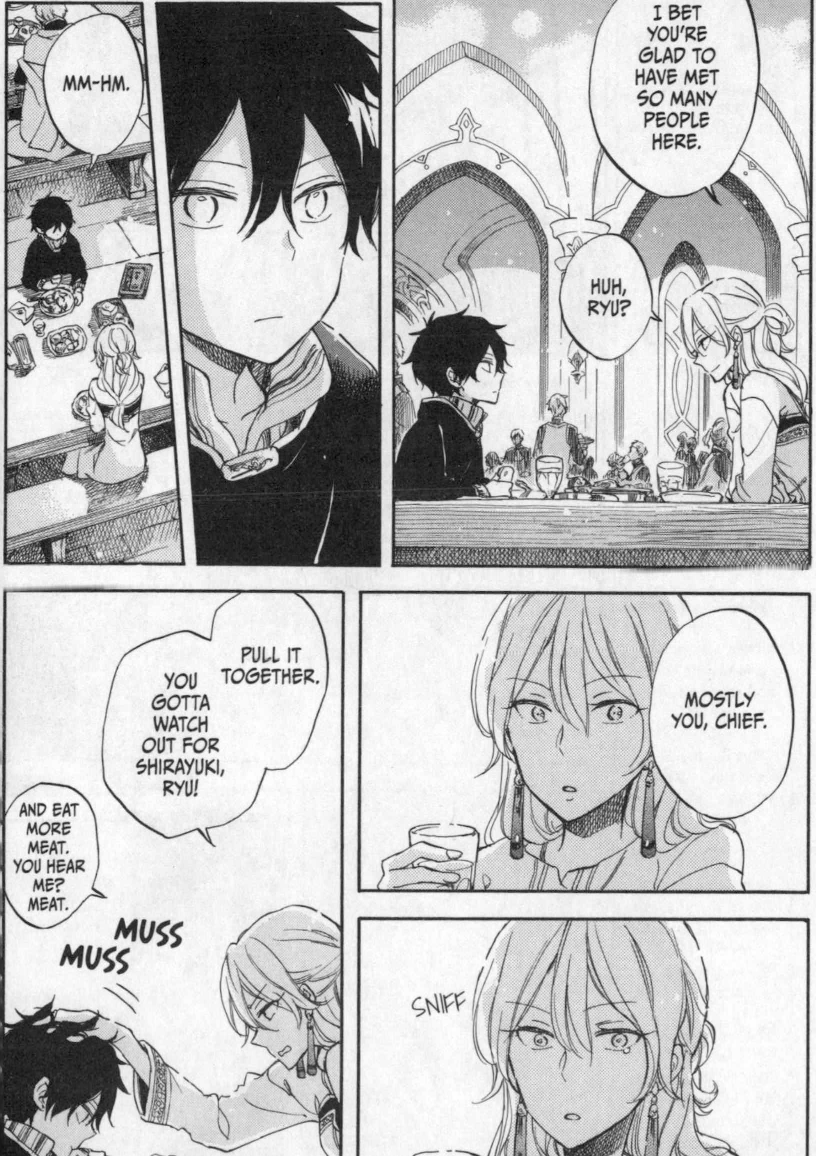
I BET YOU'RE GLAD TO HAVE MET SO MANY PEOPLE HERE.
HUH, RYU?
MM-HM.
MOSTLY YOU, CHIEF.
SNIFF
PULL IT TOGETHER.
YOU GOTTA WATCH OUT FOR SHIRAYUKI, RYU!
AND EAT MORE MEAT. YOU HEAR ME? MEAT.
MUSS MUSS

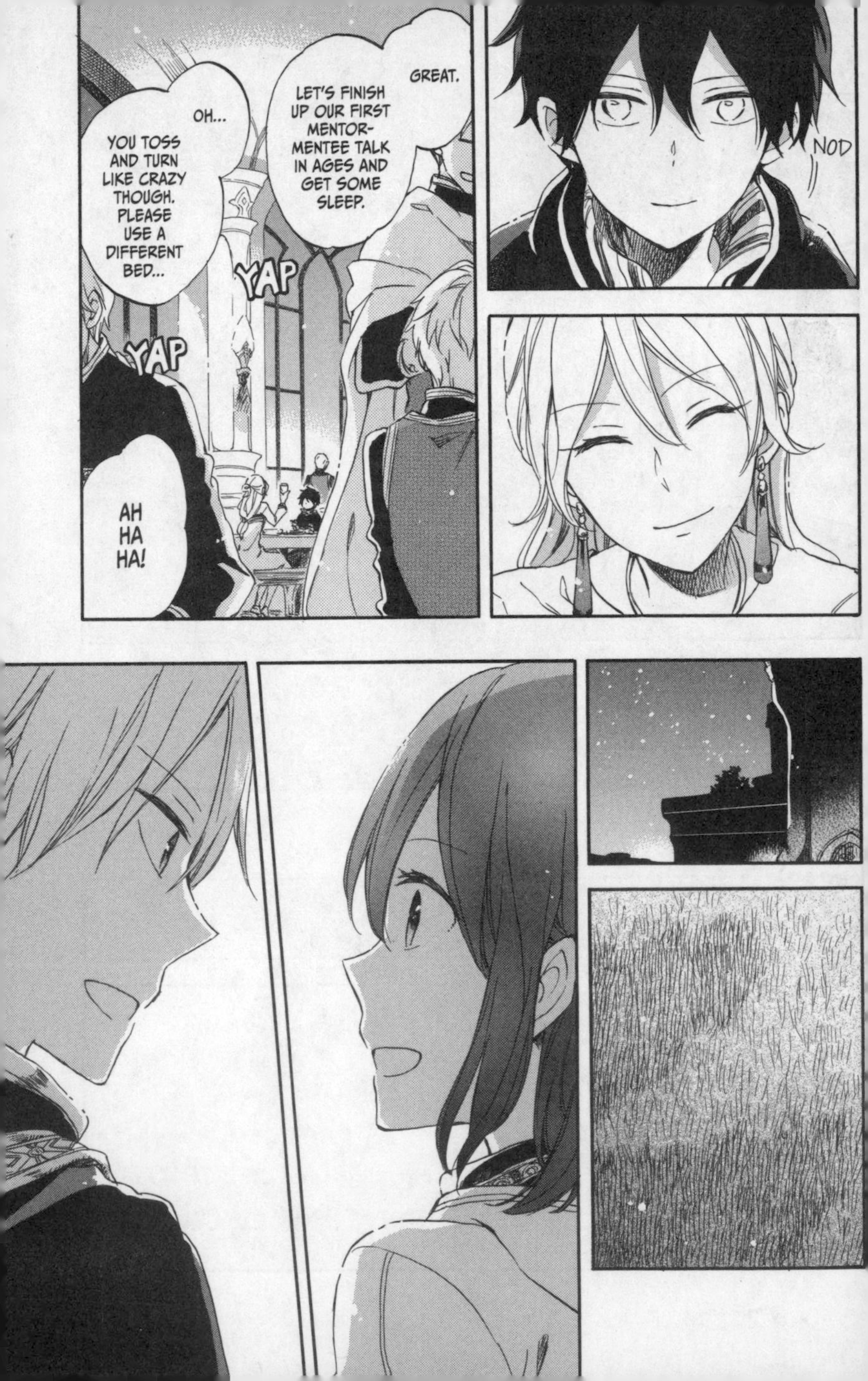
NOD
GREAT.
LET'S FINISH UP OUR FIRST MENTOR-MENTEE TALK IN AGES AND GET SOME SLEEP.
OH...
YOU TOSS AND TURN LIKE CRAZY THOUGH. PLEASE USE A DIFFERENT BED...
YAP
YAP
AH HA HA!

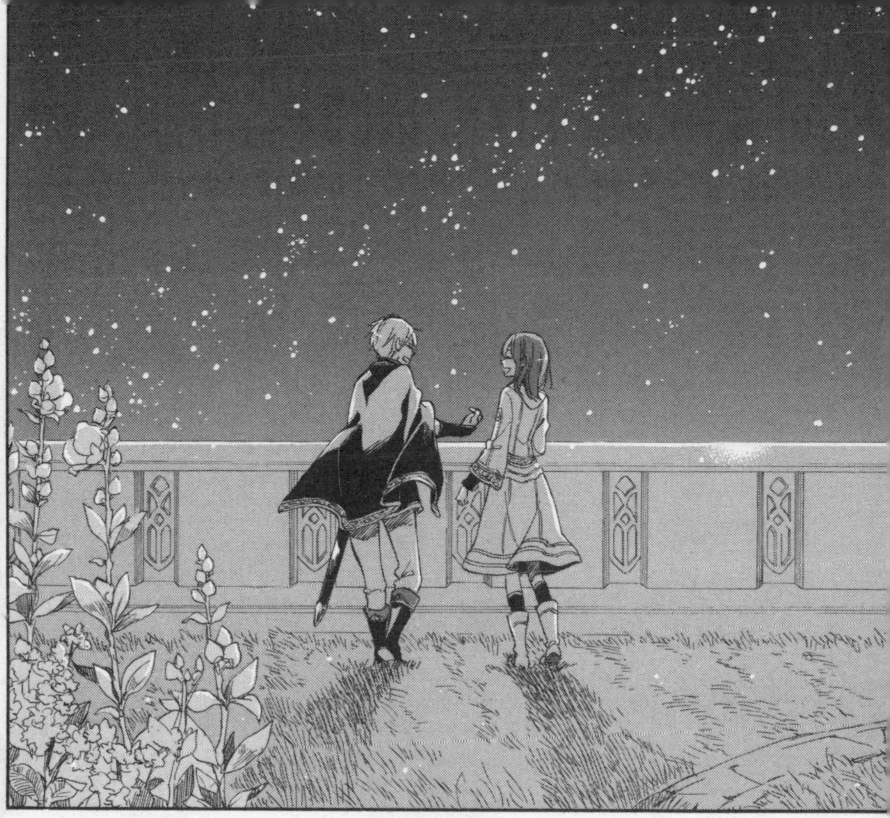

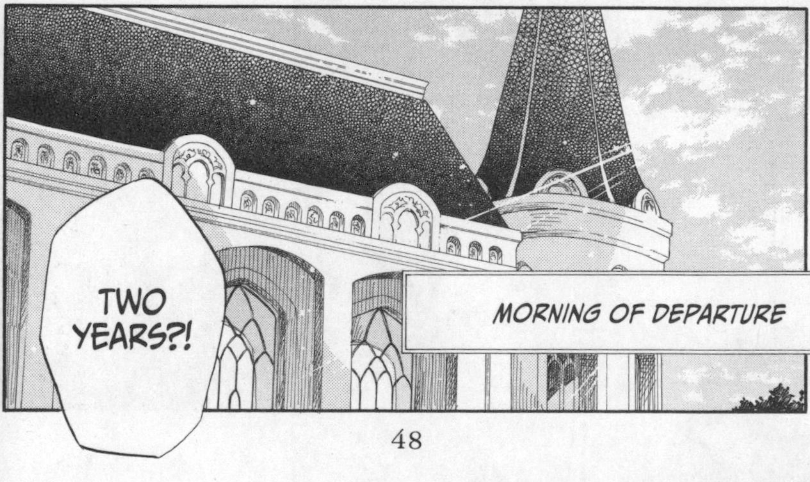
MORNING OF DEPARTURE
TWO YEARS?!

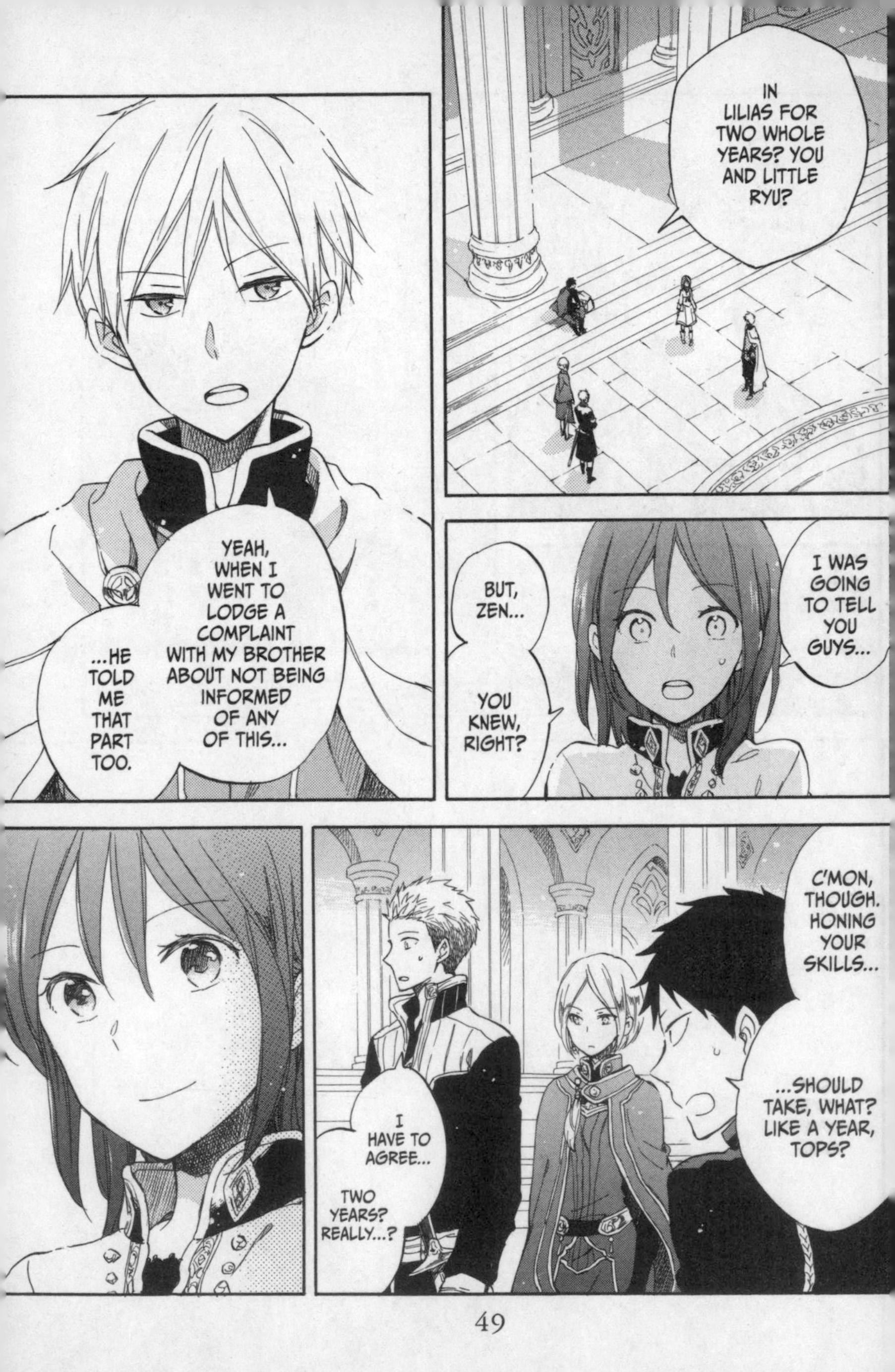
IN LILIAS FOR TWO WHOLE YEARS? YOU AND LITTLE RYU?
I WAS GOING TO TELL YOU GUYS...
BUT, ZEN...
YOU KNEW, RIGHT?
YEAH, WHEN I WENT TO LODGE A COMPLAINT WITH MY BROTHER ABOUT NOT BEING INFORMED OF ANY OF THIS...
...HE TOLD ME THAT PART TOO.
C'MON, THOUGH. HONING YOUR SKILLS...
...SHOULD TAKE, WHAT? LIKE A YEAR, TOPS?
I HAVE TO AGREE...
TWO YEARS? REALLY...?

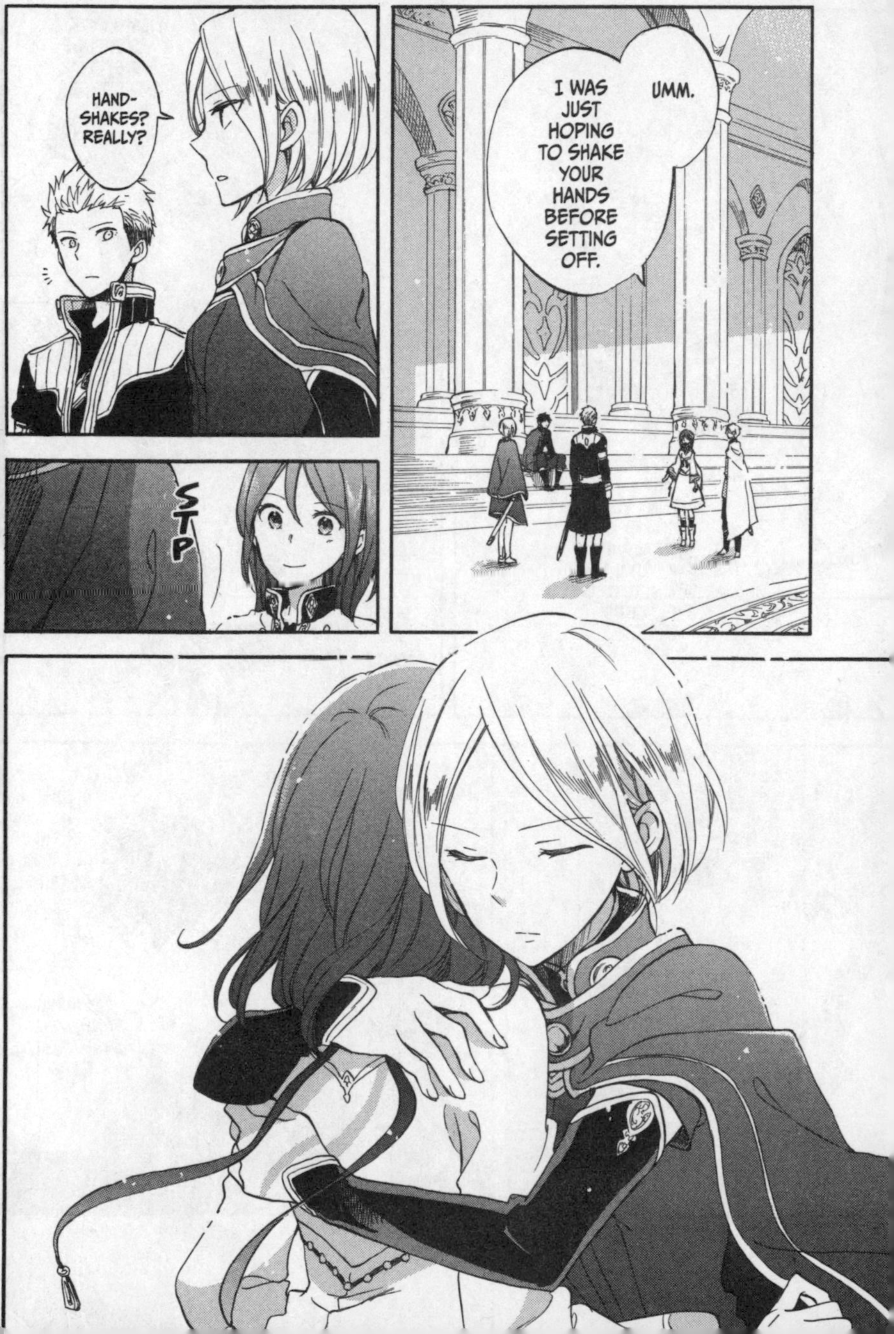
UMM.
I WAS JUST HOPING TO SHAKE YOUR HANDS BEFORE SETTING OFF.
HAND-SHAKES? REALLY?
STP

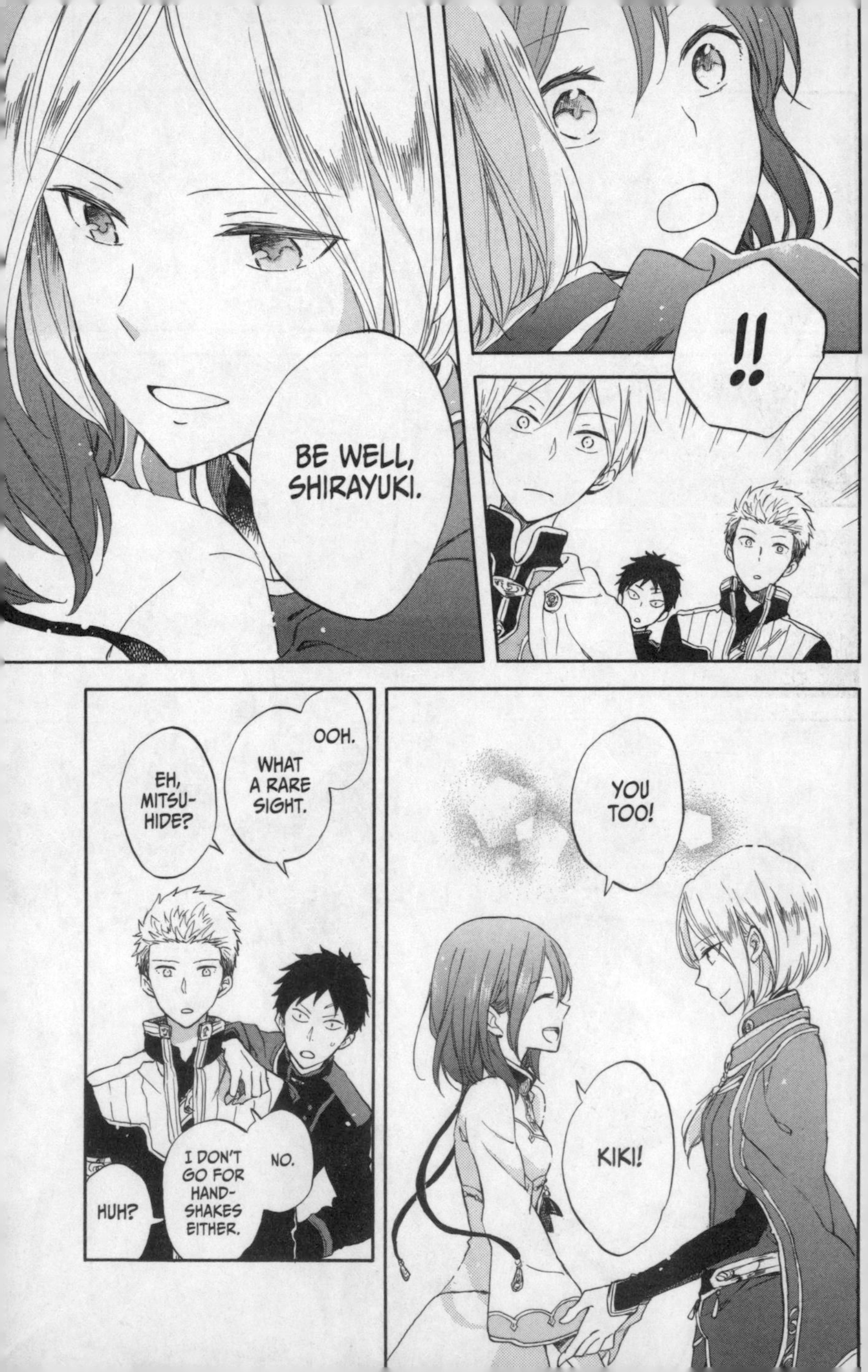
!!
BE WELL, SHIRAYUKI.
YOU TOO!
KIKI!
OOH.
WHAT A RARE SIGHT.
EH, MITSU-HIDE?
NO.
I DON'T GO FOR HAND-SHAKES EITHER.
HUH?

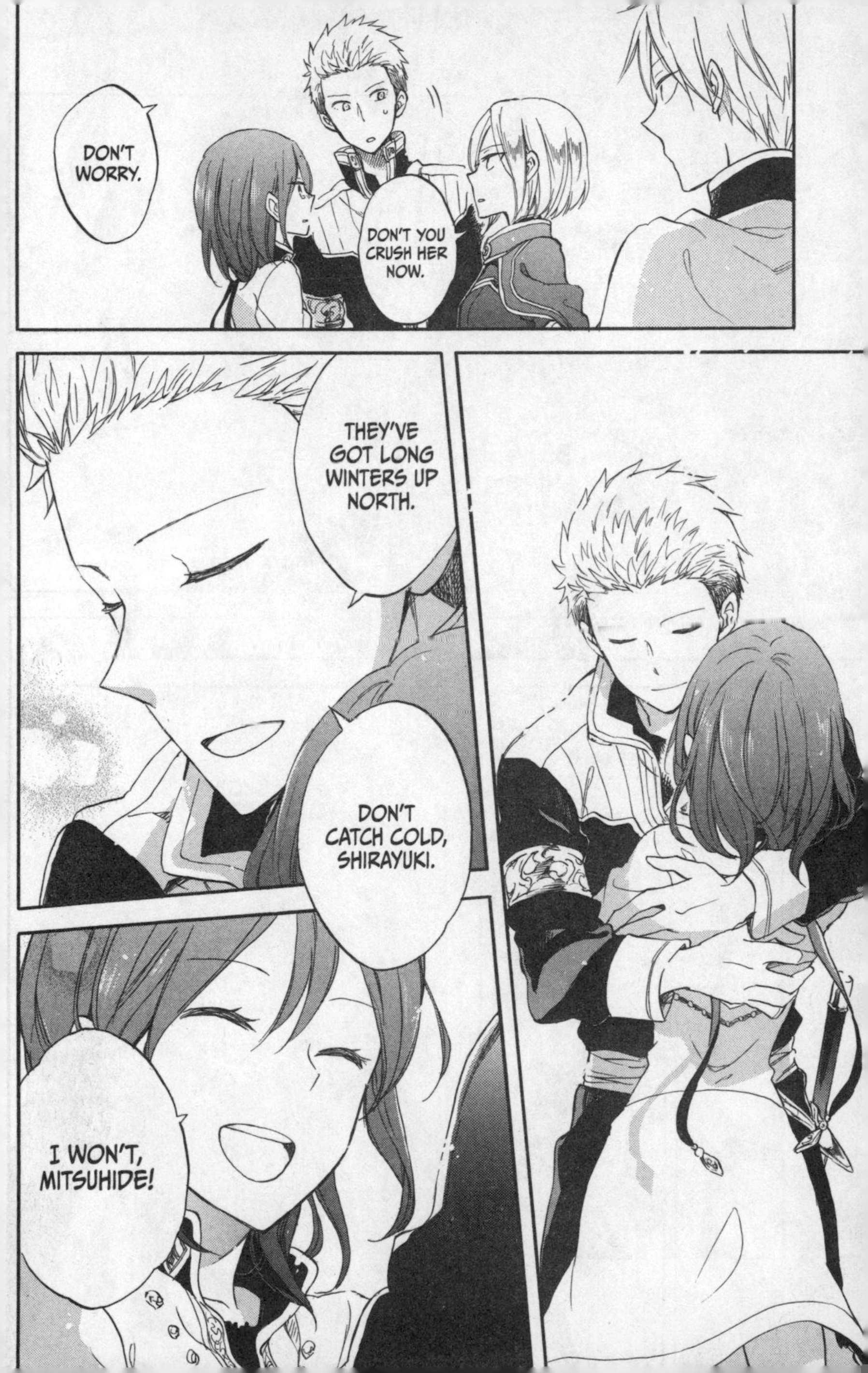
DON'T YOU CRUSH HER NOW.
DON'T WORRY.
THEY'VE GOT LONG WINTERS UP NORTH.
DON'T CATCH COLD, SHIRAYUKI.
I WON'T, MITSUHIDE!

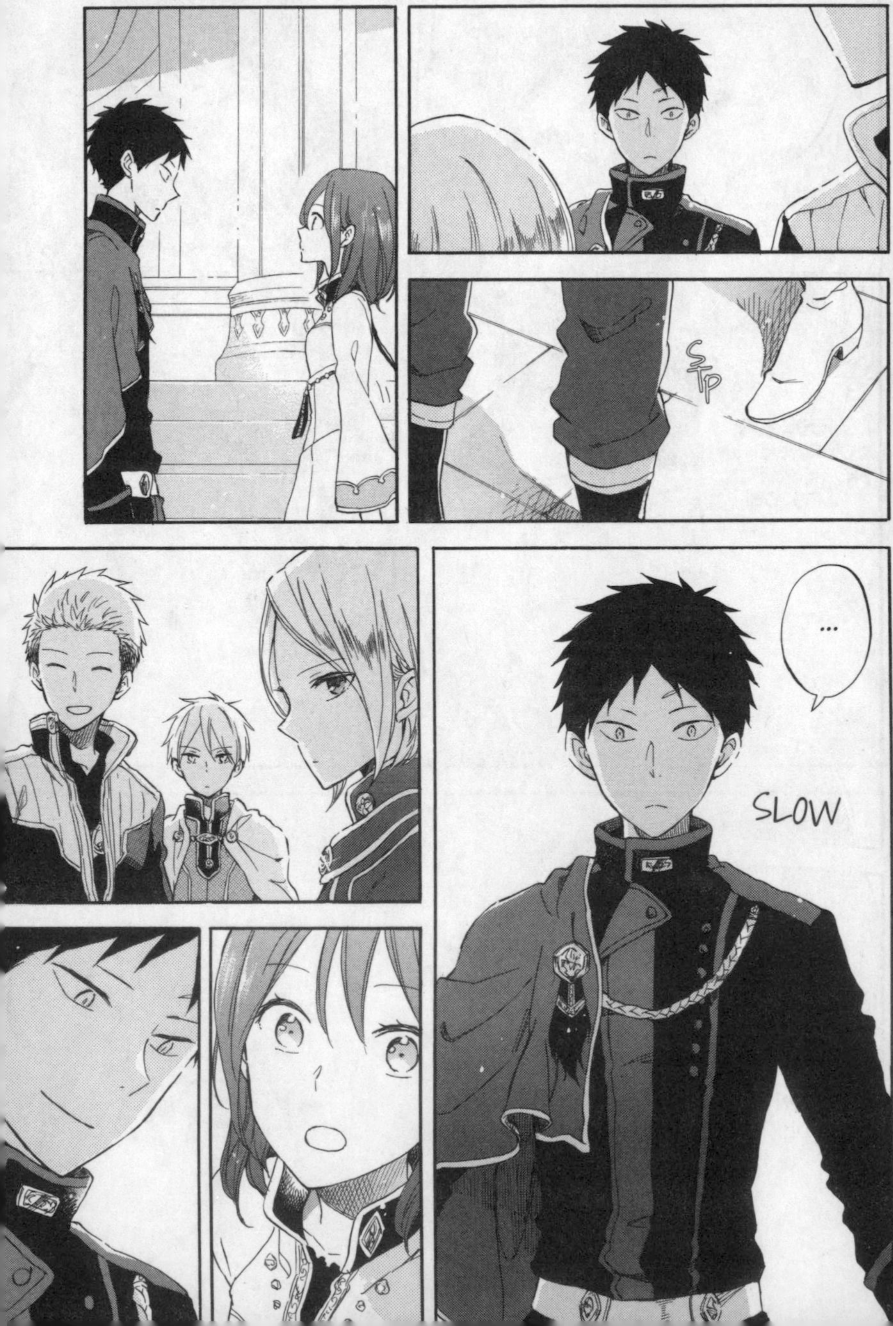
STP
...
SLOW

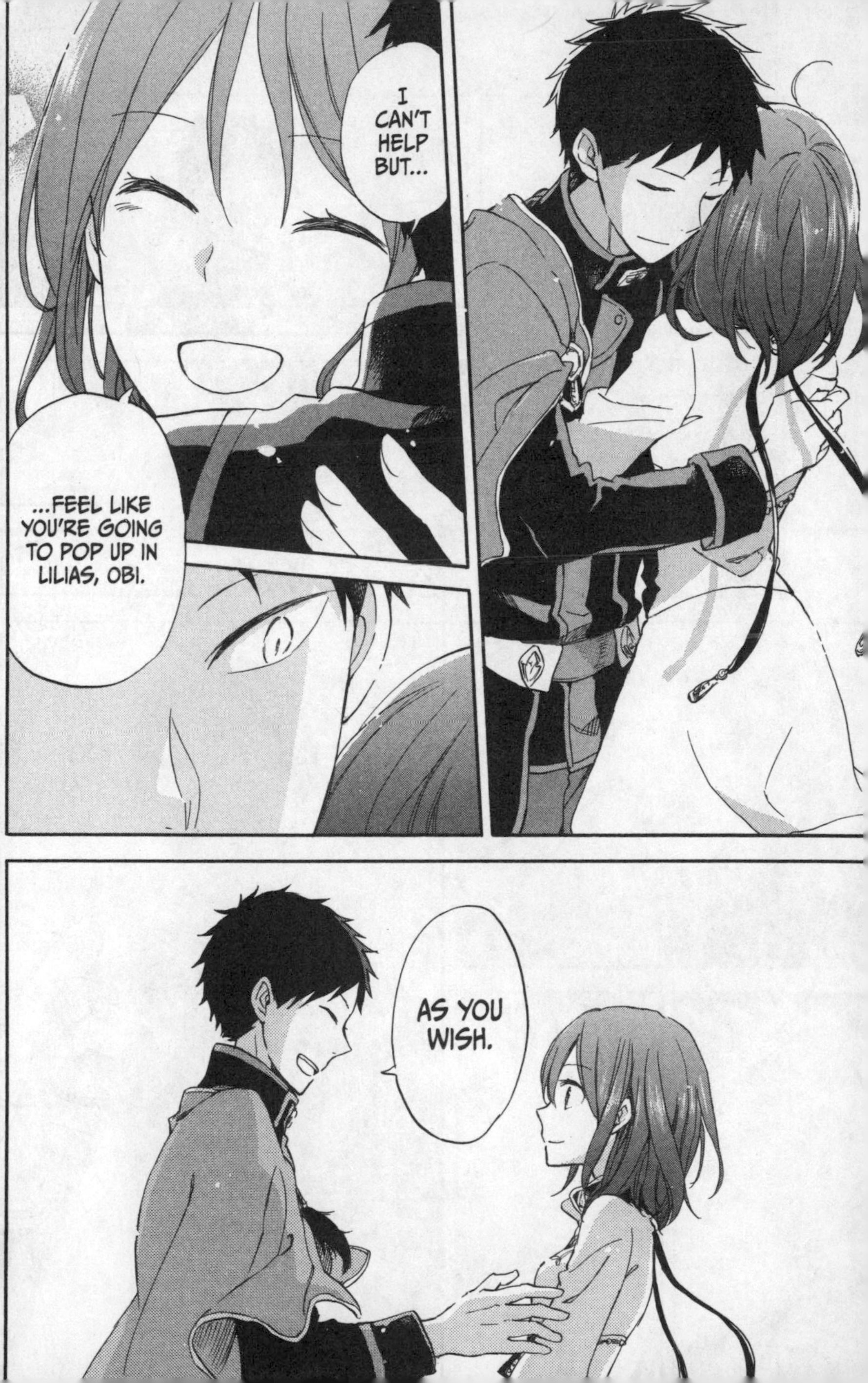
I CAN'T HELP BUT...
...FEEL LIKE YOU'RE GOING TO POP UP IN LILIAS, OBI.
AS YOU WISH.

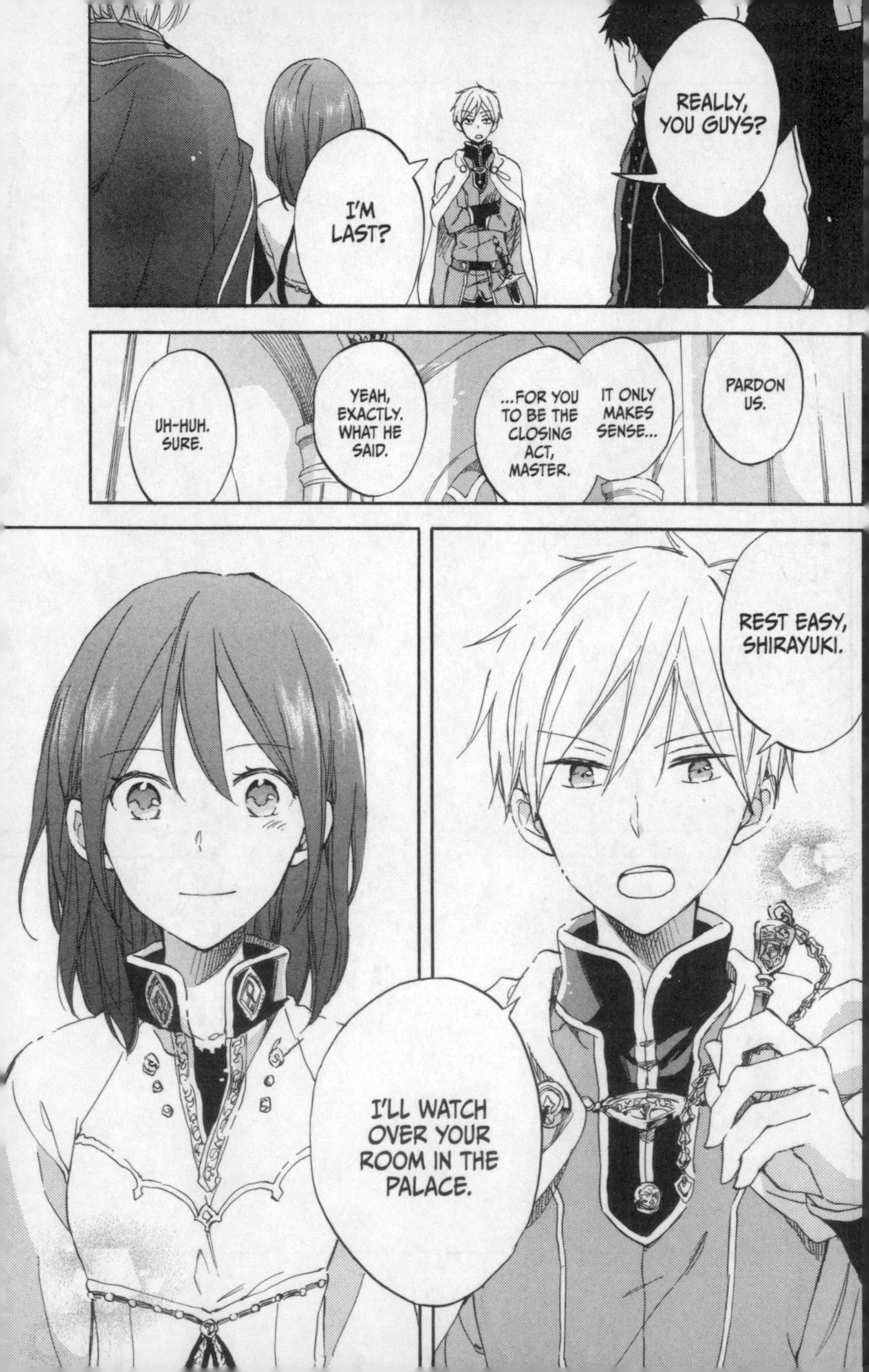
REALLY, YOU GUYS?
I'M LAST?
PARDON US.
IT ONLY MAKES SENSE...
...FOR YOU TO BE THE CLOSING ACT, MASTER.
YEAH, EXACTLY. WHAT HE SAID.
UH-HUH. SURE.
REST EASY, SHIRAYUKI.
I'LL WATCH OVER YOUR ROOM IN THE PALACE.

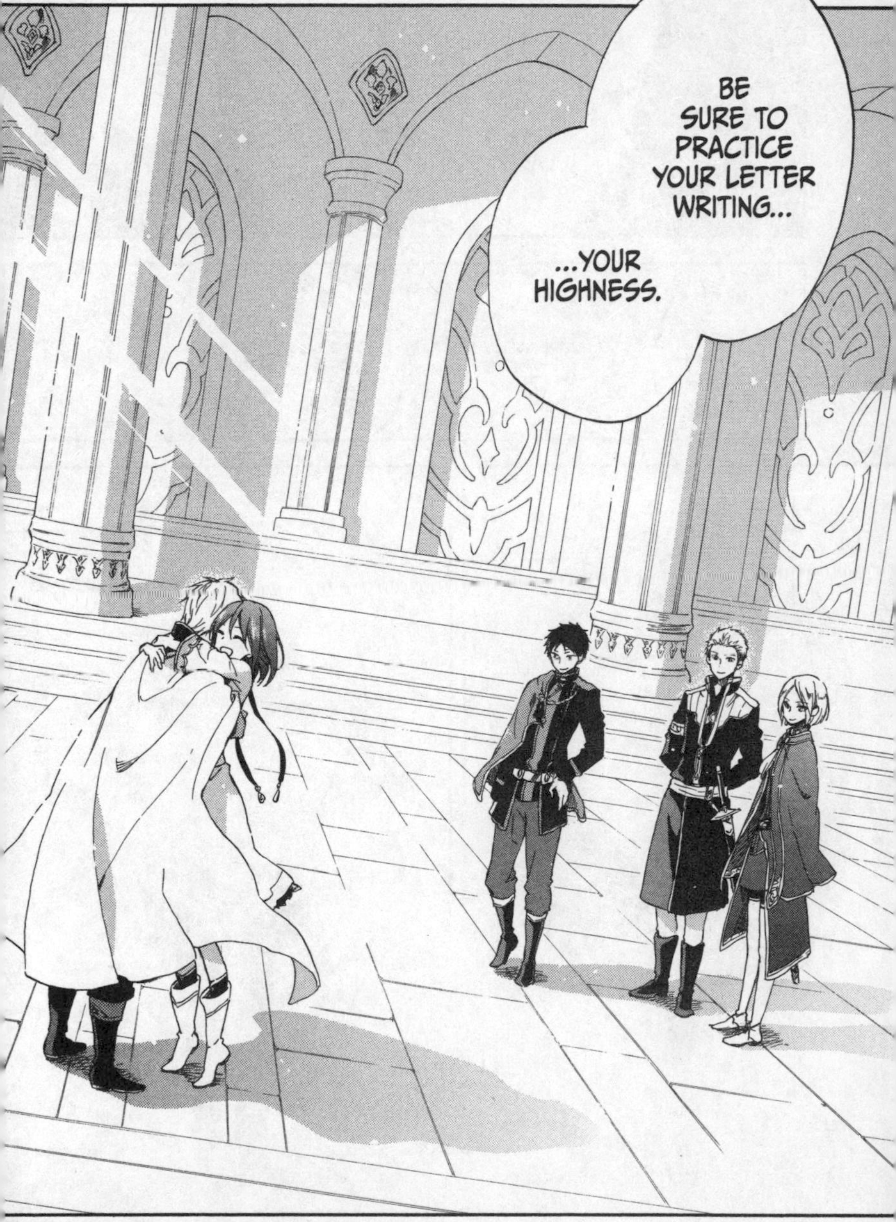
BE SURE TO PRACTICE YOUR LETTER WRITING...
...YOUR HIGHNESS.

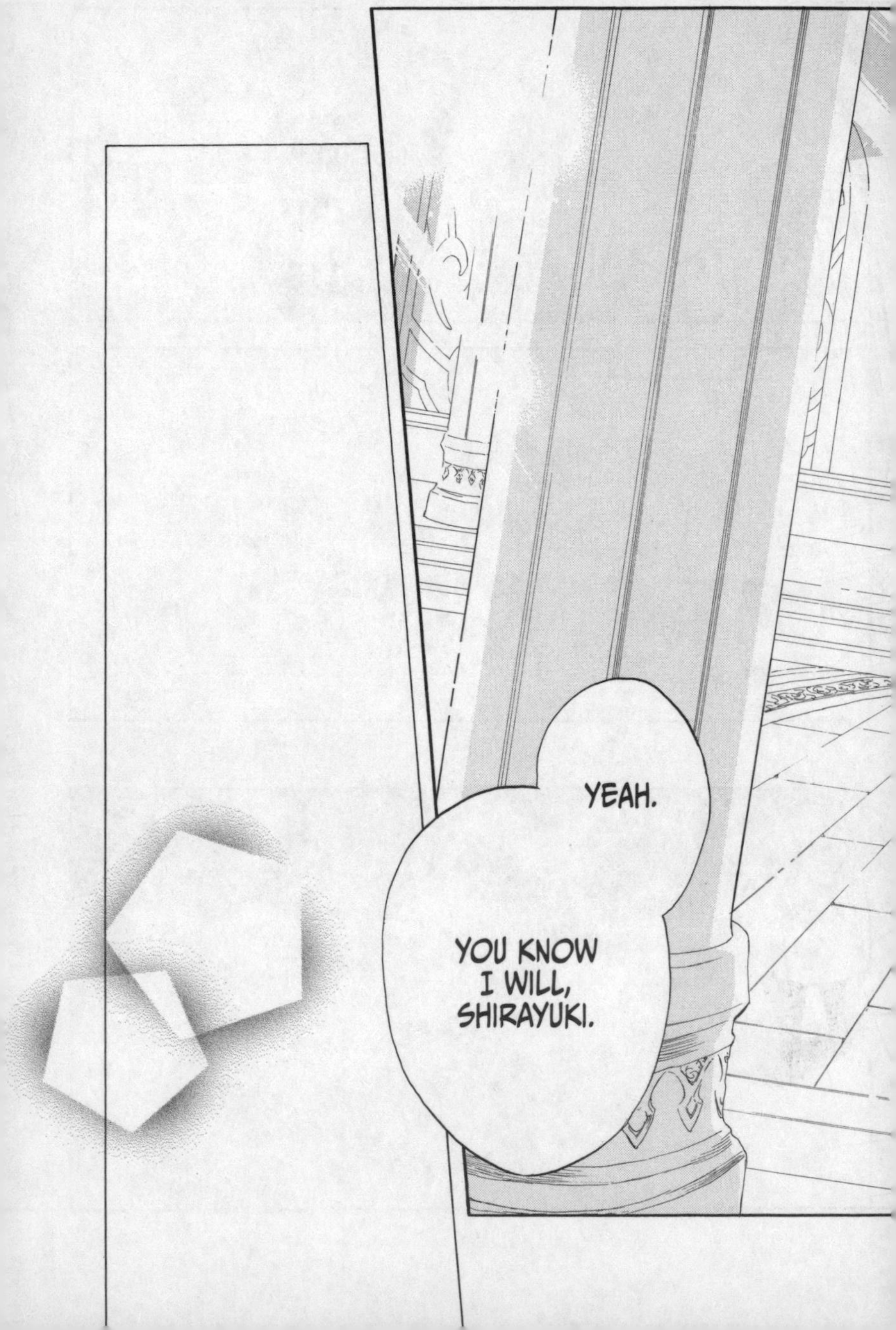
YEAH.
YOU KNOW I WILL, SHIRAYUKI.

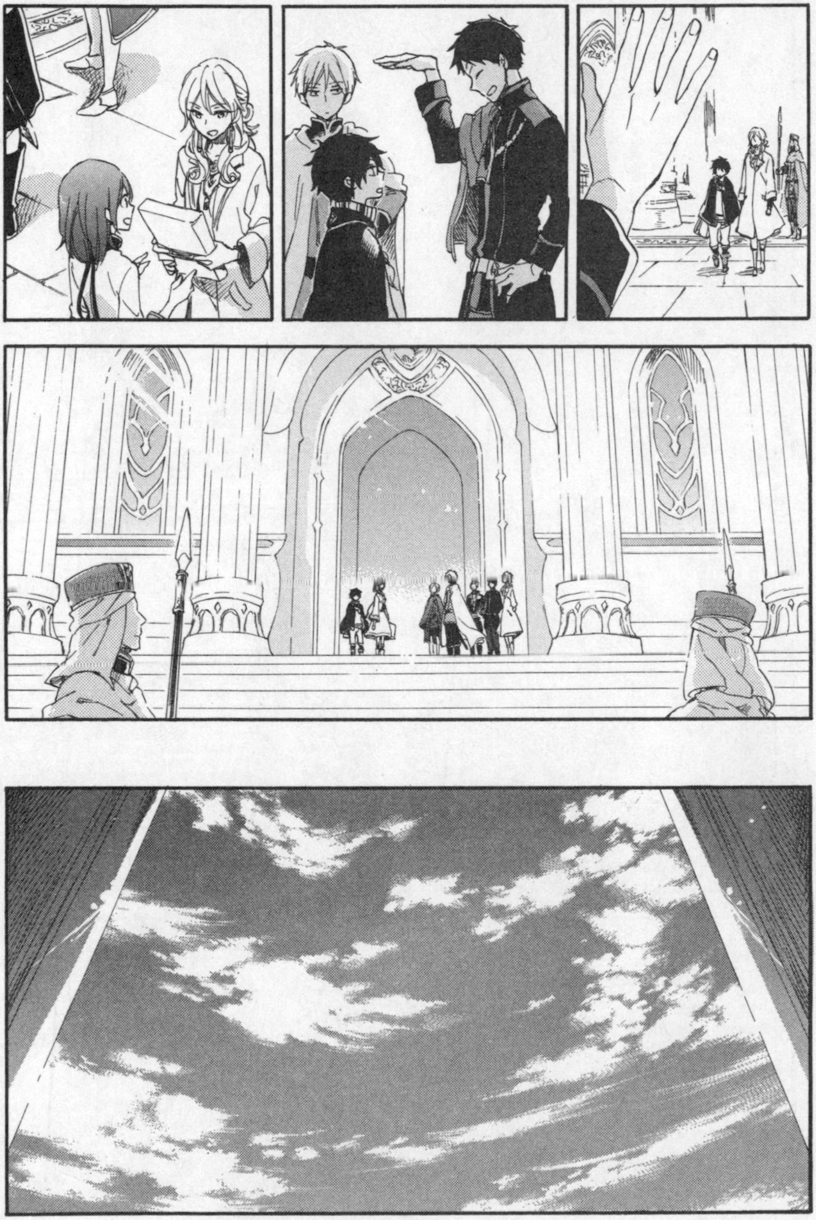

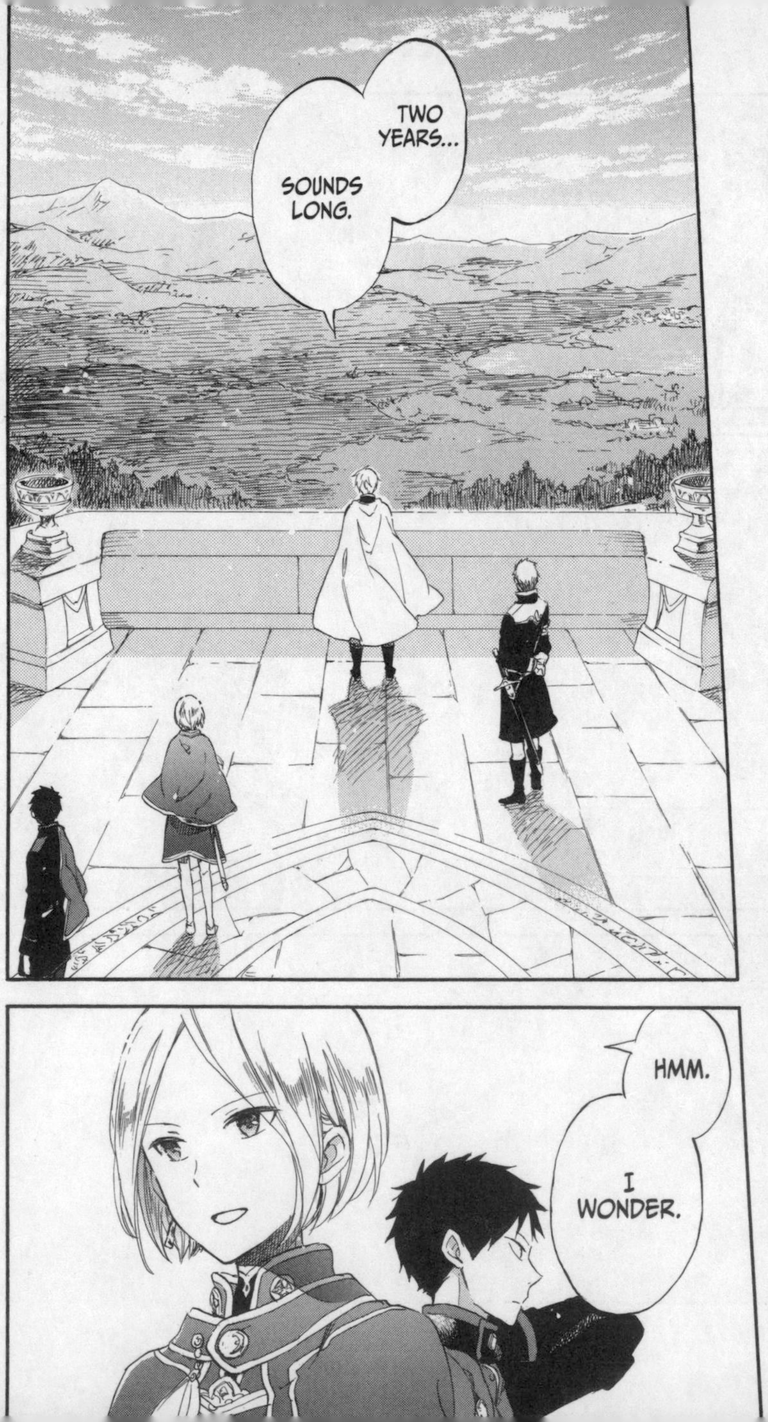
TWO YEARS... SOUNDS LONG.
HMM. I WONDER.

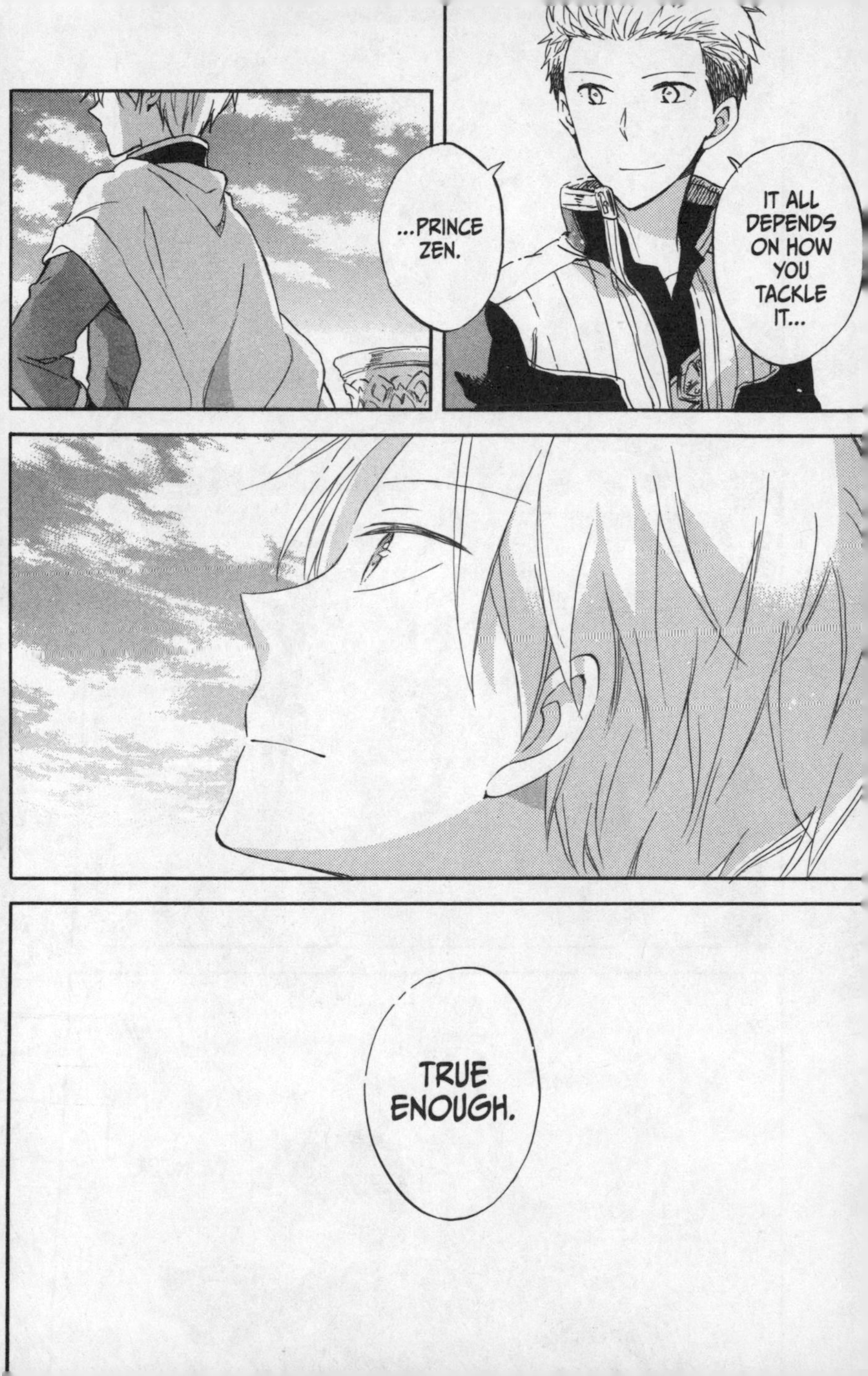
IT ALL DEPENDS ON HOW YOU TACKLE IT...
...PRINCE ZEN.
TRUE ENOUGH.

Chapter 58

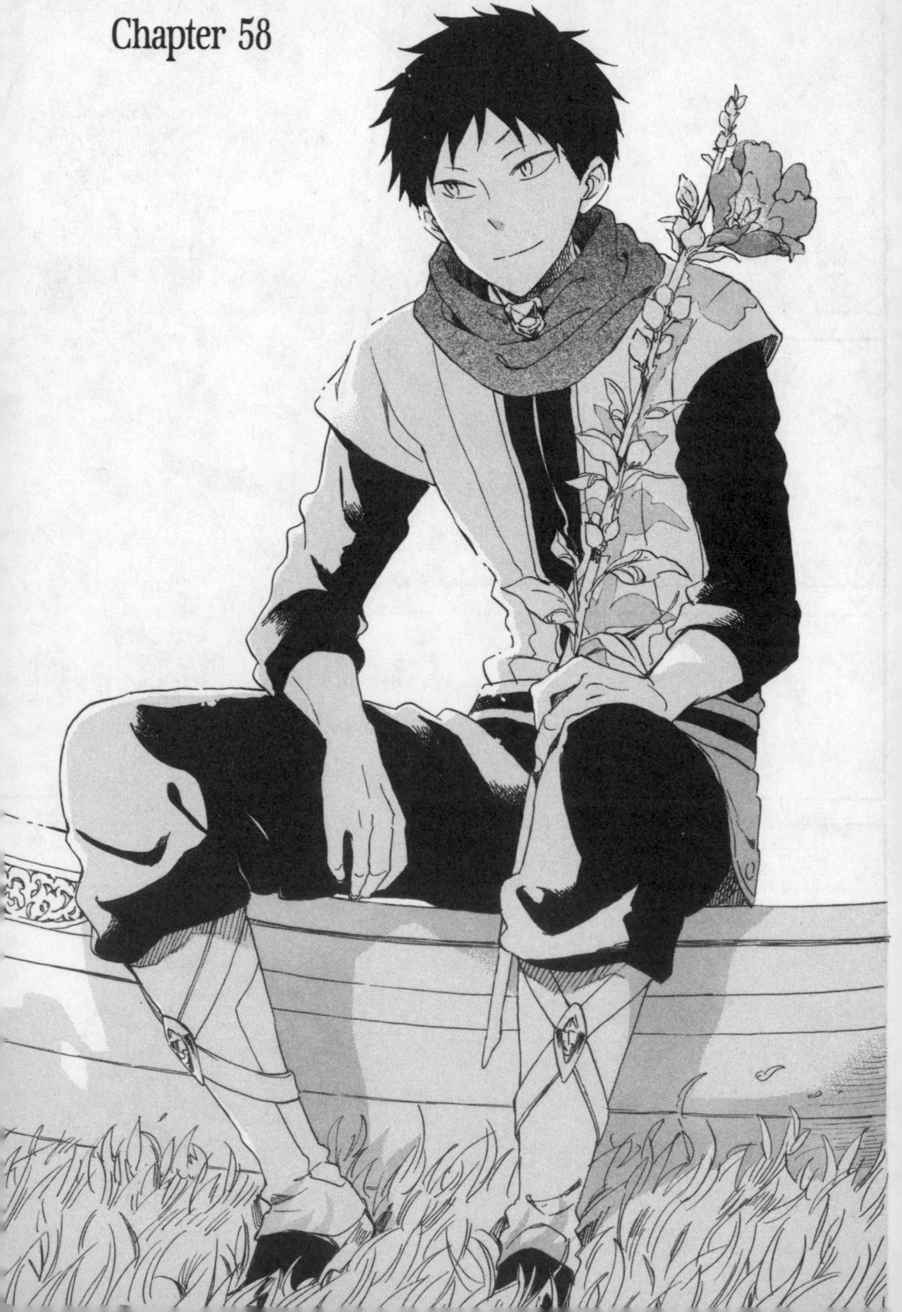

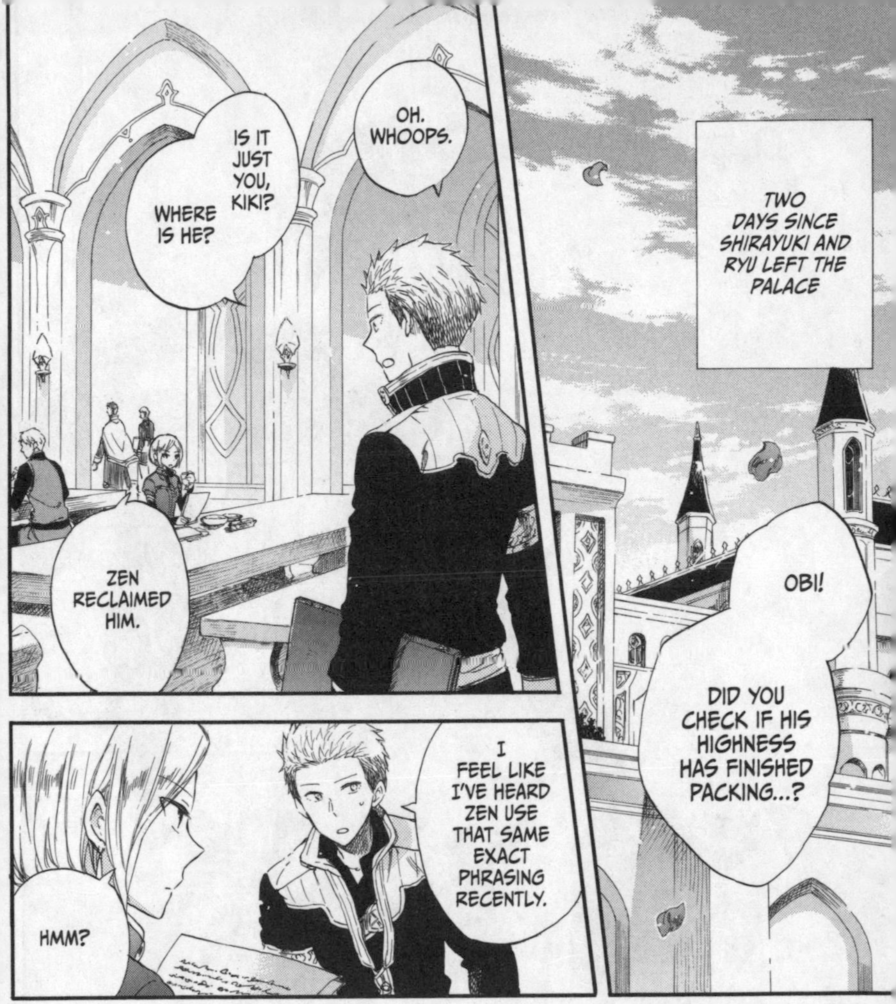
TWO DAYS SINCE SHIRAYUKI AND RYU LEFT THE PALACE
OBI!
DID YOU CHECK IF HIS HIGHNESS HAS FINISHED PACKING...?
OH. WHOOPS.
IS IT JUST YOU, KIKI?
WHERE IS HE?
ZEN RECLAIMED HIM.
I FEEL LIKE I'VE HEARD ZEN USE THAT SAME EXACT PHRASING RECENTLY.
HMM?

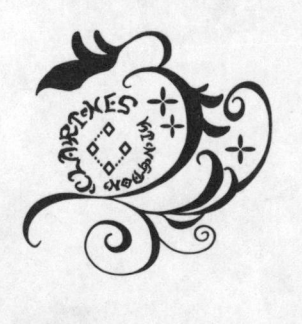

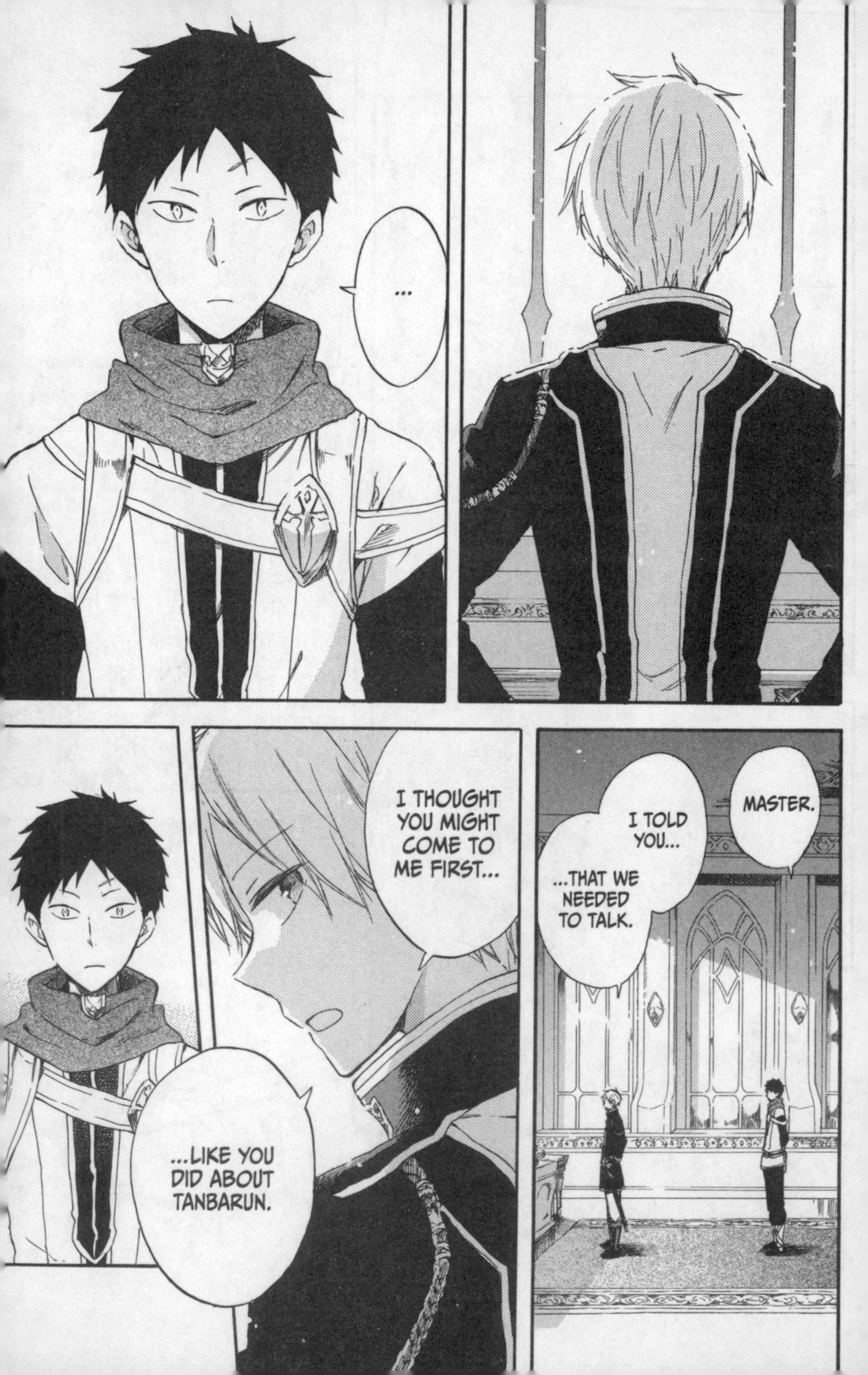
...
MASTER.
I TOLD YOU...
...THAT WE NEEDED TO TALK.
I THOUGHT YOU MIGHT COME TO ME FIRST...
...LIKE YOU DID ABOUT TANBARUN.

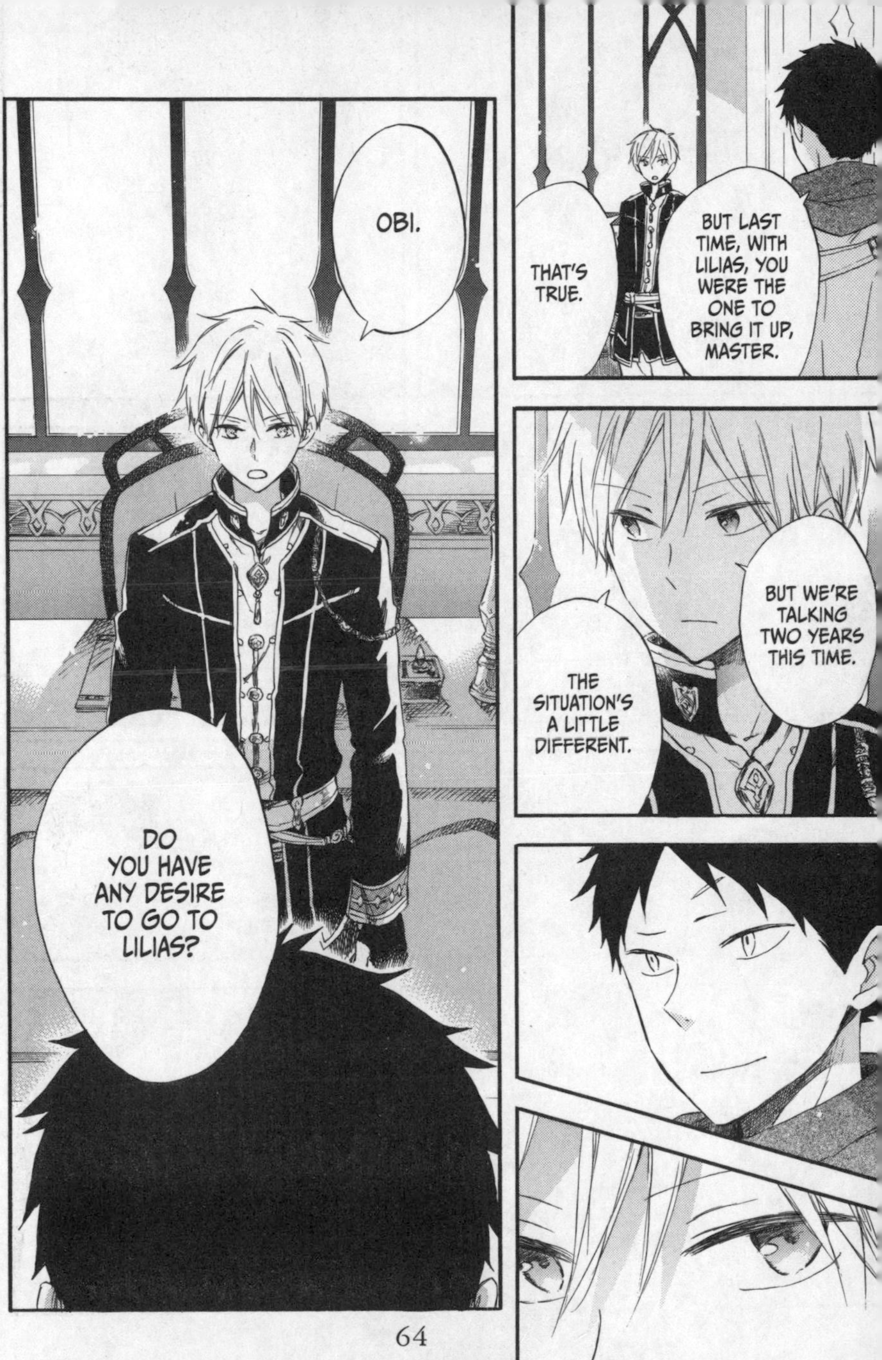
BUT LAST TIME, WITH LILIAS, YOU WERE THE ONE TO BRING IT UP, MASTER.
THAT'S TRUE.
BUT WE'RE TALKING TWO YEARS THIS TIME.
THE SITUATION'S A LITTLE DIFFERENT.
OBI.
DO YOU HAVE ANY DESIRE TO GO TO LILIAS?

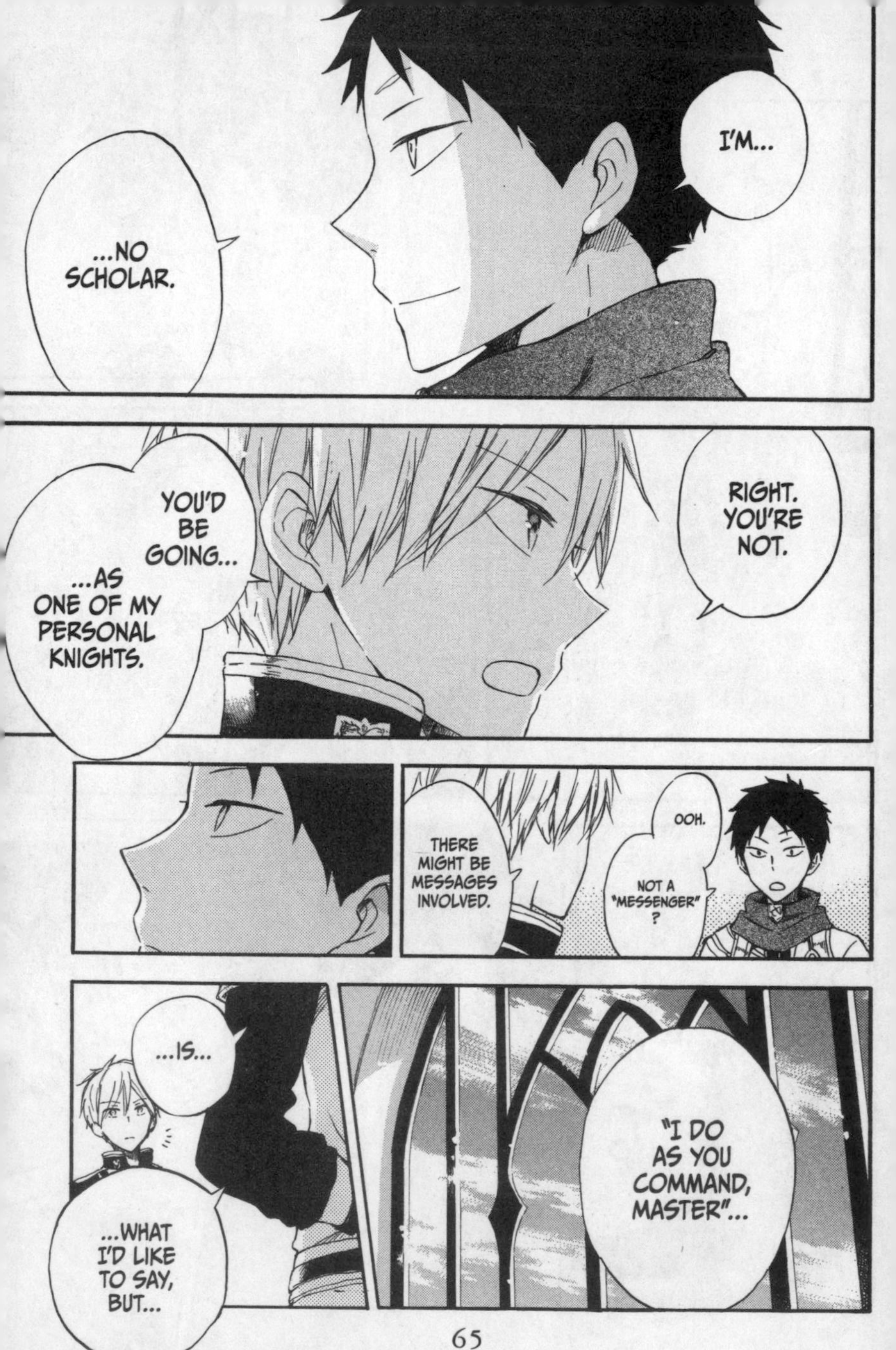
I'M...
...NO SCHOLAR.
RIGHT. YOU'RE NOT.
YOU'D BE GOING...
...AS ONE OF MY PERSONAL KNIGHTS.
OOH.
NOT A "MESSENGER"?
THERE MIGHT BE MESSAGES INVOLVED.
"I DO AS YOU COMMAND, MASTER"...
...IS...
...WHAT I'D LIKE TO SAY, BUT...

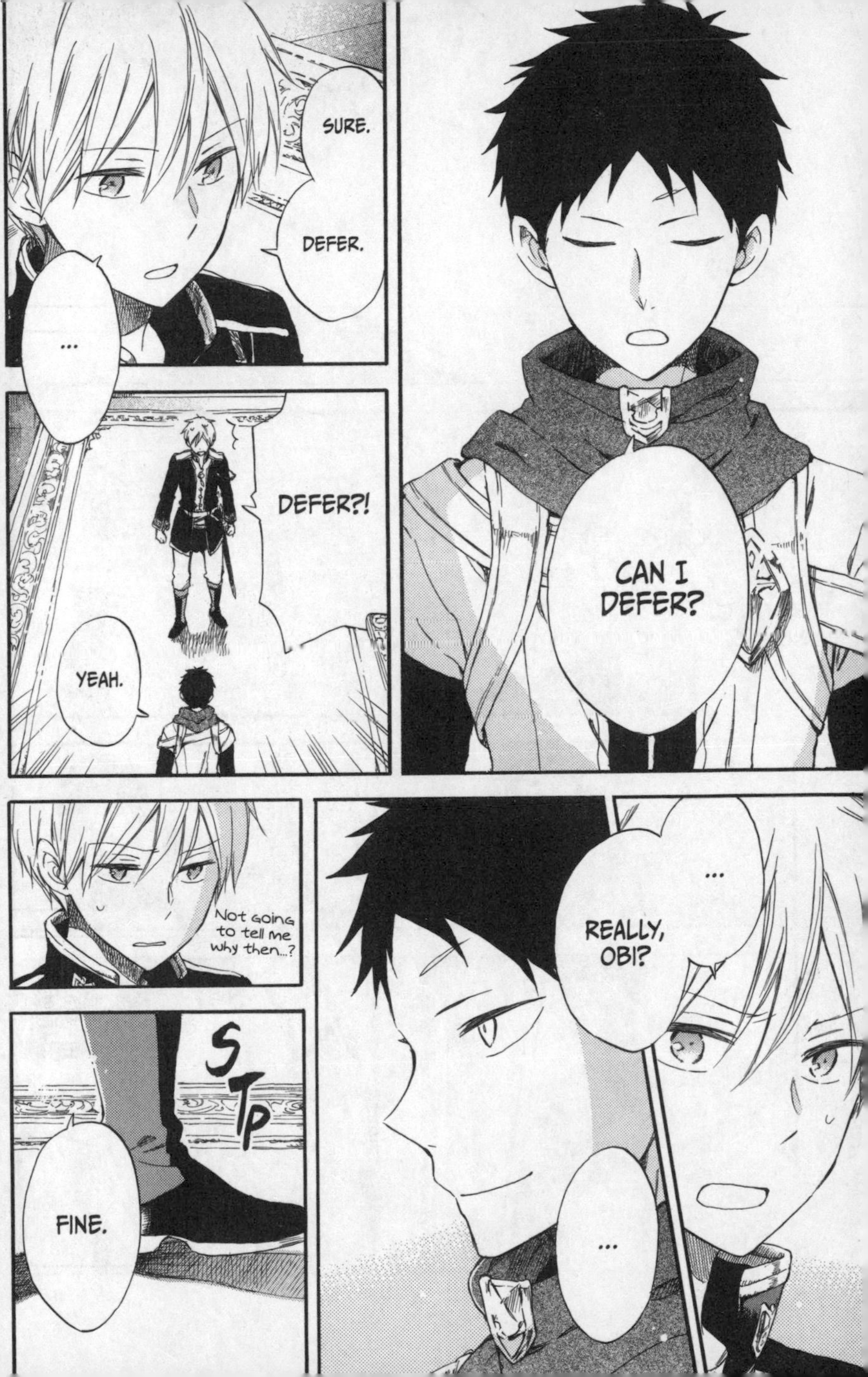
CAN I DEFER?
SURE.
DEFER.
...
DEFER?!
YEAH.
...
REALLY, OBI?
...
Not going to tell me why then...?
STP
FINE.

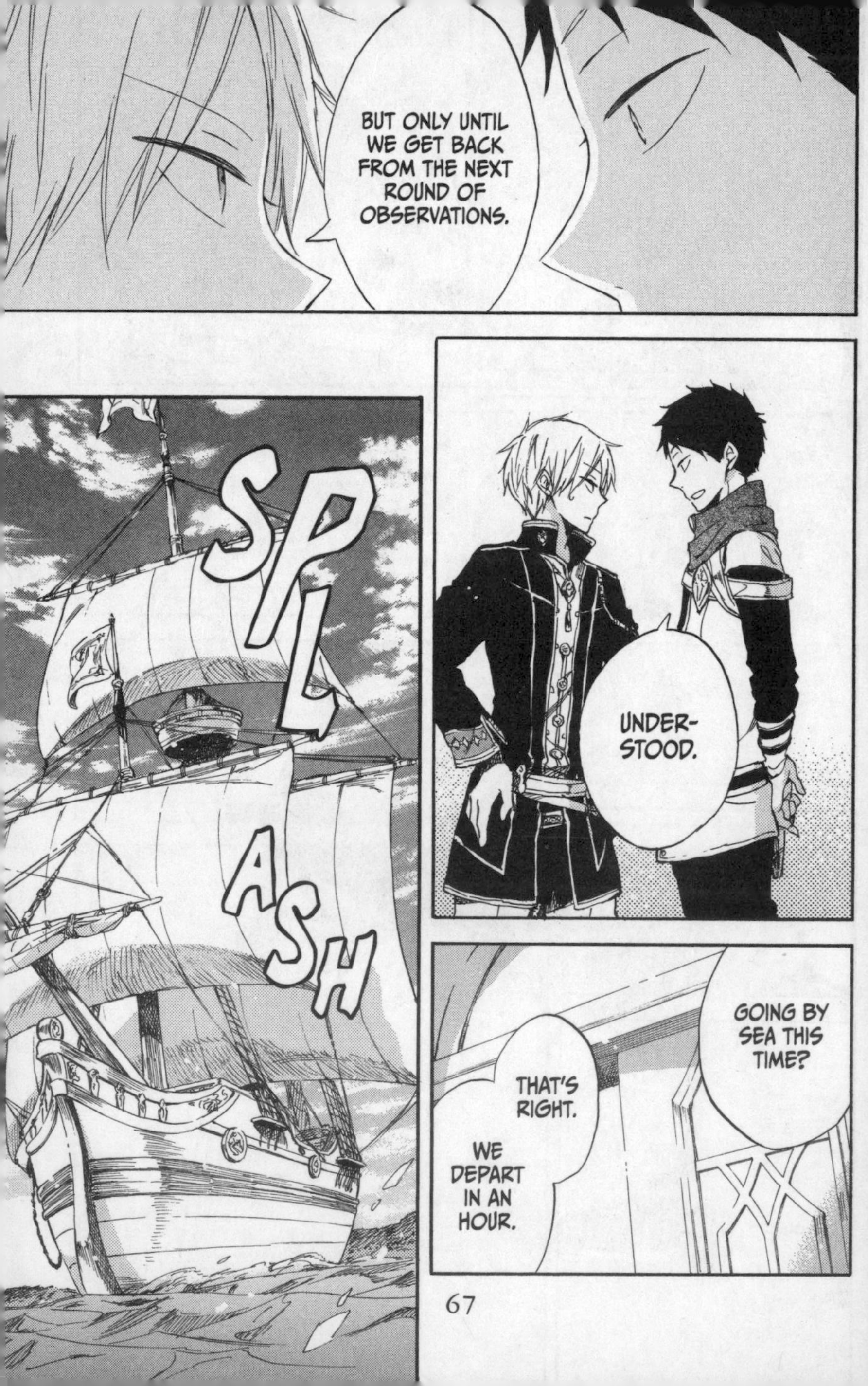
BUT ONLY UNTIL WE GET BACK FROM THE NEXT ROUND OF OBSERVATIONS.
UNDER-STOOD.
GOING BY SEA THIS TIME?
THAT'S RIGHT.
WE DEPART IN AN HOUR.
SPLASH

["

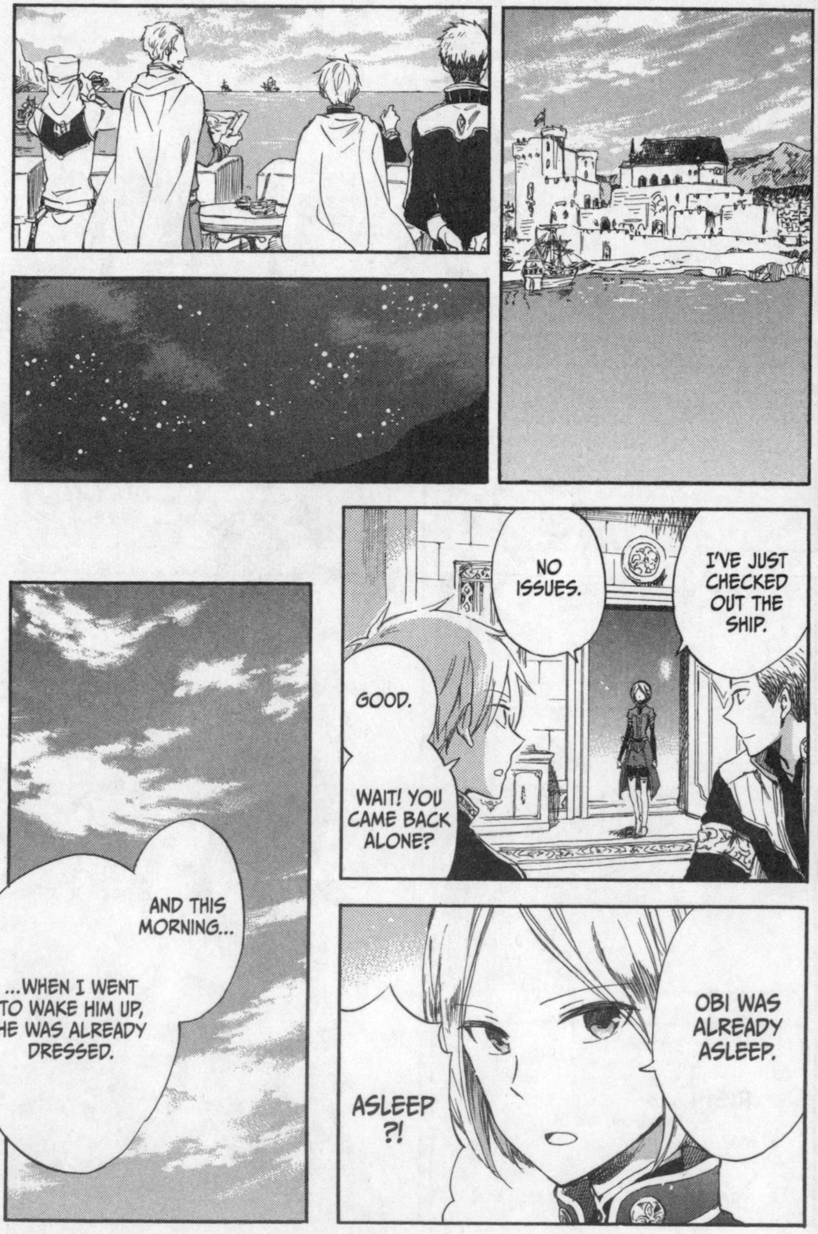
I'VE JUST CHECKED OUT THE SHIP.
NO ISSUES.
GOOD.
WAIT! YOU CAME BACK ALONE?
OBI WAS ALREADY ASLEEP.
ASLEEP ?!
AND THIS MORNING...
...WHEN I WENT TO WAKE HIM UP, HE WAS ALREADY DRESSED.

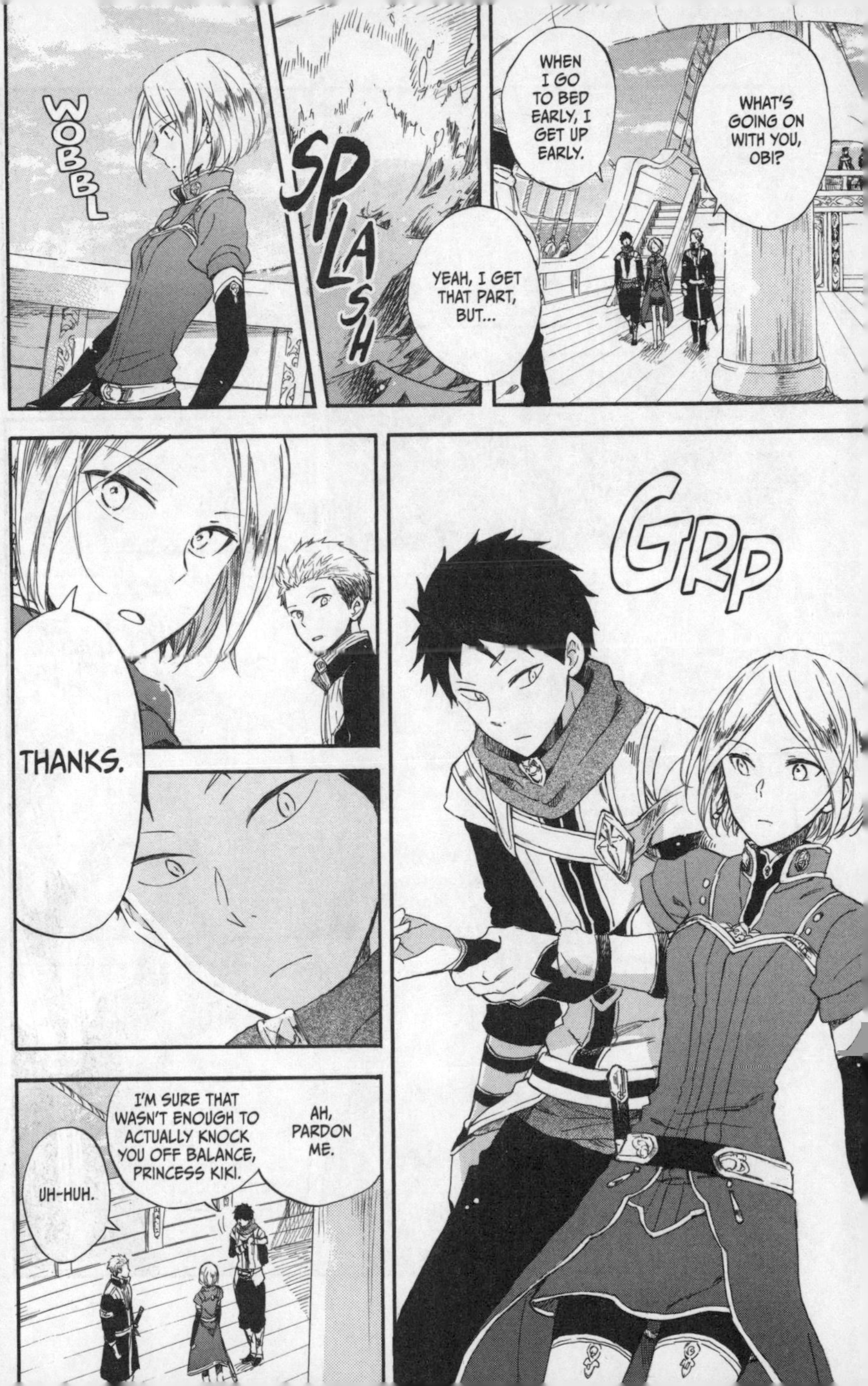
WHAT'S GOING ON WITH YOU, OBI?
WHEN I GO TO BED EARLY, I GET UP EARLY.
YEAH, I GET THAT PART, BUT...
SPLASH
WOBBL
GRP
THANKS.
AH, PARDON ME.
I'M SURE THAT WASN'T ENOUGH TO ACTUALLY KNOCK YOU OFF BALANCE, PRINCESS KIKI.
UH-HUH.

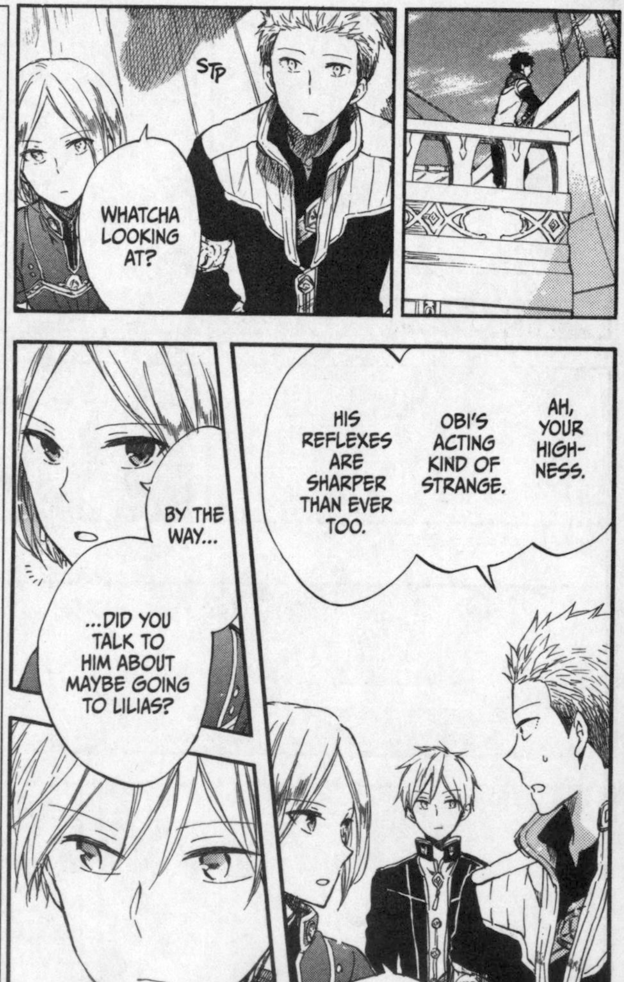

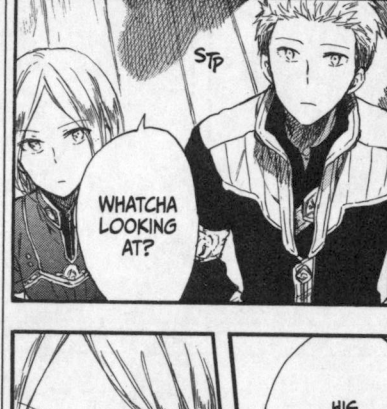

STP
WHATCHA LOOKING AT?
AH, YOUR HIGH-NESS.
OBI'S ACTING KIND OF STRANGE.
HIS REFLEXES ARE SHARPER THAN EVER TOO.
AND HE SEEMS TO BE AVOIDING YOU, YOUR HIGHNESS.
BY THE WAY...
...DID YOU TALK TO HIM ABOUT MAYBE GOING TO LILIAS?

3

TRIP (PART 2)

The best part was the tea seminar. We got a live demonstration on how to serve several types of tea (presented in Japanese), and then we got to enjoy them with snacks.

First, they poured water into the teapot, filling it nearly to the brim. Then, interestingly enough, they poured a little more on top to shift the aroma around before drinking.

I wanted to buy a whole set...

I did end up buying tea leaves—four boxes of little hardened balls of pu'er that had been aged for 20 years! "Four boxes is the perfect amount!" is how they pitched it, and before I knew it, I had four boxes in my basket. "I'll never be able to drink four whole boxes' worth!" "Nonsense! Of course you can!" That was basically the back-and-forth with the employee (in Japanese). I split those four boxes with Hibiki, and I still probably won't run out of pu'er tea for a good two years or so.

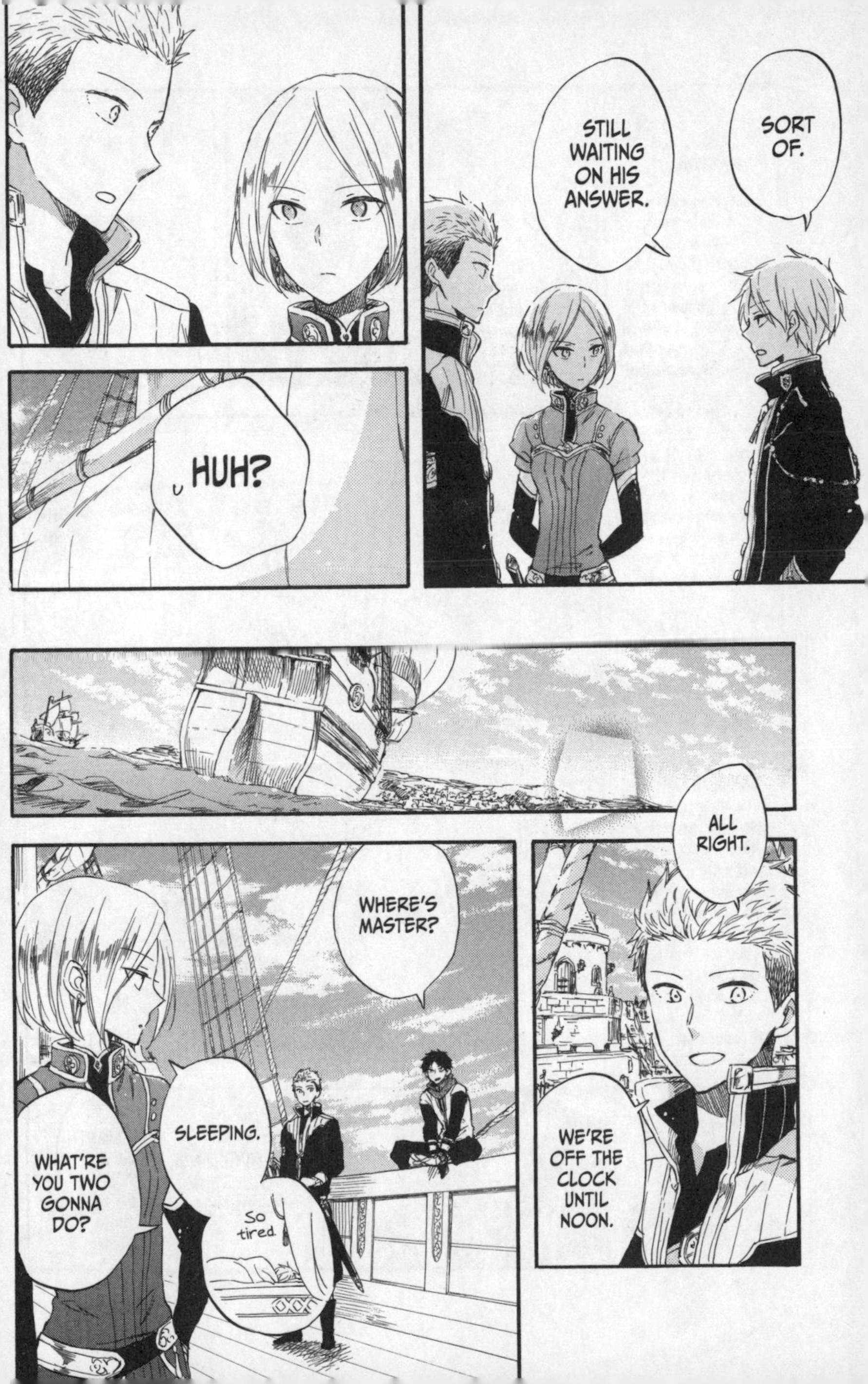
SORT OF.
STILL WAITING ON HIS ANSWER.
HUH?
ALL RIGHT.
WE'RE OFF THE CLOCK UNTIL NOON.
WHERE'S MASTER?
SLEEPING.
So tired.
WHAT'RE YOU TWO GONNA DO?

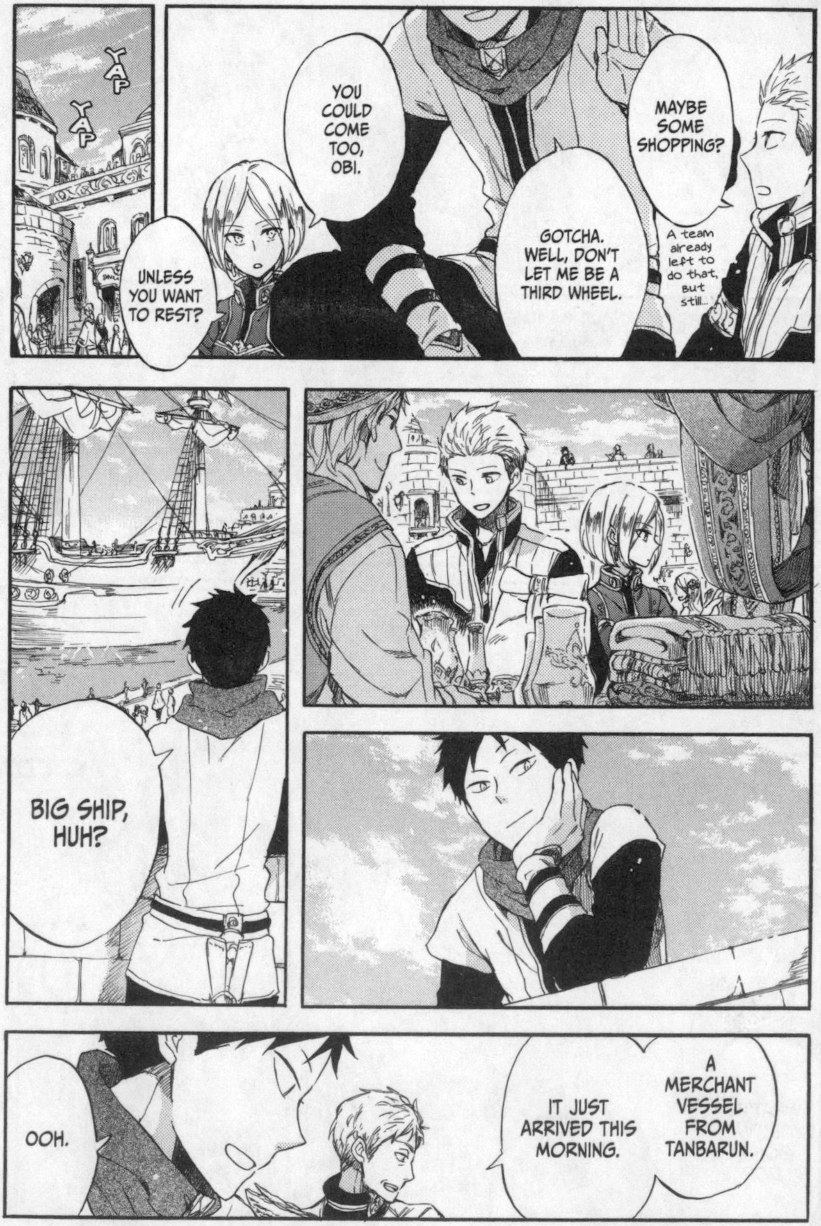
MAYBE SOME SHOPPING?
A team already left to do that, but still...
GOTCHA. WELL, DON'T LET ME BE A THIRD WHEEL.
YOU COULD COME TOO, OBI.
UNLESS YOU WANT TO REST?
YAP YAP
BIG SHIP, HUH?
A MERCHANT VESSEL FROM TANBARUN.
IT JUST ARRIVED THIS MORNING.
OOH.

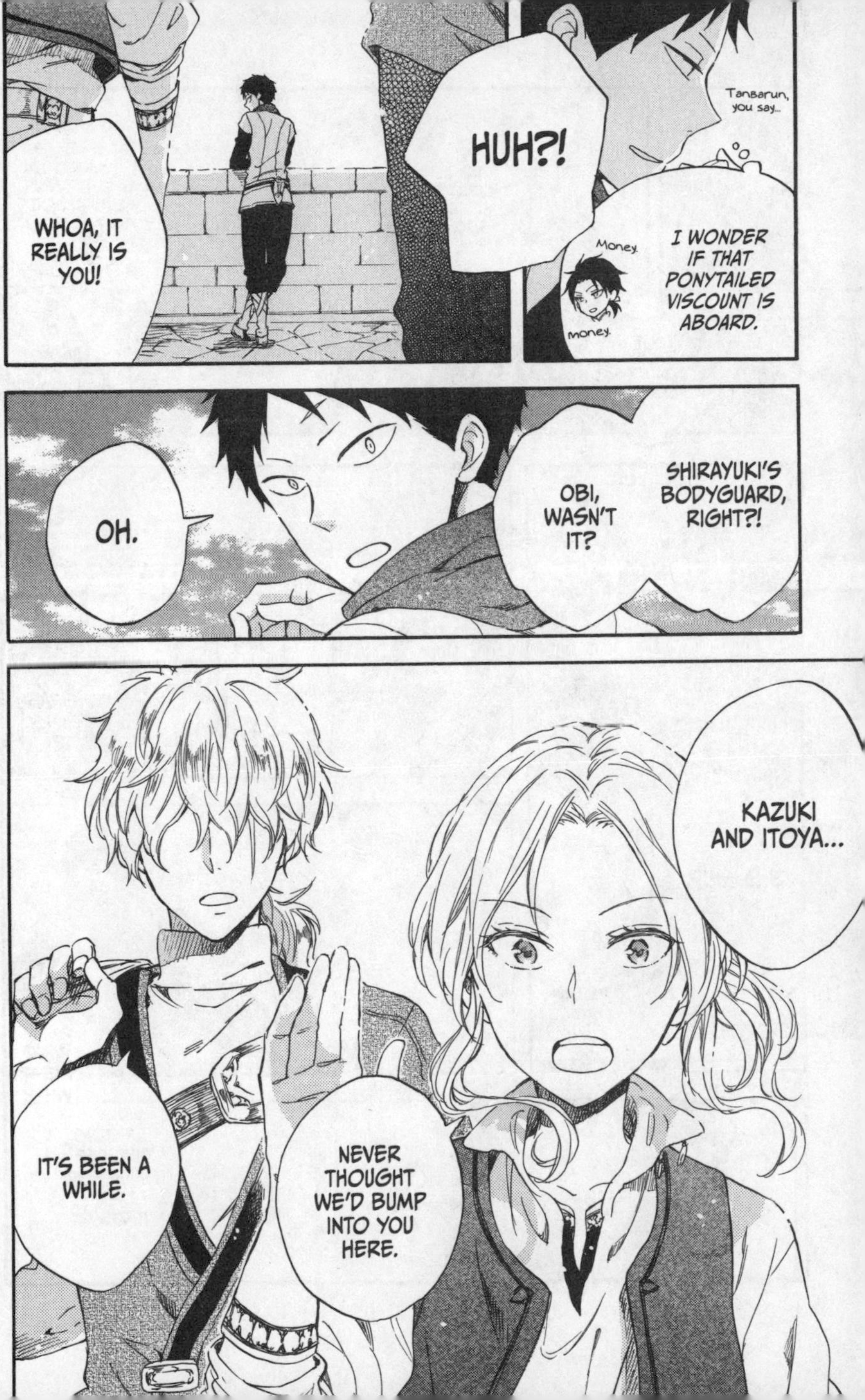
Tanbarun, you say...
I WONDER IF THAT PONYTAILED VISCOUNT IS ABOARD.
Money.
money.
HUH?!
WHOA, IT REALLY IS YOU!
SHIRAYUKI'S BODYGUARD, RIGHT?!
OBI, WASN'T IT?
OH.
KAZUKI AND ITOYA...
NEVER THOUGHT WE'D BUMP INTO YOU HERE.
IT'S BEEN A WHILE.

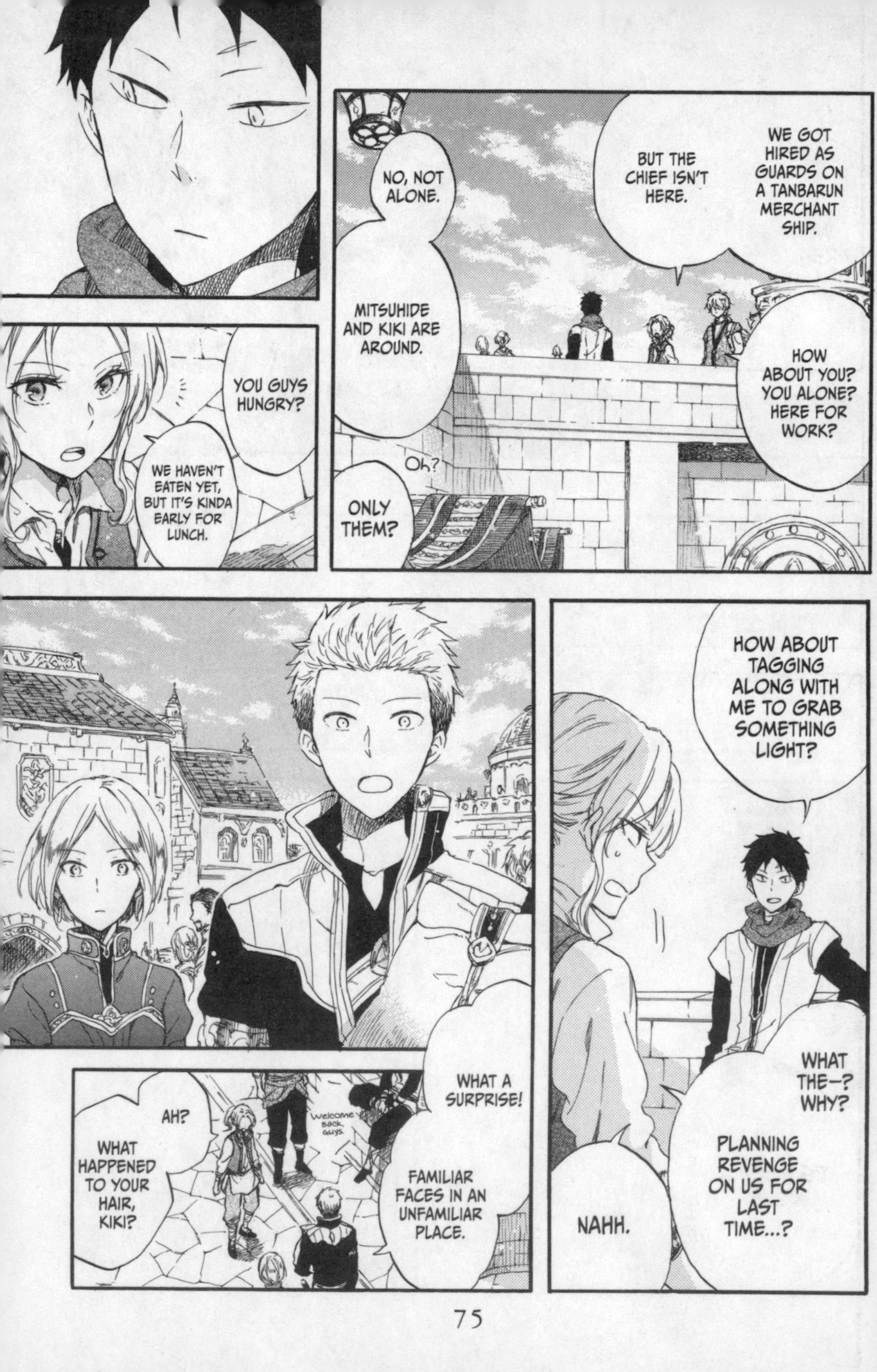
WE GOT HIRED AS GUARDS ON A TANBARUN MERCHANT SHIP.
BUT THE CHIEF ISN'T HERE.
HOW ABOUT YOU? YOU ALONE? HERE FOR WORK?
NO, NOT ALONE.
MITSUHIDE AND KIKI ARE AROUND.
Oh?
ONLY THEM?
YOU GUYS HUNGRY?
WE HAVEN'T EATEN YET, BUT IT'S KINDA EARLY FOR LUNCH.
HOW ABOUT TAGGING ALONG WITH ME TO GRAB SOMETHING LIGHT?
WHAT THE—? WHY?
PLANNING REVENGE ON US FOR LAST TIME...?
NAHH.
WHAT A SURPRISE!
FAMILIAR FACES IN AN UNFAMILIAR PLACE.
Welcome back, guys.
AH?
WHAT HAPPENED TO YOUR HAIR, KIKI?

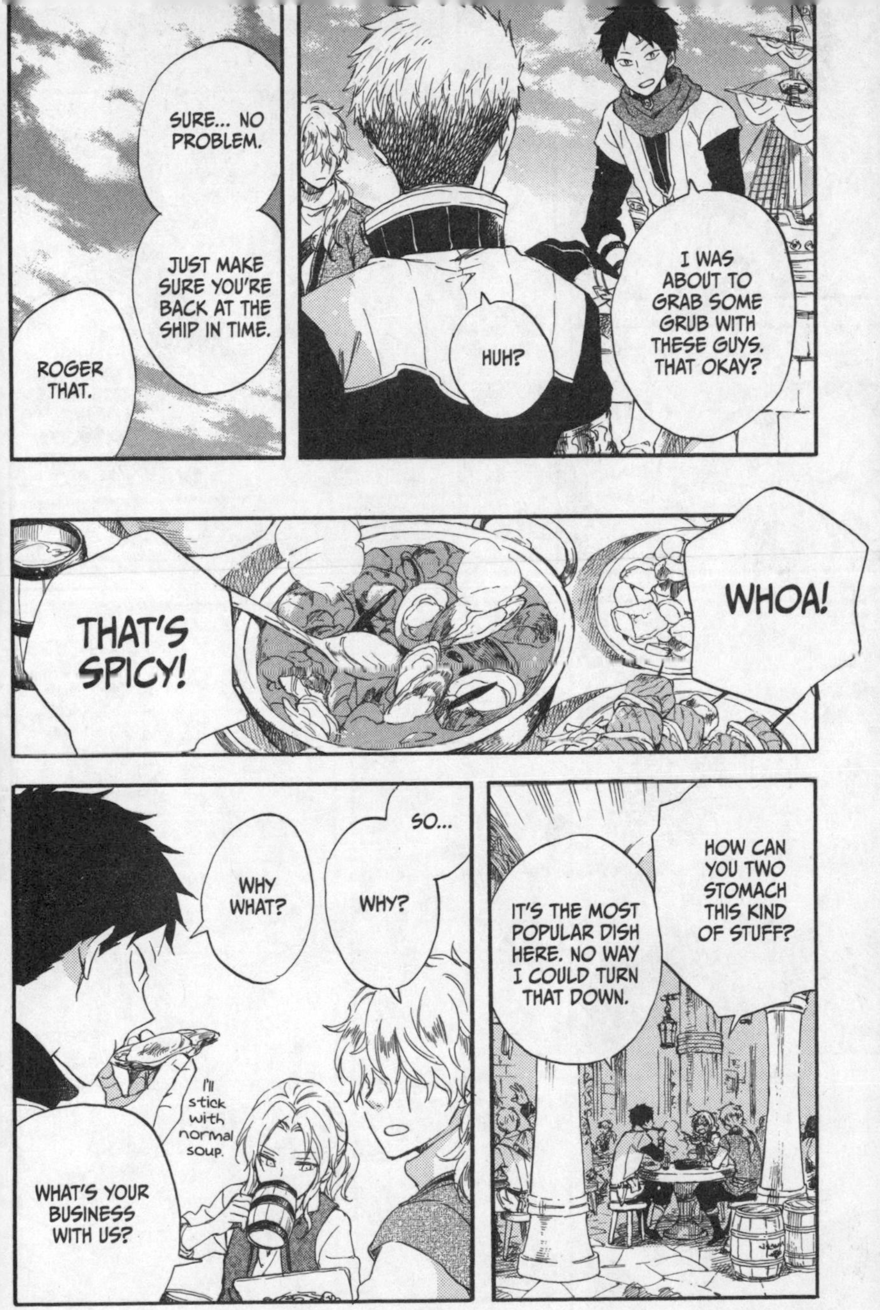
I WAS ABOUT TO GRAB SOME GRUB WITH THESE GUYS. THAT OKAY?
HUH?
SURE... NO PROBLEM.
JUST MAKE SURE YOU'RE BACK AT THE SHIP IN TIME.
ROGER THAT.
WHOA!
THAT'S SPICY!
HOW CAN YOU TWO STOMACH THIS KIND OF STUFF?
IT'S THE MOST POPULAR DISH HERE. NO WAY I COULD TURN THAT DOWN.
SO...
WHY?
WHY WHAT?
I'll stick with normal soup.
WHAT'S YOUR BUSINESS WITH US?

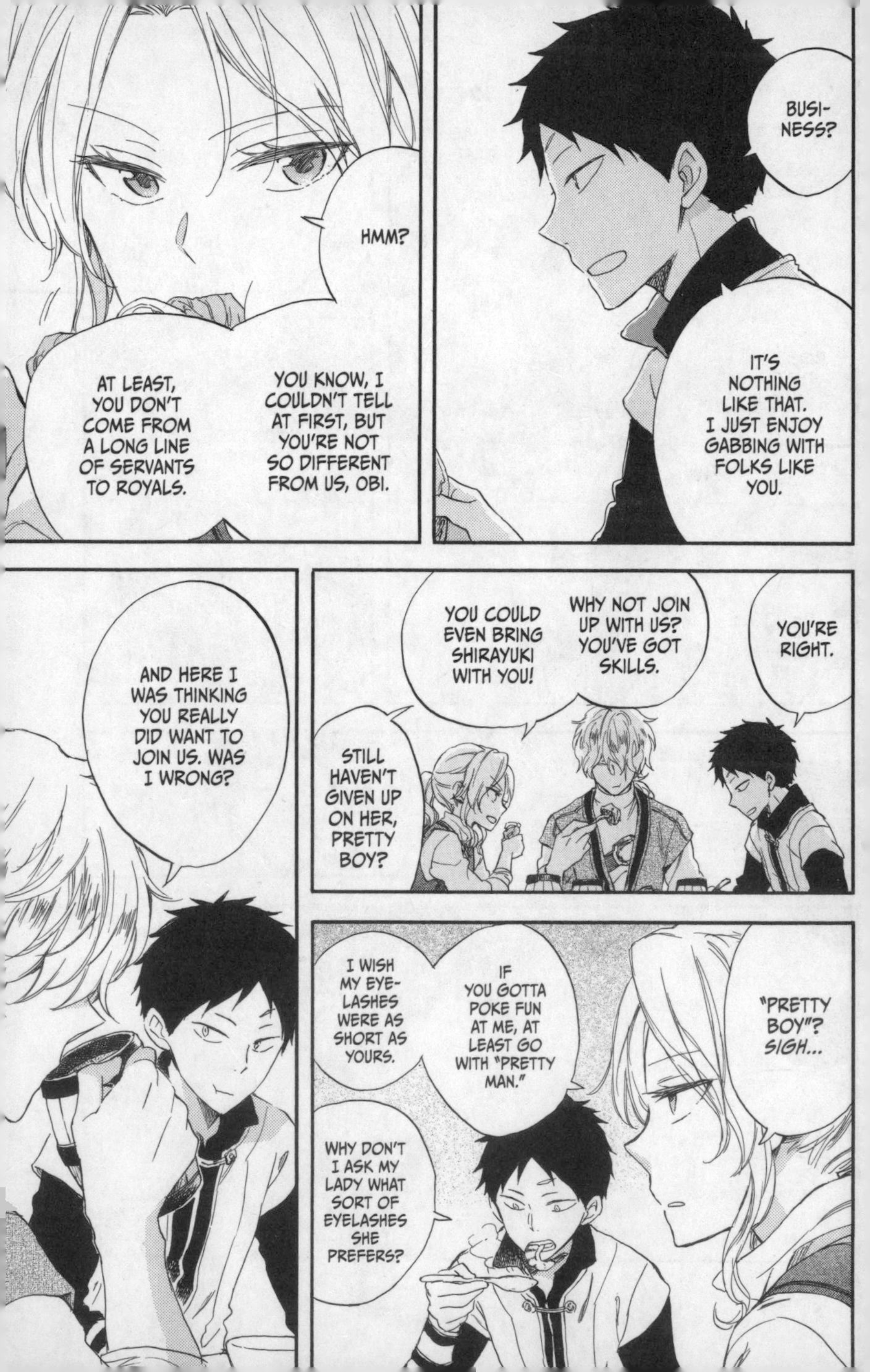
BUSI-NESS?
IT'S NOTHING LIKE THAT. I JUST ENJOY GABBING WITH FOLKS LIKE YOU.
HMM?
YOU KNOW, I COULDN'T TELL AT FIRST, BUT YOU'RE NOT SO DIFFERENT FROM US, OBI.
AT LEAST, YOU DON'T COME FROM A LONG LINE OF SERVANTS TO ROYALS.
YOU'RE RIGHT.
WHY NOT JOIN UP WITH US? YOU'VE GOT SKILLS.
YOU COULD EVEN BRING SHIRAYUKI WITH YOU!
STILL HAVEN'T GIVEN UP ON HER, PRETTY BOY?
"PRETTY BOY"? SIGH...
IF YOU GOTTA POKE FUN AT ME, AT LEAST GO WITH "PRETTY MAN."
I WISH MY EYE-LASHES WERE AS SHORT AS YOURS.
WHY DON'T I ASK MY LADY WHAT SORT OF EYELASHES SHE PREFERS?
AND HERE I WAS THINKING YOU REALLY DID WANT TO JOIN US. WAS I WRONG?

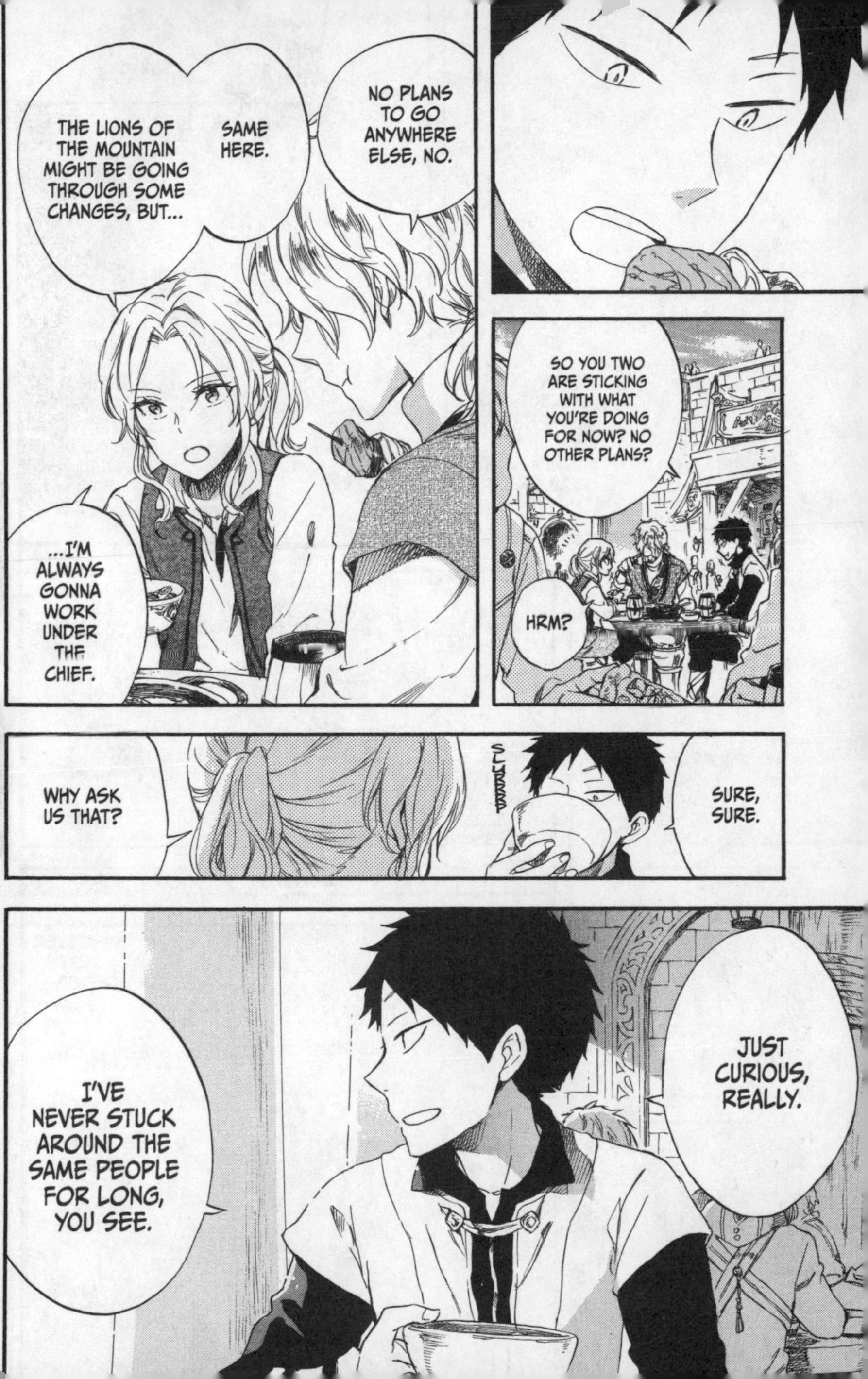
SO YOU TWO ARE STICKING WITH WHAT YOU'RE DOING FOR NOW? NO OTHER PLANS?
HRM?
NO PLANS TO GO ANYWHERE ELSE, NO.
SAME HERE.
THE LIONS OF THE MOUNTAIN MIGHT BE GOING THROUGH SOME CHANGES, BUT...
...I'M ALWAYS GONNA WORK UNDER THE CHIEF.
SURE, SURE.
SLURRRP
WHY ASK US THAT?
JUST CURIOUS, REALLY.
I'VE NEVER STUCK AROUND THE SAME PEOPLE FOR LONG, YOU SEE.

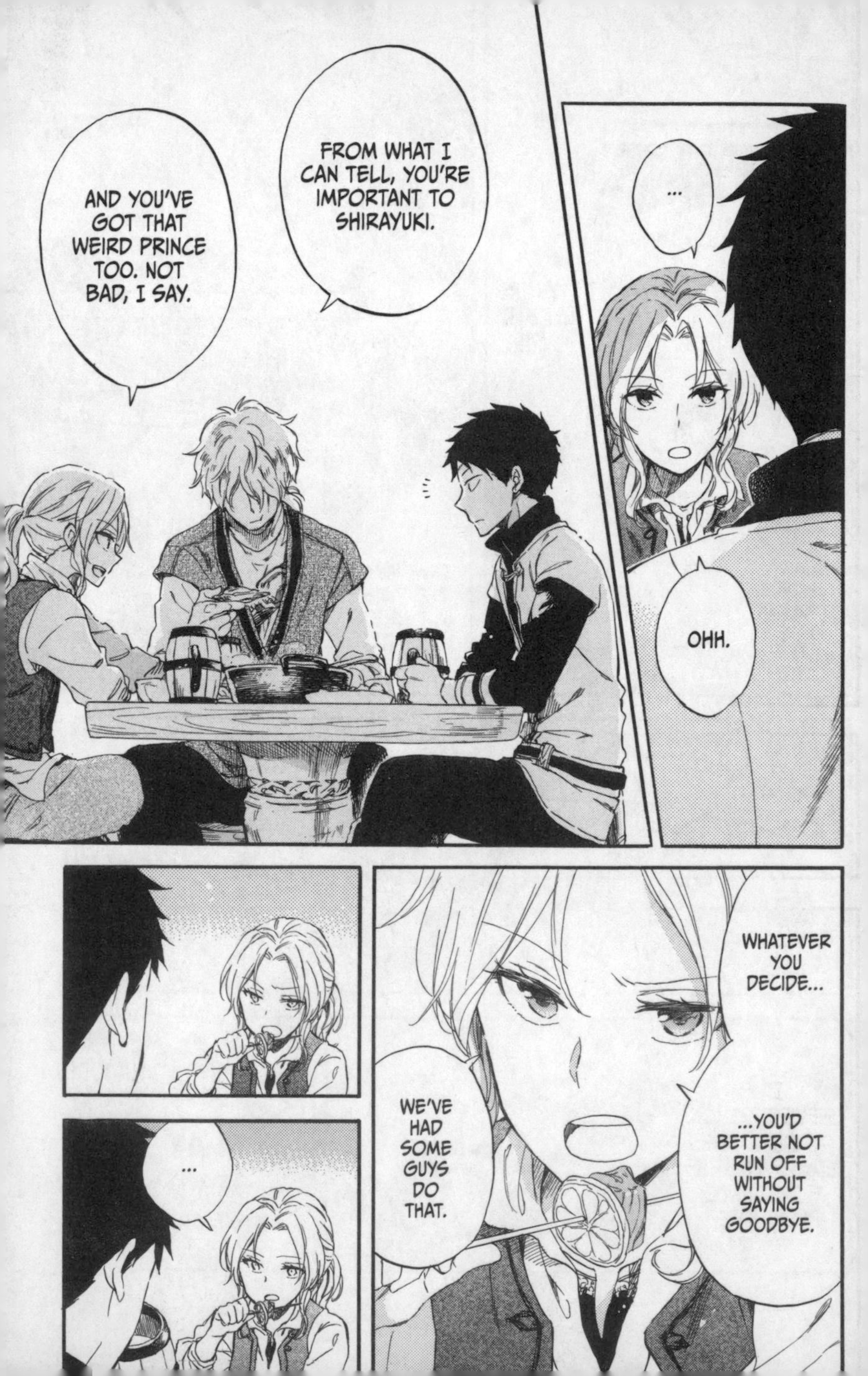
...
OHH.
FROM WHAT I CAN TELL, YOU'RE IMPORTANT TO SHIRAYUKI.
AND YOU'VE GOT THAT WEIRD PRINCE TOO. NOT BAD, I SAY.
WHATEVER YOU DECIDE...
...YOU'D BETTER NOT RUN OFF WITHOUT SAYING GOODBYE.
WE'VE HAD SOME GUYS DO THAT.
...

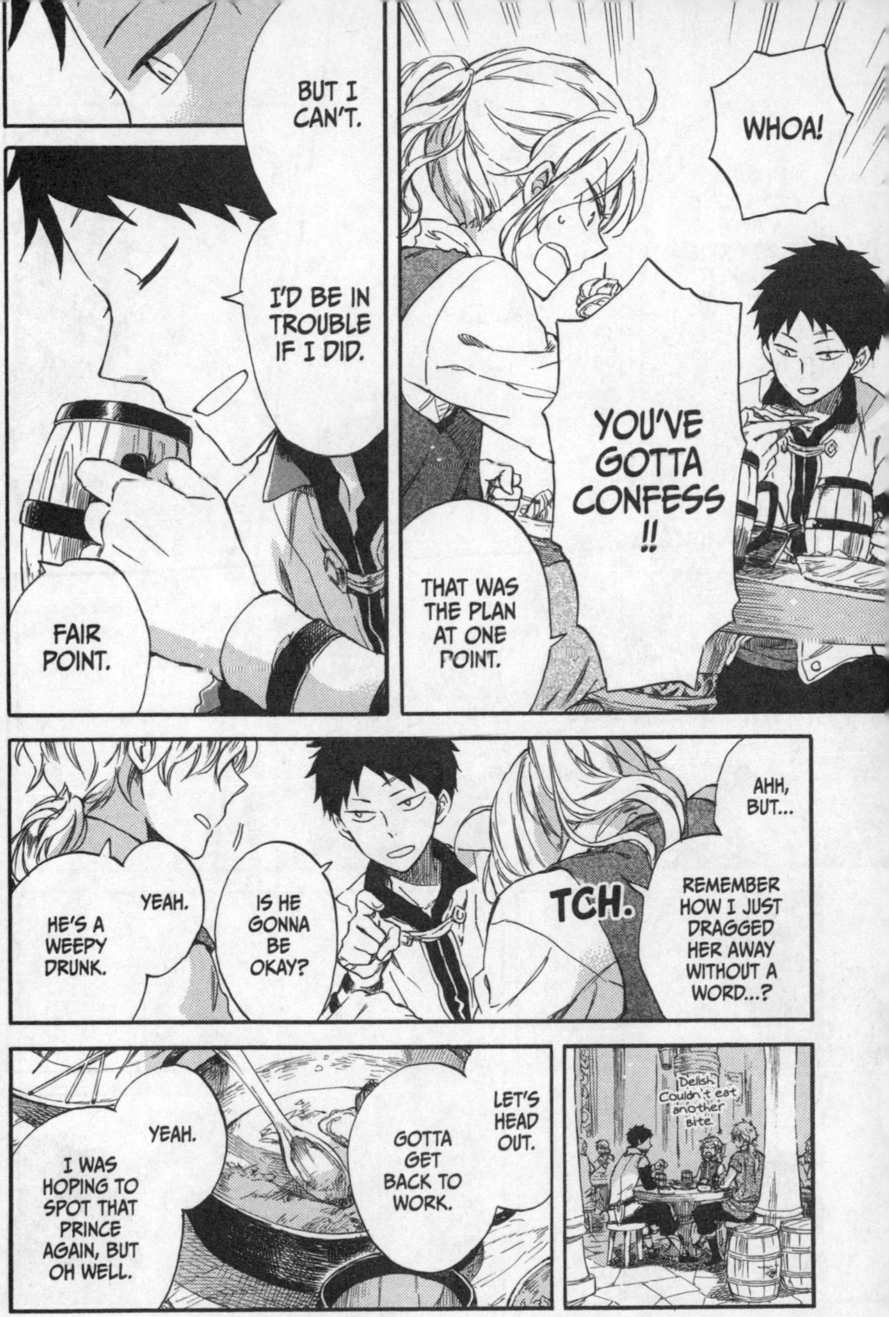
WHOA!
YOU'VE GOTTA CONFESS !!
THAT WAS THE PLAN AT ONE POINT.
BUT I CAN'T.
I'D BE IN TROUBLE IF I DID.
FAIR POINT.
AHH, BUT...
REMEMBER HOW I JUST DRAGGED HER AWAY WITHOUT A WORD...?
TCH.
IS HE GONNA BE OKAY?
YEAH.
HE'S A WEEPY DRUNK.
Delish. Couldn't eat another bite.
LET'S HEAD OUT.
GOTTA GET BACK TO WORK.
YEAH.
I WAS HOPING TO SPOT THAT PRINCE AGAIN, BUT OH WELL.

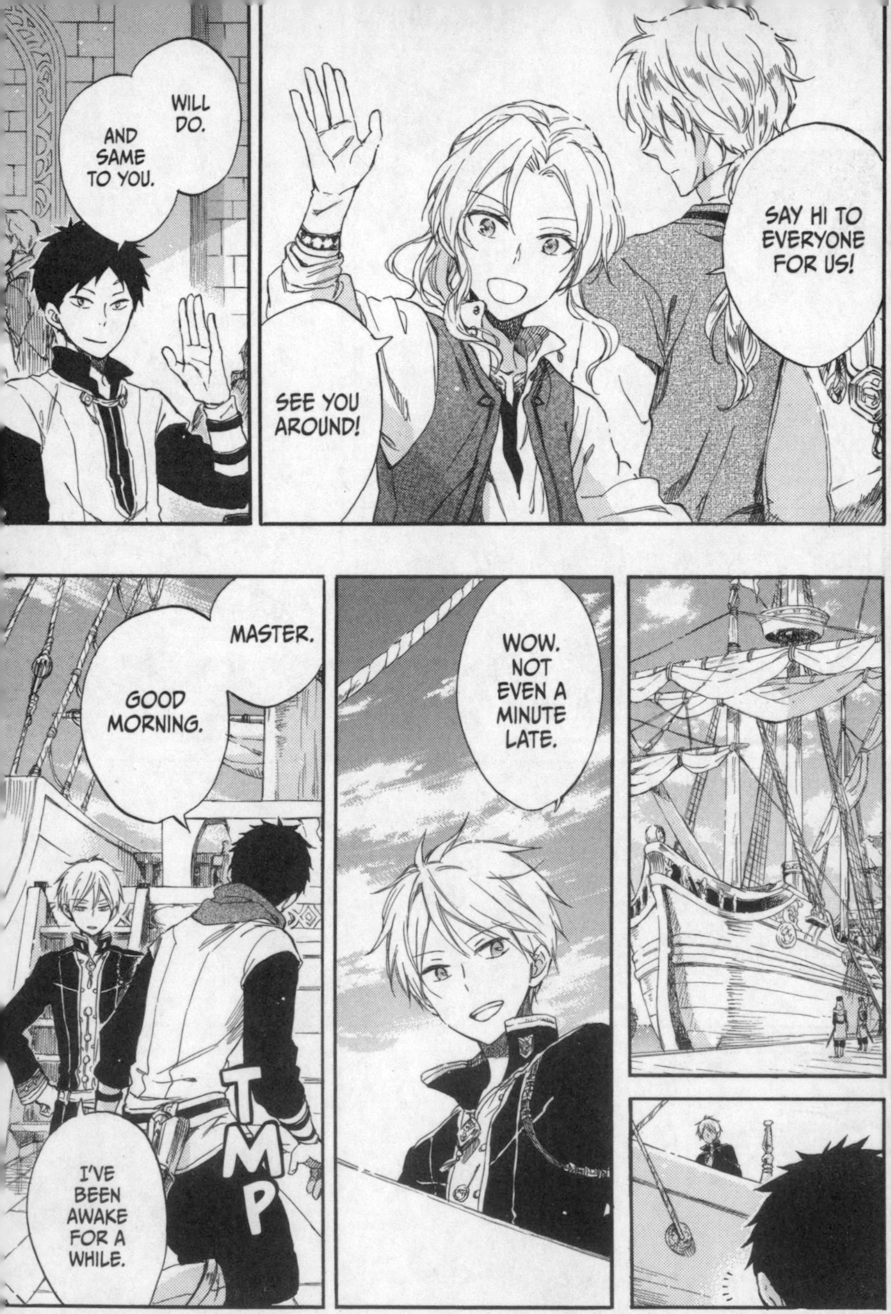
SAY HI TO EVERYONE FOR US!
SEE YOU AROUND!
WILL DO.
AND SAME TO YOU.
WOW. NOT EVEN A MINUTE LATE.
MASTER.
GOOD MORNING.
TMP
I'VE BEEN AWAKE FOR A WHILE.

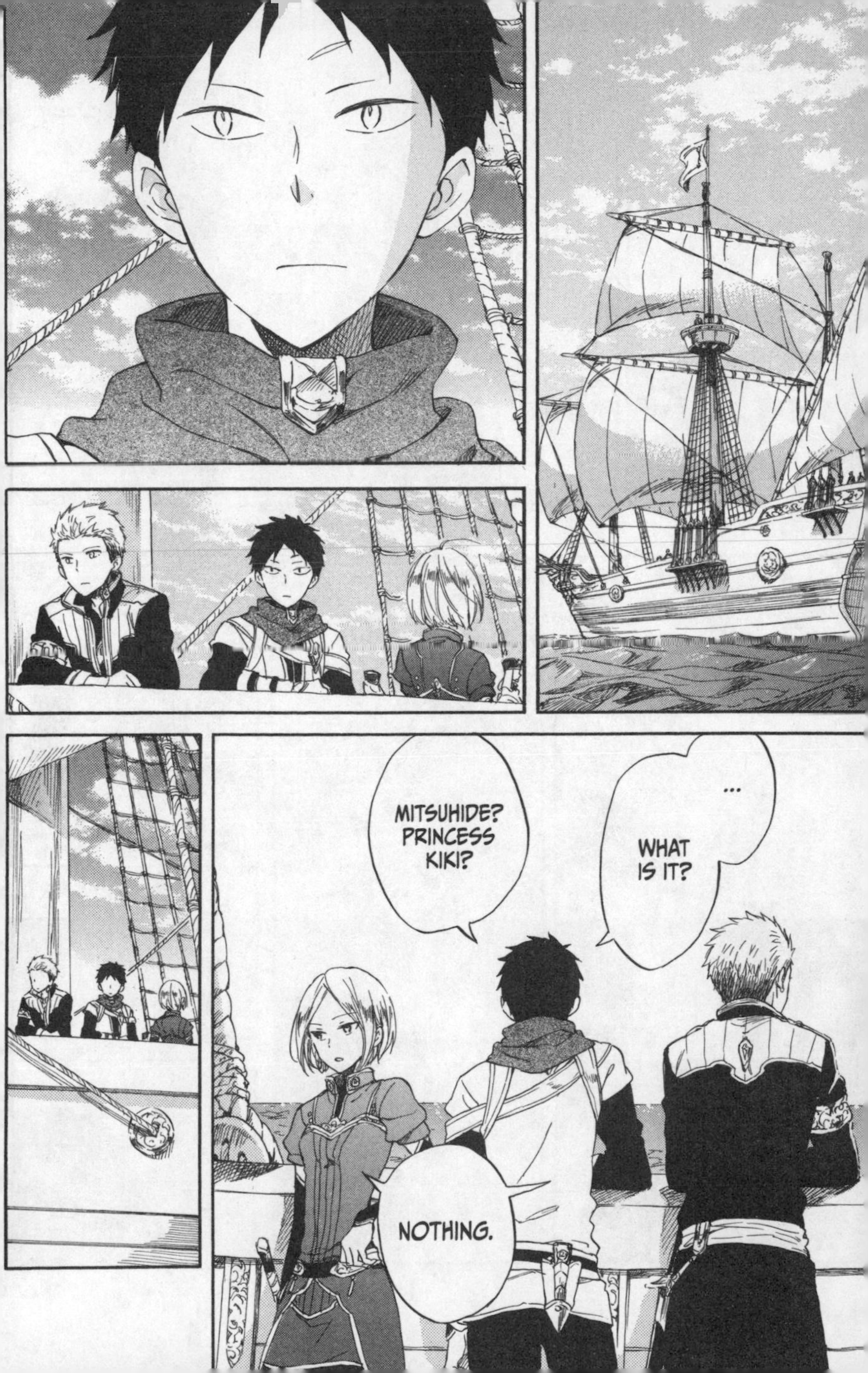
...
WHAT IS IT?
MITSUHIDE? PRINCESS KIKI?
NOTHING.

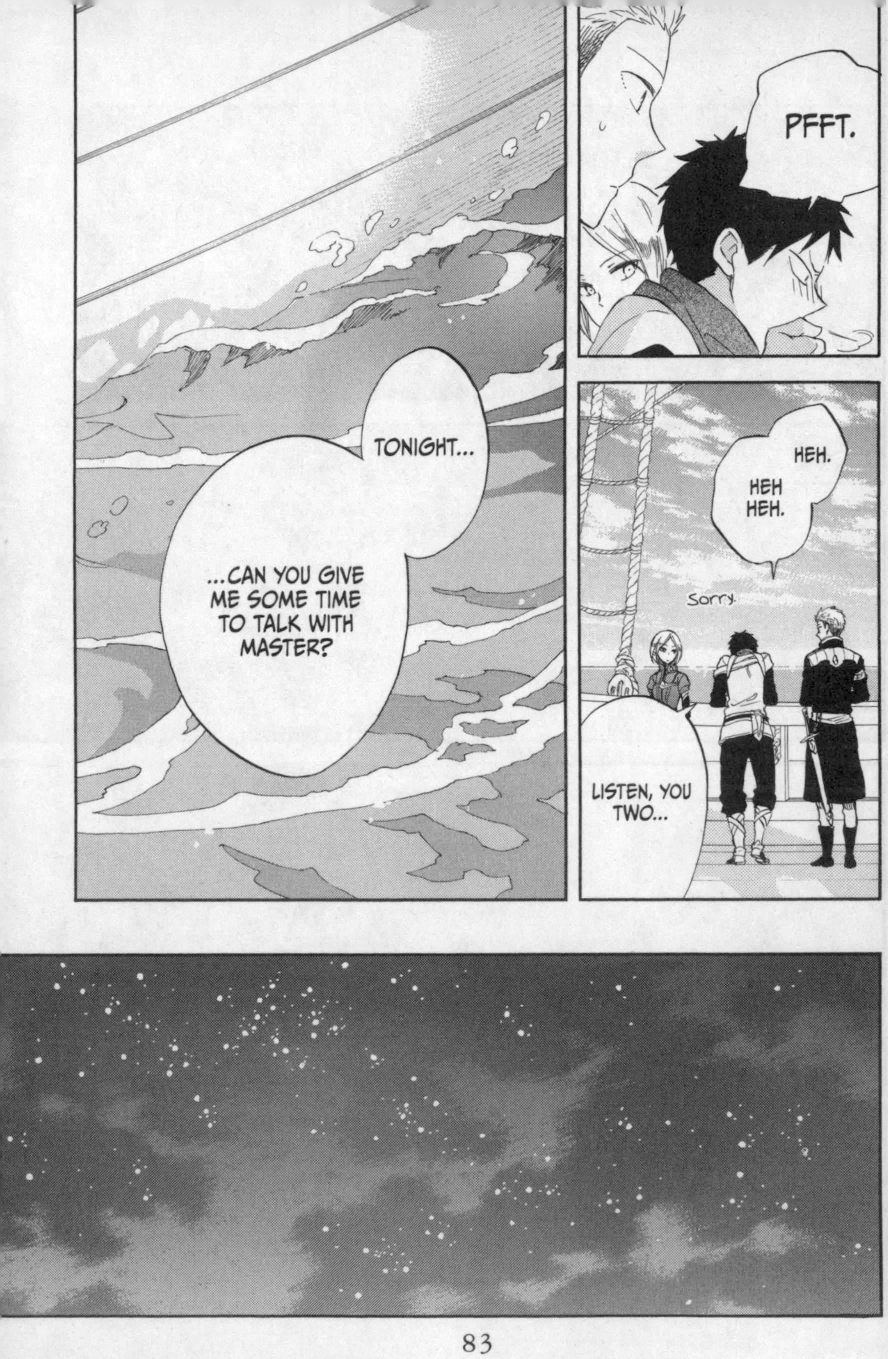
PFFT.
HEH.
HEH HEH.
Sorry.
LISTEN, YOU TWO...
TONIGHT...
...CAN YOU GIVE ME SOME TIME TO TALK WITH MASTER?

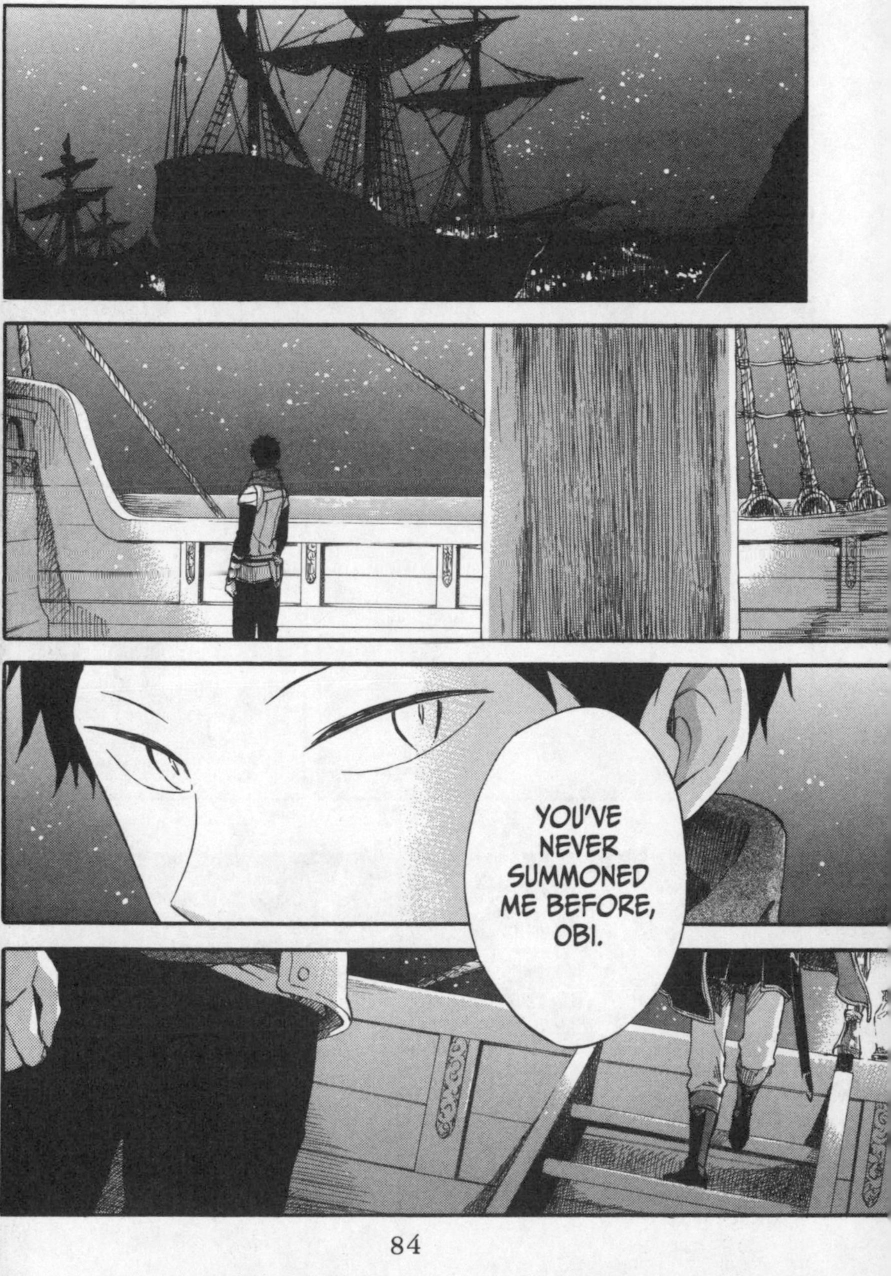
YOU'VE NEVER SUMMONED ME BEFORE, OBI.

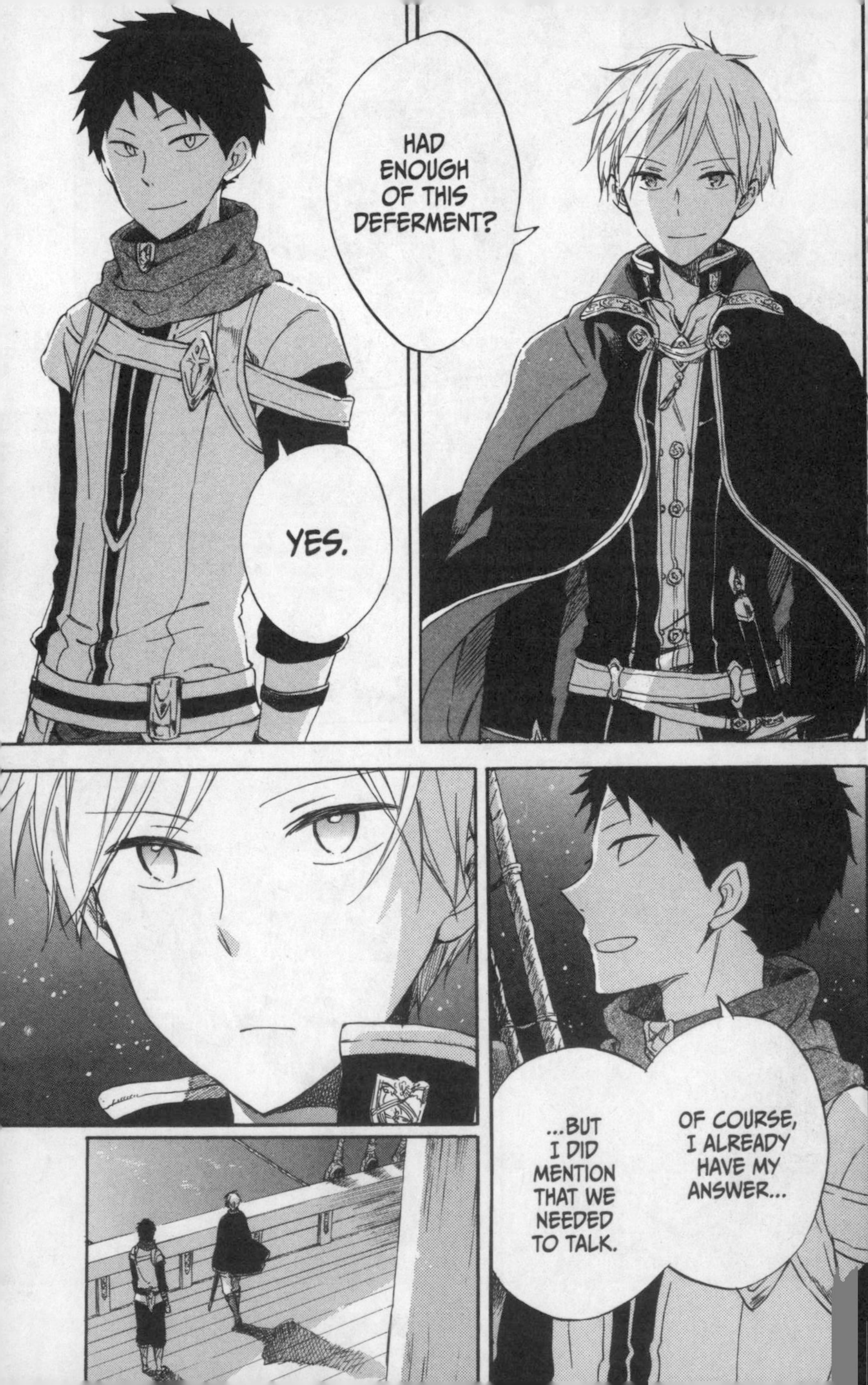
HAD ENOUGH OF THIS DEFERMENT?
YES.
OF COURSE, I ALREADY HAVE MY ANSWER...
...BUT I DID MENTION THAT WE NEEDED TO TALK.

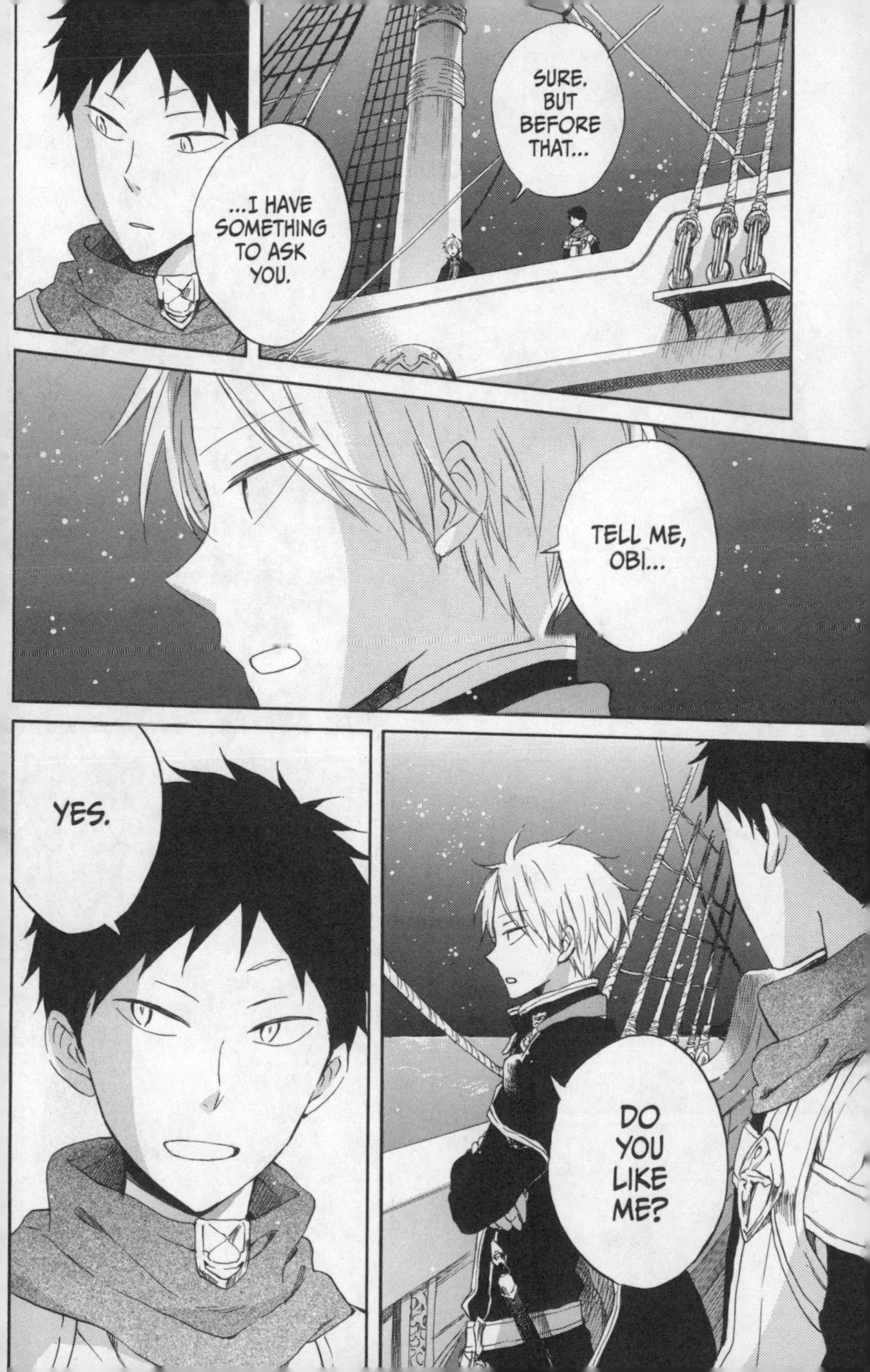
...I HAVE SOMETHING TO ASK YOU.
SURE. BUT BEFORE THAT...
TELL ME, OBI...
DO YOU LIKE ME?
YES.

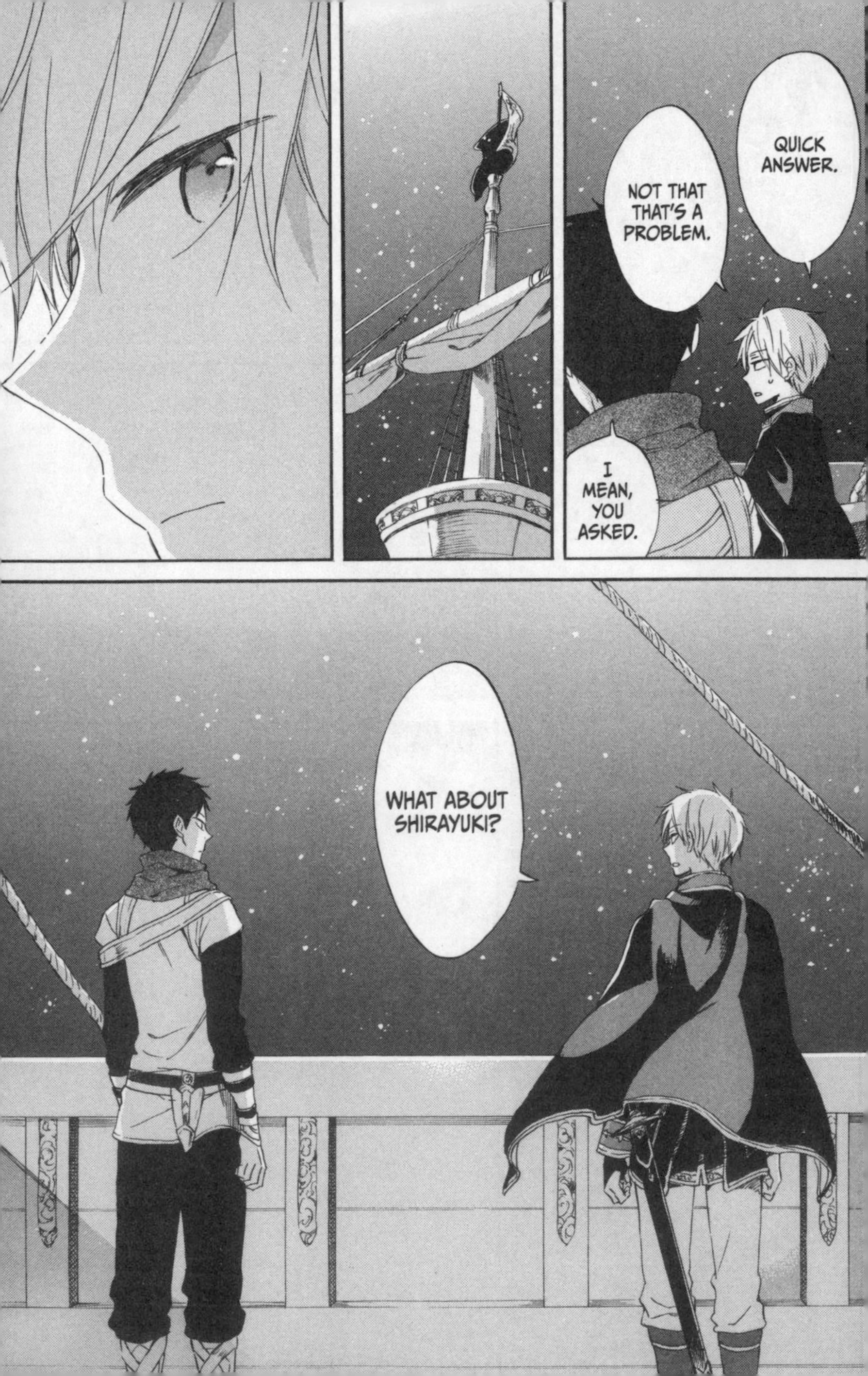
QUICK ANSWER.
NOT THAT THAT'S A PROBLEM.
I MEAN, YOU ASKED.
WHAT ABOUT SHIRAYUKI?

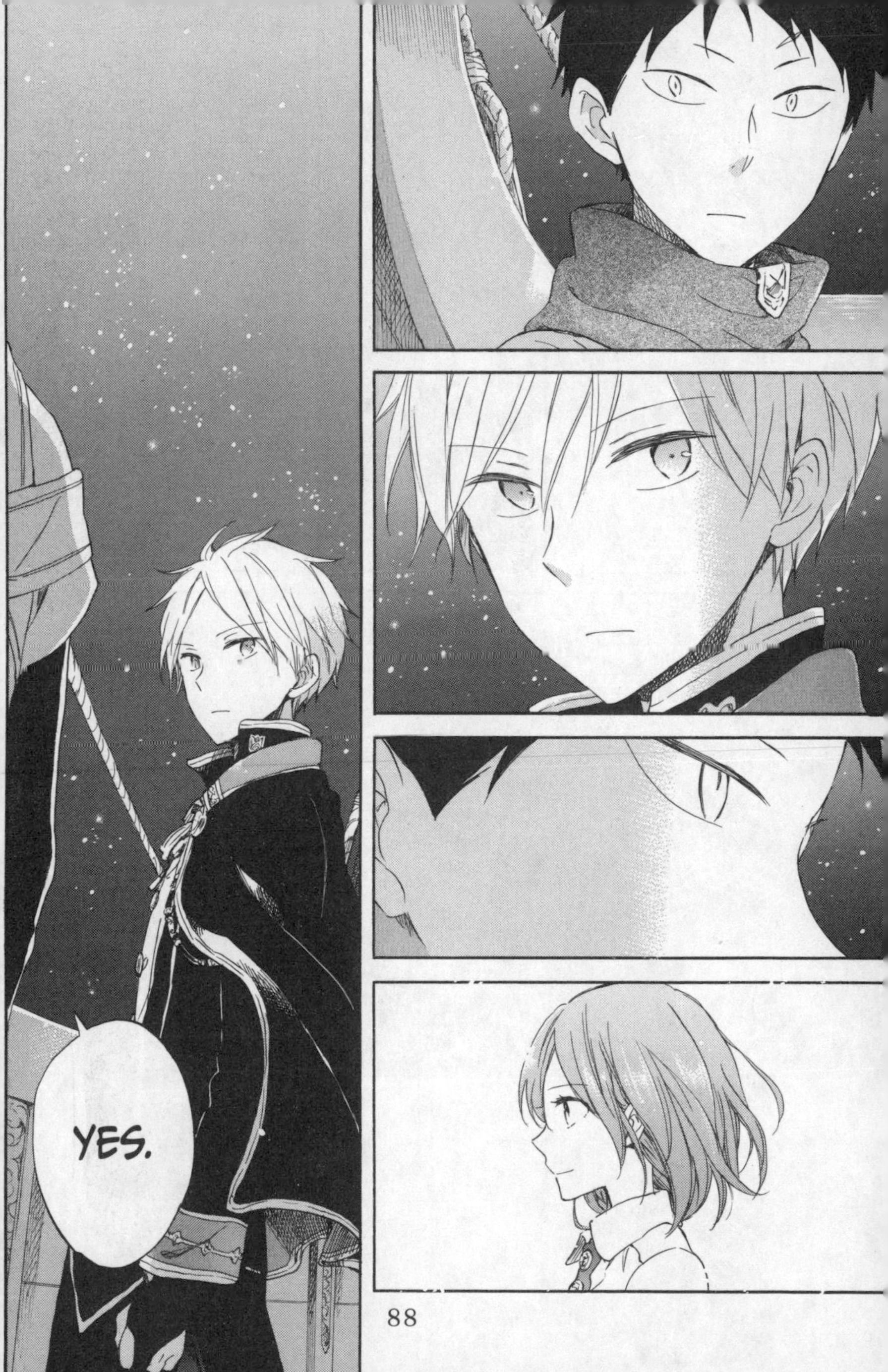
YES.

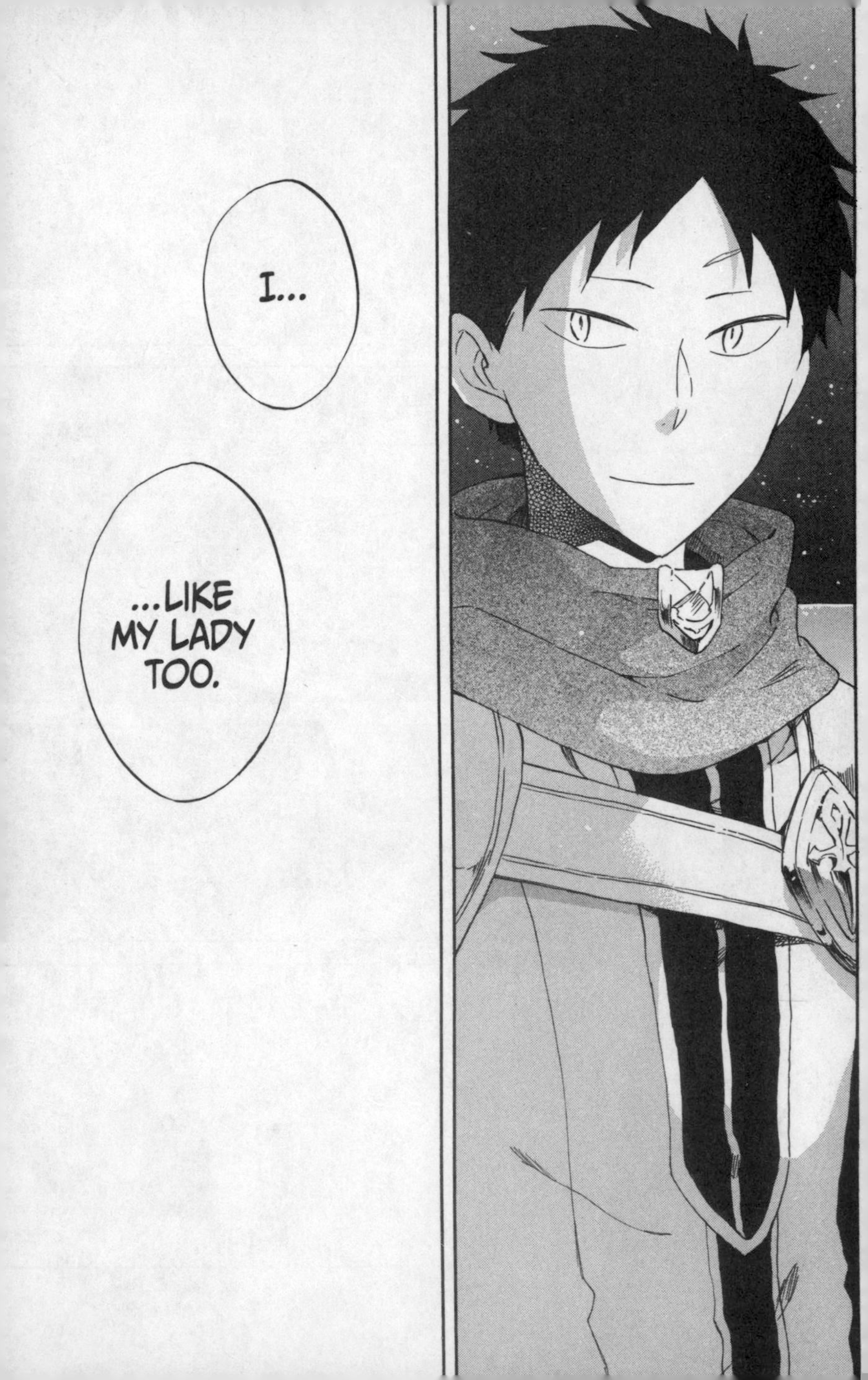
I...
...LIKE MY LADY TOO.

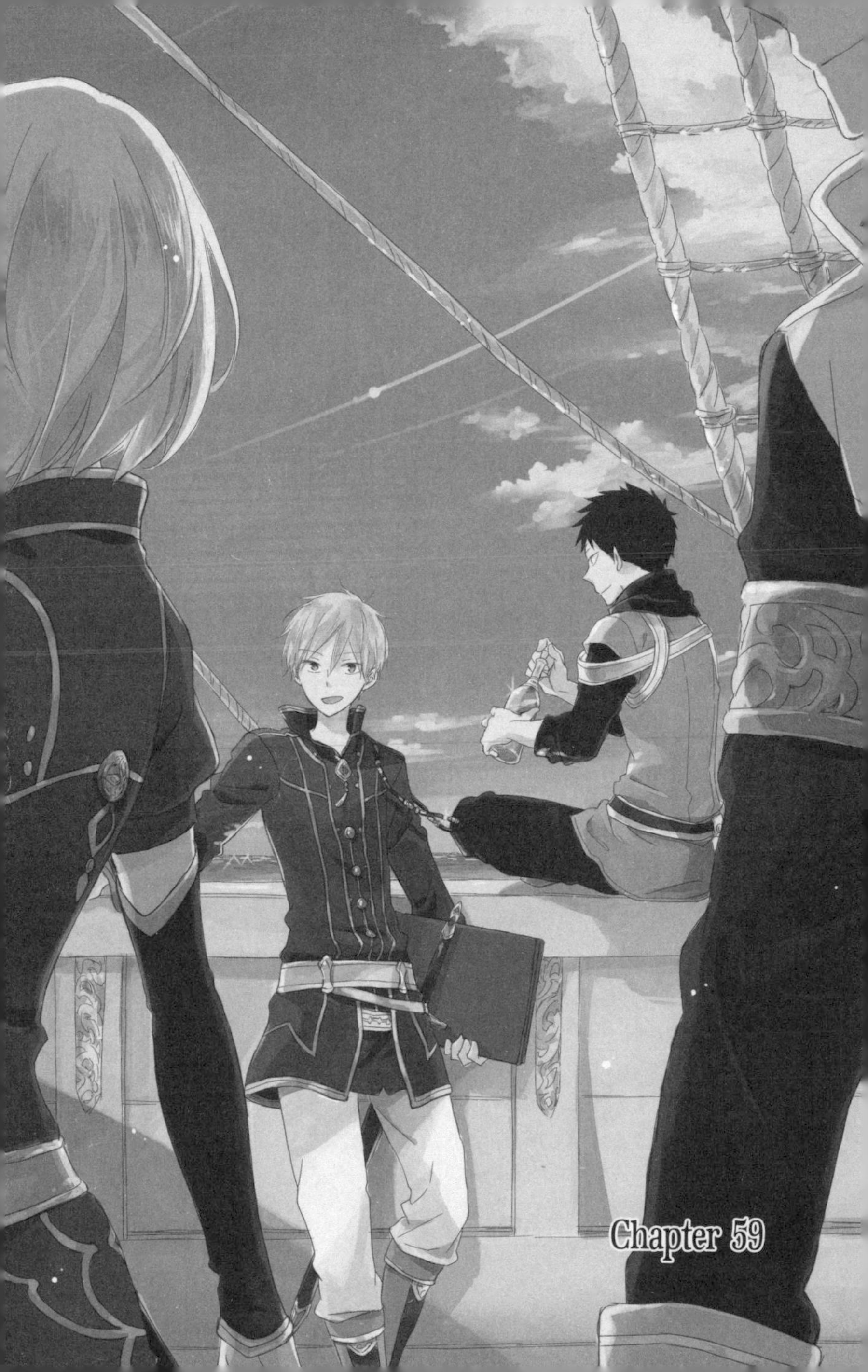
Chapter 59

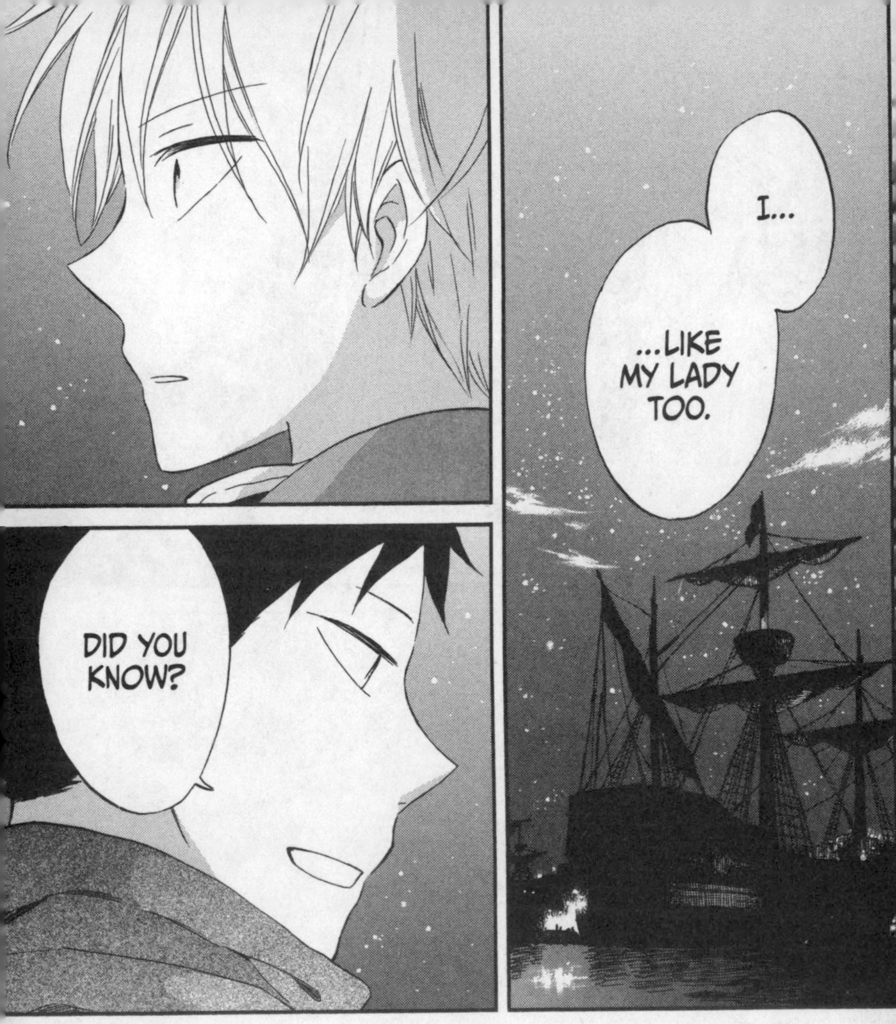
I...
...LIKE MY LADY TOO.
DID YOU KNOW?

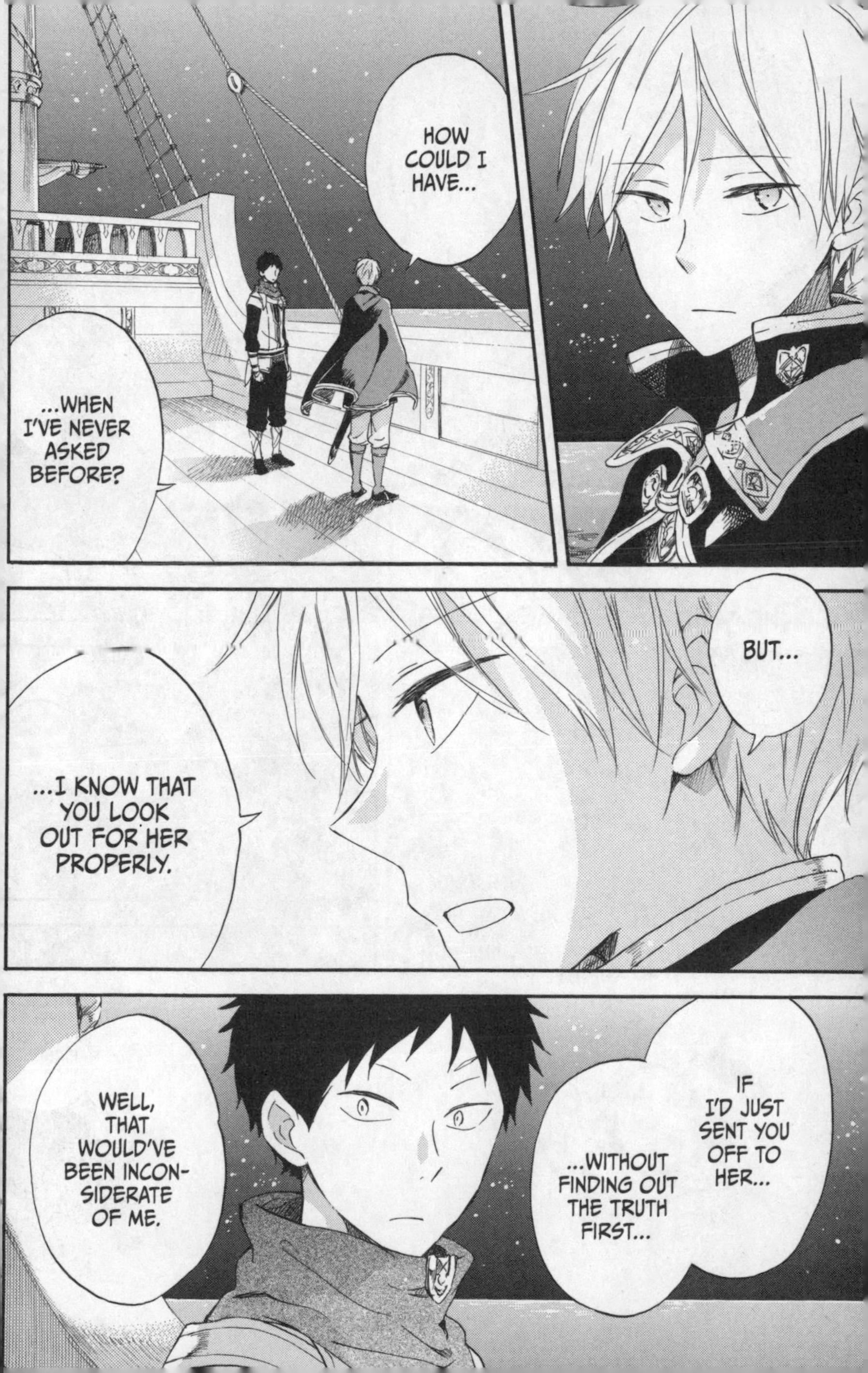
HOW COULD I HAVE...
...WHEN I'VE NEVER ASKED BEFORE?
BUT...
...I KNOW THAT YOU LOOK OUT FOR HER PROPERLY.
IF I'D JUST SENT YOU OFF TO HER...
...WITHOUT FINDING OUT THE TRUTH FIRST...
WELL, THAT WOULD'VE BEEN INCON-SIDERATE OF ME.

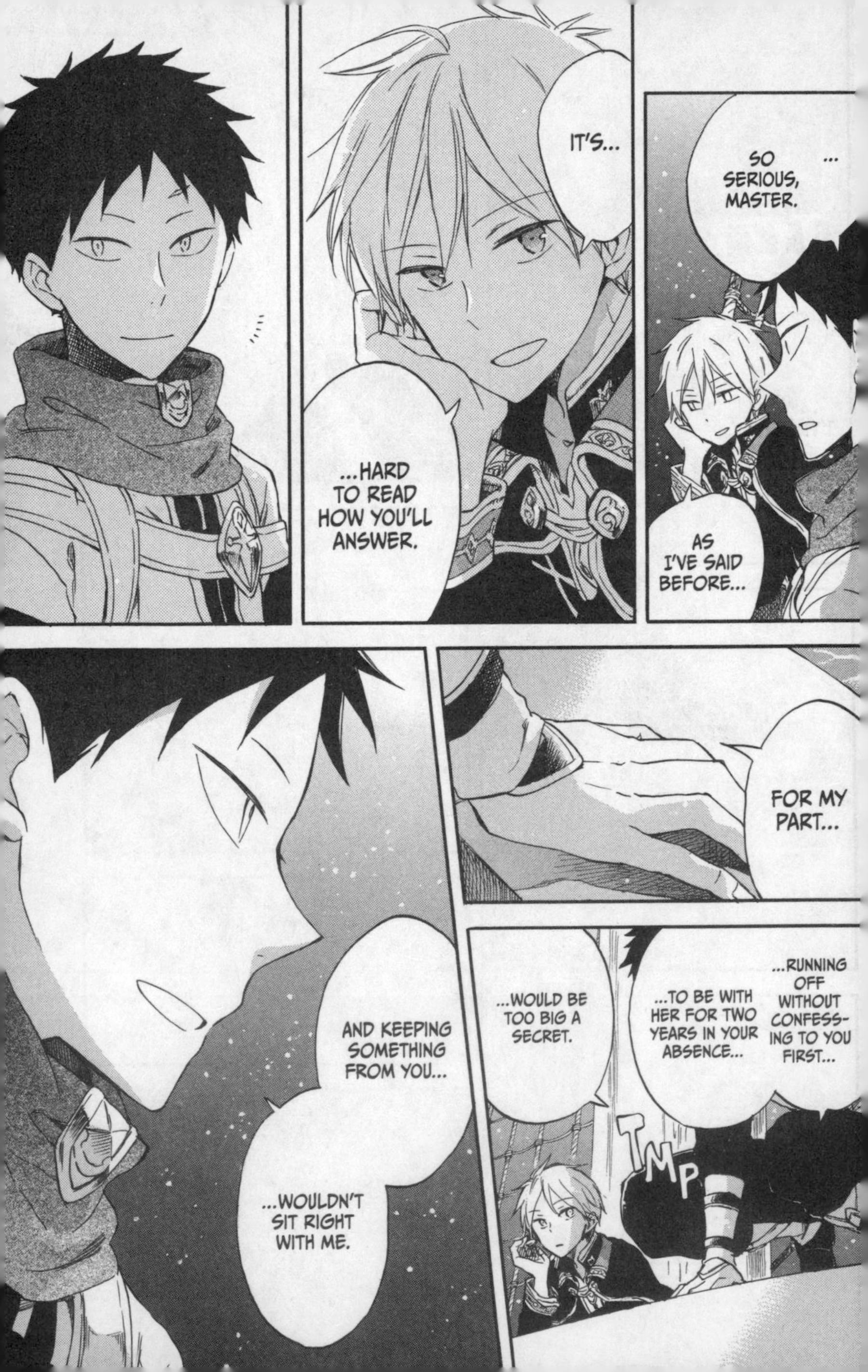
...
SO SERIOUS, MASTER.
AS I'VE SAID BEFORE...
IT'S...
...HARD TO READ HOW YOU'LL ANSWER.
FOR MY PART...
...RUNNING OFF WITHOUT CONFESSING TO YOU FIRST...
...TO BE WITH HER FOR TWO YEARS IN YOUR ABSENCE...
...WOULD BE TOO BIG A SECRET.
TMP
AND KEEPING SOMETHING FROM YOU...
...WOULDN'T SIT RIGHT WITH ME.

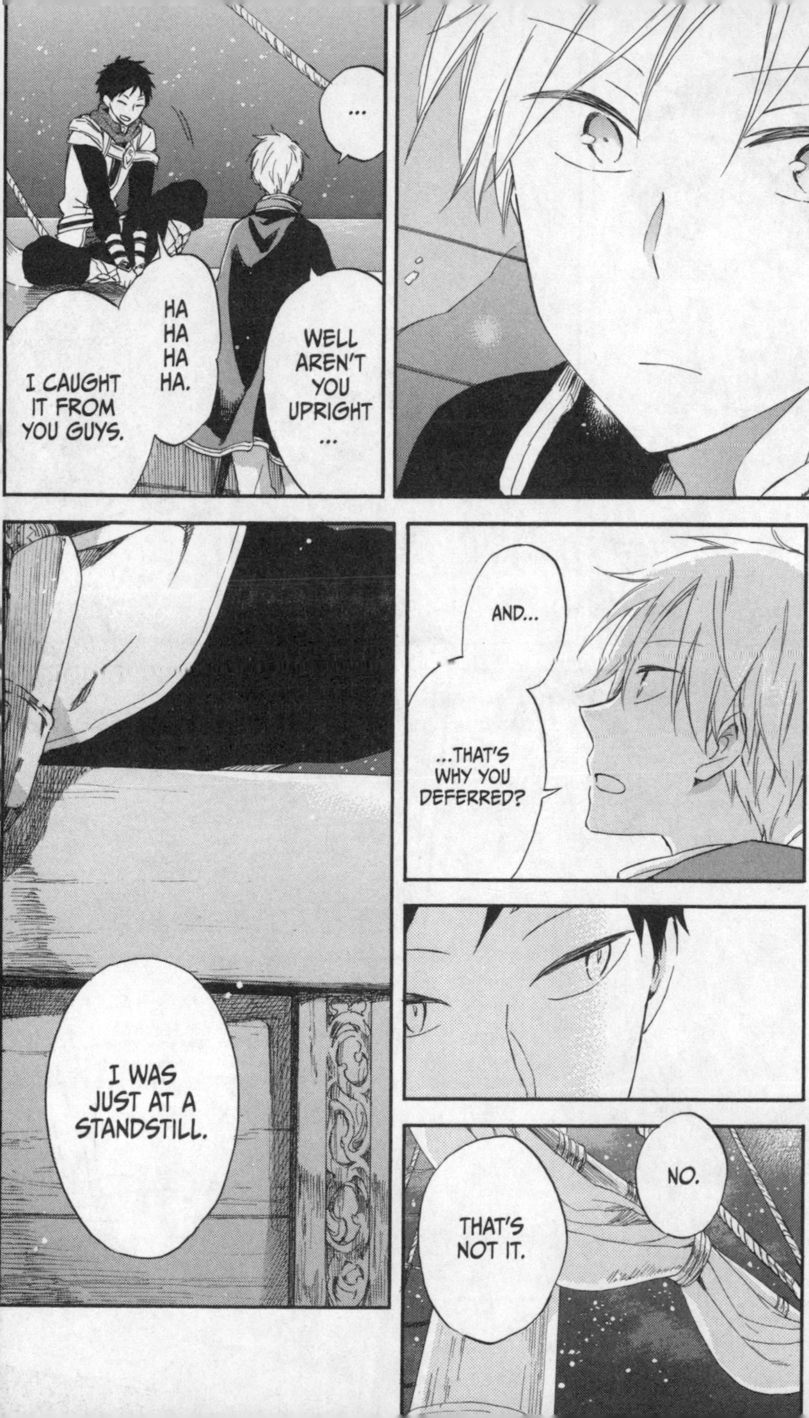
...
WELL AREN'T YOU UPRIGHT...
HA HA HA HA.
I CAUGHT IT FROM YOU GUYS.
AND...
...THAT'S WHY YOU DEFERRED?
NO.
THAT'S NOT IT.
I WAS JUST AT A STANDSTILL.

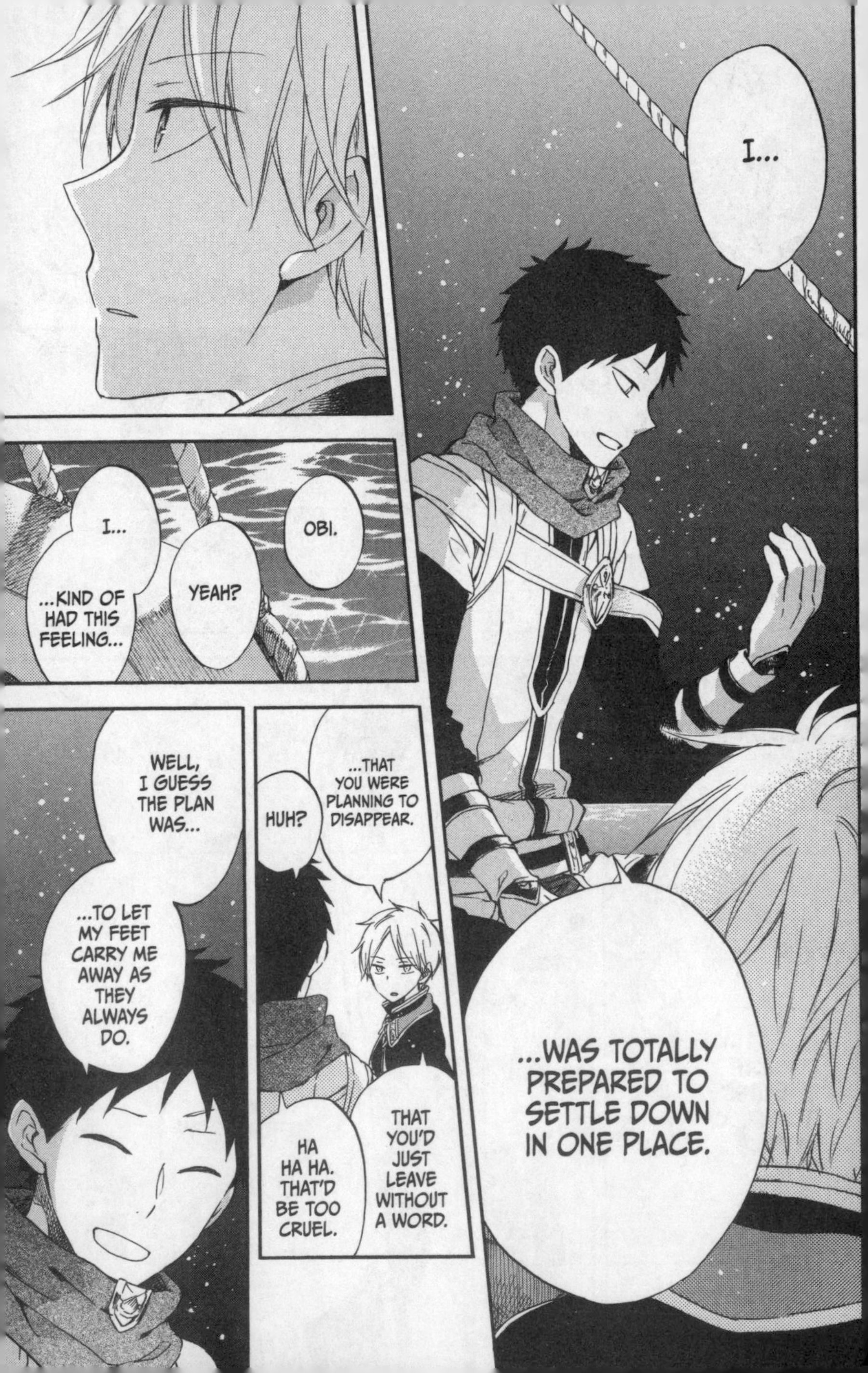
I...
...WAS TOTALLY PREPARED TO SETTLE DOWN IN ONE PLACE.
OBI.
YEAH?
I...
...KIND OF HAD THIS FEELING...
...THAT YOU WERE PLANNING TO DISAPPEAR.
HUH?
THAT YOU'D JUST LEAVE WITHOUT A WORD.
WELL, I GUESS THE PLAN WAS...
...TO LET MY FEET CARRY ME AWAY AS THEY ALWAYS DO.
HA HA HA. THAT'D BE TOO CRUEL.

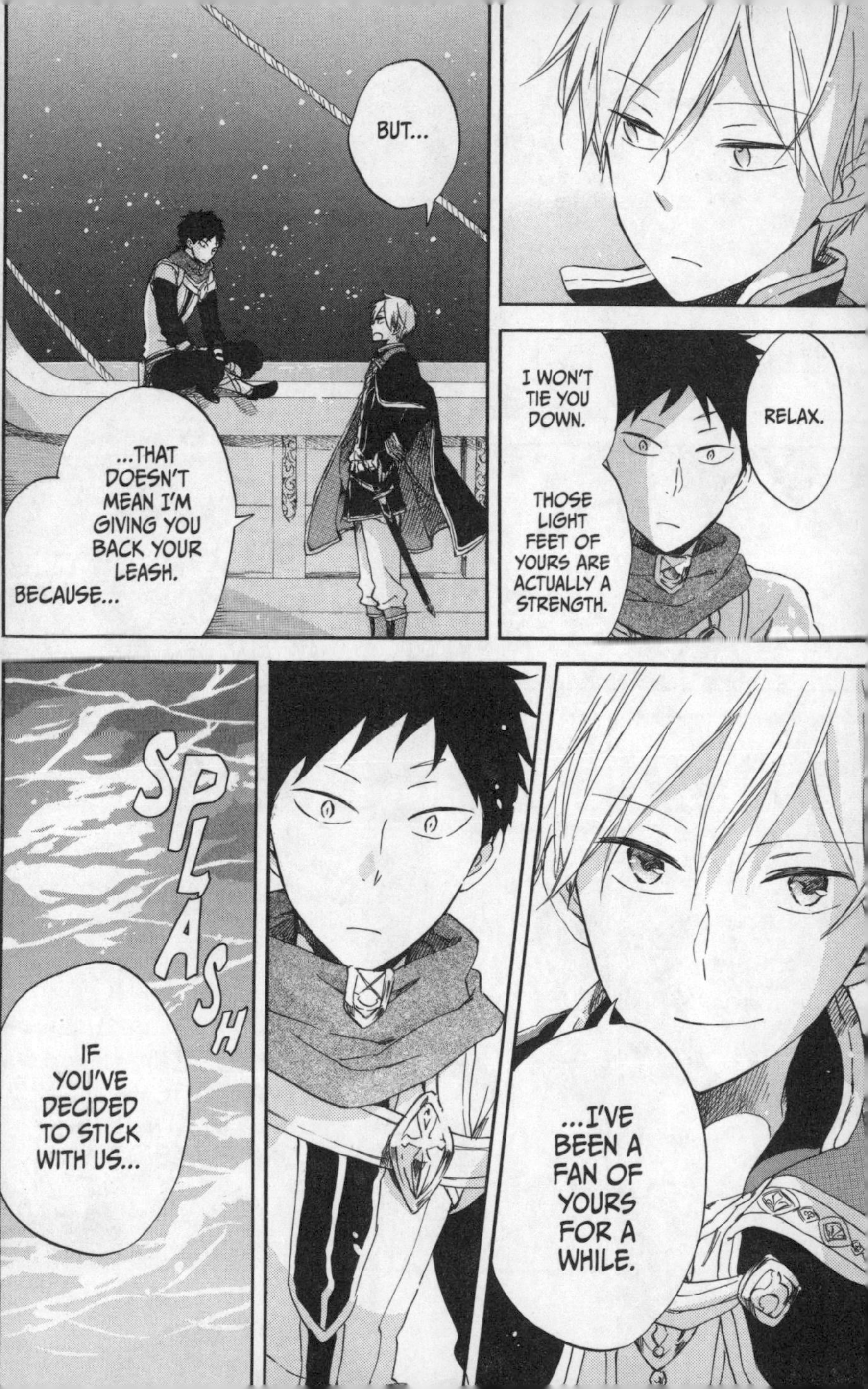
RELAX.
I WON'T TIE YOU DOWN.
THOSE LIGHT FEET OF YOURS ARE ACTUALLY A STRENGTH.
BUT...
...THAT DOESN'T MEAN I'M GIVING YOU BACK YOUR LEASH.
BECAUSE...
...I'VE BEEN A FAN OF YOURS FOR A WHILE.
SPLASH
IF YOU'VE DECIDED TO STICK WITH US...

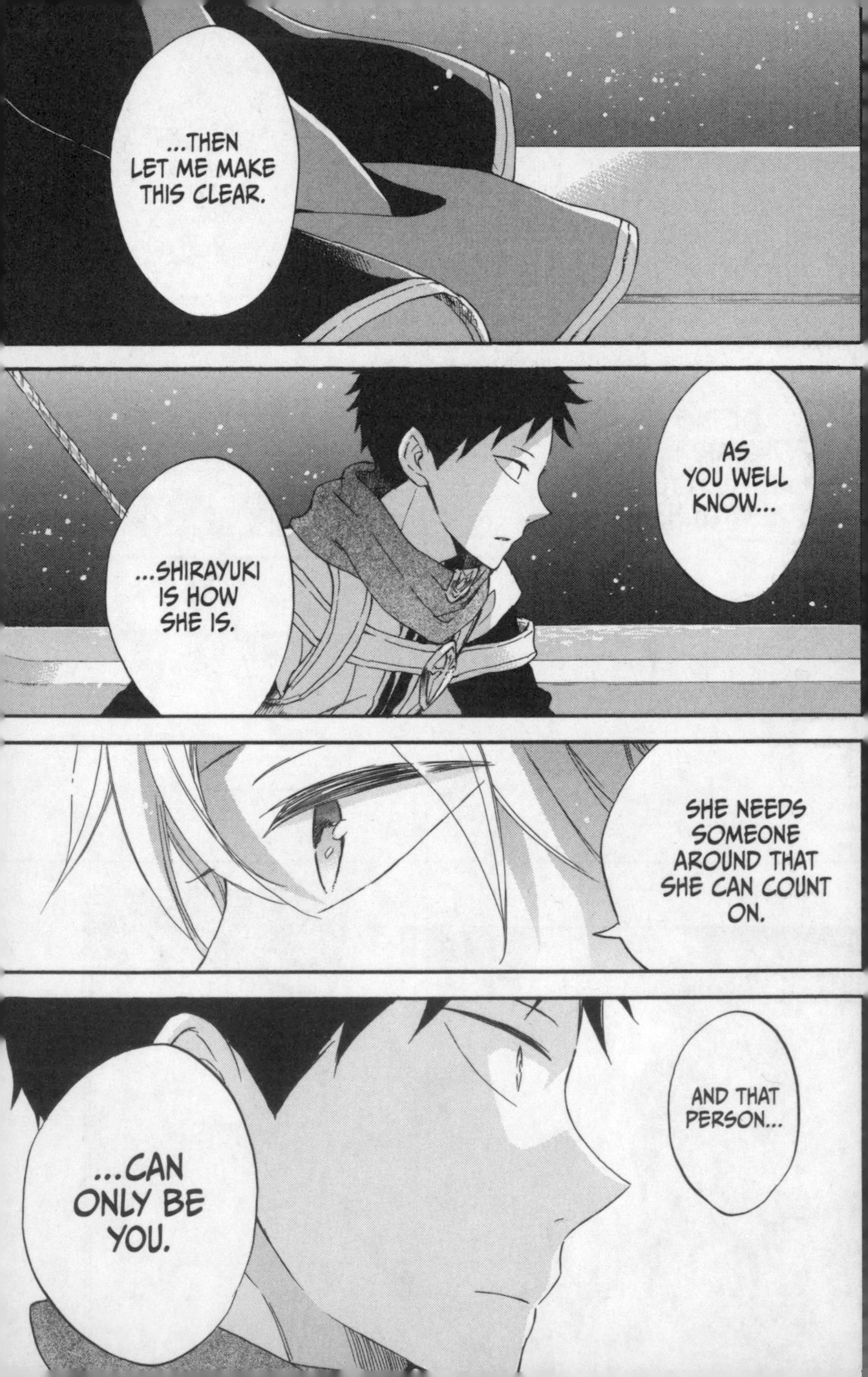
...THEN LET ME MAKE THIS CLEAR.
AS YOU WELL KNOW...
...SHIRAYUKI IS HOW SHE IS.
SHE NEEDS SOMEONE AROUND THAT SHE CAN COUNT ON.
AND THAT PERSON...
...CAN ONLY BE YOU.

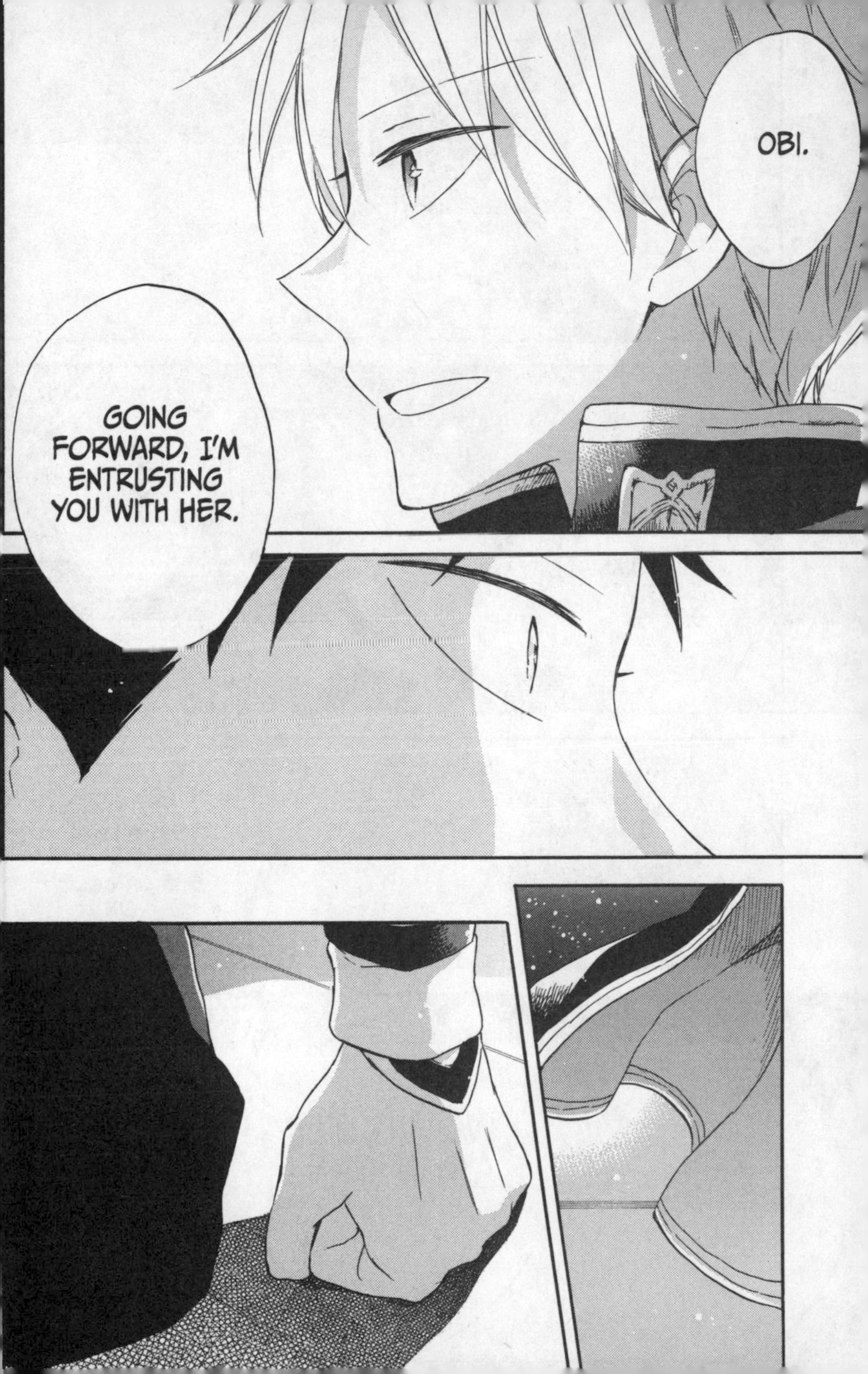
OBI.
GOING FORWARD, I'M ENTRUSTING YOU WITH HER.

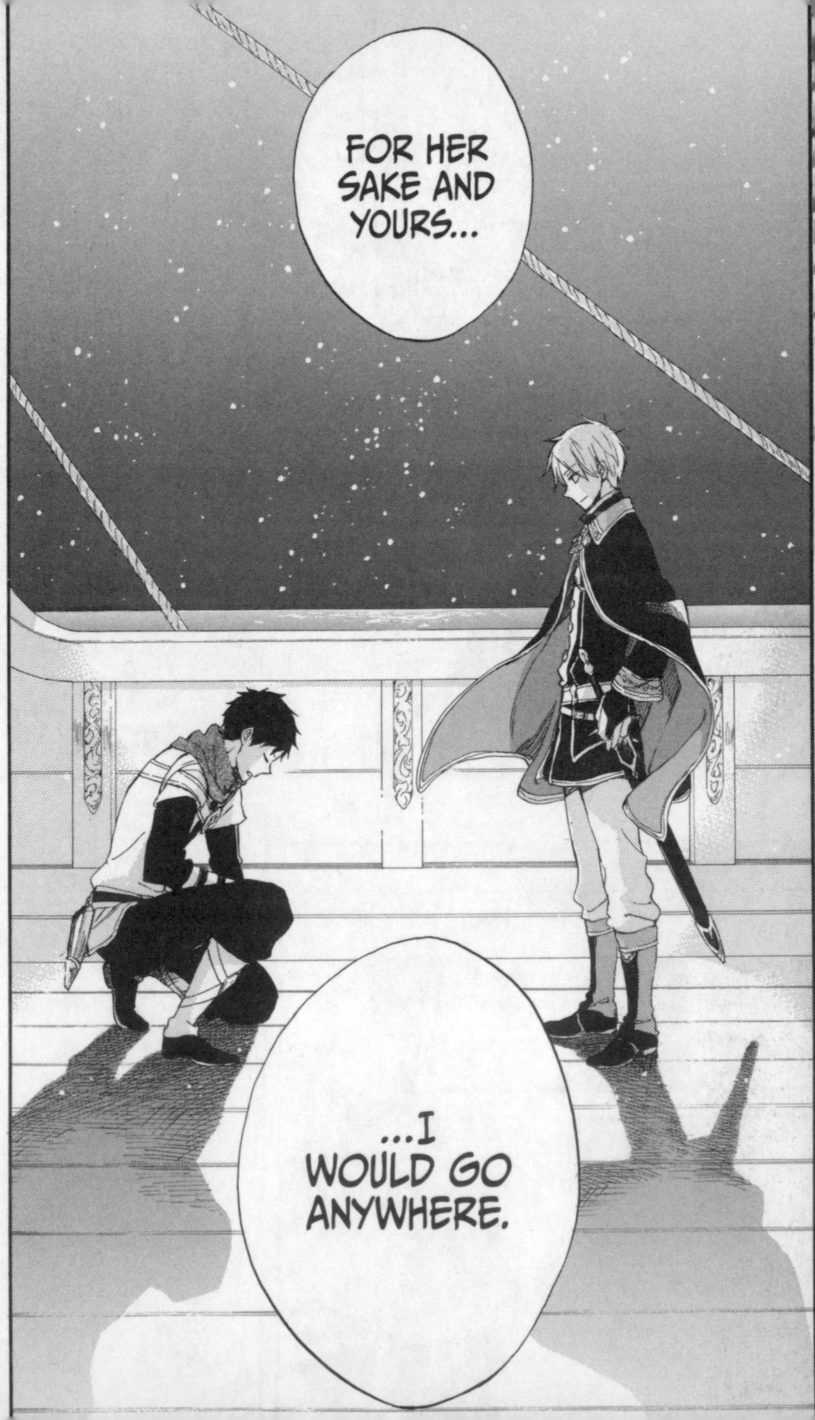
FOR HER SAKE AND YOURS...
...I WOULD GO ANYWHERE.

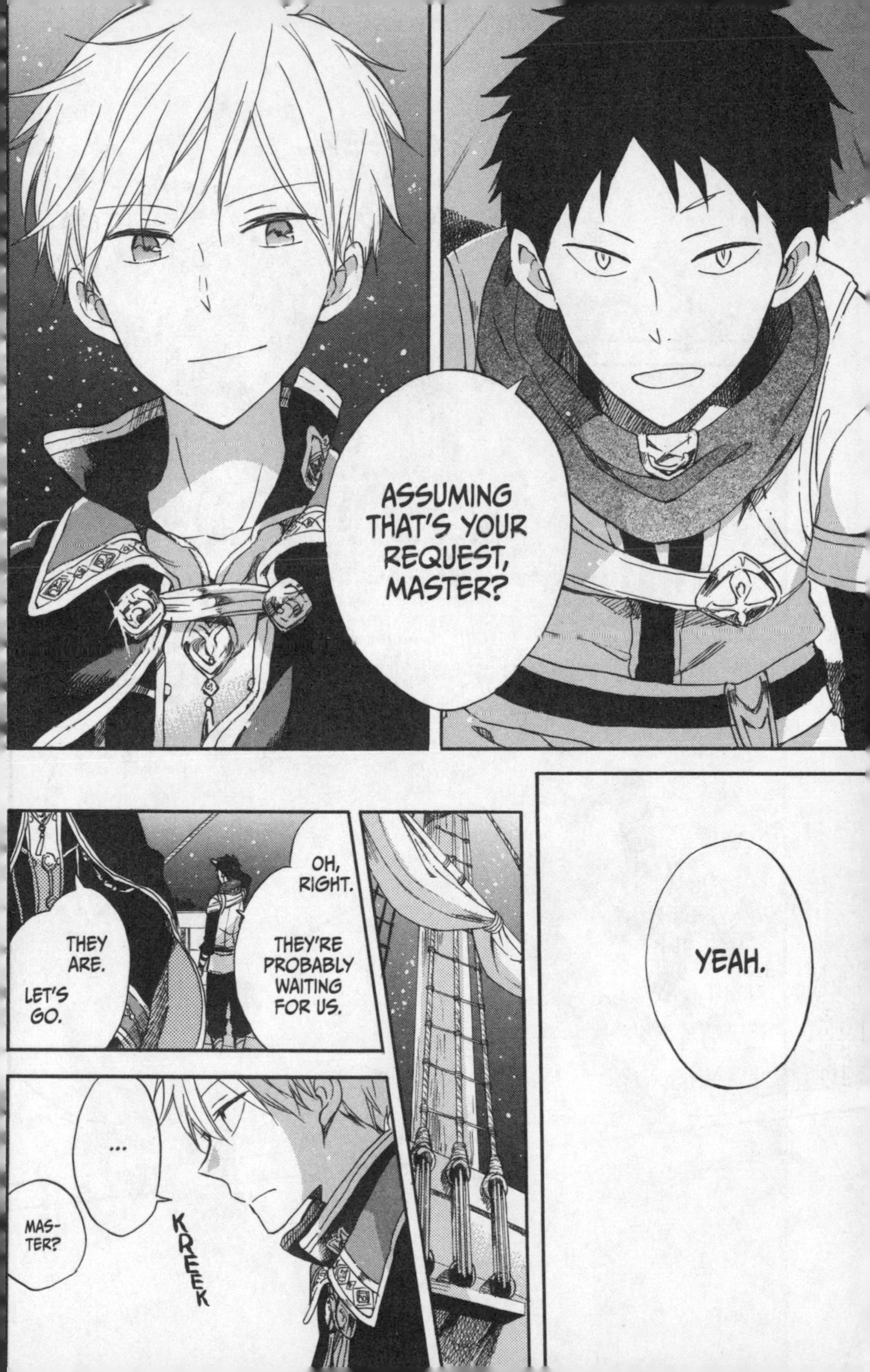
ASSUMING THAT'S YOUR REQUEST, MASTER?
YEAH.
OH, RIGHT.
THEY'RE PROBABLY WAITING FOR US.
THEY ARE.
LET'S GO.
...
MAS-TER?
KREEK

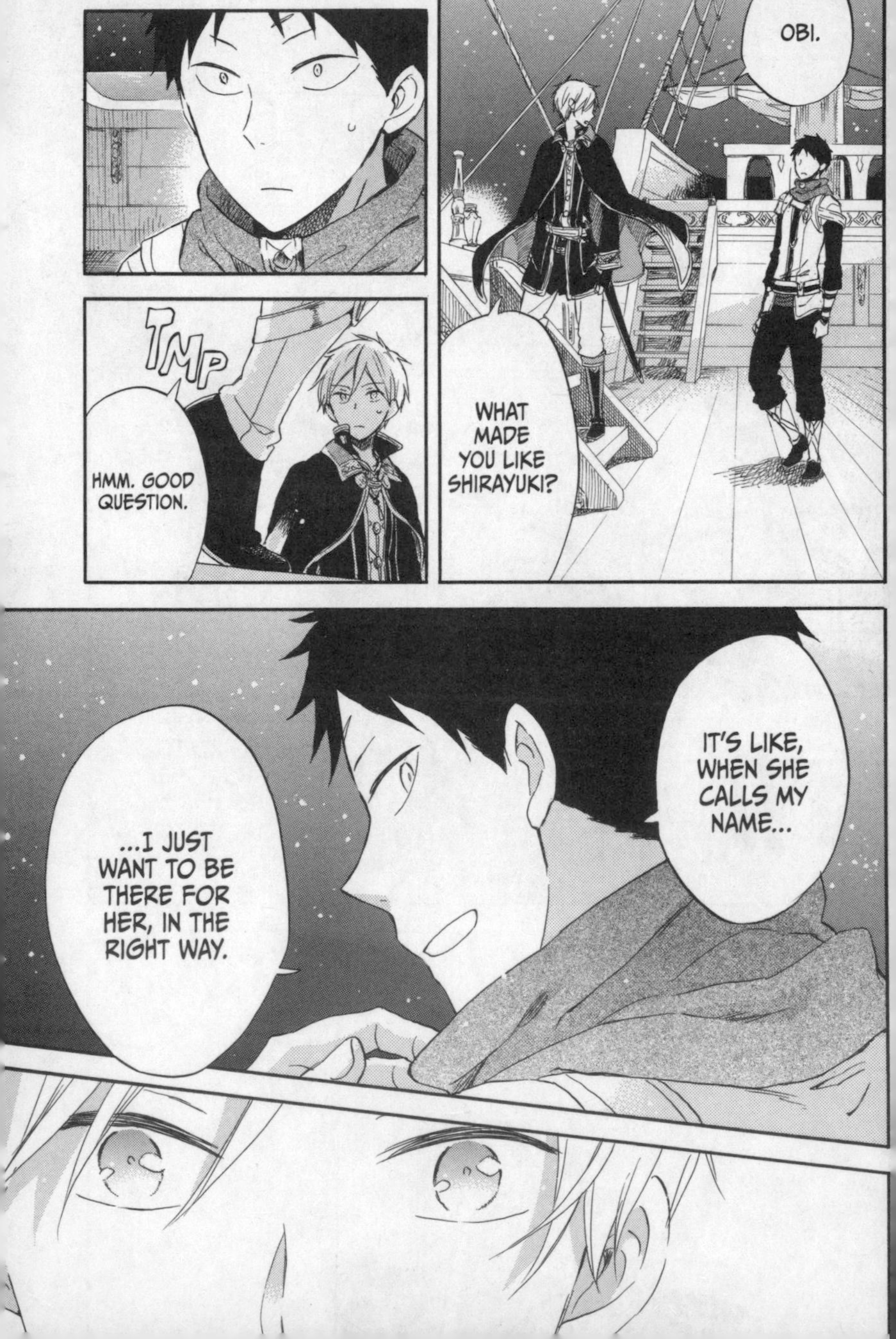
OBI.
WHAT MADE YOU LIKE SHIRAYUKI?
TMP
HMM. GOOD QUESTION.
IT'S LIKE, WHEN SHE CALLS MY NAME...
...I JUST WANT TO BE THERE FOR HER, IN THE RIGHT WAY.

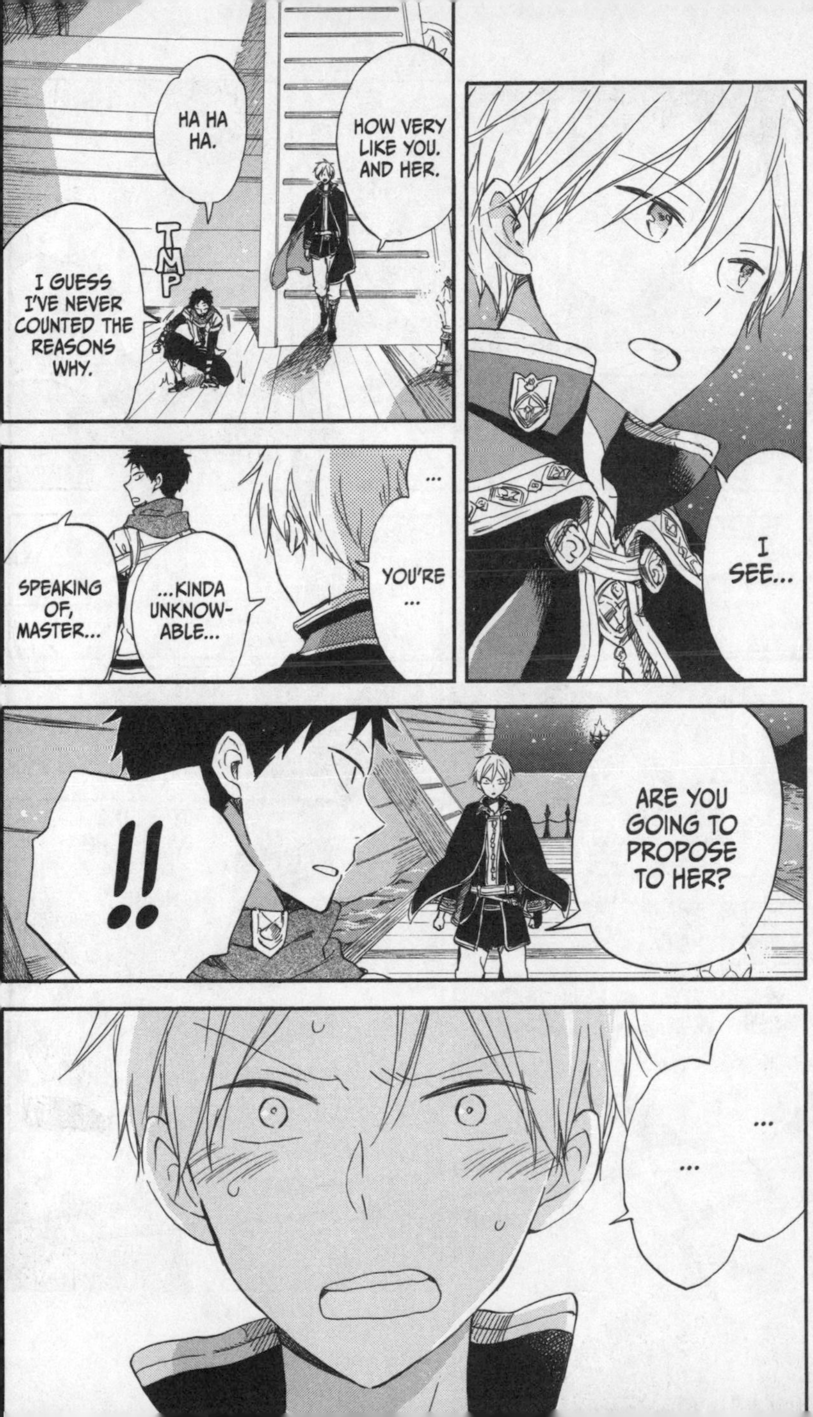
I SEE...
HOW VERY LIKE YOU. AND HER.
HA HA HA.
TMP
I GUESS I'VE NEVER COUNTED THE REASONS WHY.
...
YOU'RE ...
...KINDA UNKNOWABLE...
SPEAKING OF, MASTER...
ARE YOU GOING TO PROPOSE TO HER?
!!
...
...

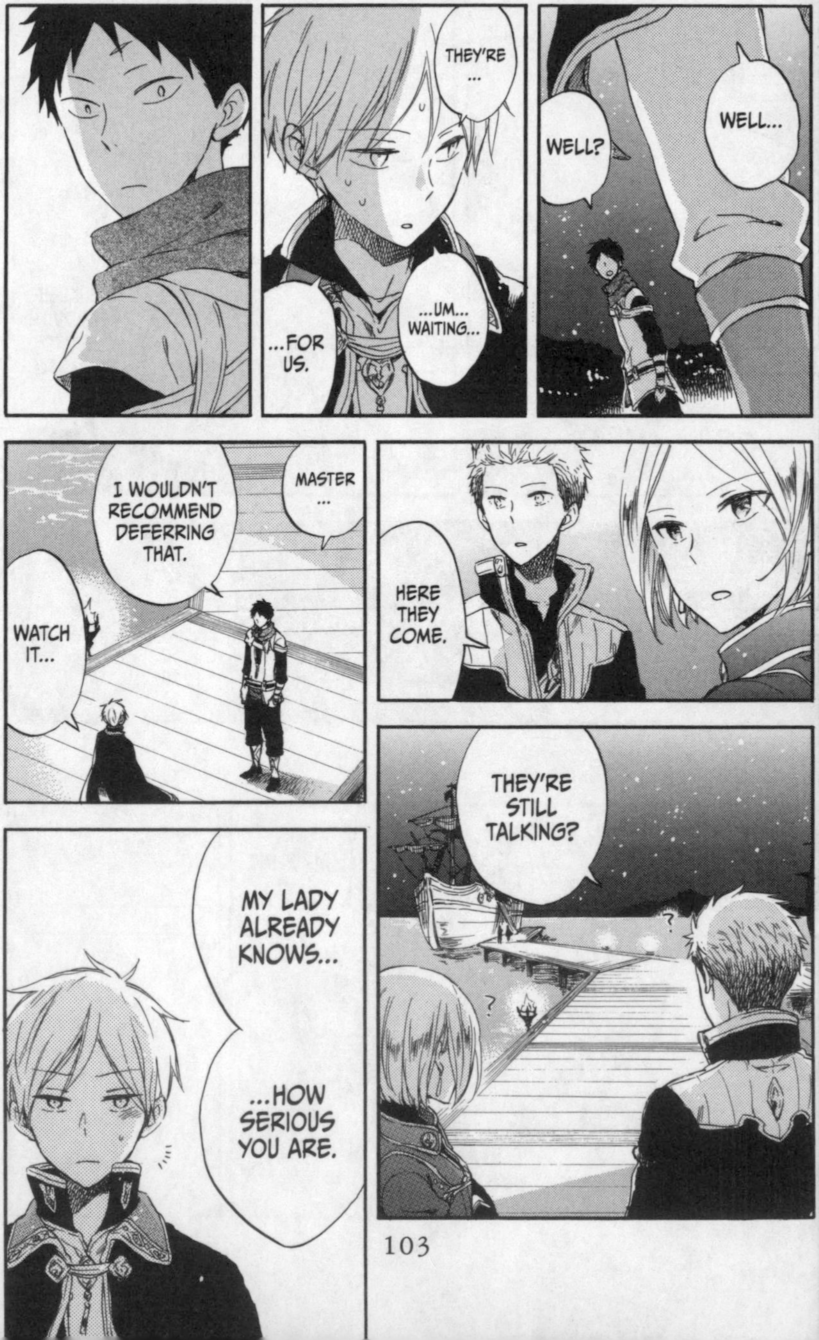
WELL...
WELL?
THEY'RE ...
...UM... WAITING...
...FOR US.
HERE THEY COME.
MASTER ...
I WOULDN'T RECOMMEND DEFERRING THAT.
WATCH IT...
THEY'RE STILL TALKING?
MY LADY ALREADY KNOWS...
...HOW SERIOUS YOU ARE.

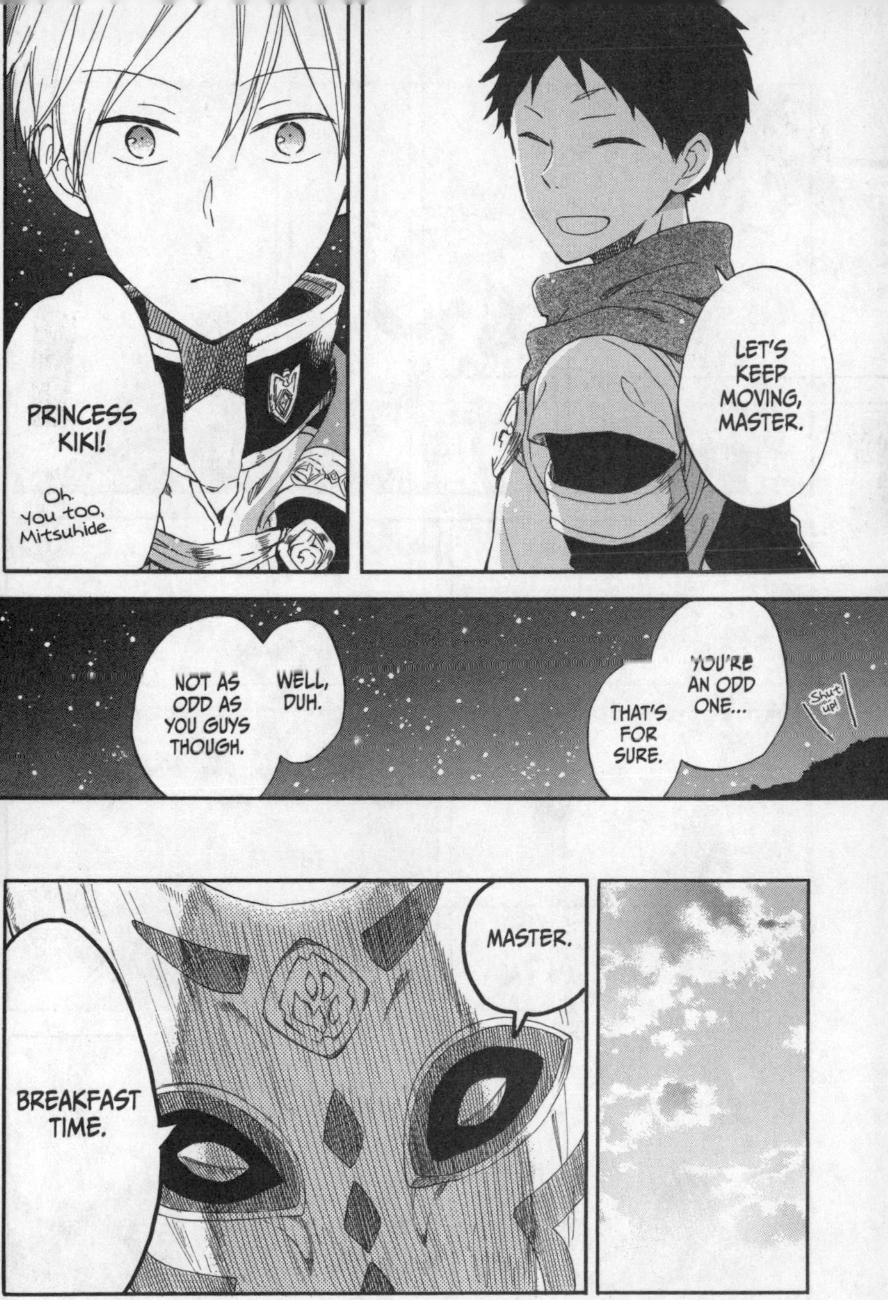
LET'S KEEP MOVING, MASTER.
PRINCESS KIKI!
Oh. You too, Mitsuhide.
Shut up!
YOU'RE AN ODD ONE...
THAT'S FOR SURE.
WELL, DUH.
NOT AS ODD AS YOU GUYS THOUGH.
MASTER.
BREAKFAST TIME.

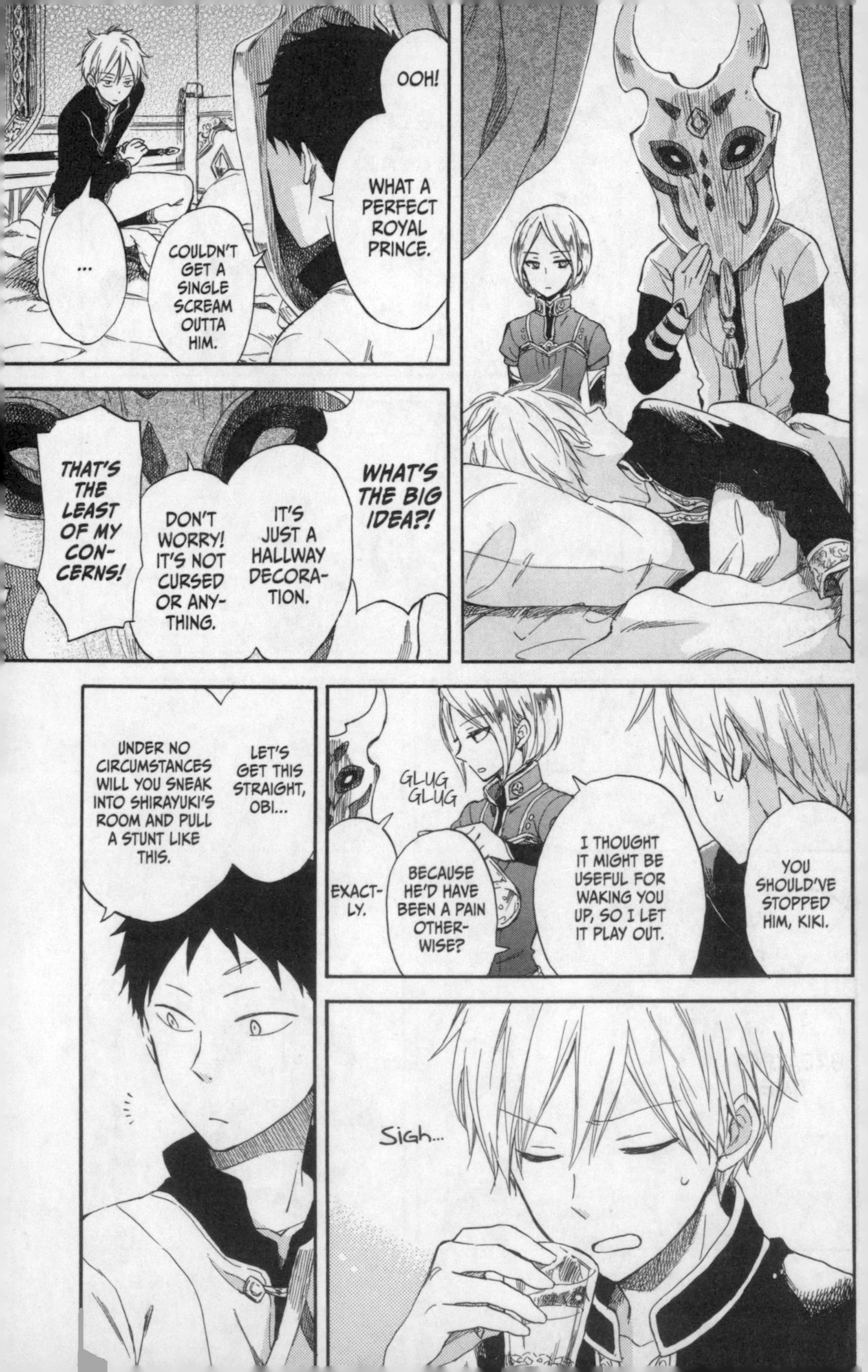
OOH!
WHAT A PERFECT ROYAL PRINCE.
COULDN'T GET A SINGLE SCREAM OUTTA HIM.
...
WHAT'S THE BIG IDEA?!
IT'S JUST A HALLWAY DECORA-TION.
DON'T WORRY! IT'S NOT CURSED OR ANY-THING.
THAT'S THE LEAST OF MY CON-CERNS!
YOU SHOULD'VE STOPPED HIM, KIKI.
I THOUGHT IT MIGHT BE USEFUL FOR WAKING YOU UP, SO I LET IT PLAY OUT.
GLUG GLUG
BECAUSE HE'D HAVE BEEN A PAIN OTHER-WISE?
EXACT-LY.
Sigh...
LET'S GET THIS STRAIGHT, OBI...
UNDER NO CIRCUMSTANCES WILL YOU SNEAK INTO SHIRAYUKI'S ROOM AND PULL A STUNT LIKE THIS.

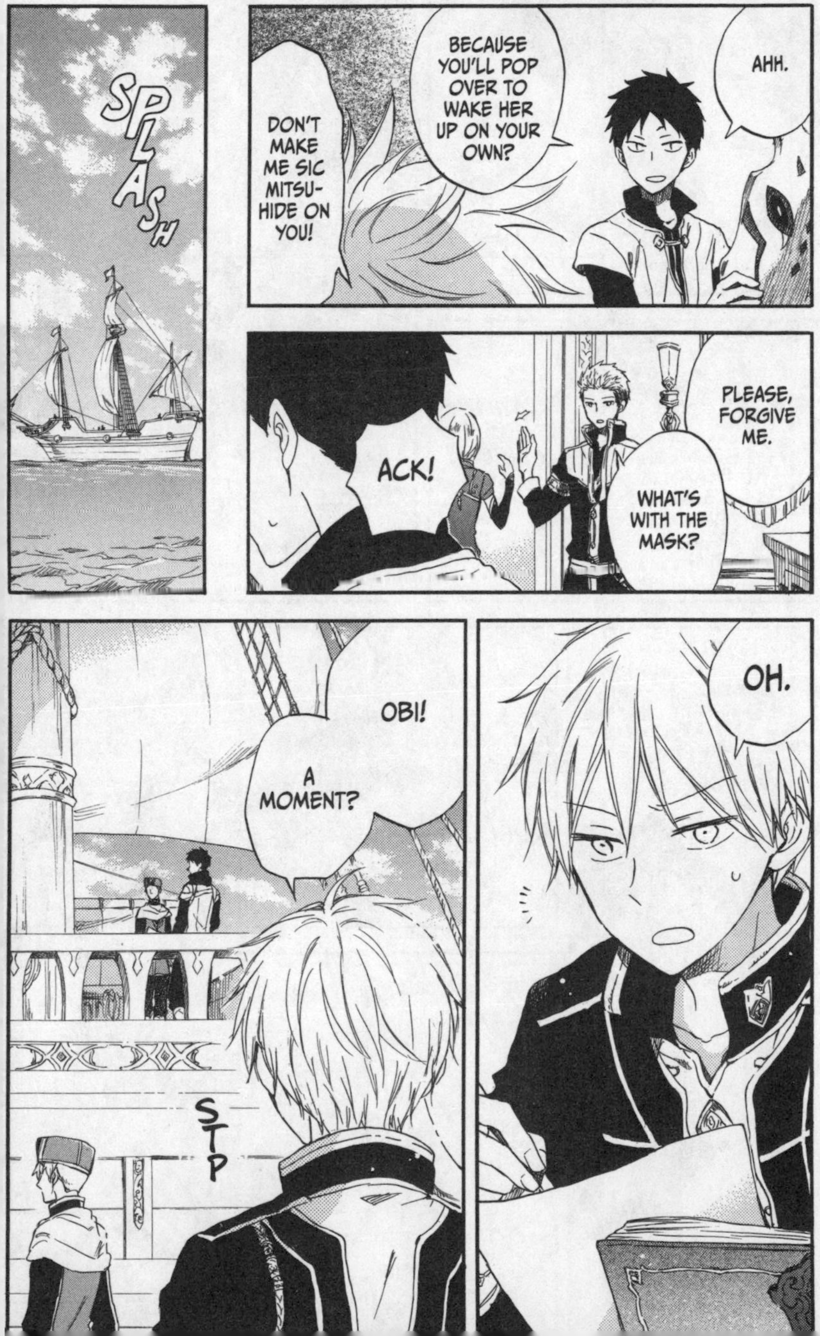
AHH.
BECAUSE YOU'LL POP OVER TO WAKE HER UP ON YOUR OWN?
DON'T MAKE ME SIC MITSU-HIDE ON YOU!
PLEASE, FORGIVE ME.
WHAT'S WITH THE MASK?
ACK!
SPLASH
OH.
OBI!
A MOMENT?
STP

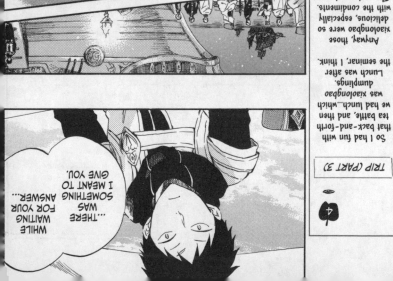

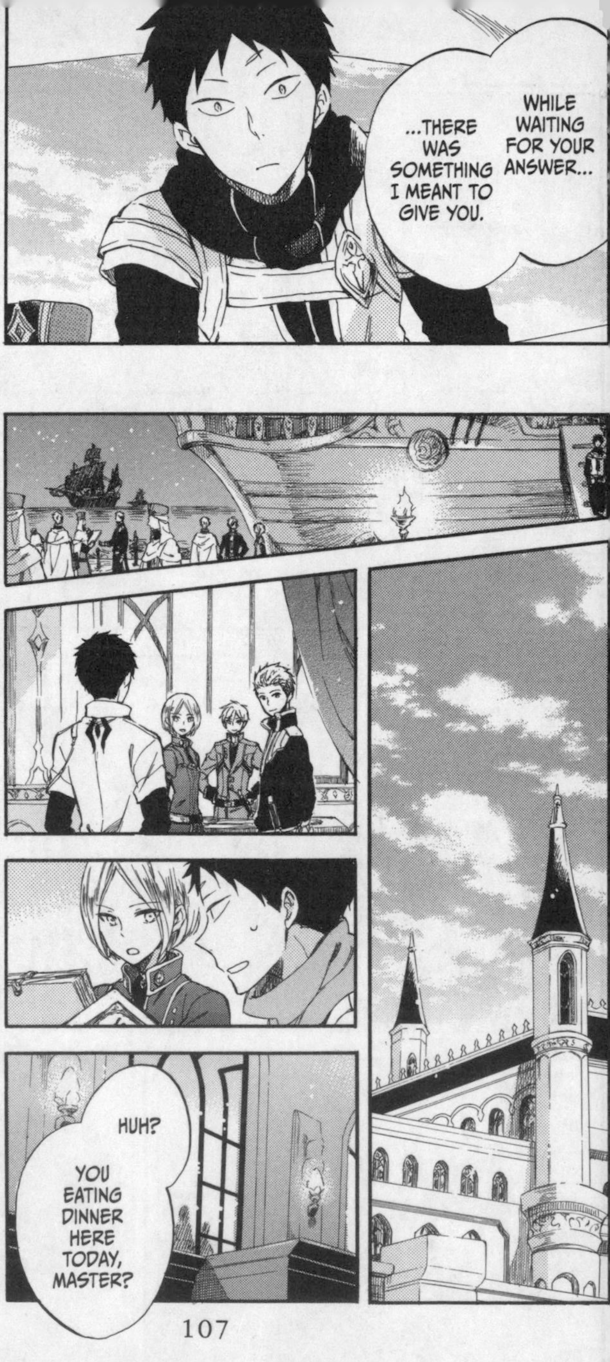
WHILE WAITING FOR YOUR ANSWER...
...THERE WAS SOMETHING I MEANT TO GIVE YOU.
HUH?
YOU EATING DINNER HERE TODAY, MASTER?

4

TRIP (PART 3)

So I had fun with that back-and-forth tea battle, and then we had lunch...which was *xiaolongbao* dumplings. Lunch was after the seminar, I think.

Anyway, those xiaolongbao were so delicious, especially with the condiments. The restaurant was so jam-packed they asked if we could finish eating in 15 minutes or less. I actually enjoyed the hustle and bustle.

The fried rice was also great. I couldn't stop talking about it after I got back home. I swear, one day I'll fly back just to eat some more fried rice.

Oops. All I've talked about is food.

Since I've come this far, I might as well mention the hotel food too...

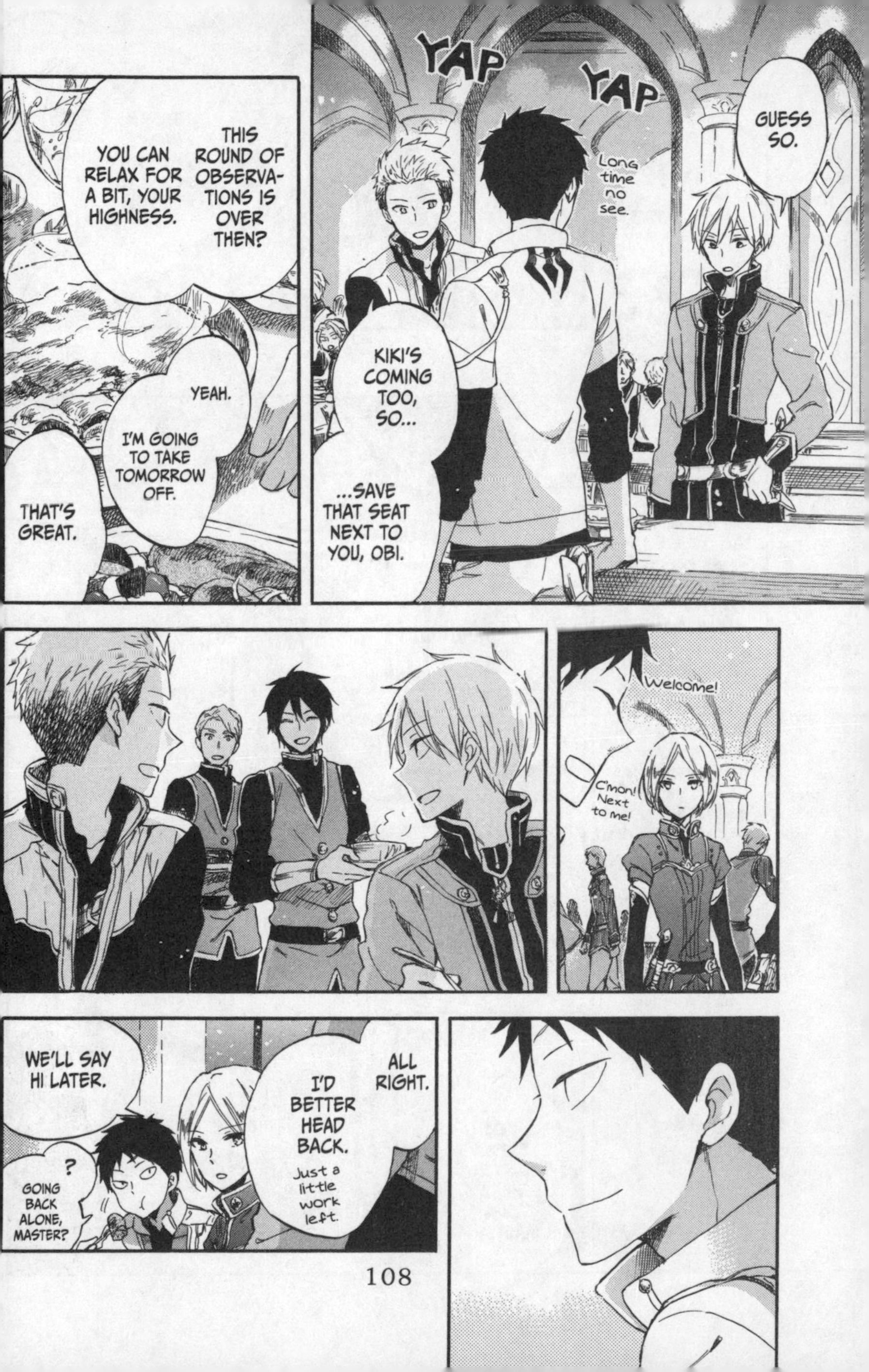
YAP
YAP
GUESS SO.
Long time no see.
KIKI'S COMING TOO, SO...
...SAVE THAT SEAT NEXT TO YOU, OBI.
THIS ROUND OF OBSERVATIONS IS OVER THEN?
YOU CAN RELAX FOR A BIT, YOUR HIGHNESS.
YEAH.
I'M GOING TO TAKE TOMORROW OFF.
THAT'S GREAT.
Welcome!
C'mon! Next to me!
ALL RIGHT.
I'D BETTER HEAD BACK.
Just a little work left.
?
GOING BACK ALONE, MASTER?
WE'LL SAY HI LATER.

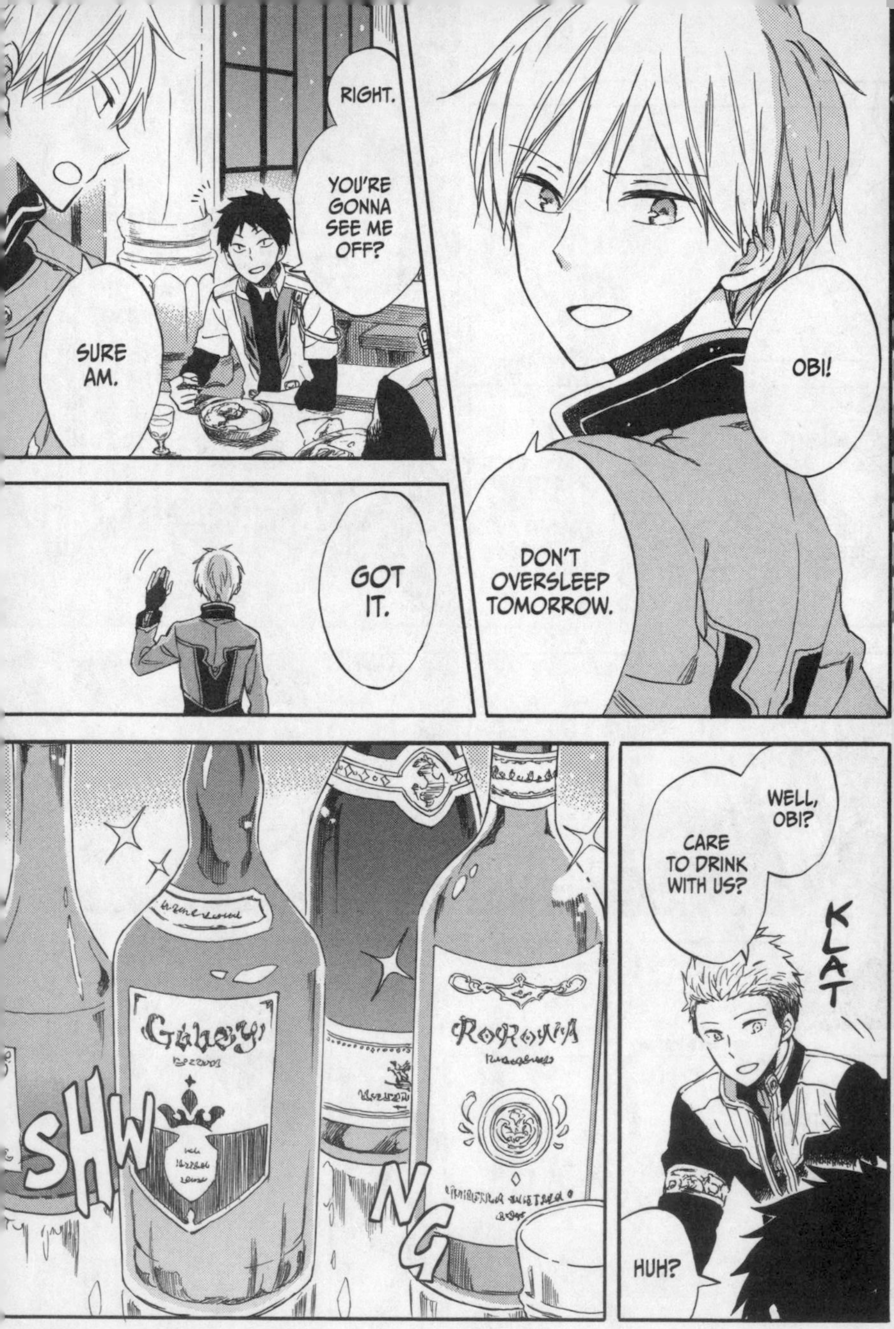
RIGHT.
YOU'RE GONNA SEE ME OFF?
SURE AM.
OBI!
DON'T OVERSLEEP TOMORROW.
GOT IT.
WELL, OBI?
CARE TO DRINK WITH US?
KLAT
HUH?
SHWNG

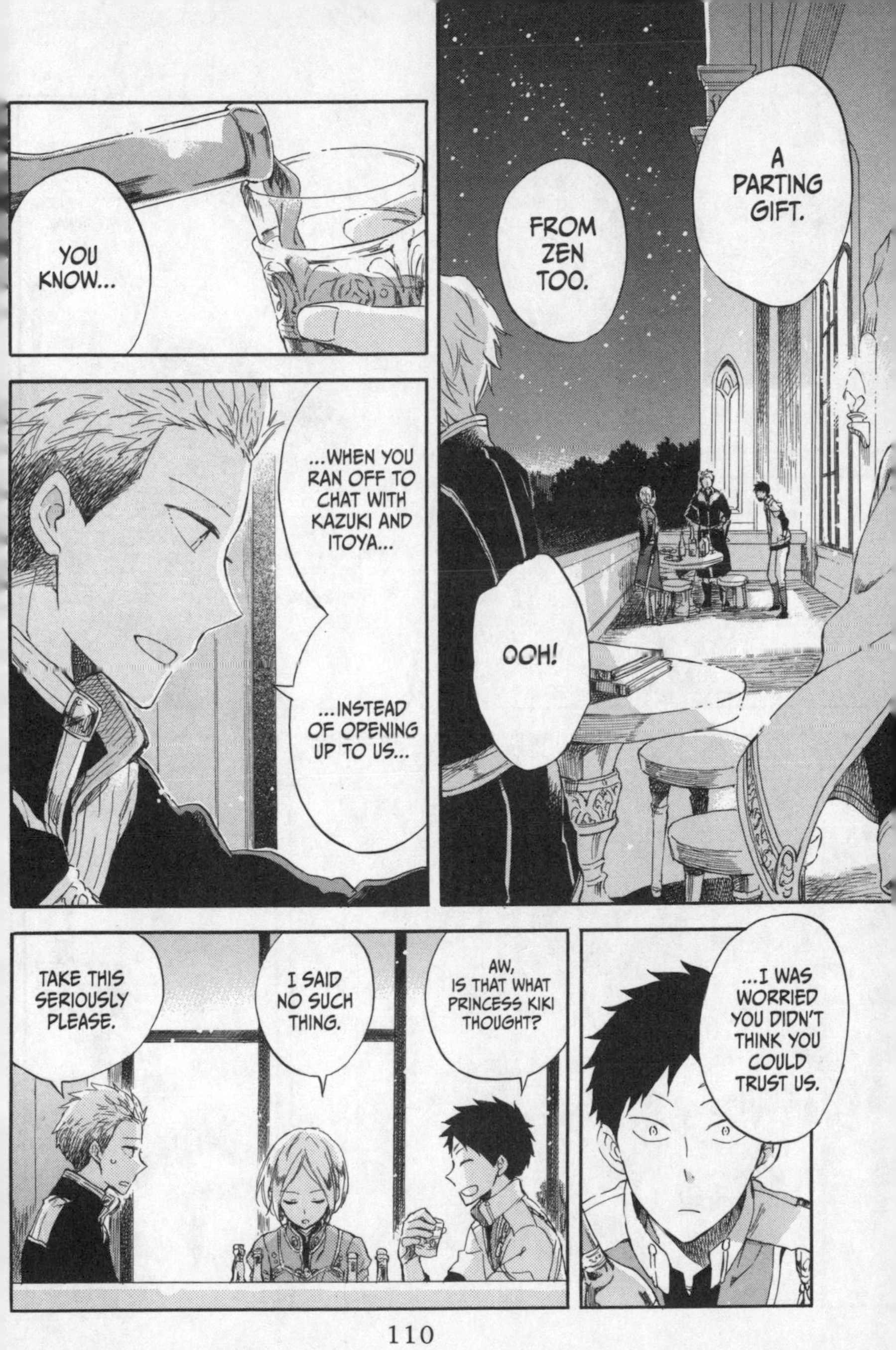
A PARTING GIFT.
FROM ZEN TOO.
OOH!
YOU KNOW...
...WHEN YOU RAN OFF TO CHAT WITH KAZUKI AND ITOYA...
...INSTEAD OF OPENING UP TO US...
...I WAS WORRIED YOU DIDN'T THINK YOU COULD TRUST US.
AW, IS THAT WHAT PRINCESS KIKI THOUGHT?
I SAID NO SUCH THING.
TAKE THIS SERIOUSLY PLEASE.

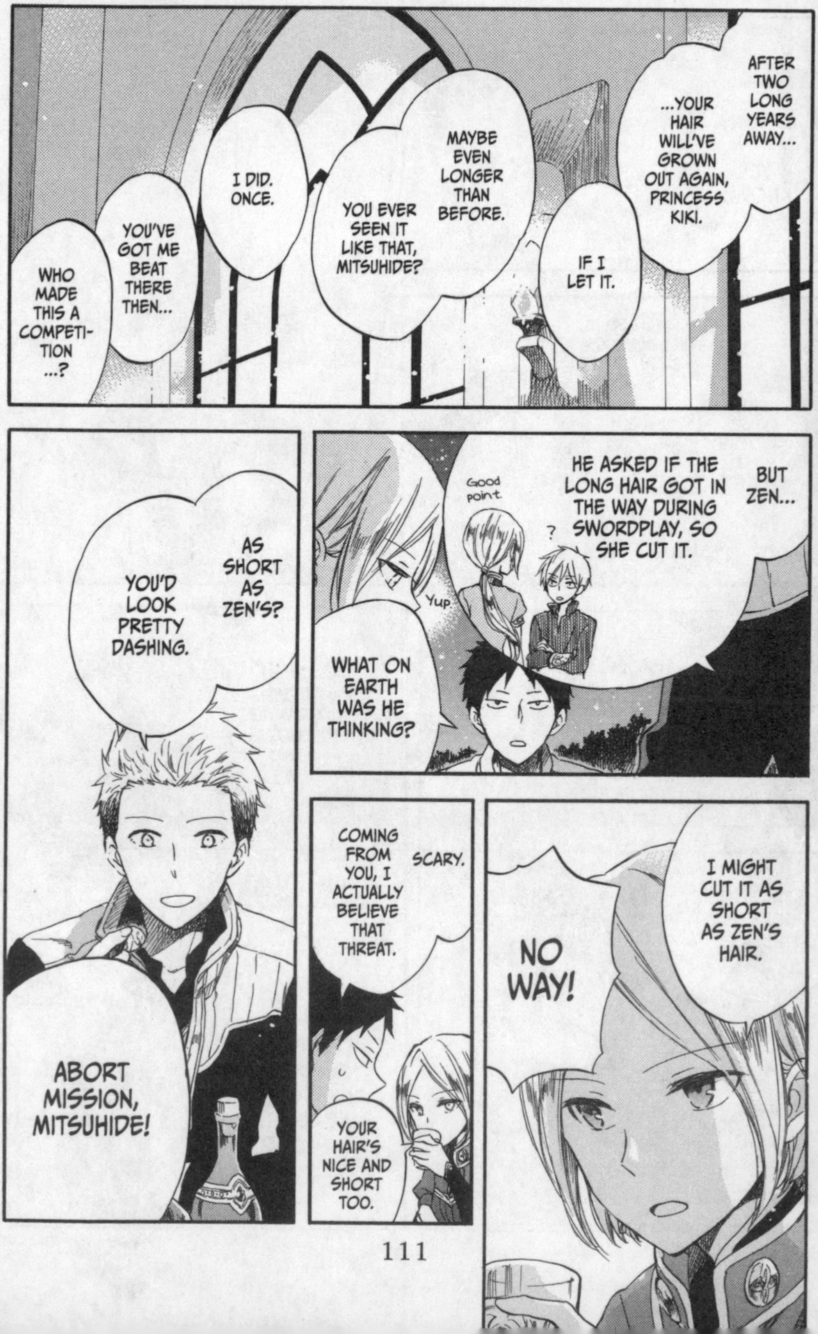
AFTER TWO LONG YEARS AWAY...
...YOUR HAIR WILL'VE GROWN OUT AGAIN, PRINCESS KIKI.
IF I LET IT.
MAYBE EVEN LONGER THAN BEFORE.
YOU EVER SEEN IT LIKE THAT, MITSUHIDE?
I DID. ONCE.
YOU'VE GOT ME BEAT THERE THEN...
WHO MADE THIS A COMPETITION ...?
BUT ZEN...
HE ASKED IF THE LONG HAIR GOT IN THE WAY DURING SWORDPLAY, SO SHE CUT IT.
Good point.
?
Yup.
WHAT ON EARTH WAS HE THINKING?
I MIGHT CUT IT AS SHORT AS ZEN'S HAIR.
NO WAY!
SCARY.
COMING FROM YOU, I ACTUALLY BELIEVE THAT THREAT.
YOUR HAIR'S NICE AND SHORT TOO.
AS SHORT AS ZEN'S?
YOU'D LOOK PRETTY DASHING.
ABORT MISSION, MITSUHIDE!

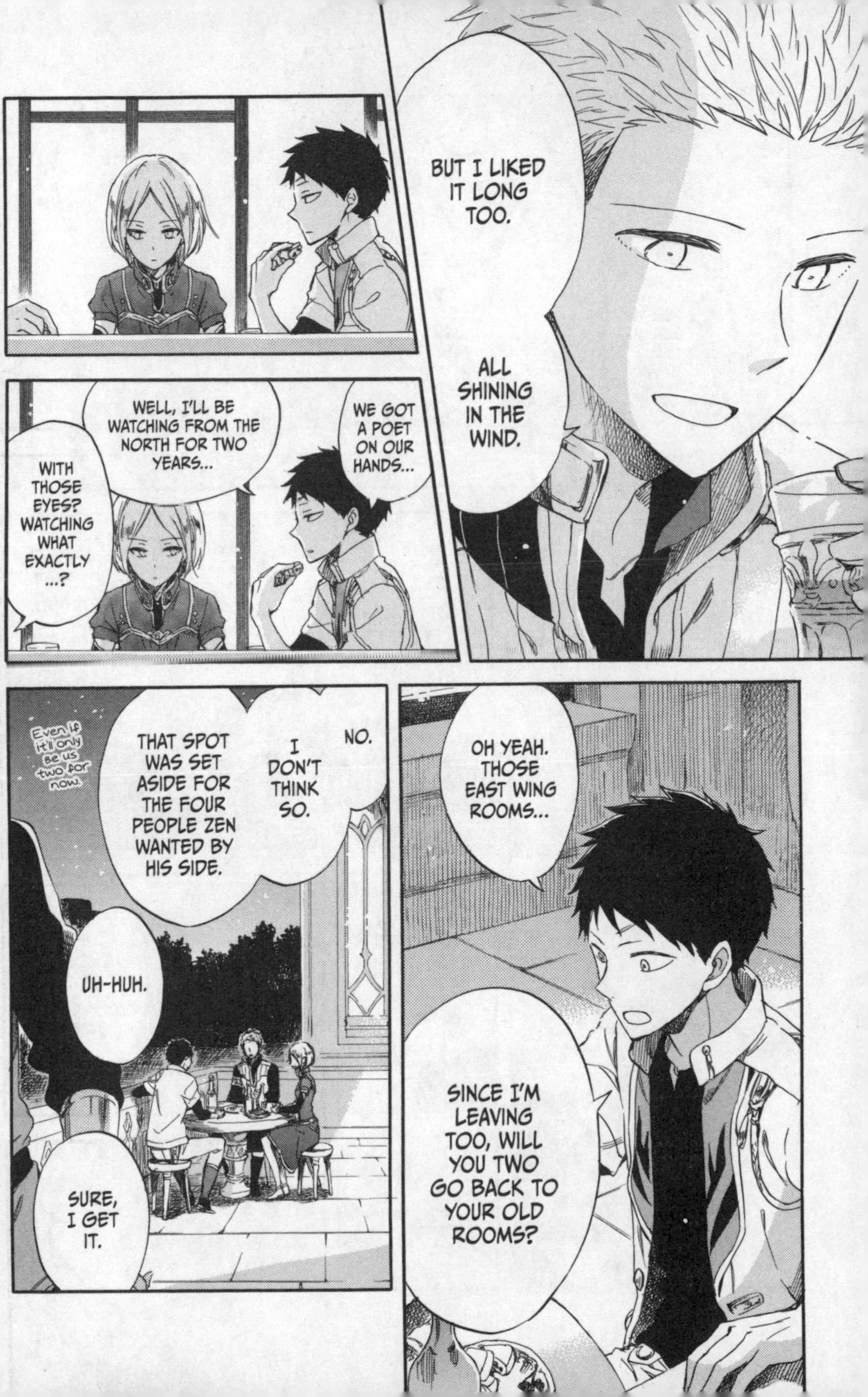
BUT I LIKED IT LONG TOO.
ALL SHINING IN THE WIND.
WE GOT A POET ON OUR HANDS...
WELL, I'LL BE WATCHING FROM THE NORTH FOR TWO YEARS...
WITH THOSE EYES? WATCHING WHAT EXACTLY ...?
OH YEAH. THOSE EAST WING ROOMS...
SINCE I'M LEAVING TOO, WILL YOU TWO GO BACK TO YOUR OLD ROOMS?
NO.
I DON'T THINK SO.
THAT SPOT WAS SET ASIDE FOR THE FOUR PEOPLE ZEN WANTED BY HIS SIDE.
Even if it'll only be us two for now.
UH-HUH.
SURE, I GET IT.

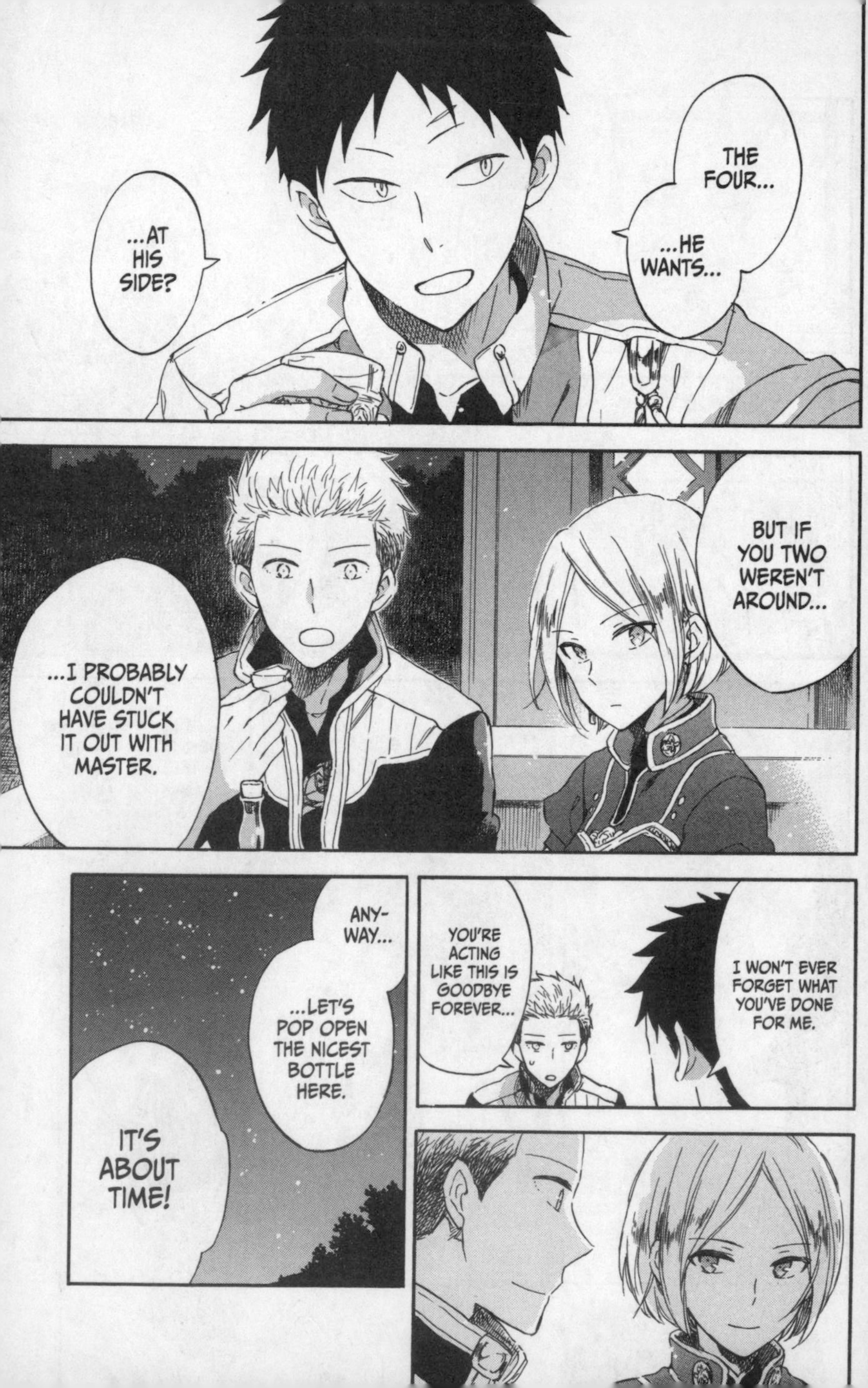
THE FOUR...
...HE WANTS...
...AT HIS SIDE?
BUT IF YOU TWO WEREN'T AROUND...
...I PROBABLY COULDN'T HAVE STUCK IT OUT WITH MASTER.
I WON'T EVER FORGET WHAT YOU'VE DONE FOR ME.
YOU'RE ACTING LIKE THIS IS GOODBYE FOREVER...
ANY-WAY...
...LET'S POP OPEN THE NICEST BOTTLE HERE.
IT'S ABOUT TIME!

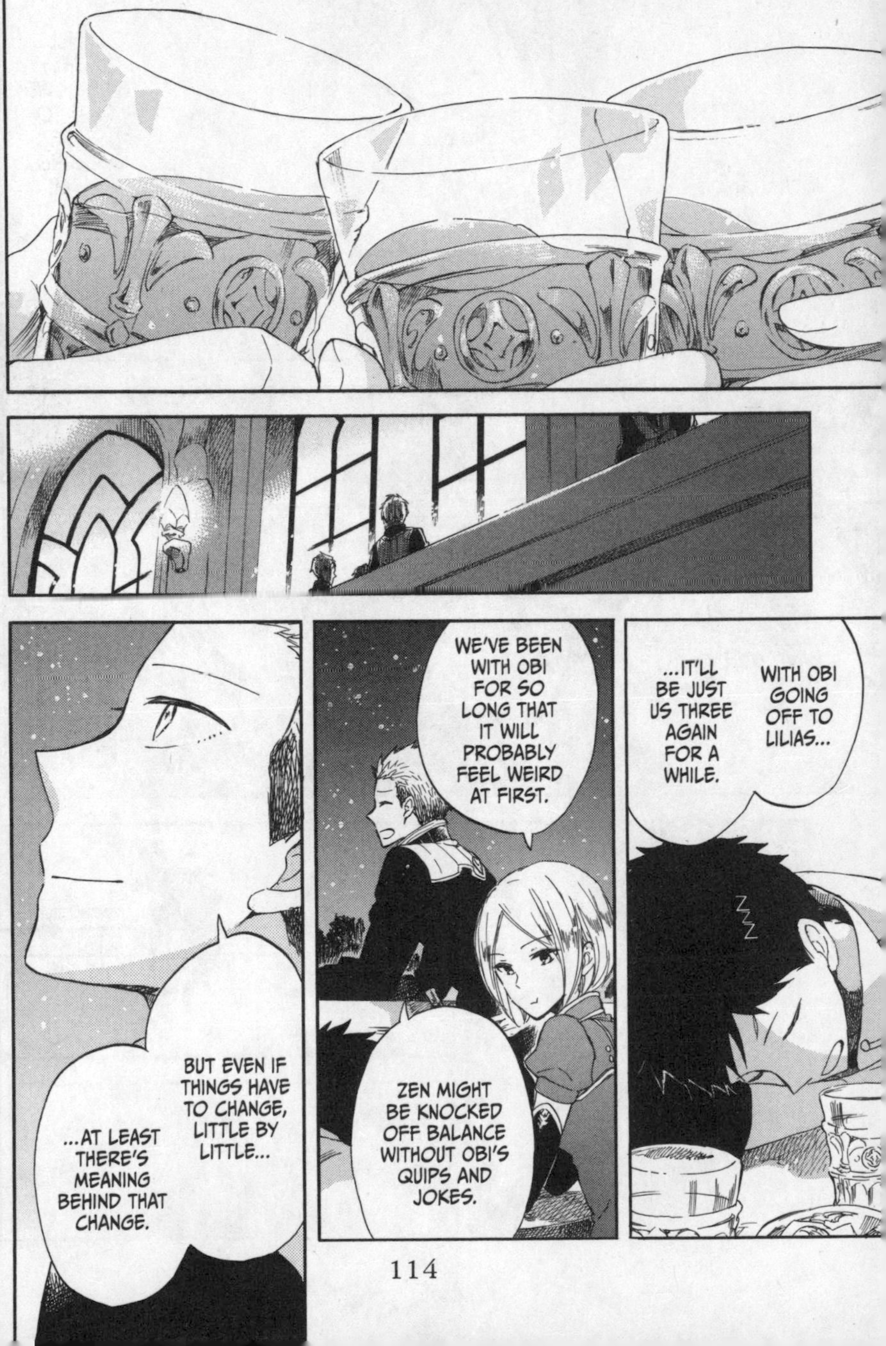
WITH OBI GOING OFF TO LILIAS...
...IT'LL BE JUST US THREE AGAIN FOR A WHILE.
WE'VE BEEN WITH OBI FOR SO LONG THAT IT WILL PROBABLY FEEL WEIRD AT FIRST.
ZEN MIGHT BE KNOCKED OFF BALANCE WITHOUT OBI'S QUIPS AND JOKES.
BUT EVEN IF THINGS HAVE TO CHANGE, LITTLE BY LITTLE...
...AT LEAST THERE'S MEANING BEHIND THAT CHANGE.

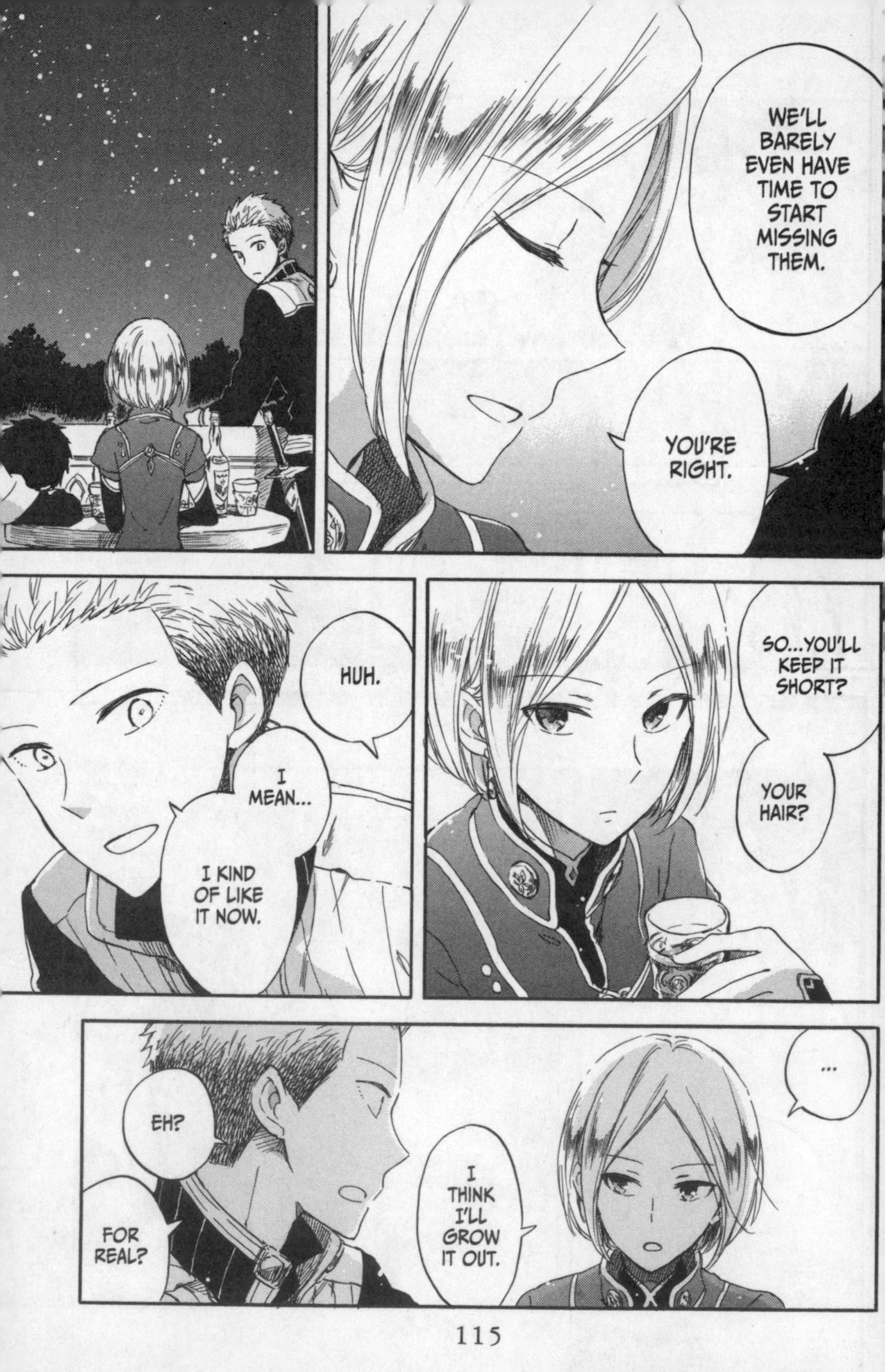
WE'LL BARELY EVEN HAVE TIME TO START MISSING THEM.
YOU'RE RIGHT.
SO...YOU'LL KEEP IT SHORT?
YOUR HAIR?
HUH.
I MEAN...
I KIND OF LIKE IT NOW.
...
I THINK I'LL GROW IT OUT.
EH?
FOR REAL?

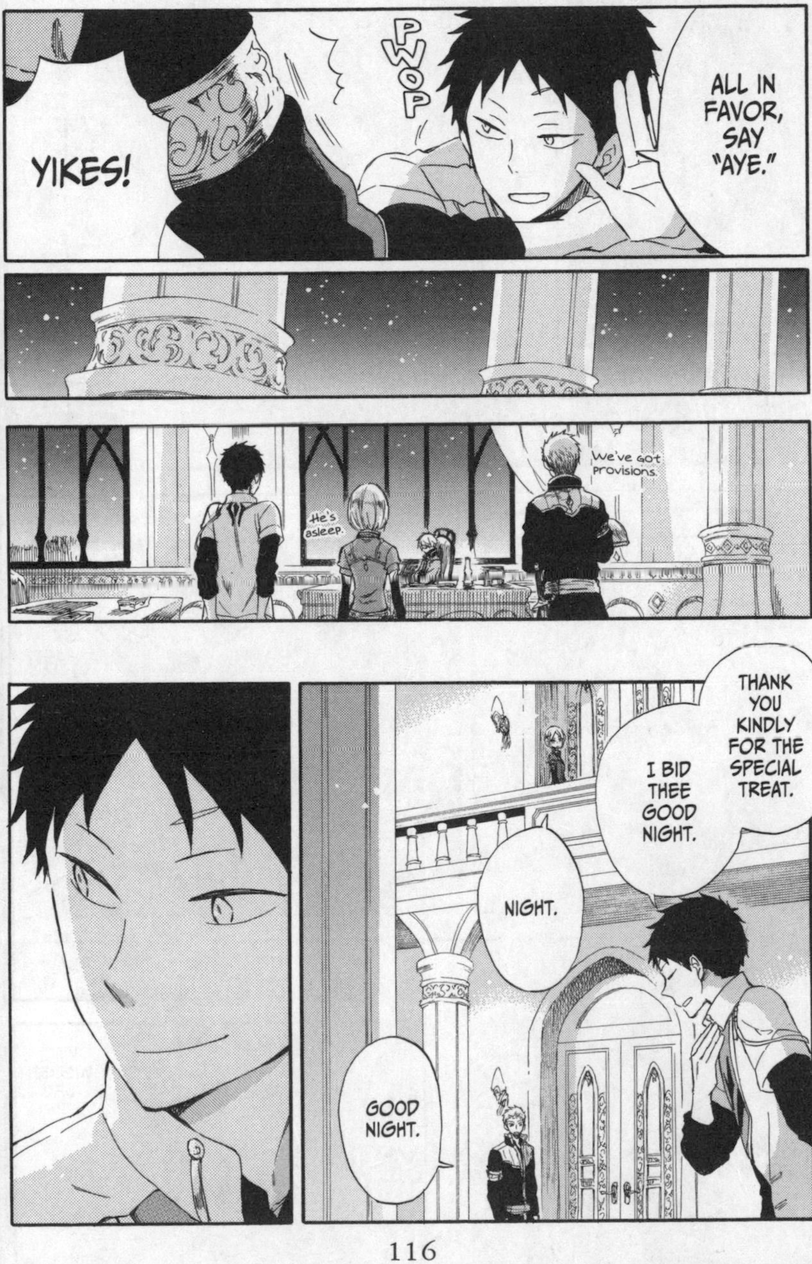
ALL IN FAVOR, SAY "AYE."
PWOP
YIKES!
We've got provisions.
He's asleep.
THANK YOU KINDLY FOR THE SPECIAL TREAT.
I BID THEE GOOD NIGHT.
NIGHT.
GOOD NIGHT.

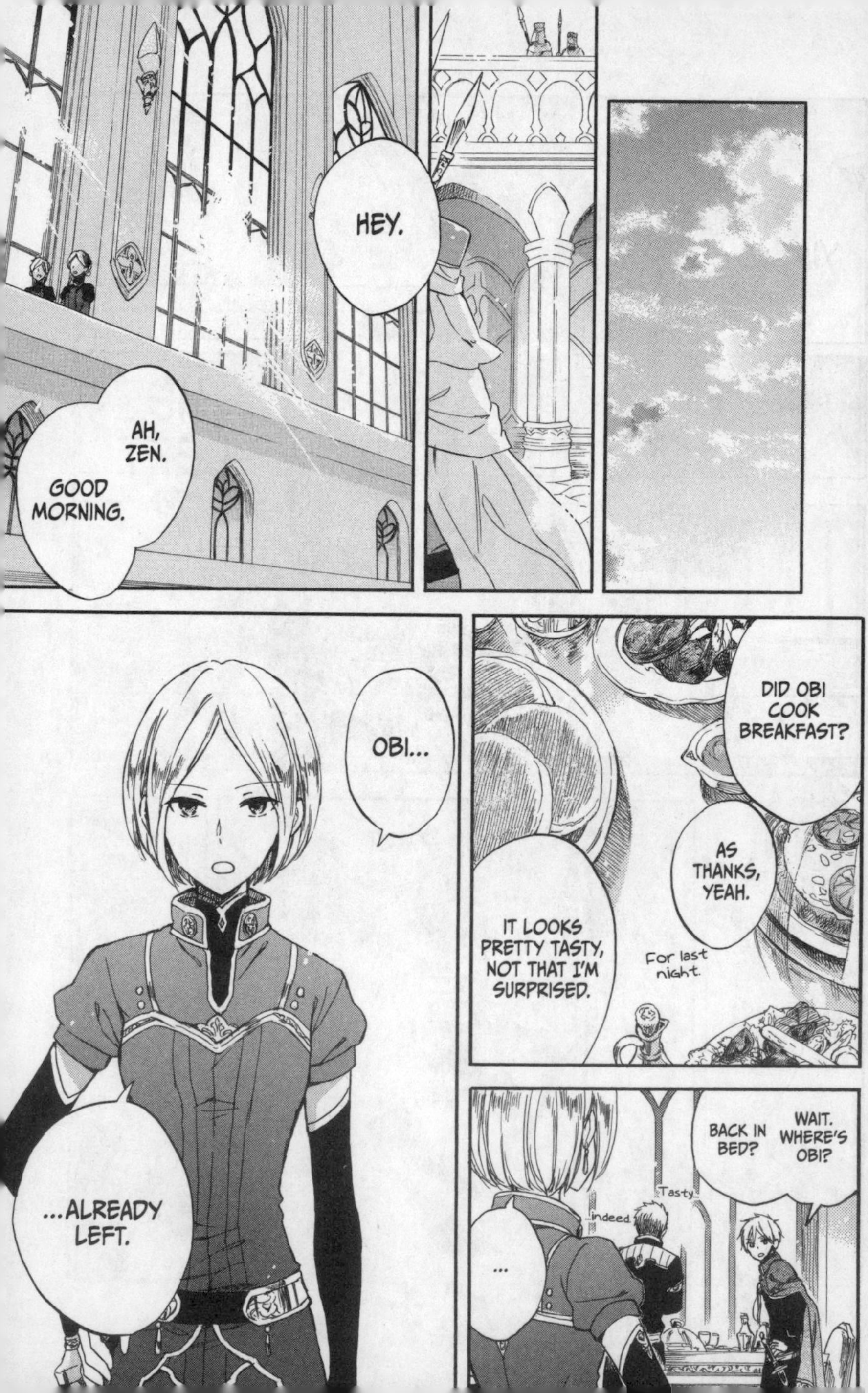
HEY.
AH, ZEN.
GOOD MORNING.
DID OBI COOK BREAKFAST?
AS THANKS, YEAH.
For last night.
IT LOOKS PRETTY TASTY, NOT THAT I'M SURPRISED.
WAIT. WHERE'S OBI?
BACK IN BED?
Tasty...
...indeed.
...
OBI...
...ALREADY LEFT.

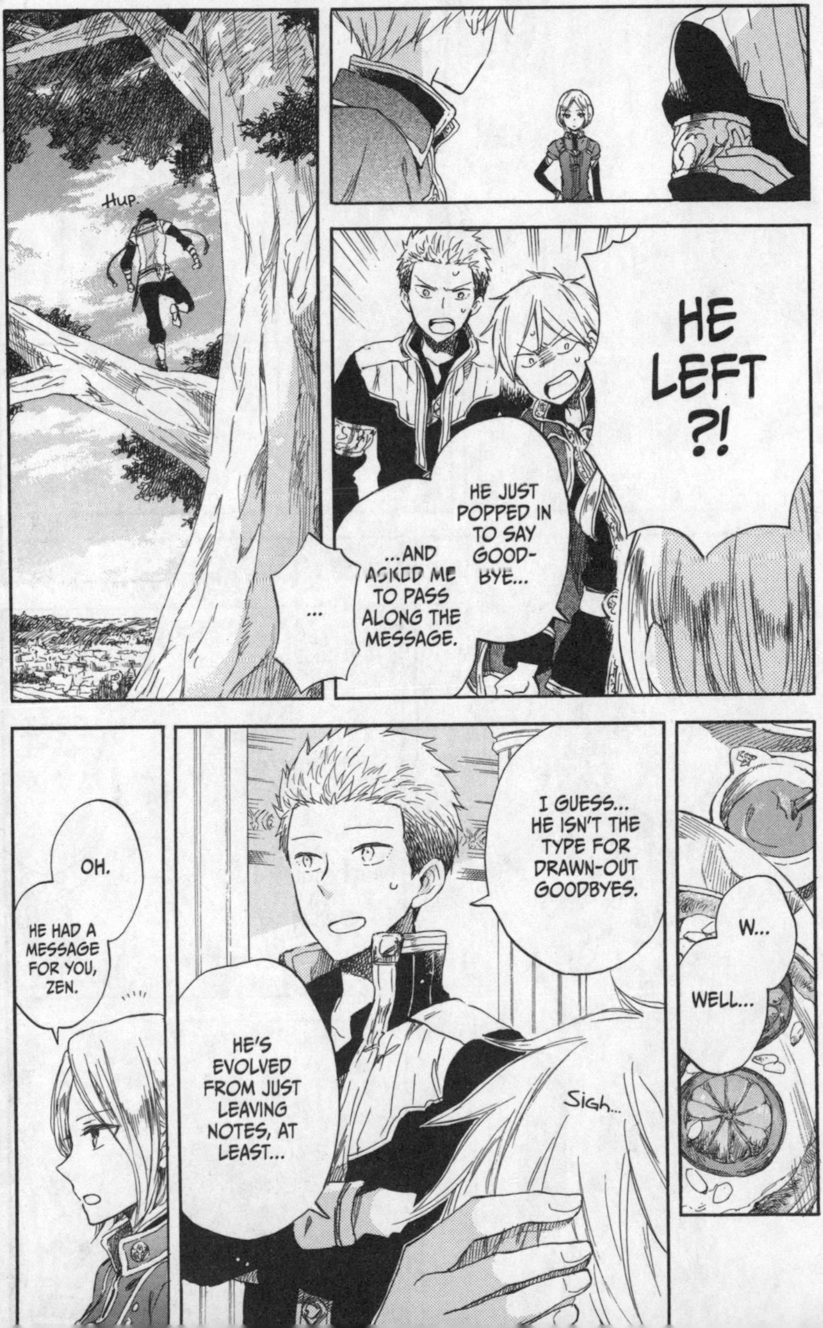
HE LEFT ?!
HE JUST POPPED IN TO SAY GOOD-BYE...
...AND ASKED ME TO PASS ALONG THE MESSAGE.
...
Hup.
W...
WELL...
I GUESS... HE ISN'T THE TYPE FOR DRAWN-OUT GOODBYES.
HE'S EVOLVED FROM JUST LEAVING NOTES, AT LEAST...
Sigh...
OH.
HE HAD A MESSAGE FOR YOU, ZEN.

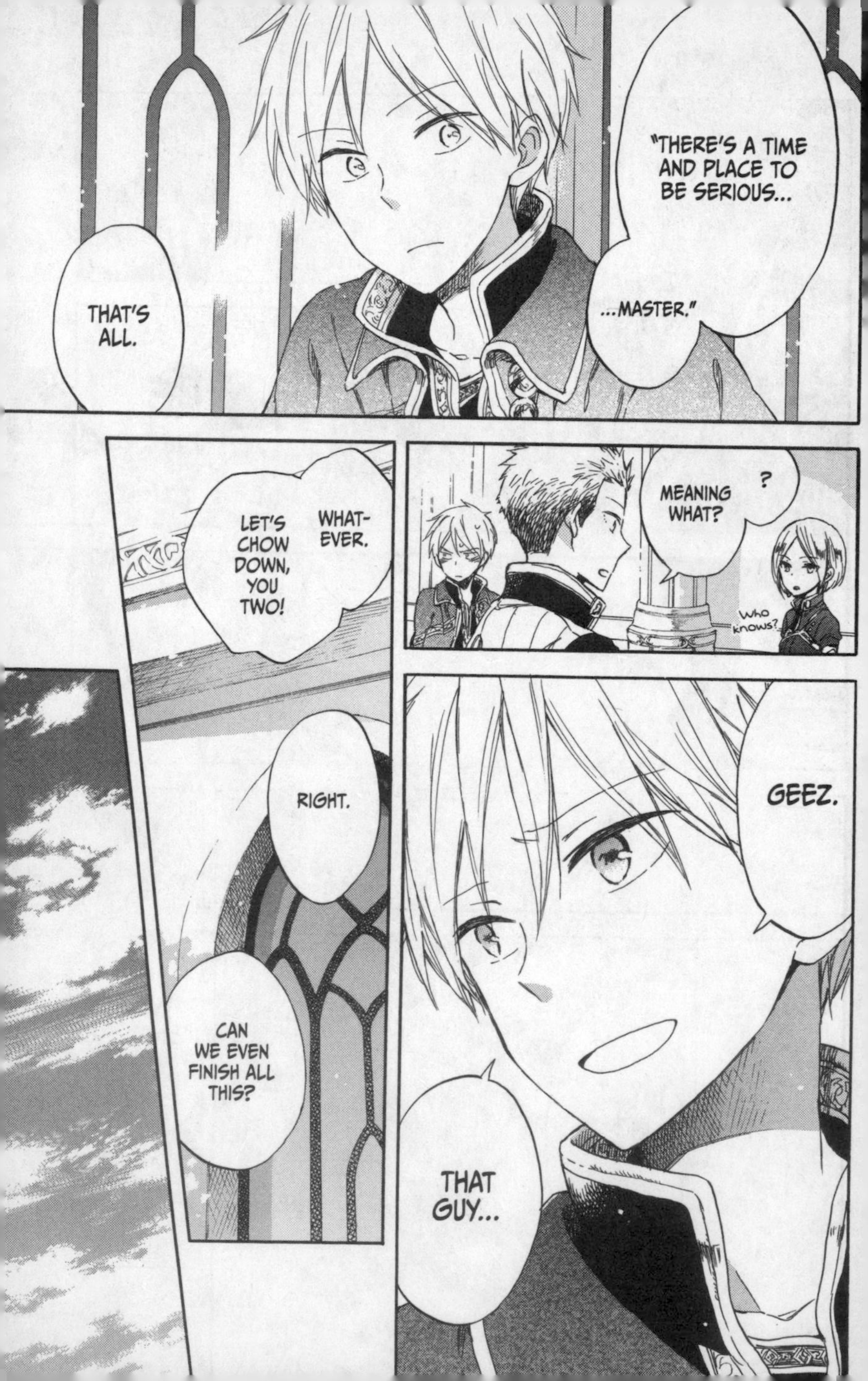
"THERE'S A TIME AND PLACE TO BE SERIOUS...
...MASTER."
THAT'S ALL.
?
MEANING WHAT?
Who knows?
WHAT-EVER.
LET'S CHOW DOWN, YOU TWO!
GEEZ.
THAT GUY...
RIGHT.
CAN WE EVEN FINISH ALL THIS?

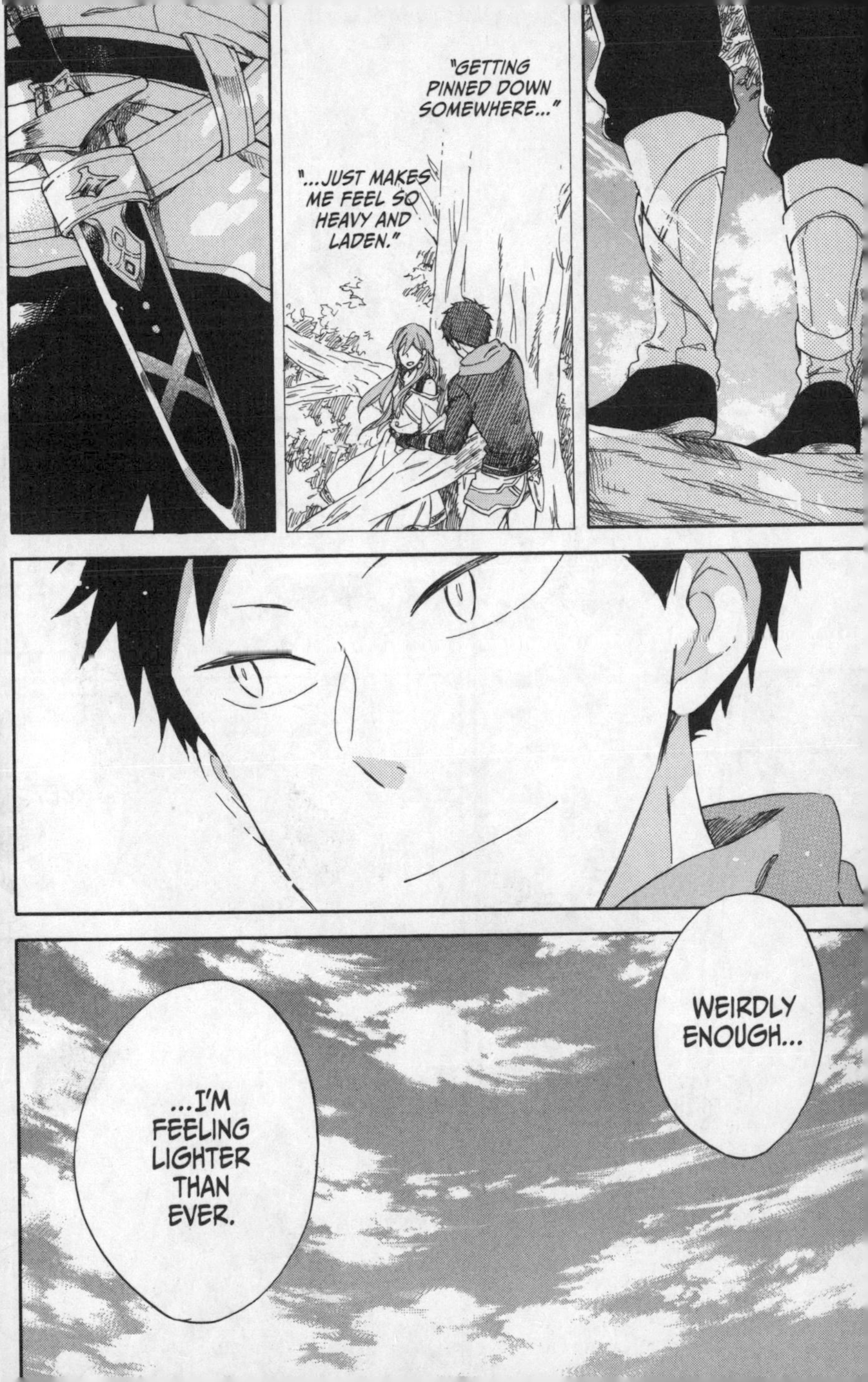
"GETTING PINNED DOWN SOMEWHERE..."
"...JUST MAKES ME FEEL SO HEAVY AND LADEN."
WEIRDLY ENOUGH...
...I'M FEELING LIGHTER THAN EVER.

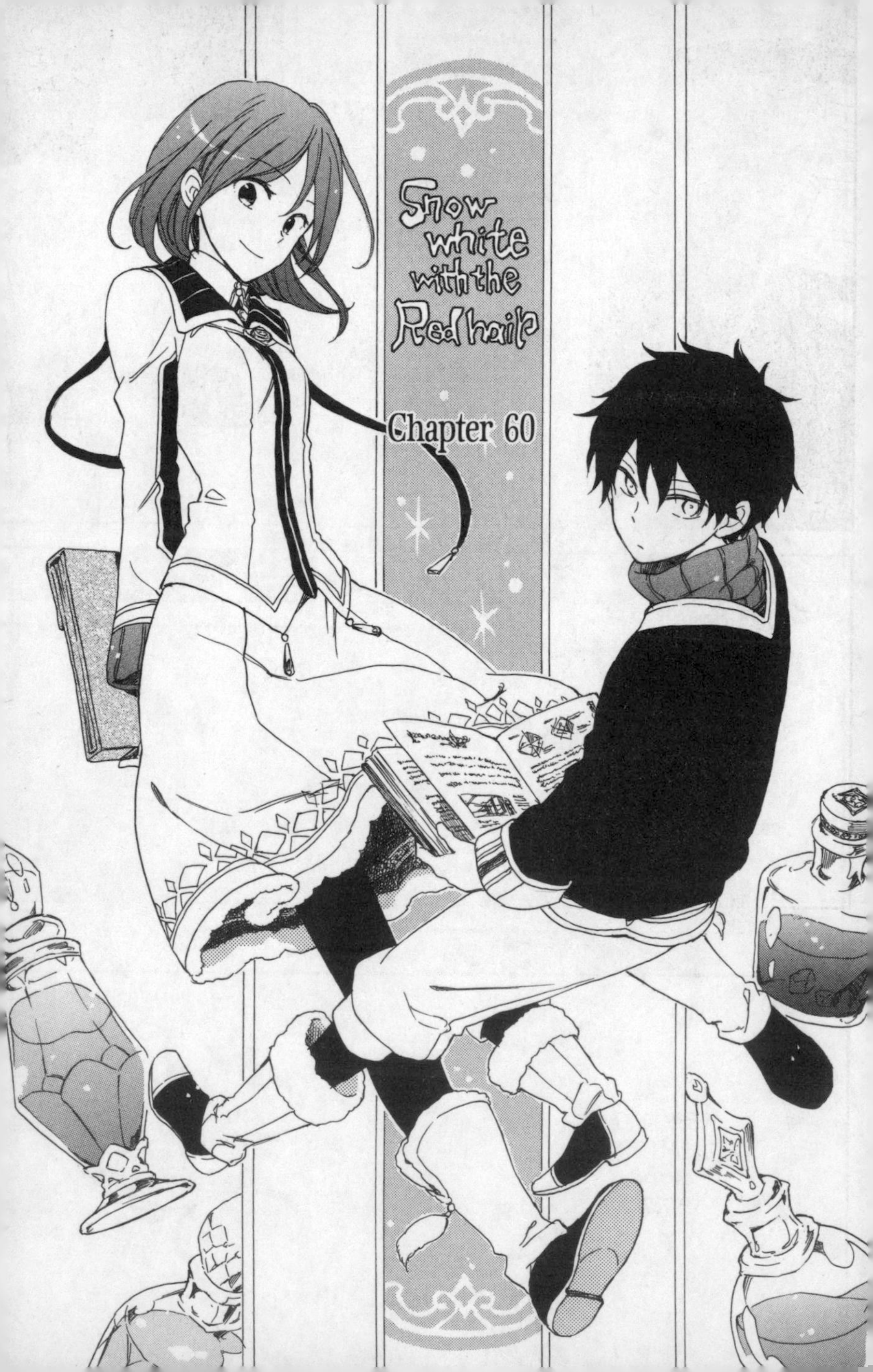
Snow white with the Red hair
Chapter 60

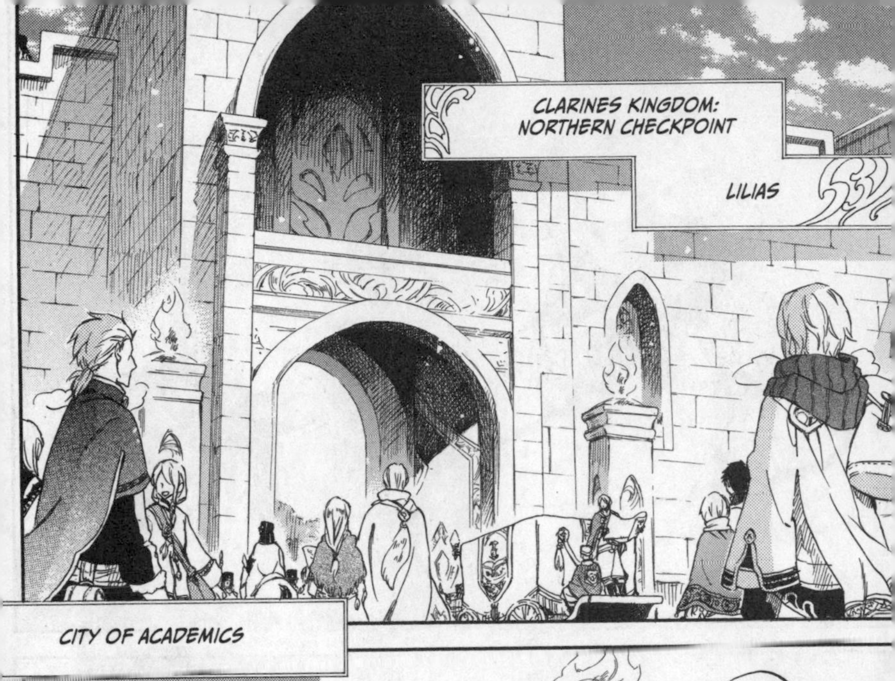
CLARINES KINGDOM:
NORTHERN CHECKPOINT
LILIAS
CITY OF ACADEMICS

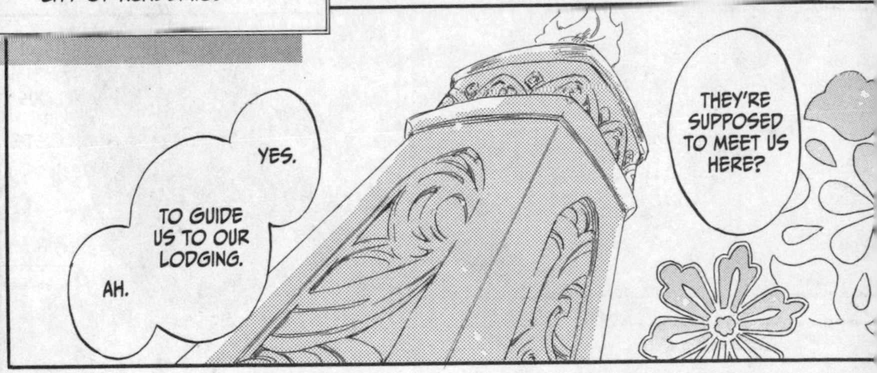
THEY'RE SUPPOSED TO MEET US HERE?
YES.
TO GUIDE US TO OUR LODGING.
AH.

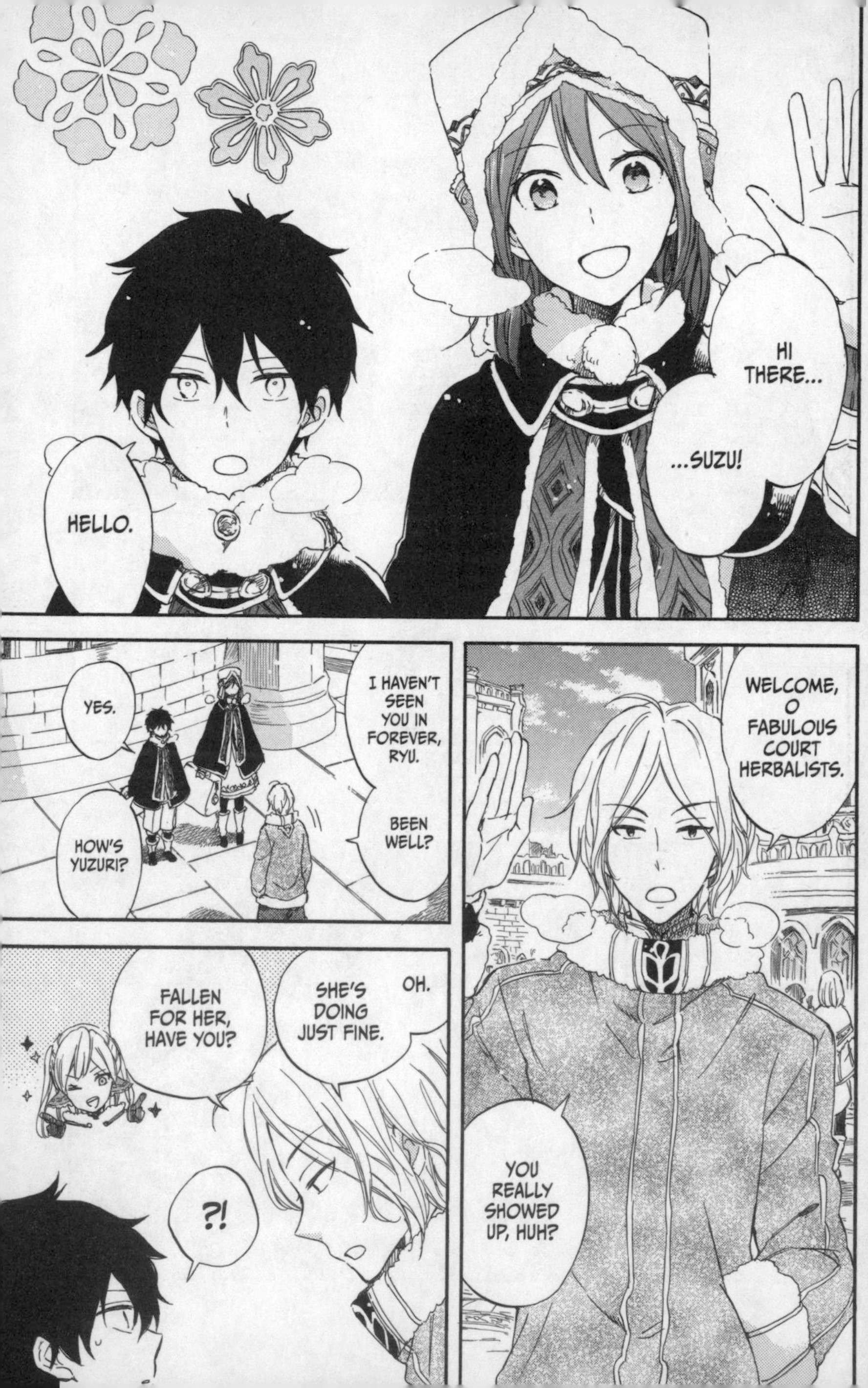
HI THERE...
...SUZU!
HELLO.
WELCOME, O FABULOUS COURT HERBALISTS.
YOU REALLY SHOWED UP, HUH?
I HAVEN'T SEEN YOU IN FOREVER, RYU.
BEEN WELL?
YES.
HOW'S YUZURI?
OH.
SHE'S DOING JUST FINE.
FALLEN FOR HER, HAVE YOU?
?!

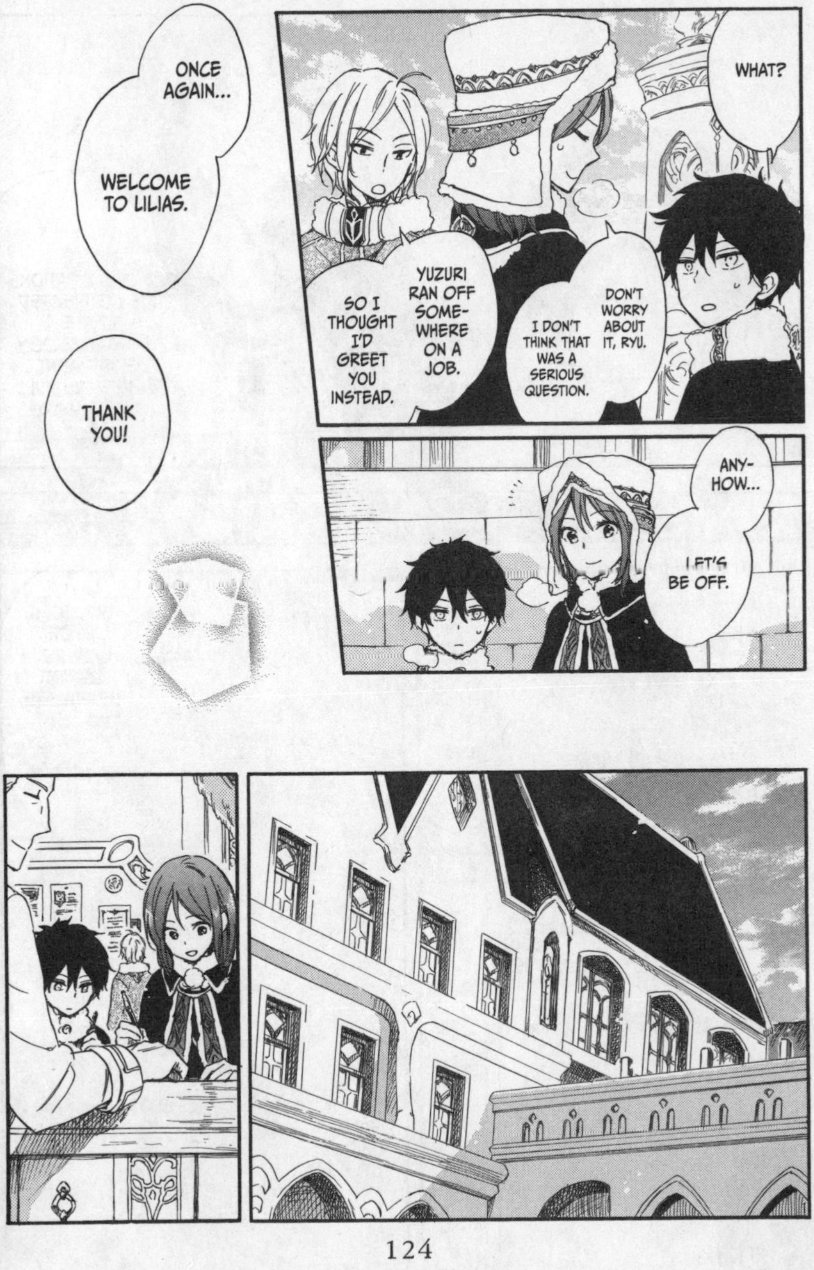
WHAT?
DON'T WORRY ABOUT IT, RYU.
I DON'T THINK THAT WAS A SERIOUS QUESTION.
YUZURI RAN OFF SOME-WHERE ON A JOB.
SO I THOUGHT I'D GREET YOU INSTEAD.
ONCE AGAIN...
WELCOME TO LILIAS.
THANK YOU!
ANY-HOW...
LET'S BE OFF.

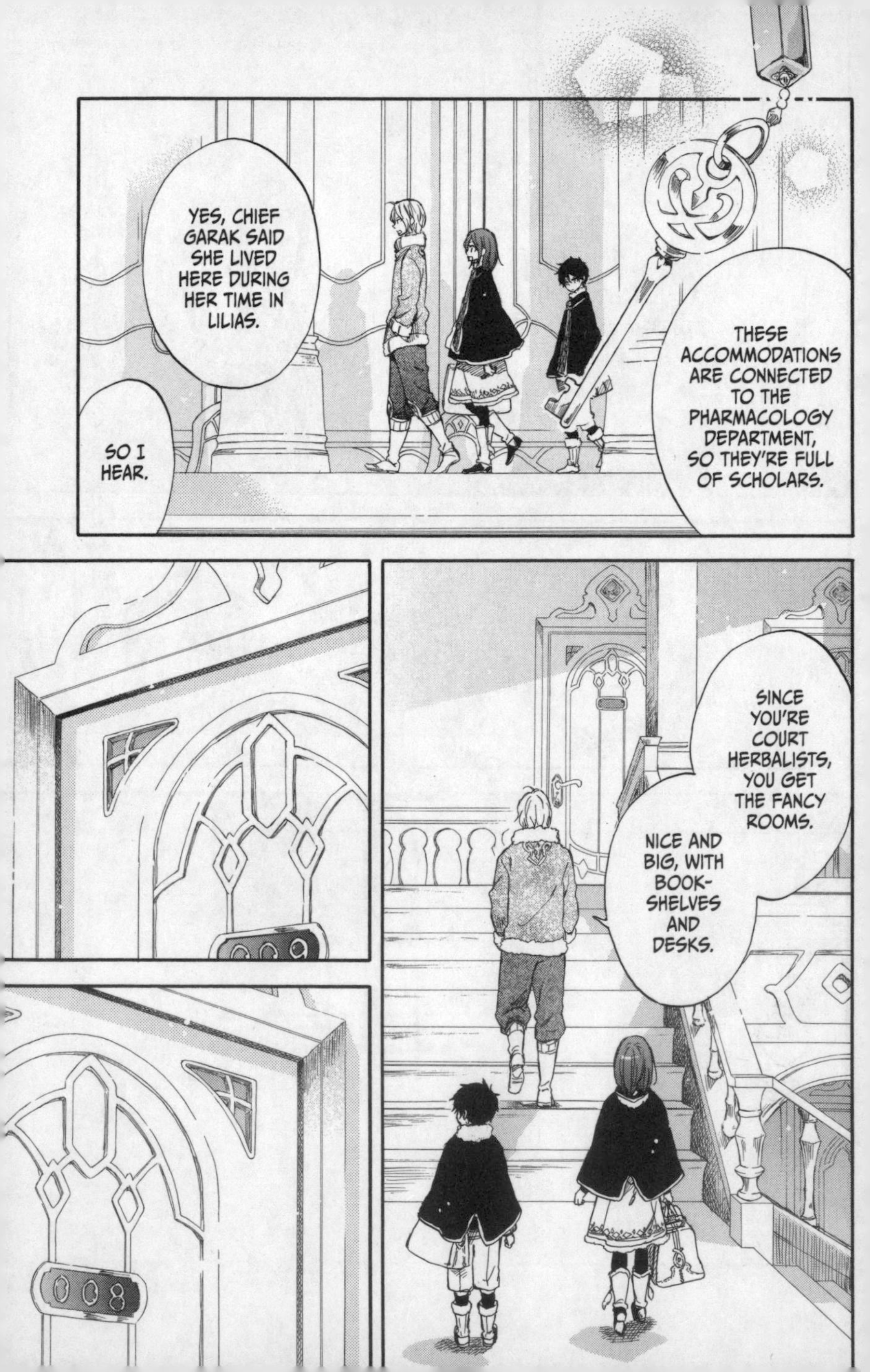
THESE ACCOMMODATIONS ARE CONNECTED TO THE PHARMACOLOGY DEPARTMENT, SO THEY'RE FULL OF SCHOLARS.
YES, CHIEF GARAK SAID SHE LIVED HERE DURING HER TIME IN LILIAS.
SO I HEAR.
SINCE YOU'RE COURT HERBALISTS, YOU GET THE FANCY ROOMS.
NICE AND BIG, WITH BOOK-SHELVES AND DESKS.
008

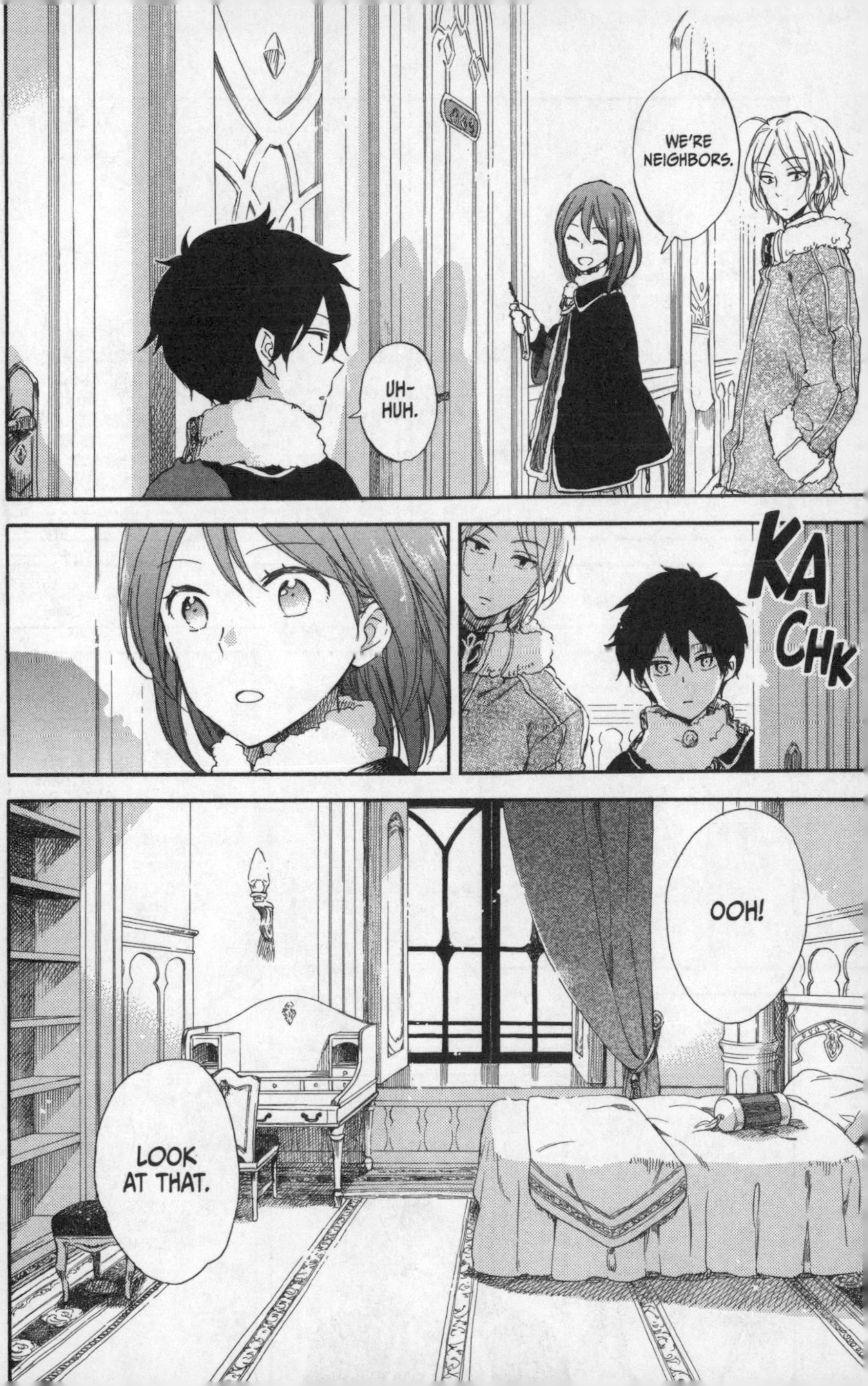
WE'RE NEIGHBORS.
UH-HUH.
KA CHK
OOH!
LOOK AT THAT.

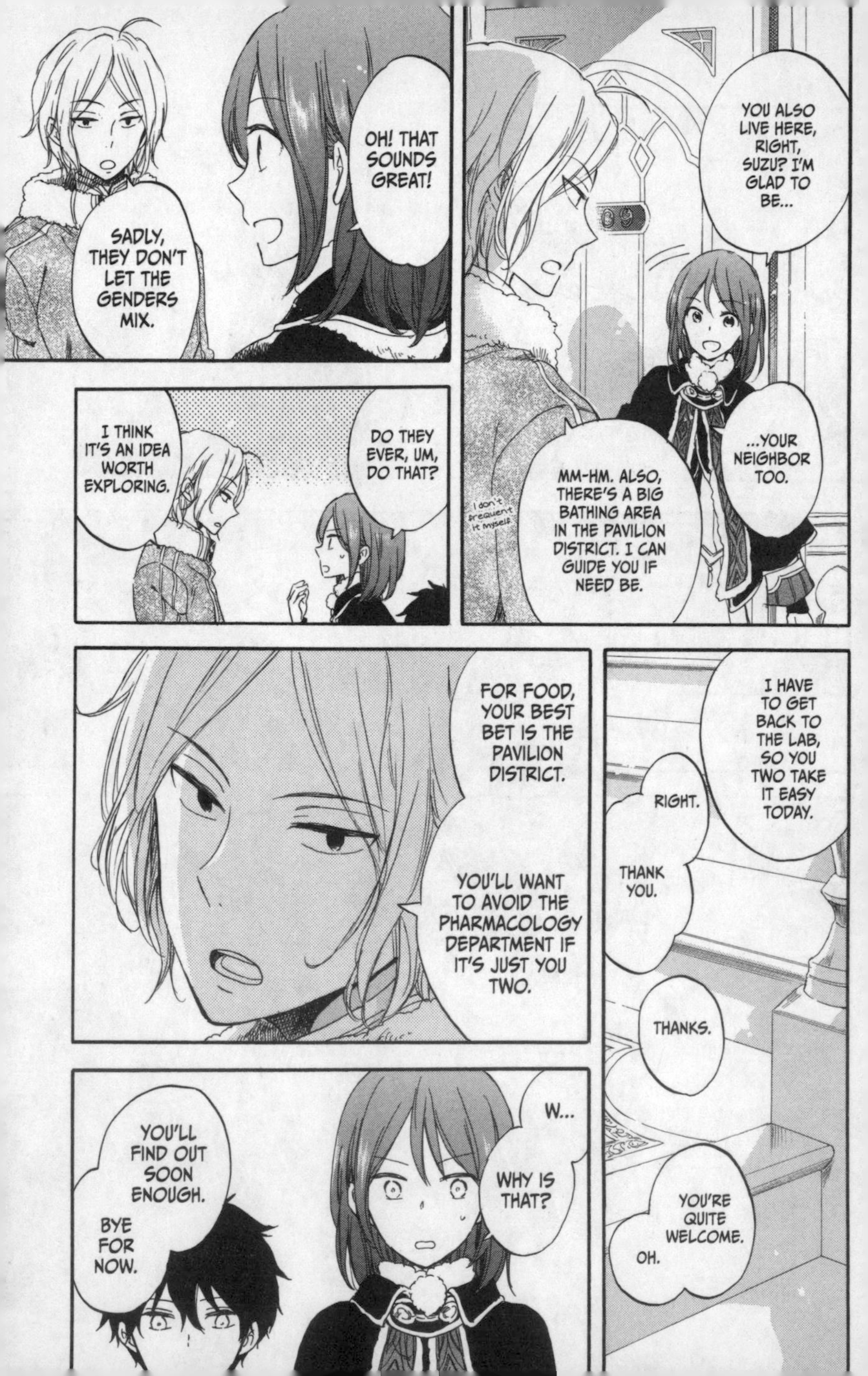
YOU ALSO LIVE HERE, RIGHT, SUZU? I'M GLAD TO BE...
...YOUR NEIGHBOR TOO.
MM-HM. ALSO, THERE'S A BIG BATHING AREA IN THE PAVILION DISTRICT. I CAN GUIDE YOU IF NEED BE.
I don't frequent it myself.
OH! THAT SOUNDS GREAT!
SADLY, THEY DON'T LET THE GENDERS MIX.
DO THEY EVER, UM, DO THAT?
I THINK IT'S AN IDEA WORTH EXPLORING.
I HAVE TO GET BACK TO THE LAB, SO YOU TWO TAKE IT EASY TODAY.
RIGHT.
THANK YOU.
THANKS.
YOU'RE QUITE WELCOME.
OH.
FOR FOOD, YOUR BEST BET IS THE PAVILION DISTRICT.
YOU'LL WANT TO AVOID THE PHARMACOLOGY DEPARTMENT IF IT'S JUST YOU TWO.
W...
WHY IS THAT?
YOU'LL FIND OUT SOON ENOUGH.
BYE FOR NOW.

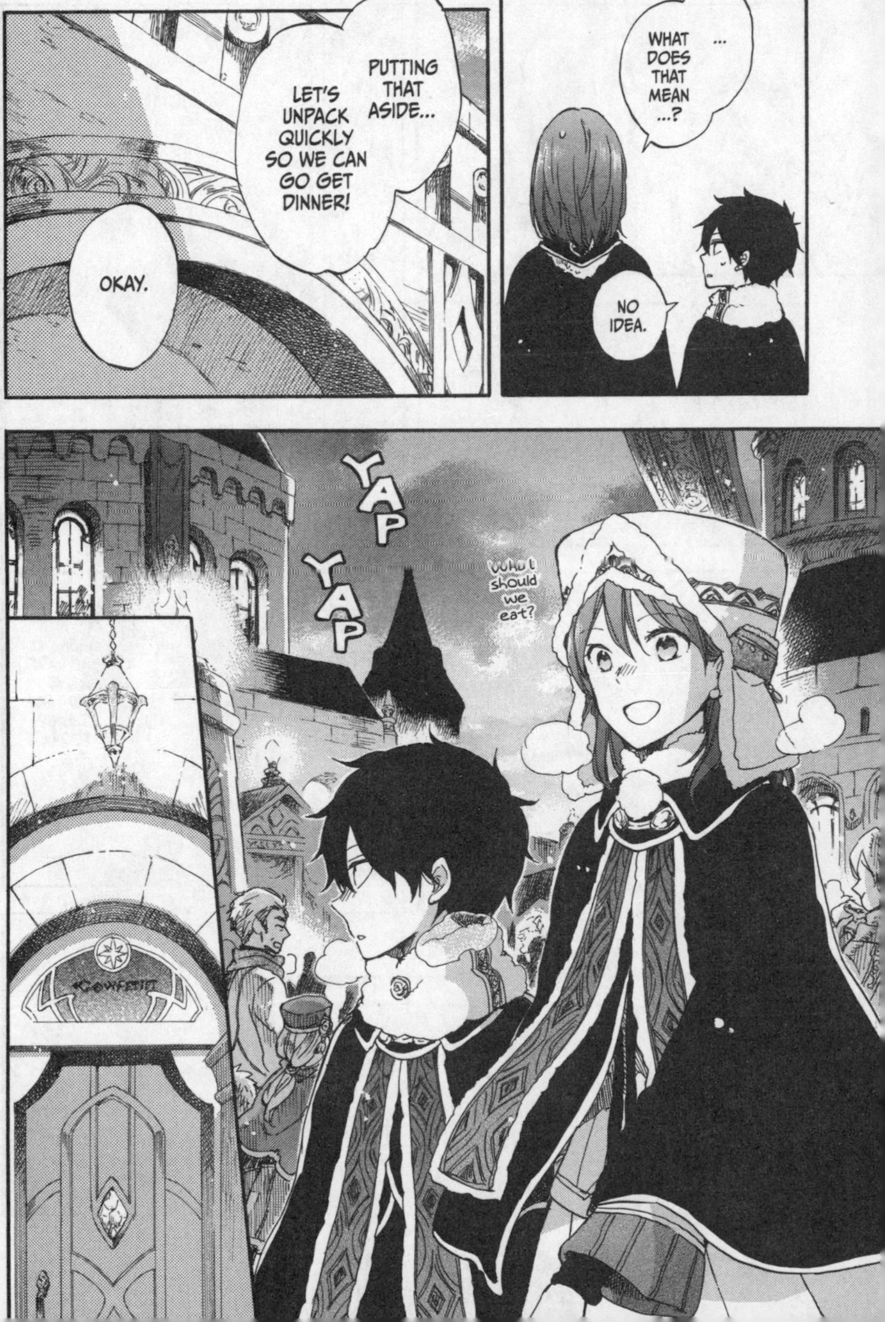
... WHAT DOES THAT MEAN ...?
NO IDEA.
PUTTING THAT ASIDE...
LET'S UNPACK QUICKLY SO WE CAN GO GET DINNER!
OKAY.
YAP YAP
should we eat?

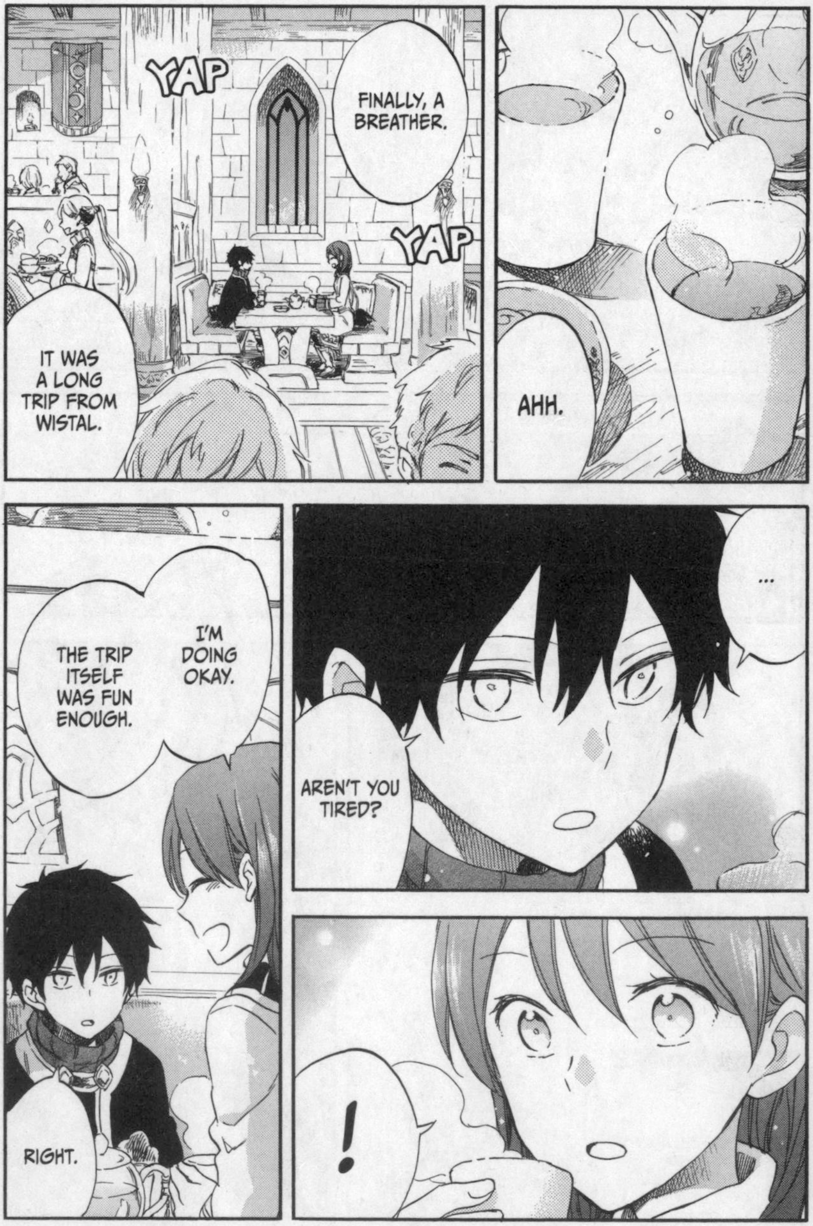
AHH.
FINALLY, A BREATHER.
YAP
YAP
IT WAS A LONG TRIP FROM WISTAL.
...
AREN'T YOU TIRED?
!
I'M DOING OKAY.
THE TRIP ITSELF WAS FUN ENOUGH.
RIGHT.

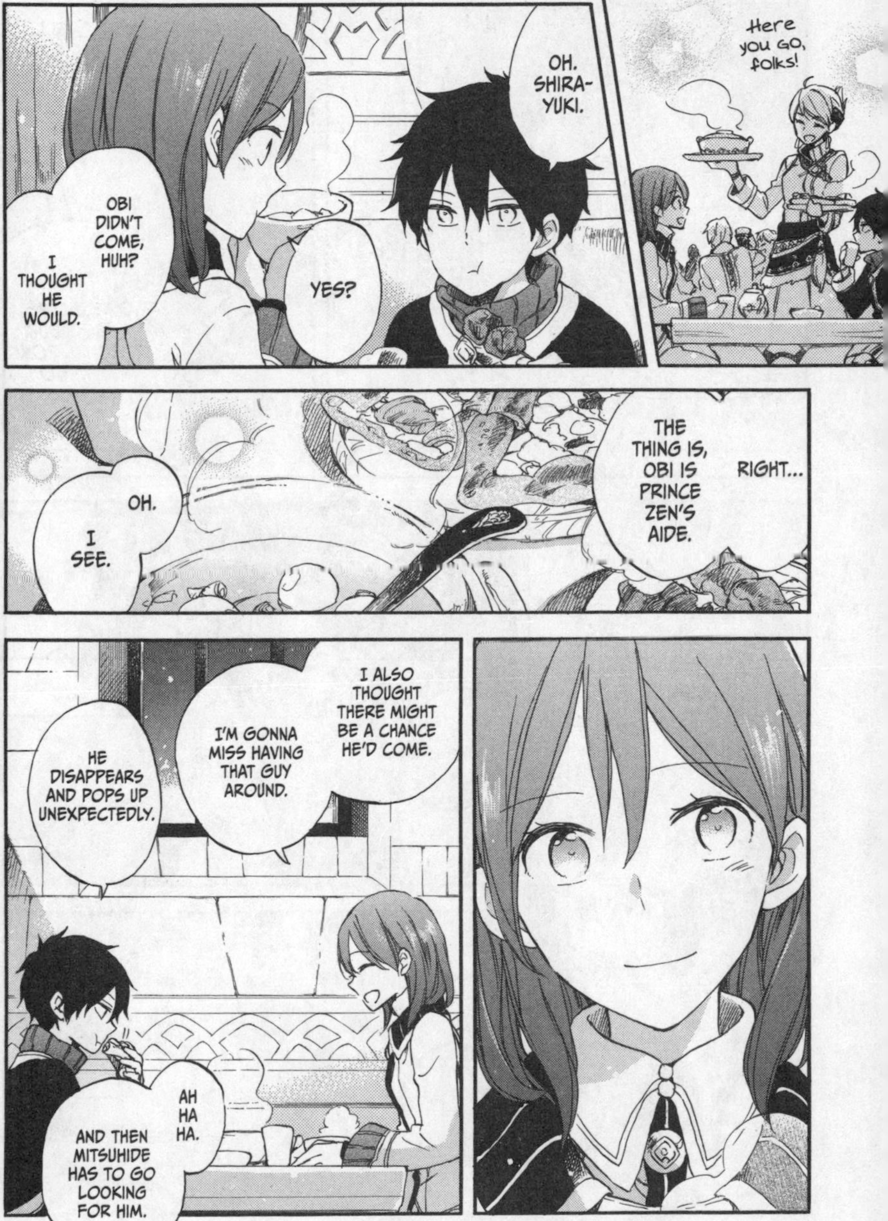
Here you go, folks!
OH. SHIRA-YUKI.
YES?
OBI DIDN'T COME, HUH?
I THOUGHT HE WOULD.
RIGHT...
THE THING IS, OBI IS PRINCE ZEN'S AIDE.
OH.
I SEE.
I ALSO THOUGHT THERE MIGHT BE A CHANCE HE'D COME.
I'M GONNA MISS HAVING THAT GUY AROUND.
HE DISAPPEARS AND POPS UP UNEXPECTEDLY.
AH HA HA.
AND THEN MITSUHIDE HAS TO GO LOOKING FOR HIM.

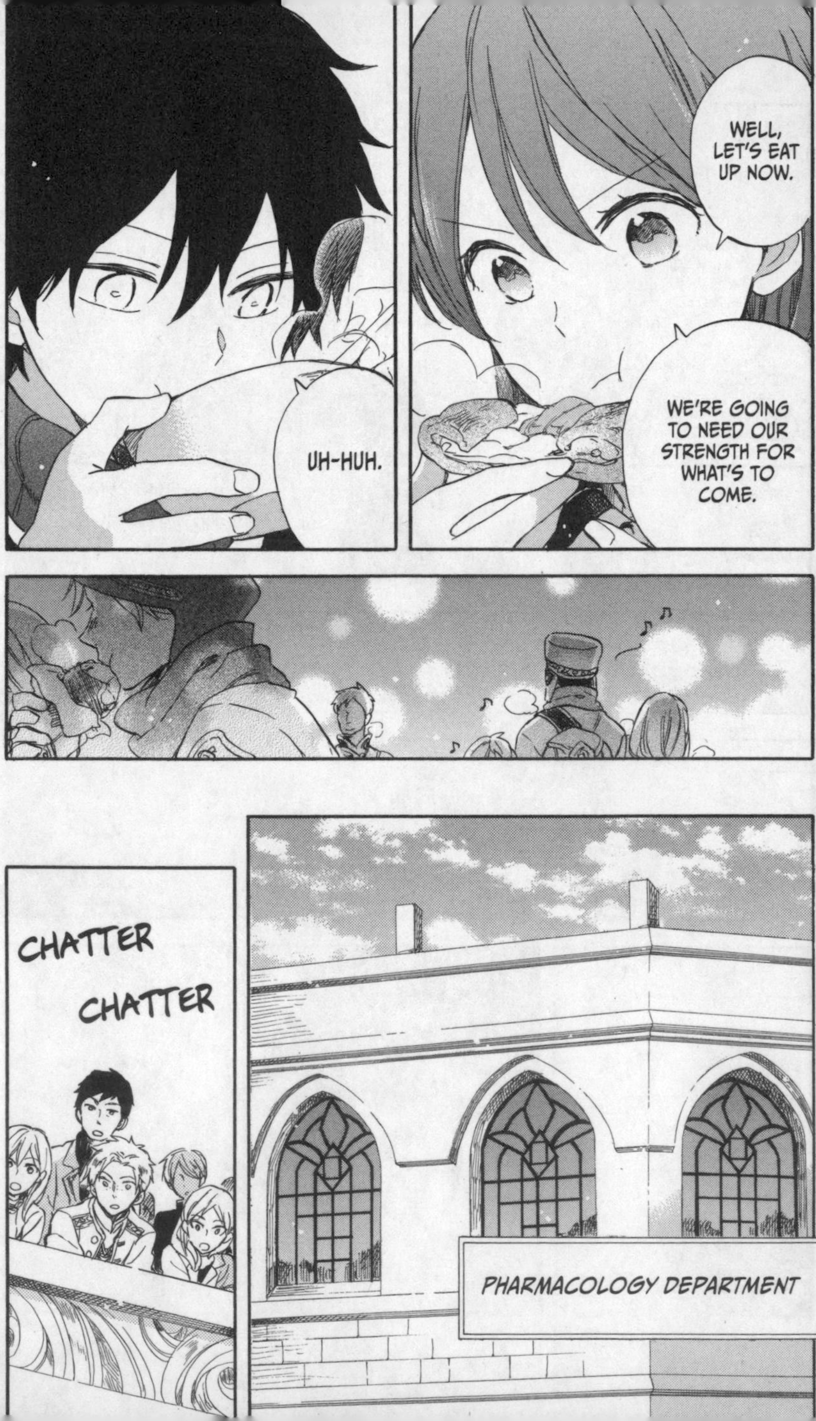
WELL, LET'S EAT UP NOW.
WE'RE GOING TO NEED OUR STRENGTH FOR WHAT'S TO COME.
UH-HUH.
PHARMACOLOGY DEPARTMENT
CHATTER
CHATTER

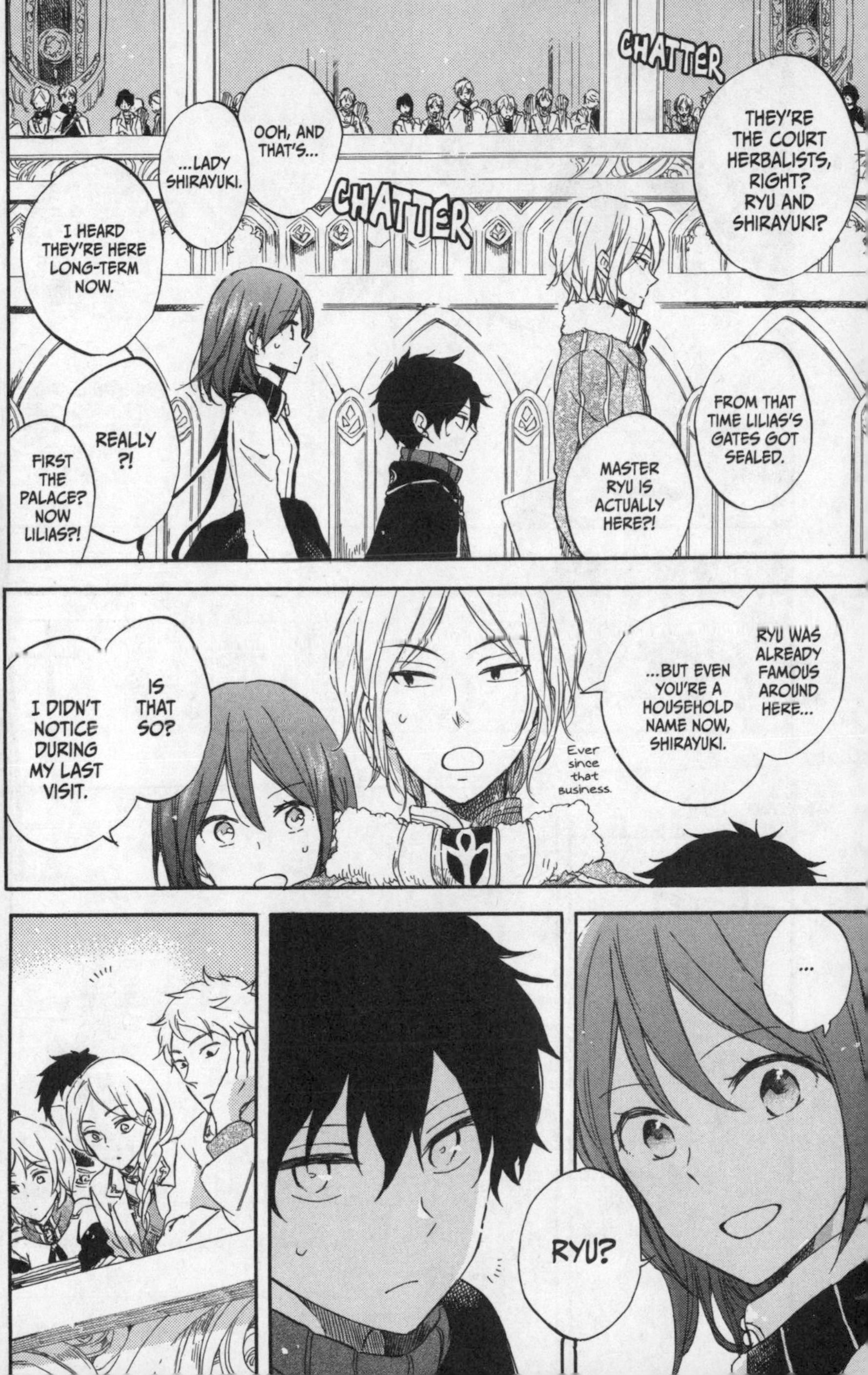
CHATTER
THEY'RE THE COURT HERBALISTS, RIGHT? RYU AND SHIRAYUKI?
OOH, AND THAT'S...
...LADY SHIRAYUKI.
CHATTER
I HEARD THEY'RE HERE LONG-TERM NOW.
FROM THAT TIME LILIAS'S GATES GOT SEALED.
MASTER RYU IS ACTUALLY HERE?!
REALLY ?!
FIRST THE PALACE? NOW LILIAS?!
RYU WAS ALREADY FAMOUS AROUND HERE...
...BUT EVEN YOU'RE A HOUSEHOLD NAME NOW, SHIRAYUKI.
Ever since that business.
IS THAT SO?
I DIDN'T NOTICE DURING MY LAST VISIT.
...
RYU?

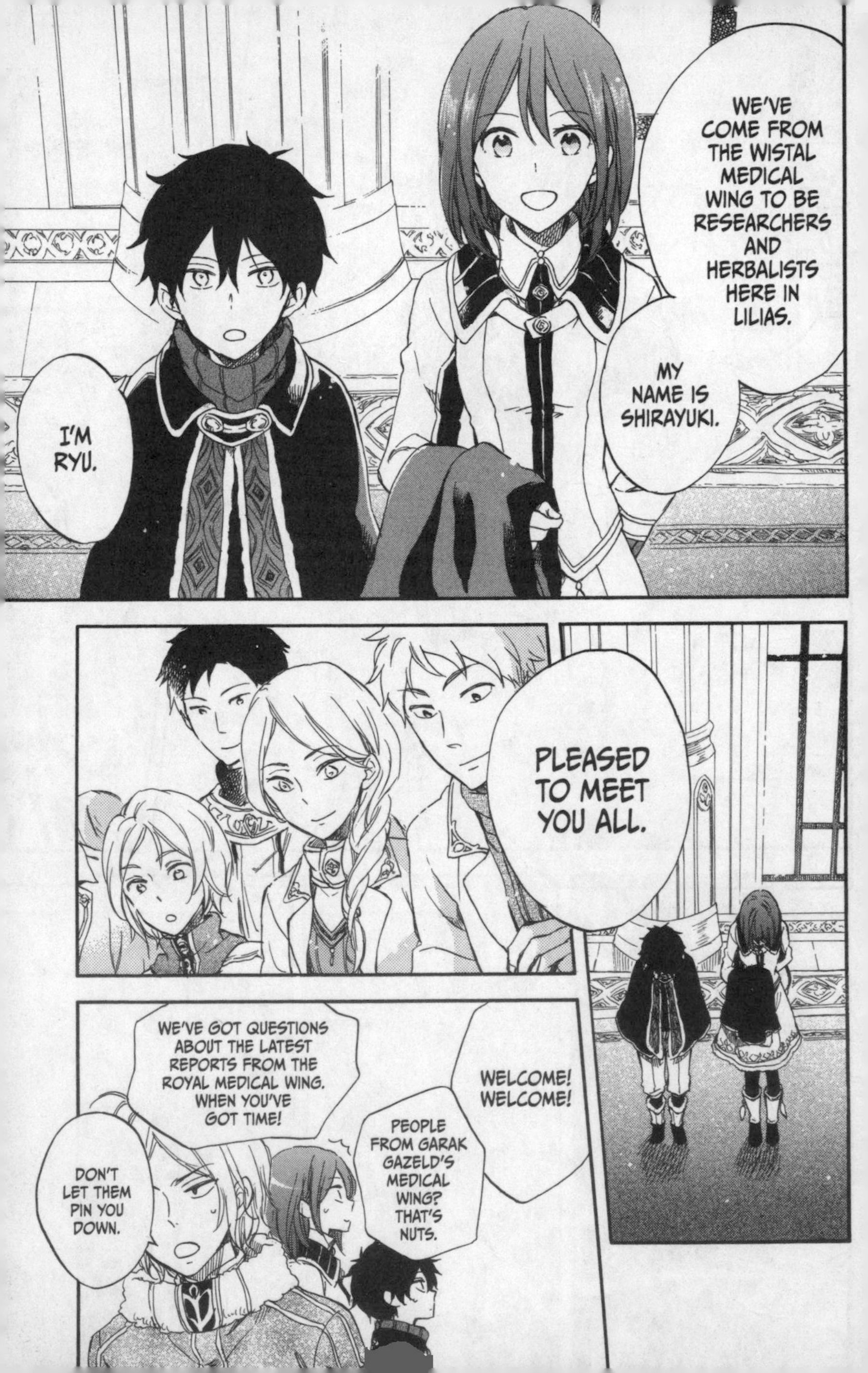
WE'VE COME FROM THE WISTAL MEDICAL WING TO BE RESEARCHERS AND HERBALISTS HERE IN LILIAS.
MY NAME IS SHIRAYUKI.
I'M RYU.
PLEASED TO MEET YOU ALL.
WELCOME! WELCOME!
WE'VE GOT QUESTIONS ABOUT THE LATEST REPORTS FROM THE ROYAL MEDICAL WING. WHEN YOU'VE GOT TIME!
PEOPLE FROM GARAK GAZELD'S MEDICAL WING? THAT'S NUTS.
DON'T LET THEM PIN YOU DOWN.

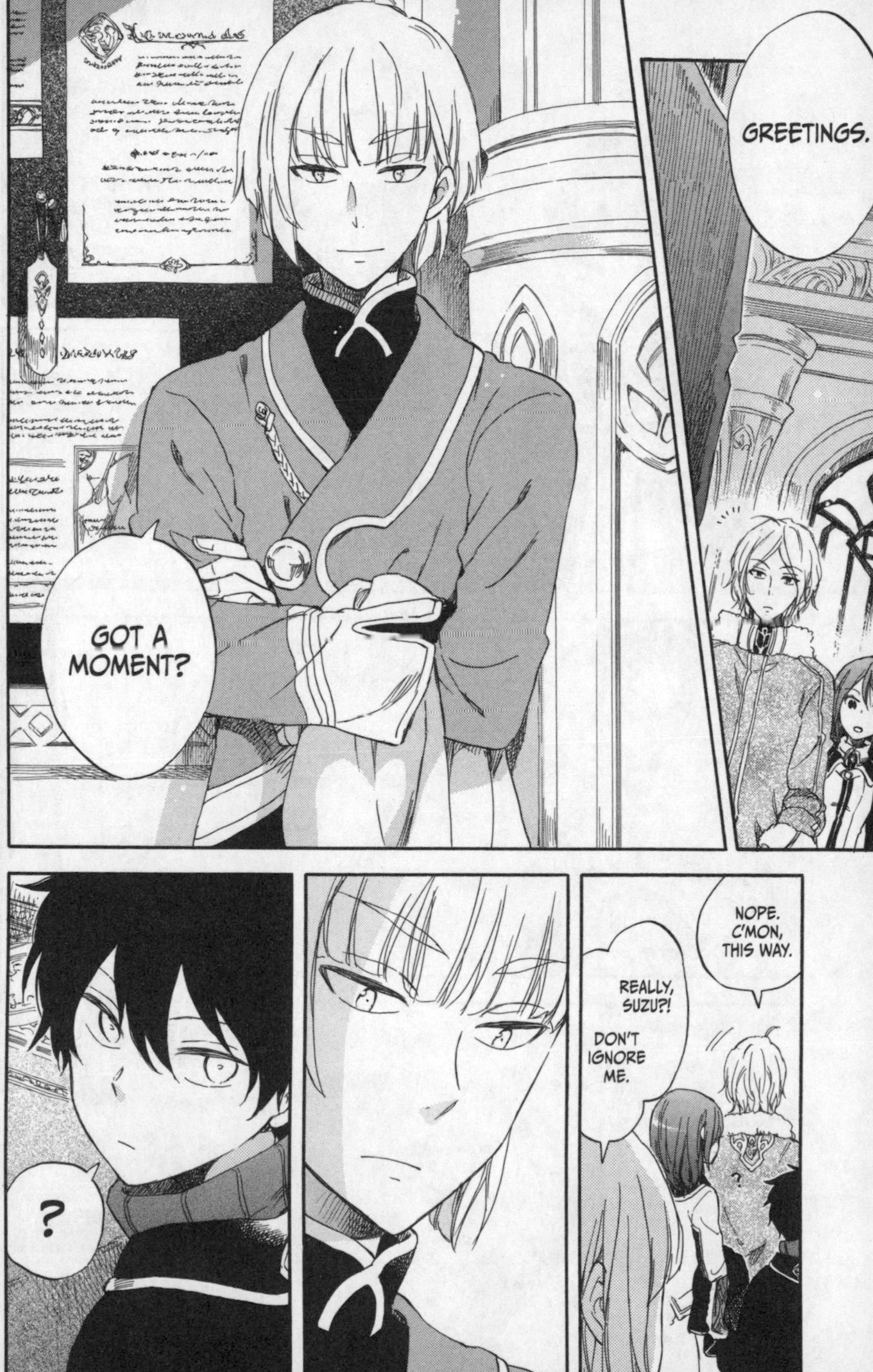
GREETINGS.
GOT A MOMENT?
NOPE. C'MON, THIS WAY.
REALLY, SUZU?!
DON'T IGNORE ME.
?

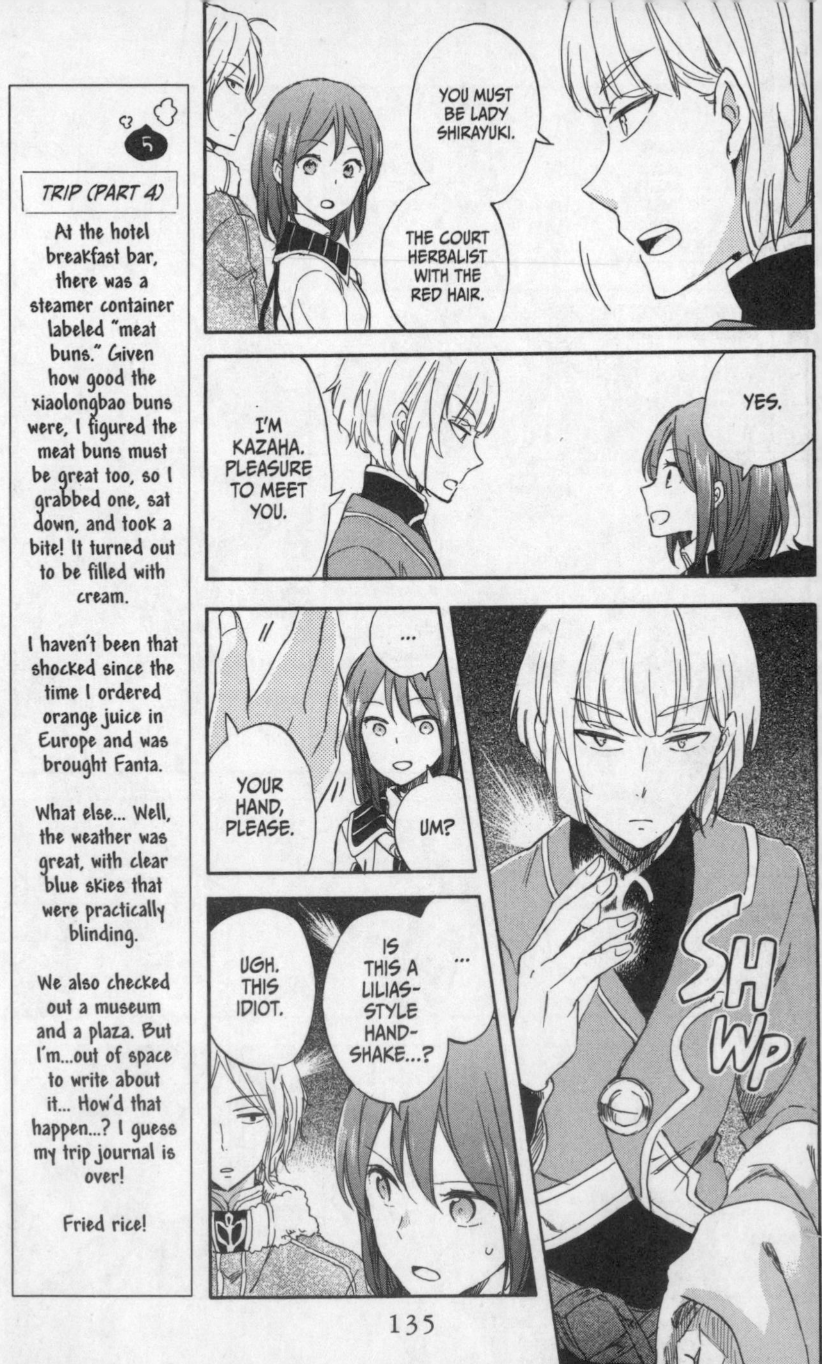
YOU MUST BE LADY SHIRAYUKI.
THE COURT HERBALIST WITH THE RED HAIR.
YES.
I'M KAZAHA. PLEASURE TO MEET YOU.
SHWP
...
YOUR HAND, PLEASE.
UM?
...
IS THIS A LILIAS-STYLE HANDSHAKE...?
UGH. THIS IDIOT.

5

TRIP (PART 4)

At the hotel breakfast bar, there was a steamer container labeled "meat buns." Given how good the xiaolongbao buns were, I figured the meat buns must be great too, so I grabbed one, sat down, and took a bite! It turned out to be filled with cream.

I haven't been that shocked since the time I ordered orange juice in Europe and was brought Fanta.

What else... Well, the weather was great, with clear blue skies that were practically blinding.

We also checked out a museum and a plaza. But I'm...out of space to write about it... How'd that happen...? I guess my trip journal is over!

Fried rice!

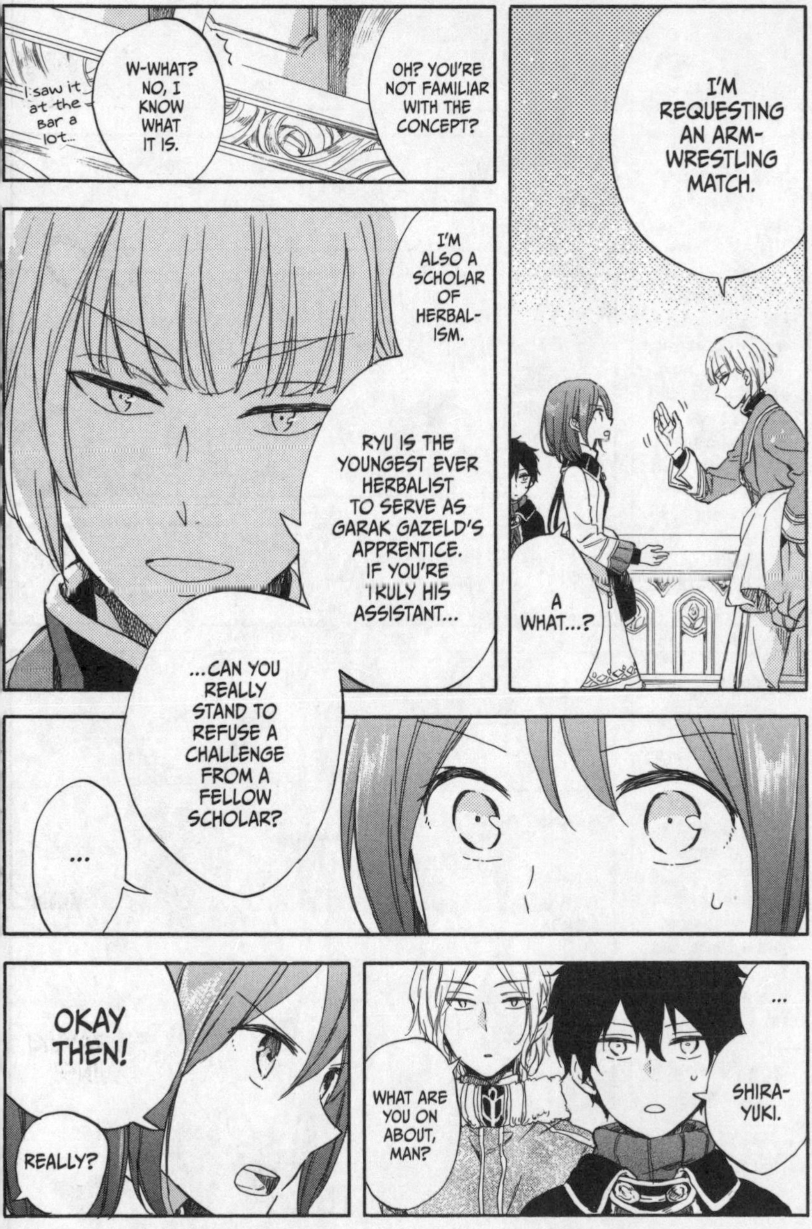
I'M REQUESTING AN ARM-WRESTLING MATCH.
A WHAT...?
OH? YOU'RE NOT FAMILIAR WITH THE CONCEPT?
W-WHAT? NO, I KNOW WHAT IT IS.
I saw it at the bar a lot...
I'M ALSO A SCHOLAR OF HERBAL-ISM.
RYU IS THE YOUNGEST EVER HERBALIST TO SERVE AS GARAK GAZELD'S APPRENTICE. IF YOU'RE TRULY HIS ASSISTANT...
...CAN YOU REALLY STAND TO REFUSE A CHALLENGE FROM A FELLOW SCHOLAR?
...
...
SHIRA-YUKI.
WHAT ARE YOU ON ABOUT, MAN?
OKAY THEN!
REALLY?

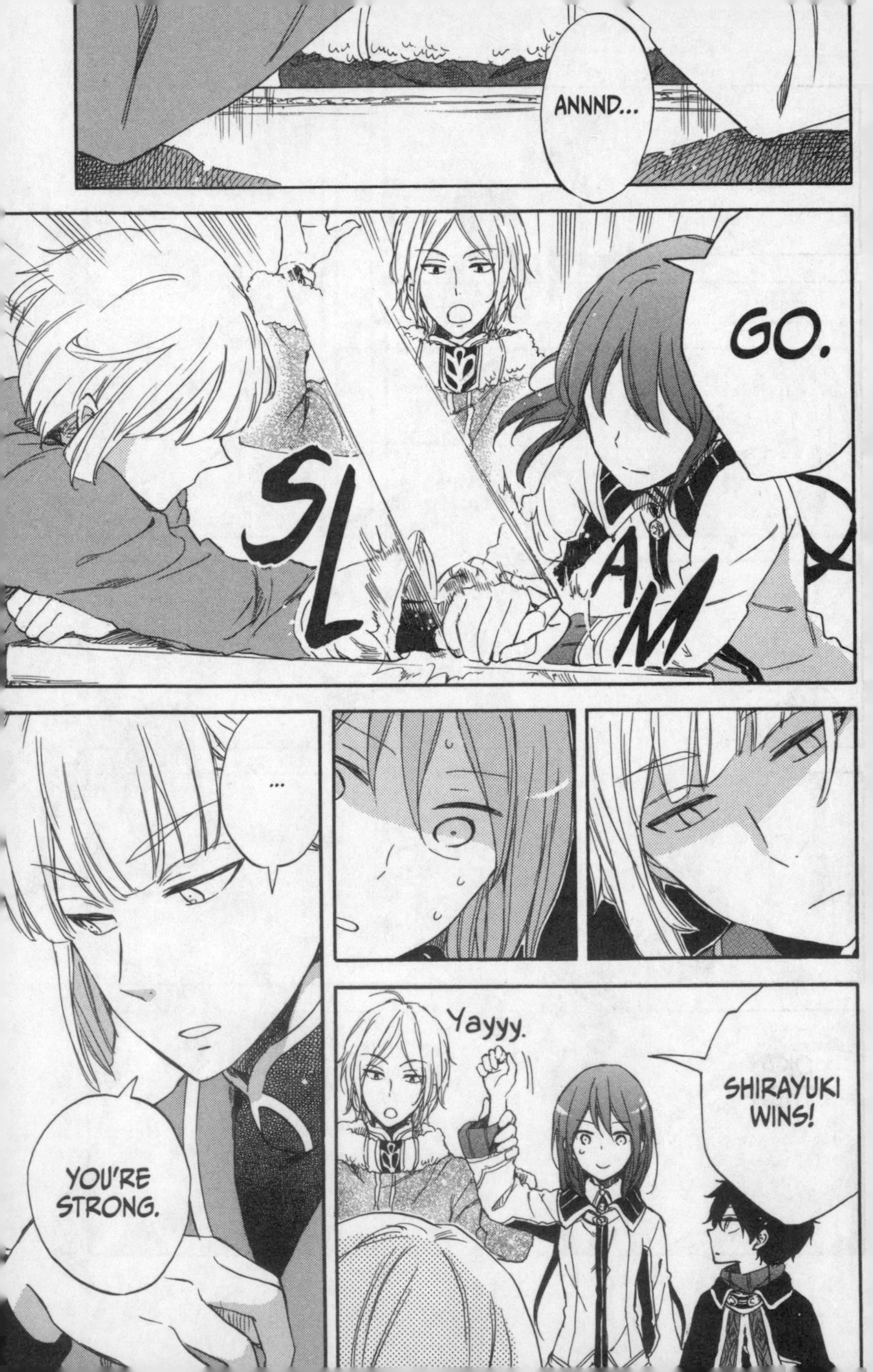
ANNND...
GO.
SLAM
SHIRAYUKI WINS!
Yayyy.
...
YOU'RE STRONG.

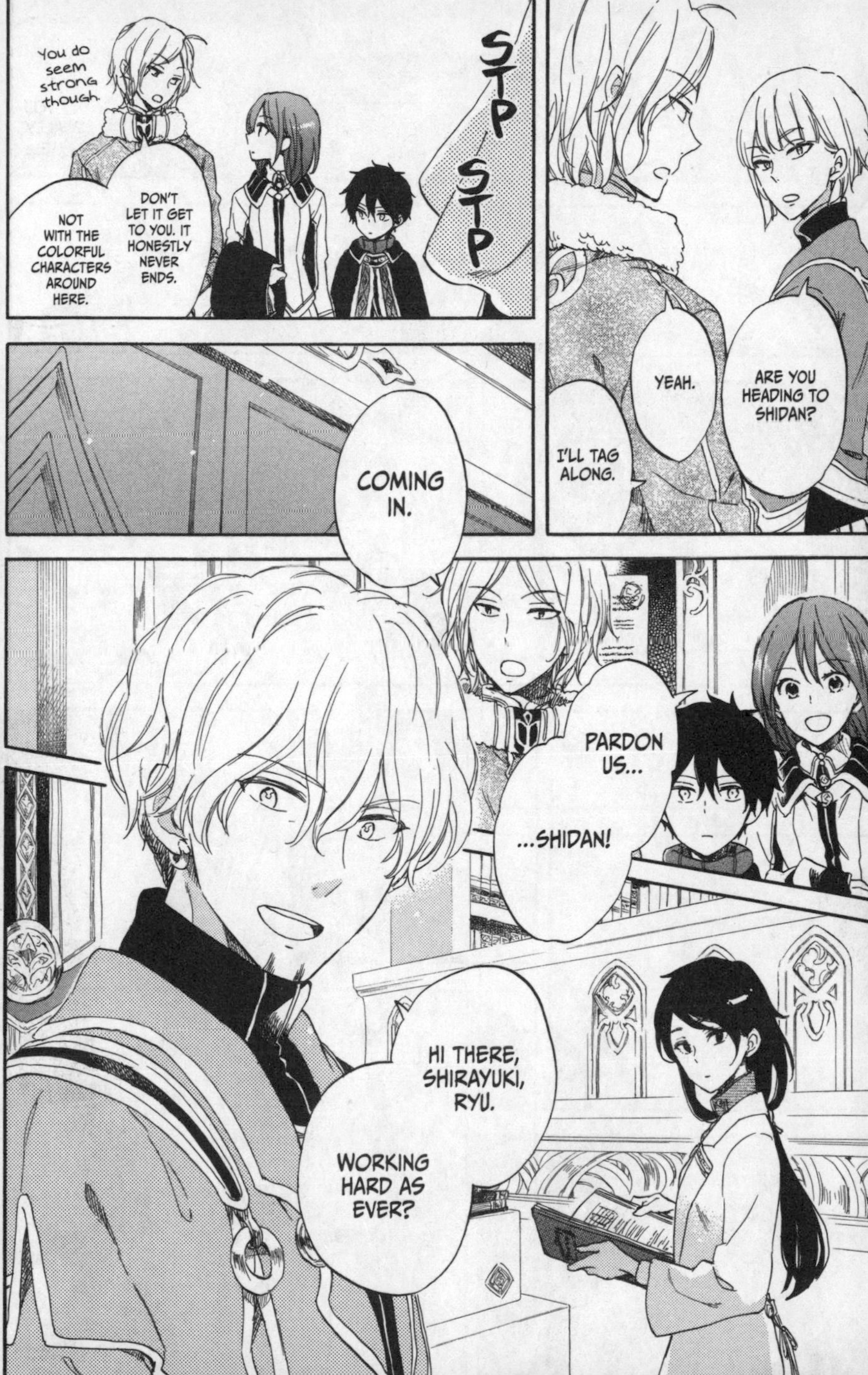
ARE YOU HEADING TO SHIDAN?
YEAH.
I'LL TAG ALONG.
STP STP
DON'T LET IT GET TO YOU. IT HONESTLY NEVER ENDS.
NOT WITH THE COLORFUL CHARACTERS AROUND HERE.
You do seem strong though.
COMING IN.
PARDON US...
...SHIDAN!
HI THERE, SHIRAYUKI, RYU.
WORKING HARD AS EVER?

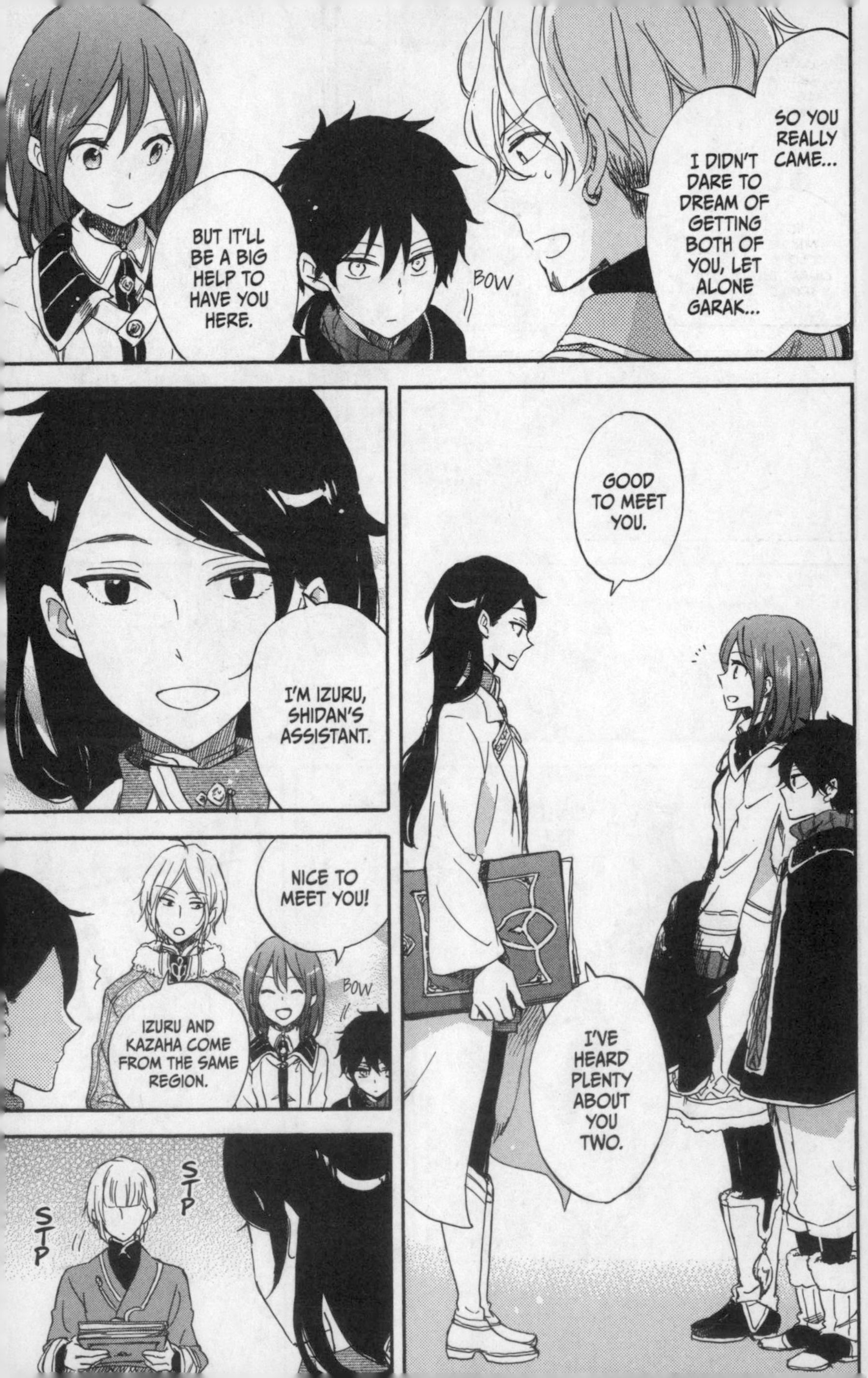
SO YOU REALLY CAME...
I DIDN'T DARE TO DREAM OF GETTING BOTH OF YOU, LET ALONE GARAK...
BOW
BUT IT'LL BE A BIG HELP TO HAVE YOU HERE.
GOOD TO MEET YOU.
I'VE HEARD PLENTY ABOUT YOU TWO.
I'M IZURU, SHIDAN'S ASSISTANT.
NICE TO MEET YOU!
BOW
IZURU AND KAZAHA COME FROM THE SAME REGION.
STP
STP

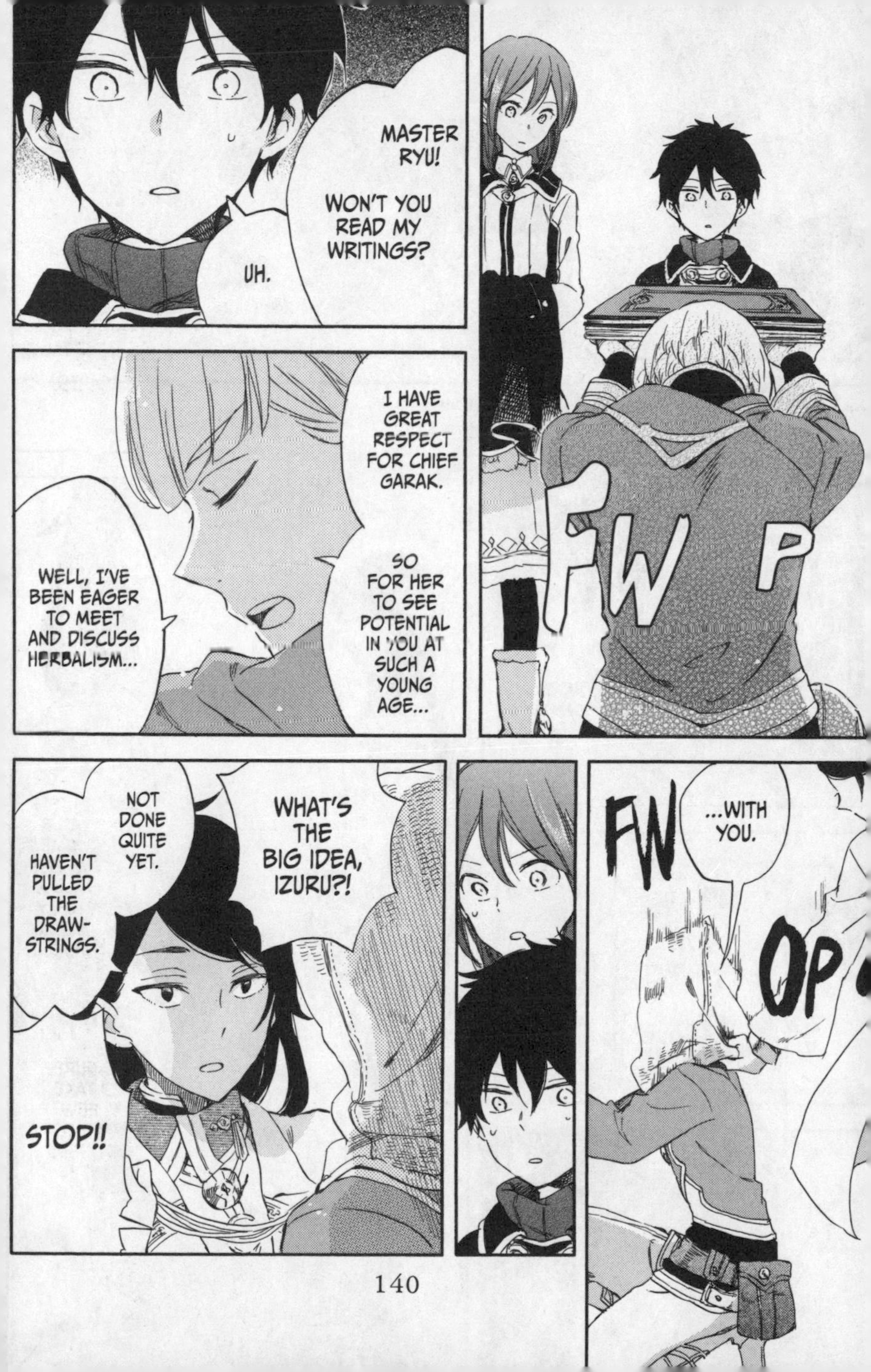
FW P
MASTER RYU!
WON'T YOU READ MY WRITINGS?
UH.
I HAVE GREAT RESPECT FOR CHIEF GARAK.
SO FOR HER TO SEE POTENTIAL IN YOU AT SUCH A YOUNG AGE...
WELL, I'VE BEEN EAGER TO MEET AND DISCUSS HERBALISM...
...WITH YOU.
FW
OP
WHAT'S THE BIG IDEA, IZURU?!
NOT DONE QUITE YET.
HAVEN'T PULLED THE DRAW-STRINGS.
STOP!!

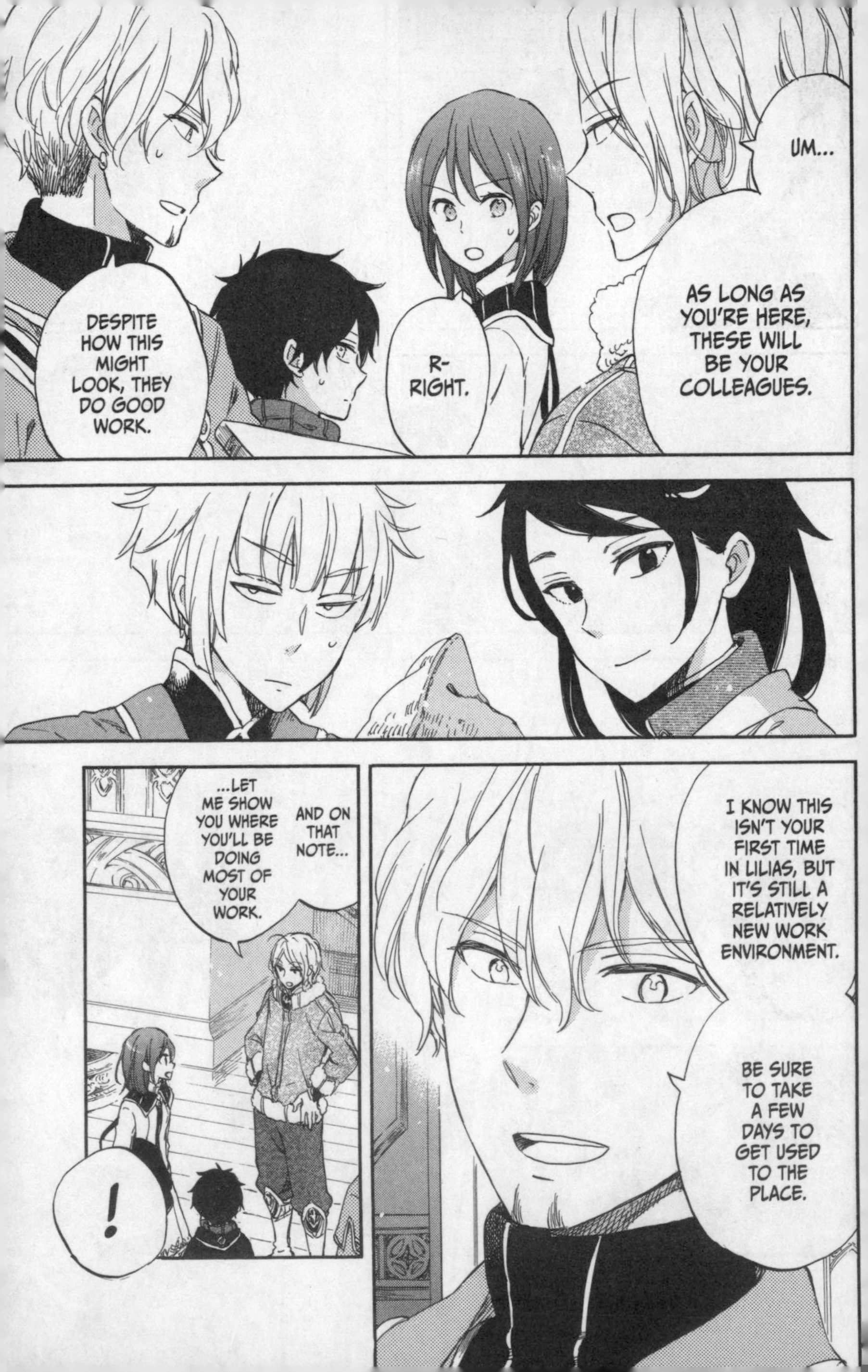
UM...
AS LONG AS YOU'RE HERE, THESE WILL BE YOUR COLLEAGUES.
R-RIGHT.
DESPITE HOW THIS MIGHT LOOK, THEY DO GOOD WORK.
I KNOW THIS ISN'T YOUR FIRST TIME IN LILIAS, BUT IT'S STILL A RELATIVELY NEW WORK ENVIRONMENT.
BE SURE TO TAKE A FEW DAYS TO GET USED TO THE PLACE.
AND ON THAT NOTE...
...LET ME SHOW YOU WHERE YOU'LL BE DOING MOST OF YOUR WORK.
!

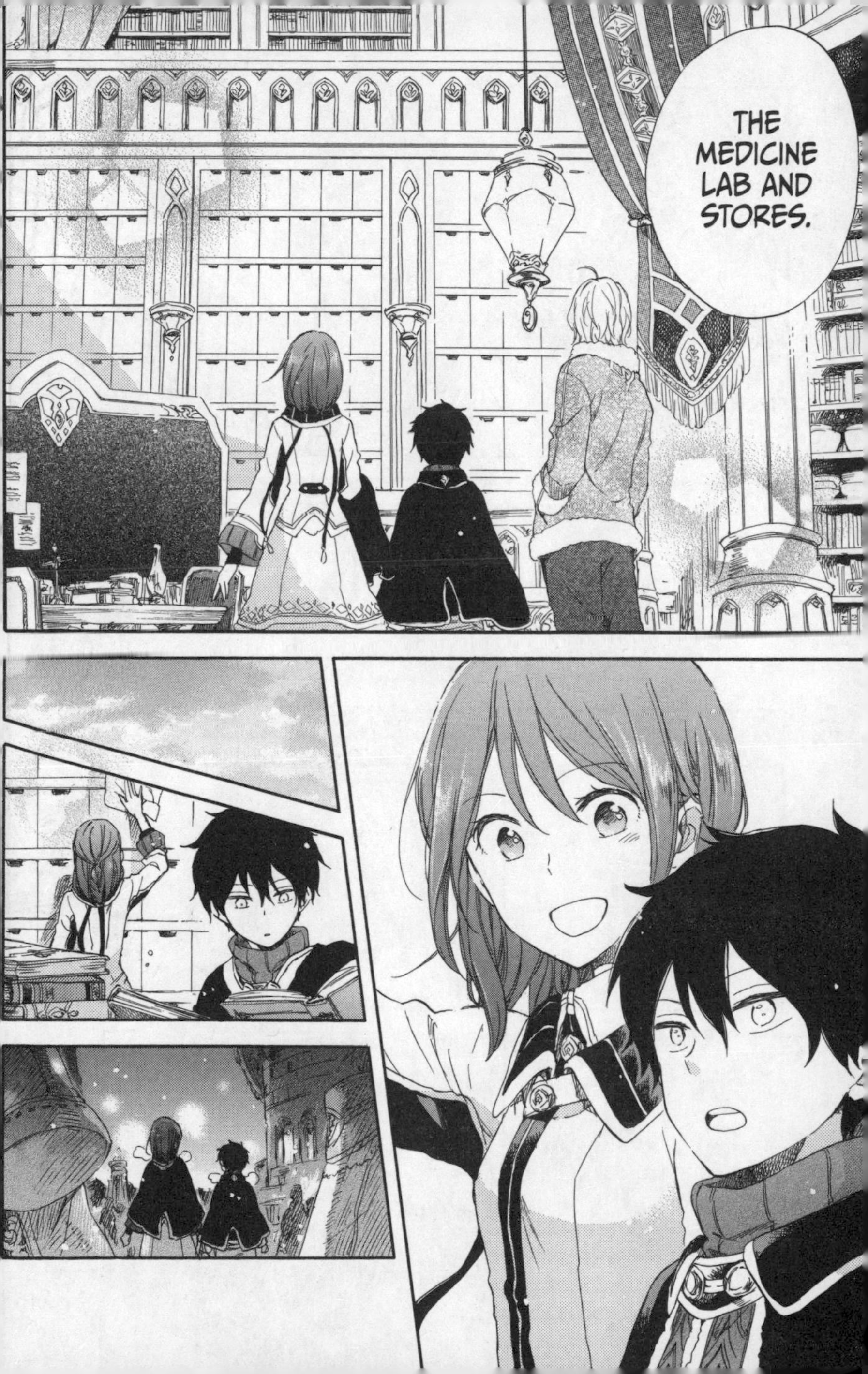
THE MEDICINE LAB AND STORES.

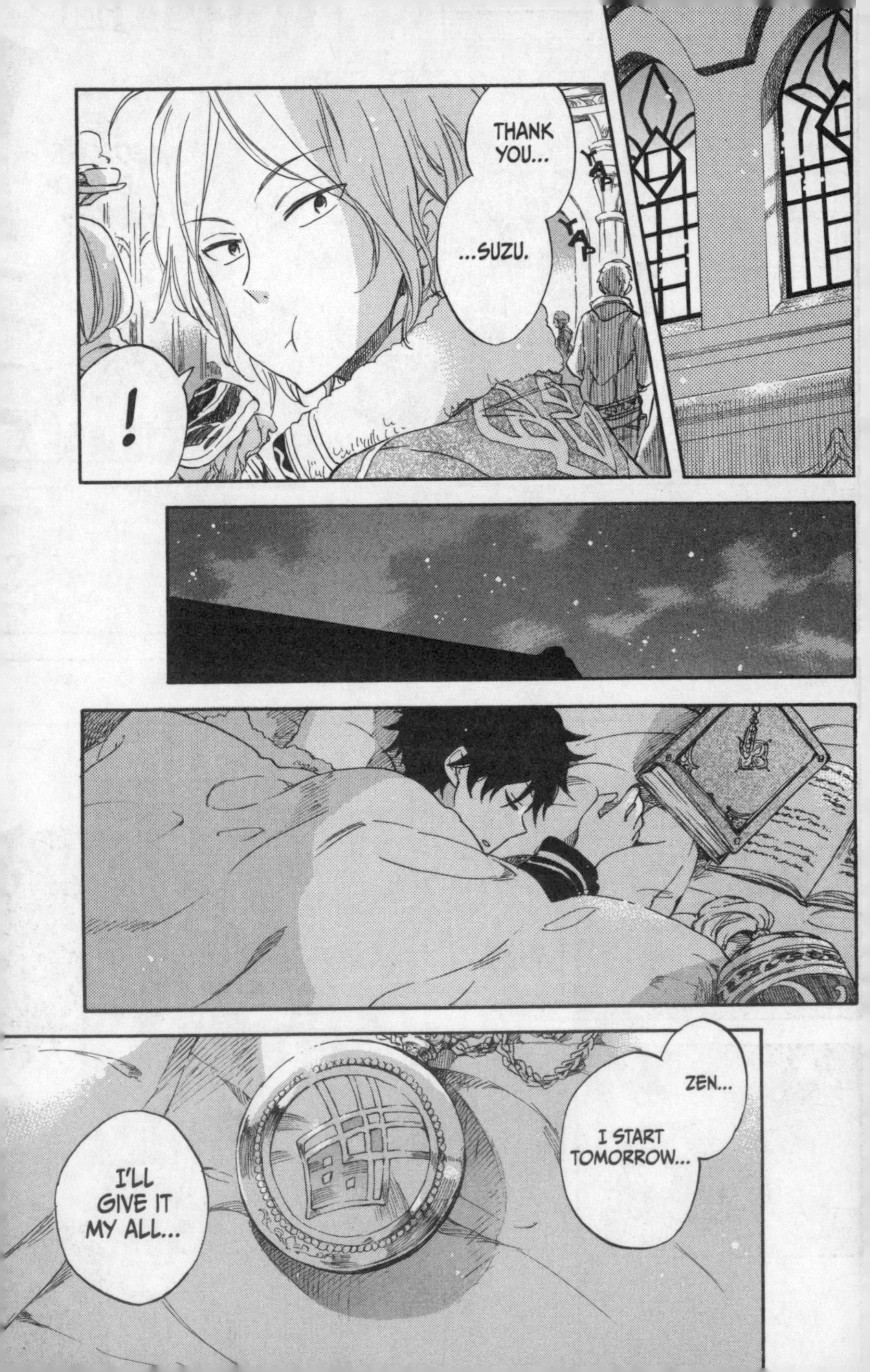
YAP YAP
THANK YOU... ...SUZU.
!
ZEN...
I START TOMORROW...
I'LL GIVE IT MY ALL...

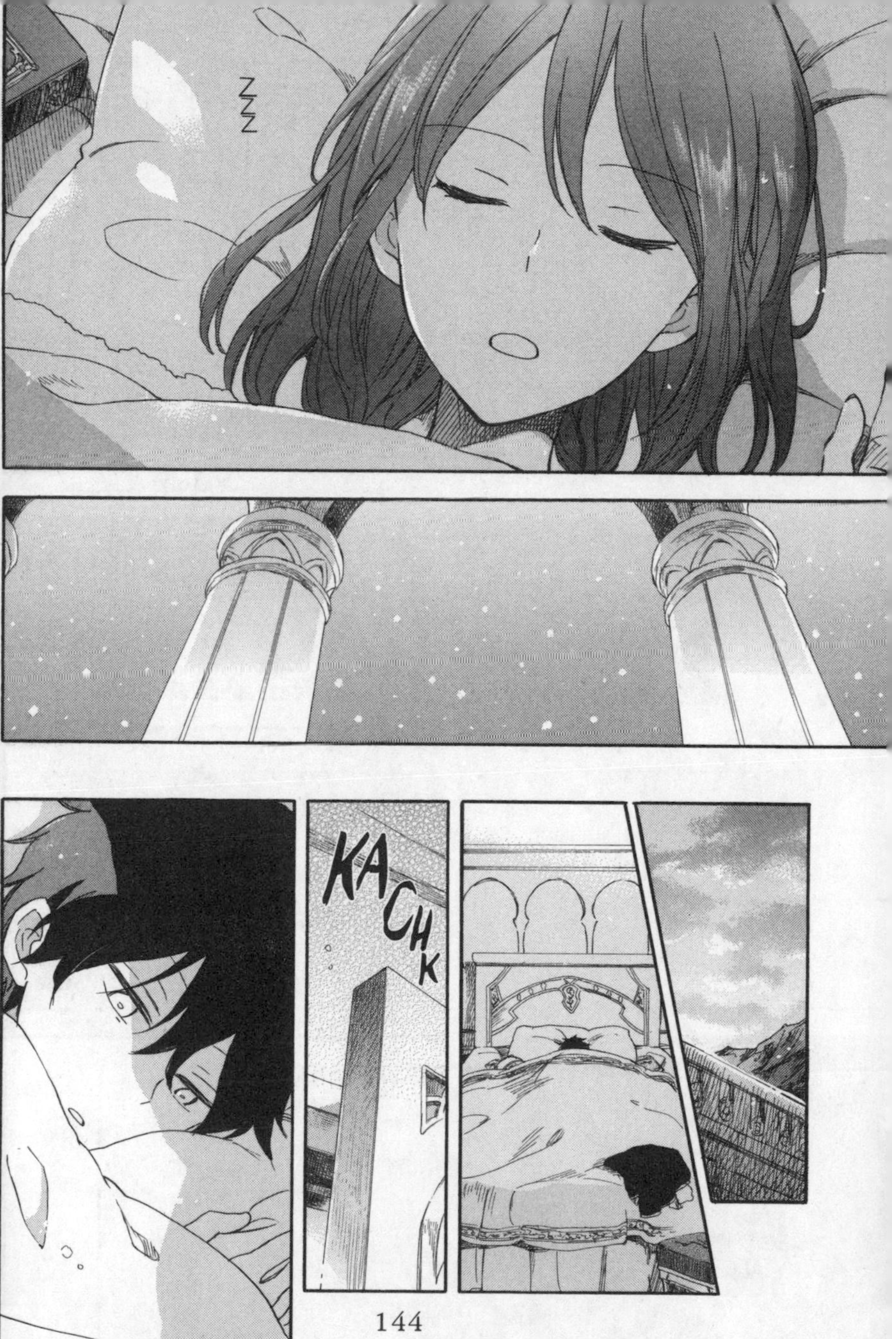
ZZZ
KACHK

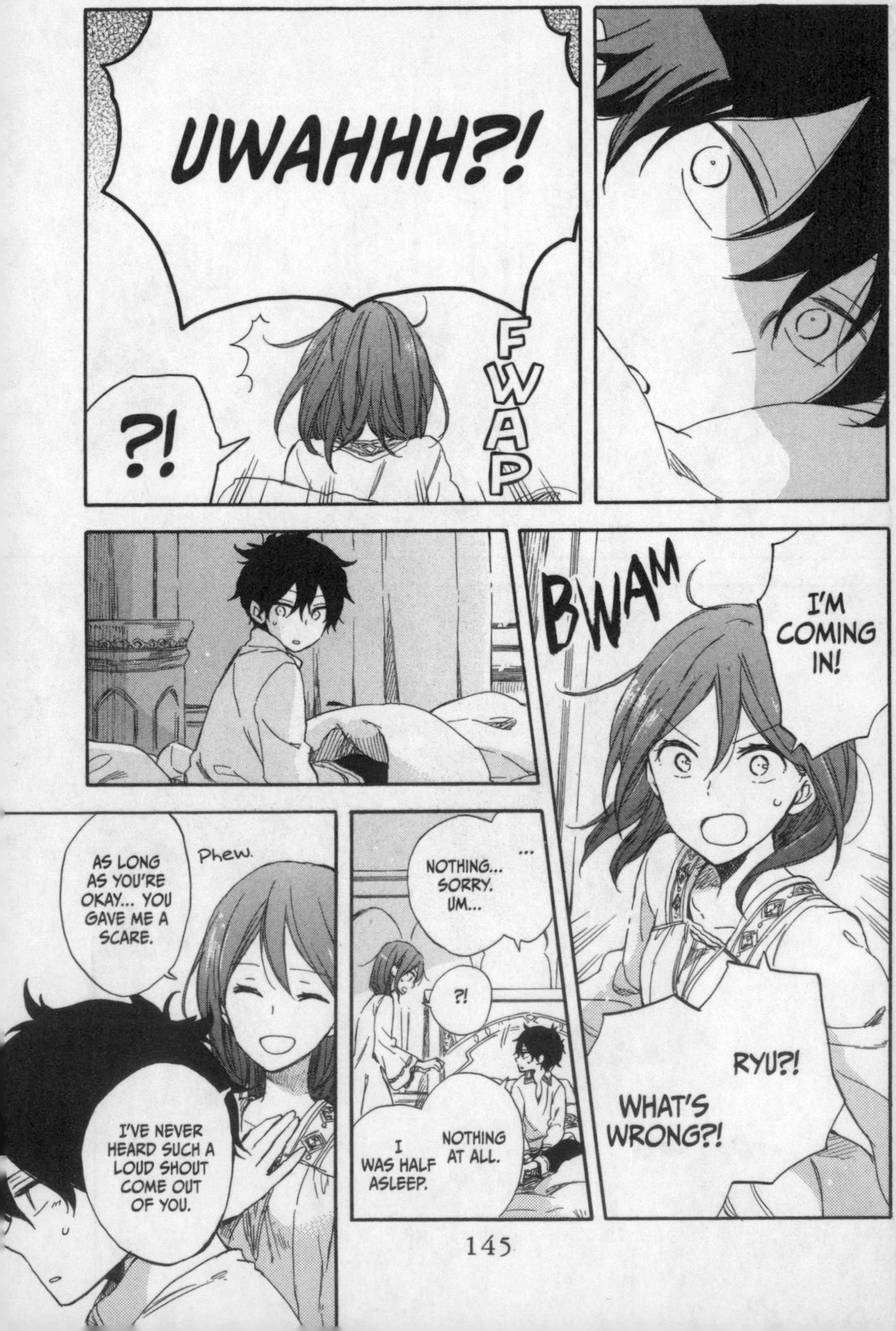
UWAHHH?!
FWAP
?!
BWAM
I'M COMING IN!
RYU?!
WHAT'S WRONG?!
...
NOTHING... SORRY. UM...
?!
NOTHING AT ALL.
I WAS HALF ASLEEP.
Phew.
AS LONG AS YOU'RE OKAY... YOU GAVE ME A SCARE.
I'VE NEVER HEARD SUCH A LOUD SHOUT COME OUT OF YOU.

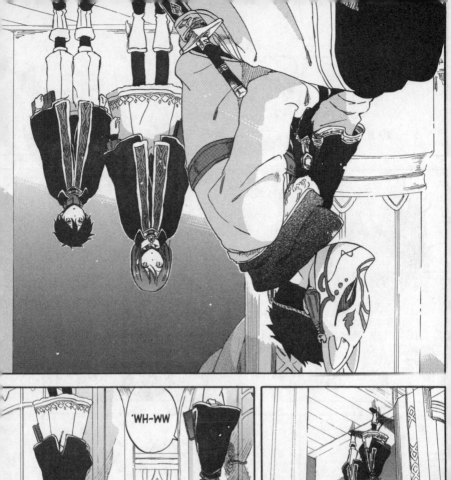

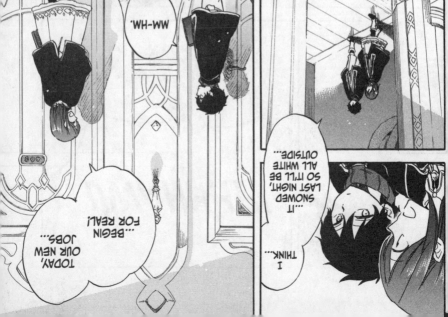

WH-WW.

...TODAY, OUR NEW JOBS.... ...BEGIN FOR REAL!

I THINK.... ...IT SNOWED LAST NIGHT, SO IT'LL BE ALL WHITE OUTSIDE....

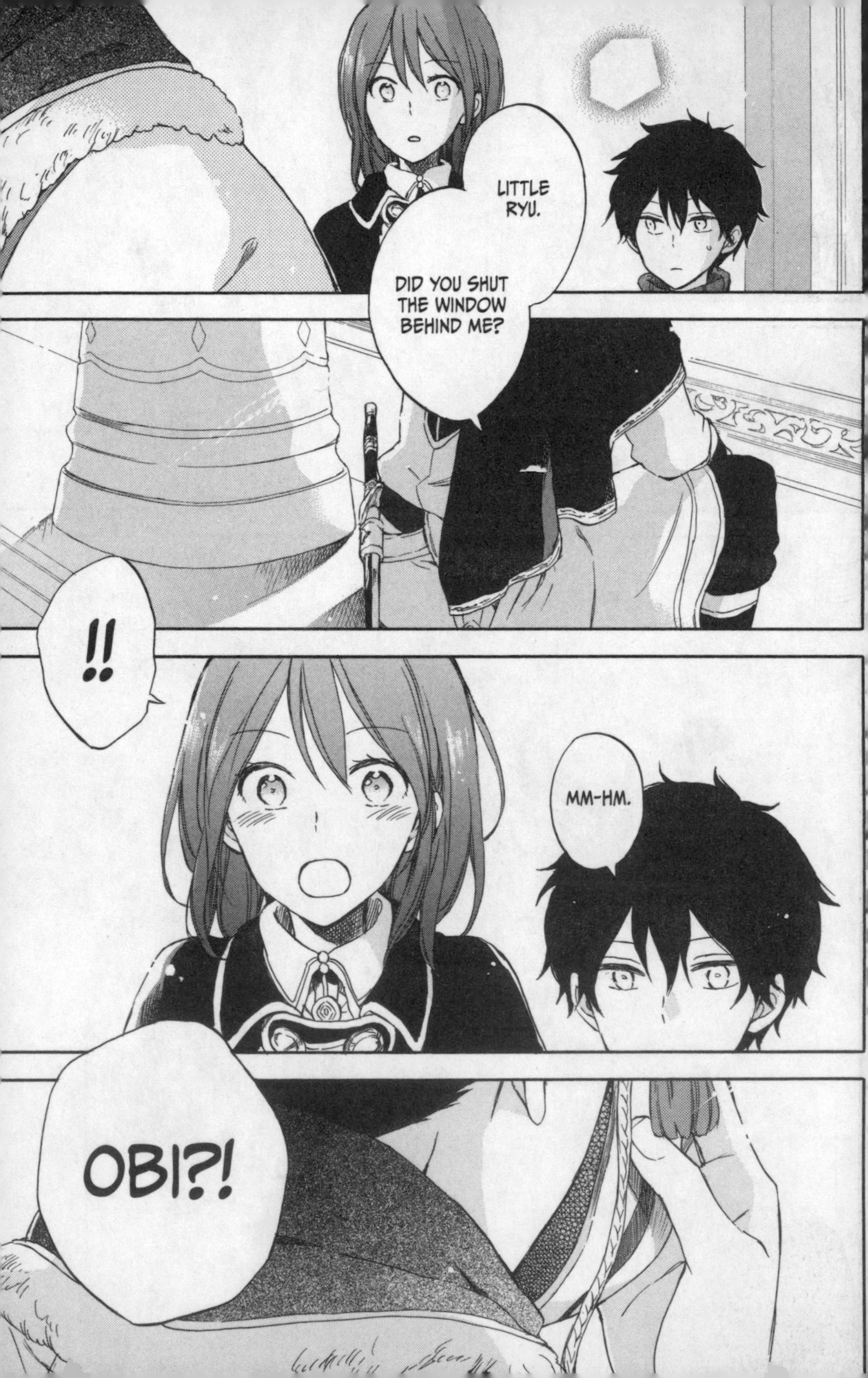
LITTLE RYU.
DID YOU SHUT THE WINDOW BEHIND ME?
MM-HM.
!!
OBI?!

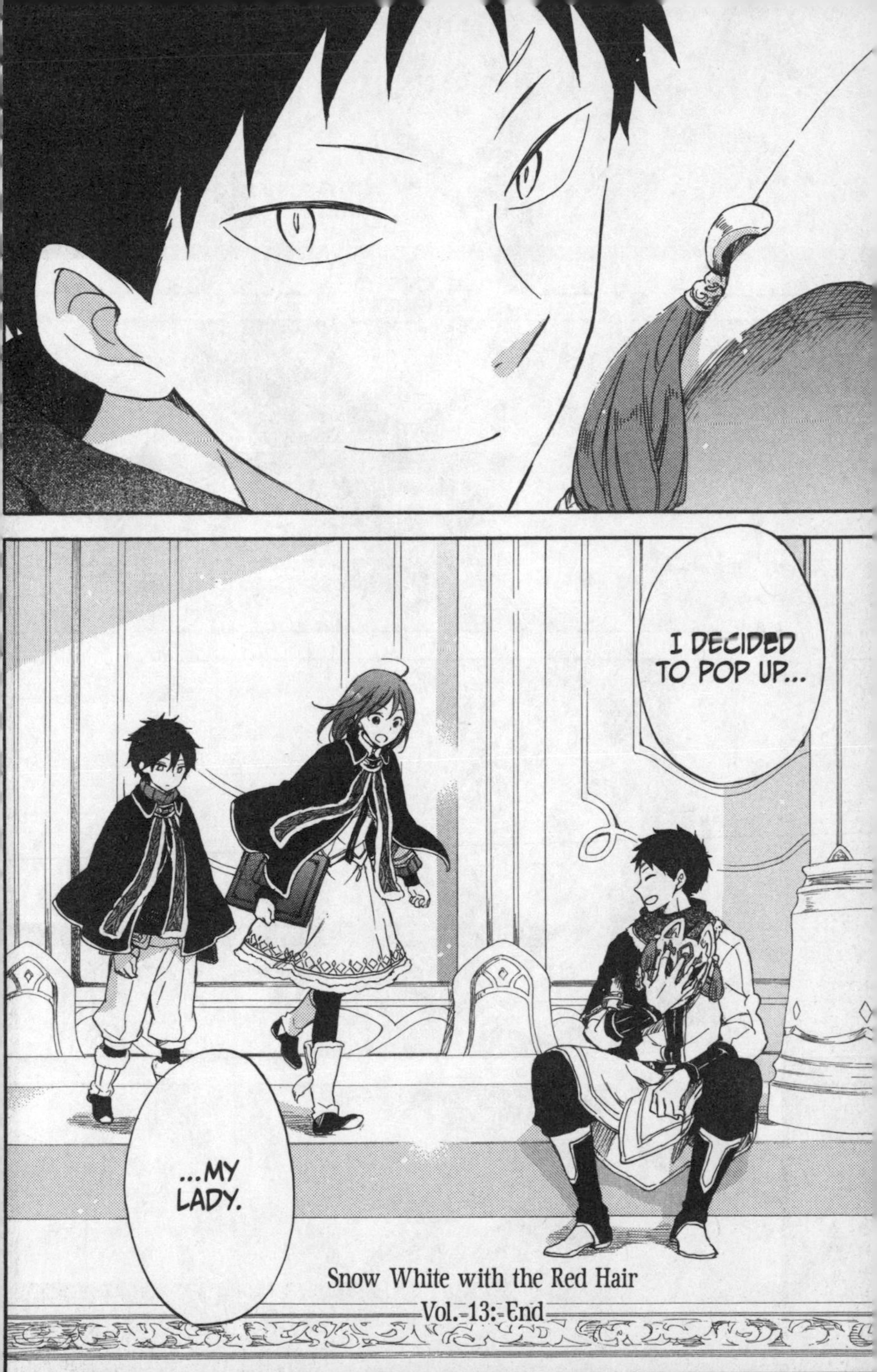
I DECIDED TO POP UP...
...MY LADY.
Snow White with the Red Hair
Vol. 13: End

HOW COULD I NOT?
I MEAN...

...YOU'RE MY BEST FRIEND, LON.

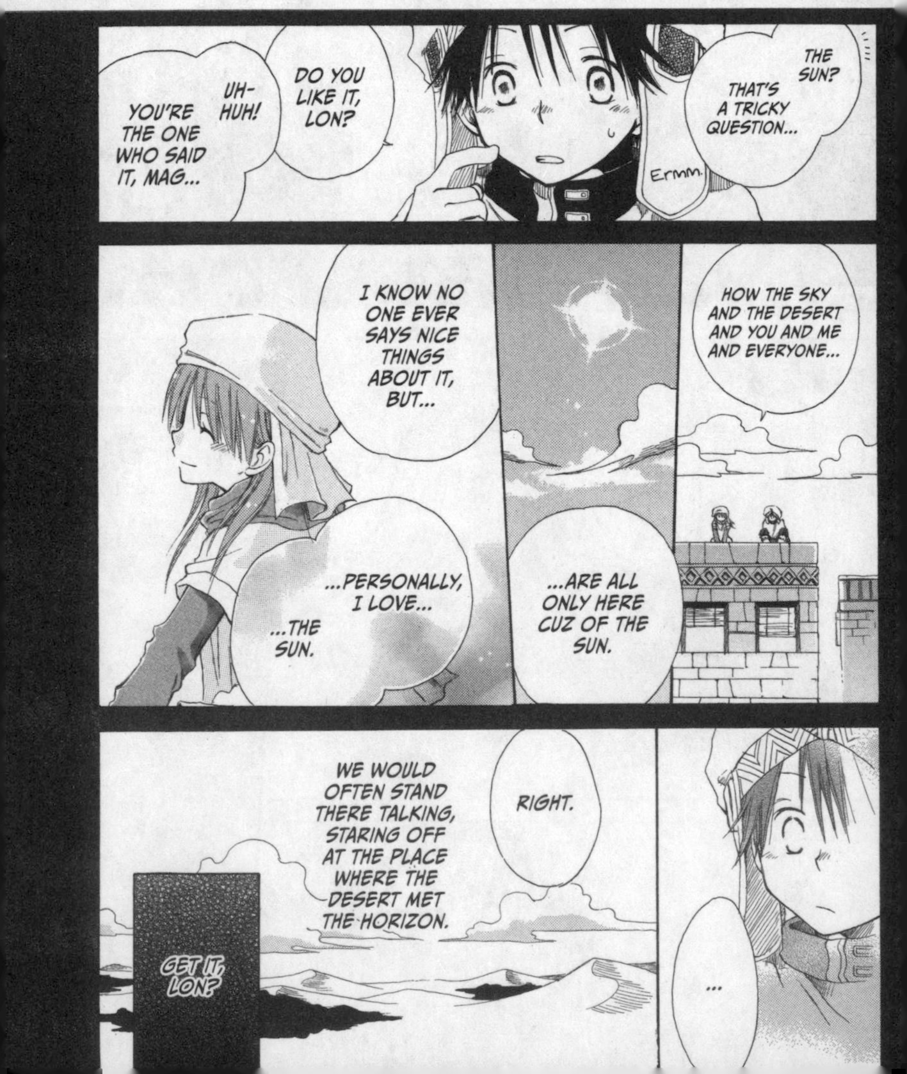
THE SUN? THAT'S A TRICKY QUESTION...
Ermm.
DO YOU LIKE IT, LON?
UH-HUH!
YOU'RE THE ONE WHO SAID IT, MAG...
HOW THE SKY AND THE DESERT AND YOU AND ME AND EVERYONE...
...ARE ALL ONLY HERE CUZ OF THE SUN.
I KNOW NO ONE EVER SAYS NICE THINGS ABOUT IT, BUT...
...PERSONALLY, I LOVE...
...THE SUN.
...
RIGHT.
WE WOULD OFTEN STAND THERE TALKING, STARING OFF AT THE PLACE WHERE THE DESERT MET THE HORIZON.
GET IT, LON?

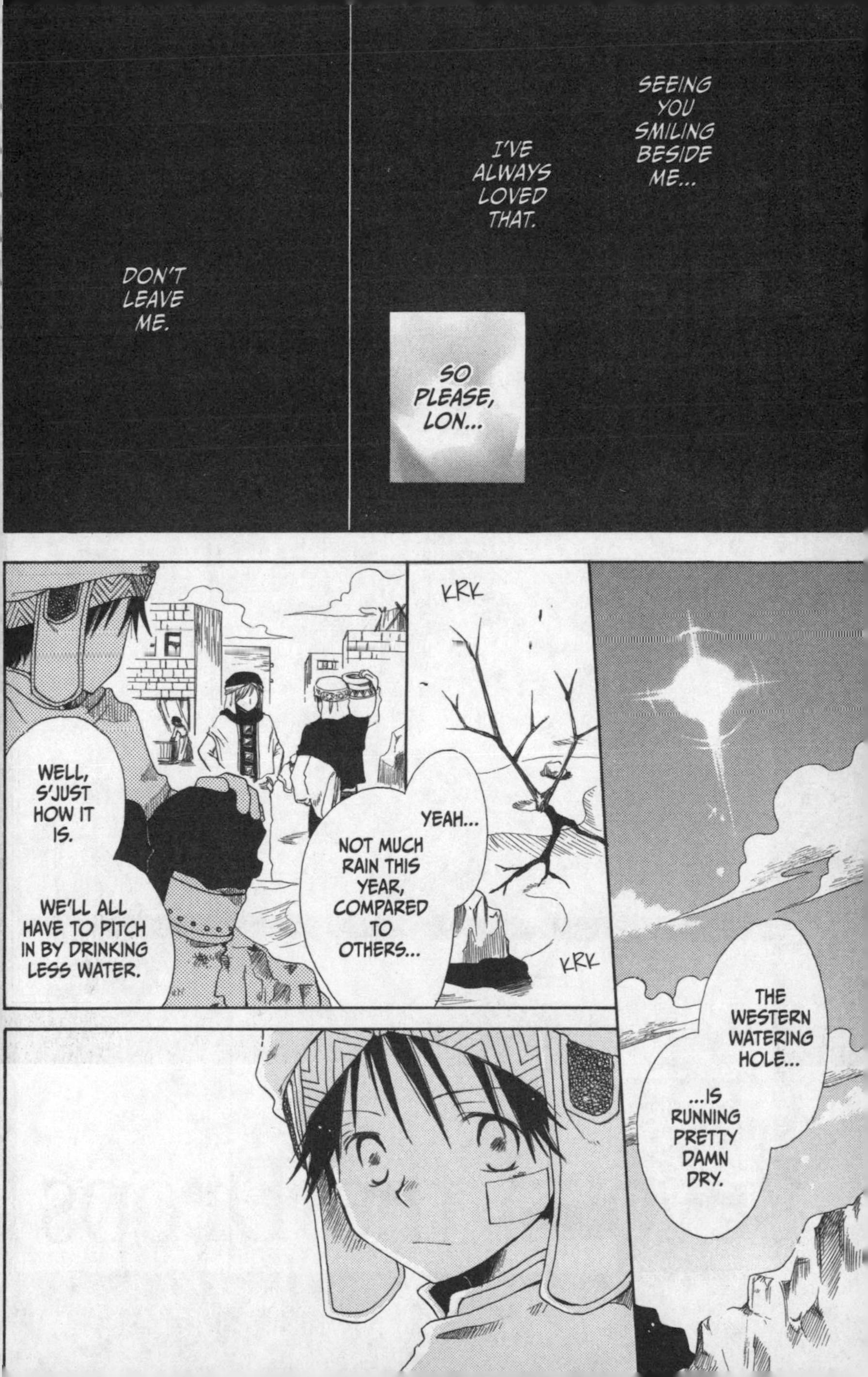
SEEING YOU SMILING BESIDE ME...
I'VE ALWAYS LOVED THAT.
SO PLEASE, LON...
DON'T LEAVE ME.
THE WESTERN WATERING HOLE...
...IS RUNNING PRETTY DAMN DRY.
KRK
KRK
YEAH...
NOT MUCH RAIN THIS YEAR, COMPARED TO OTHERS...
WELL, S'JUST HOW IT IS.
WE'LL ALL HAVE TO PITCH IN BY DRINKING LESS WATER.

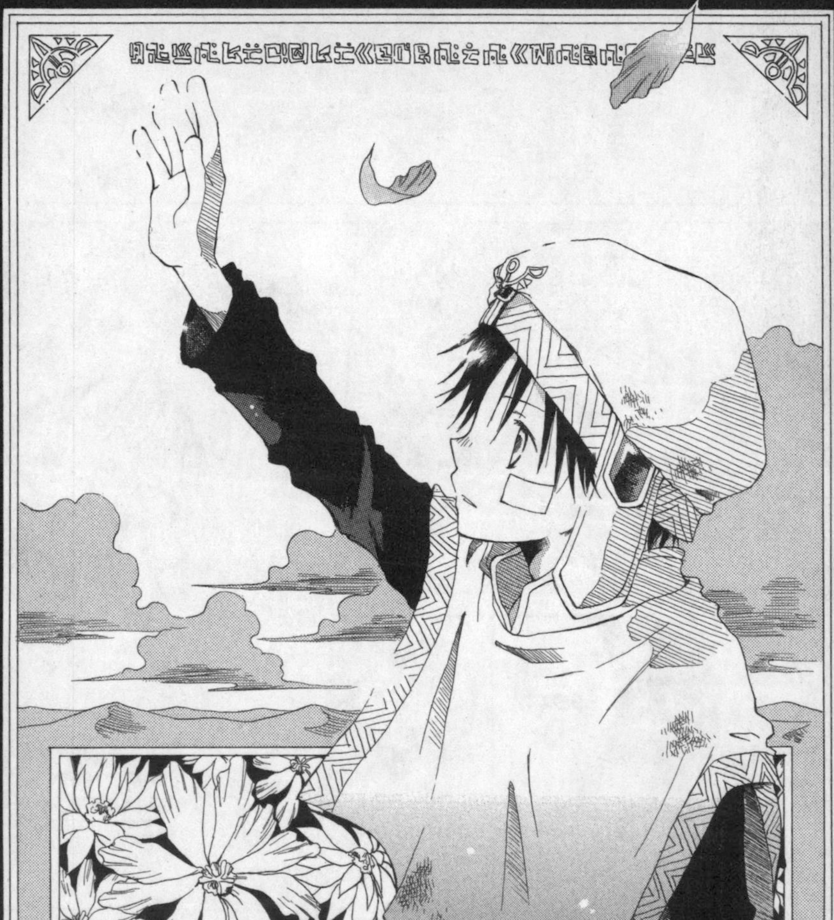

Beyond the Drops

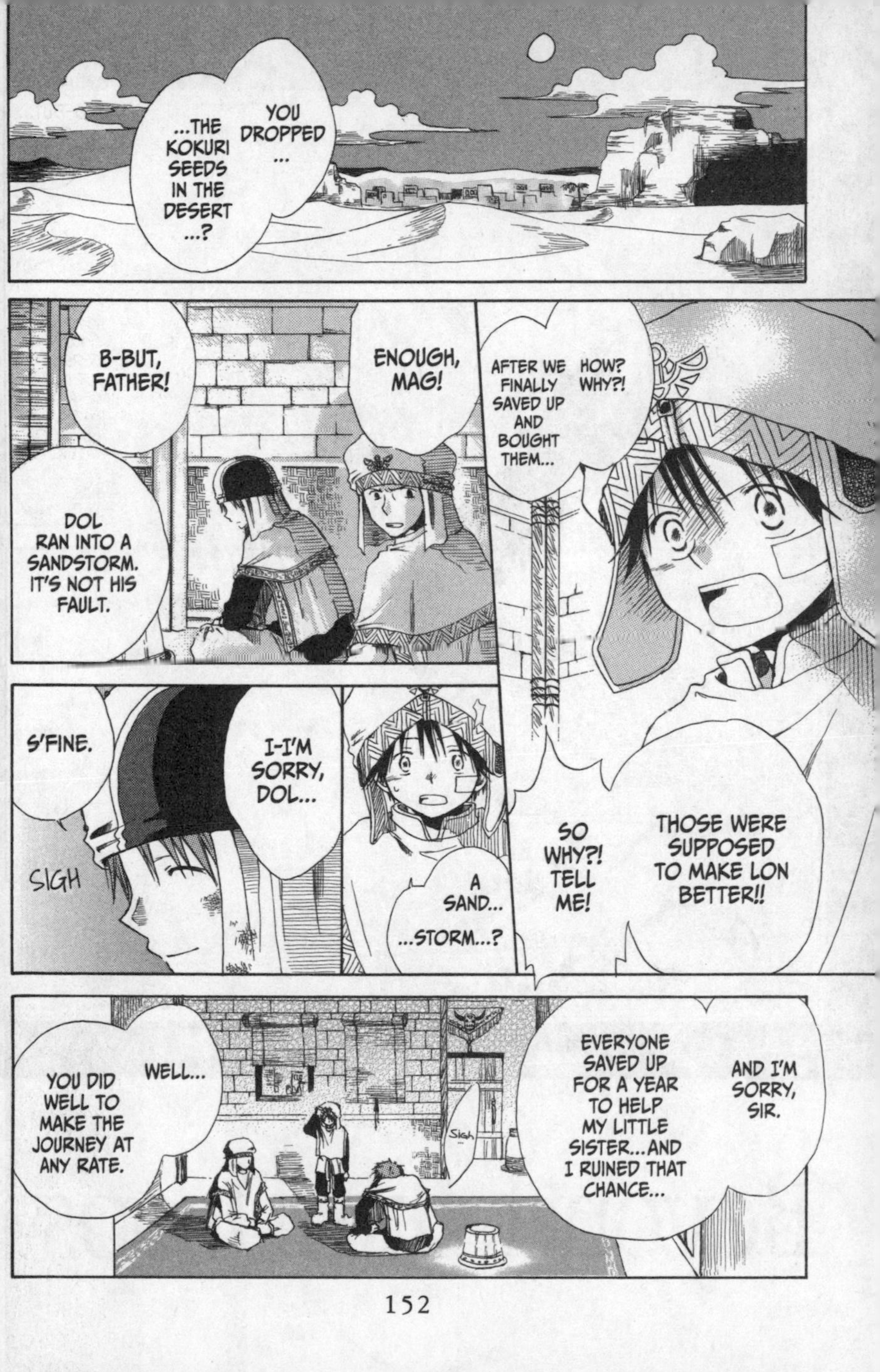
YOU DROPPED ...
...THE KOKURI SEEDS IN THE DESERT ...?
HOW? WHY?!
AFTER WE FINALLY SAVED UP AND BOUGHT THEM...
THOSE WERE SUPPOSED TO MAKE LON BETTER!!
SO WHY?! TELL ME!
ENOUGH, MAG!
B-BUT, FATHER!
DOL RAN INTO A SANDSTORM. IT'S NOT HIS FAULT.
A SAND...
...STORM...?
I-I'M SORRY, DOL...
S'FINE.
SIGH
AND I'M SORRY, SIR.
EVERYONE SAVED UP FOR A YEAR TO HELP MY LITTLE SISTER...AND I RUINED THAT CHANCE...
Sigh...
WELL...
YOU DID WELL TO MAKE THE JOURNEY AT ANY RATE.

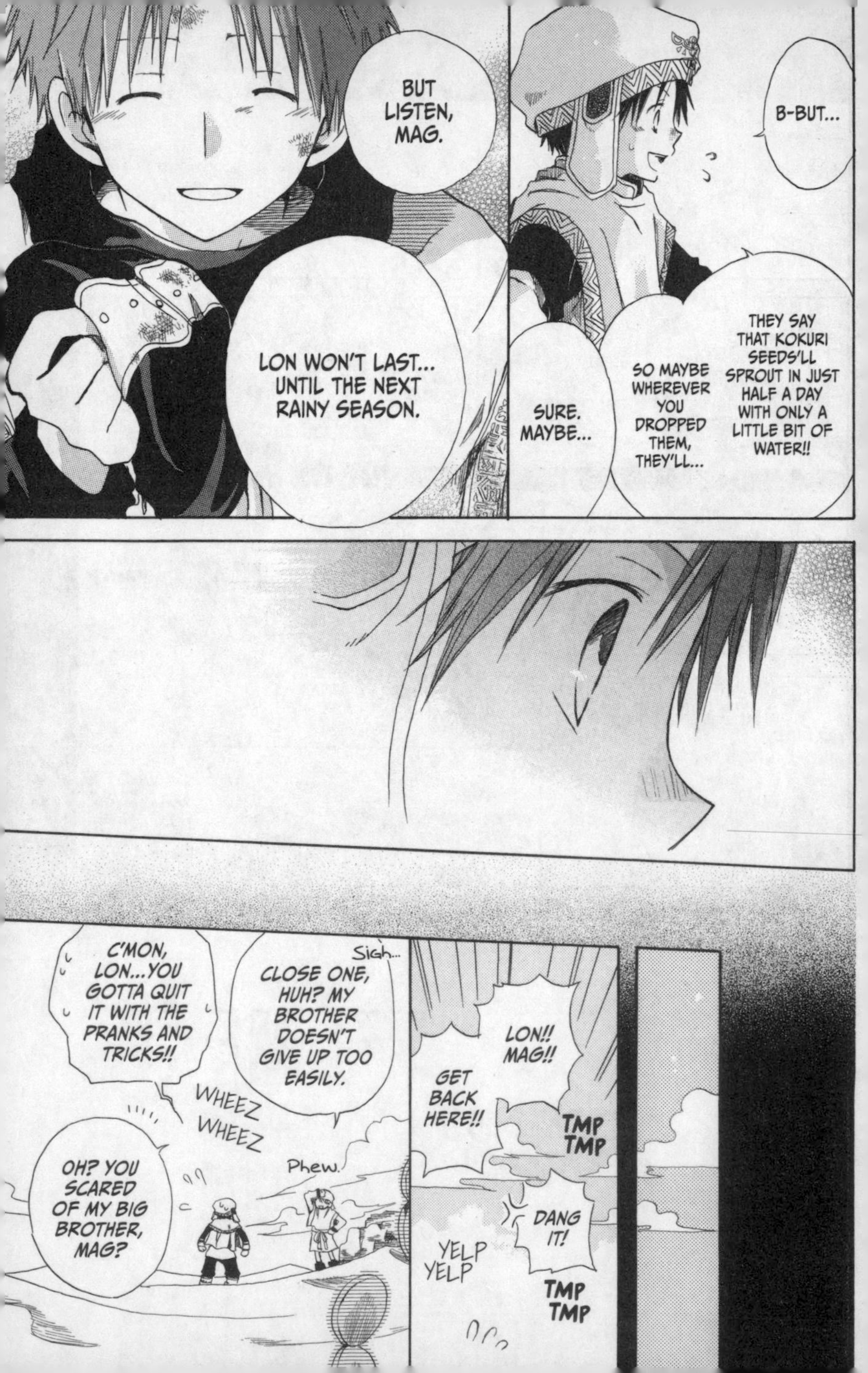
B-BUT...
THEY SAY THAT KOKURI SEEDS'LL SPROUT IN JUST HALF A DAY WITH ONLY A LITTLE BIT OF WATER!!
SO MAYBE WHEREVER YOU DROPPED THEM, THEY'LL...
SURE. MAYBE...
BUT LISTEN, MAG.
LON WON'T LAST... UNTIL THE NEXT RAINY SEASON.
LON!! MAG!!
GET BACK HERE!!
TMP TMP
DANG IT!
YELP YELP
TMP TMP
C'MON, LON...YOU GOTTA QUIT IT WITH THE PRANKS AND TRICKS!!
Sigh...
CLOSE ONE, HUH? MY BROTHER DOESN'T GIVE UP TOO EASILY.
WHEEZ WHEEZ
OH? YOU SCARED OF MY BIG BROTHER, MAG?
Phew.

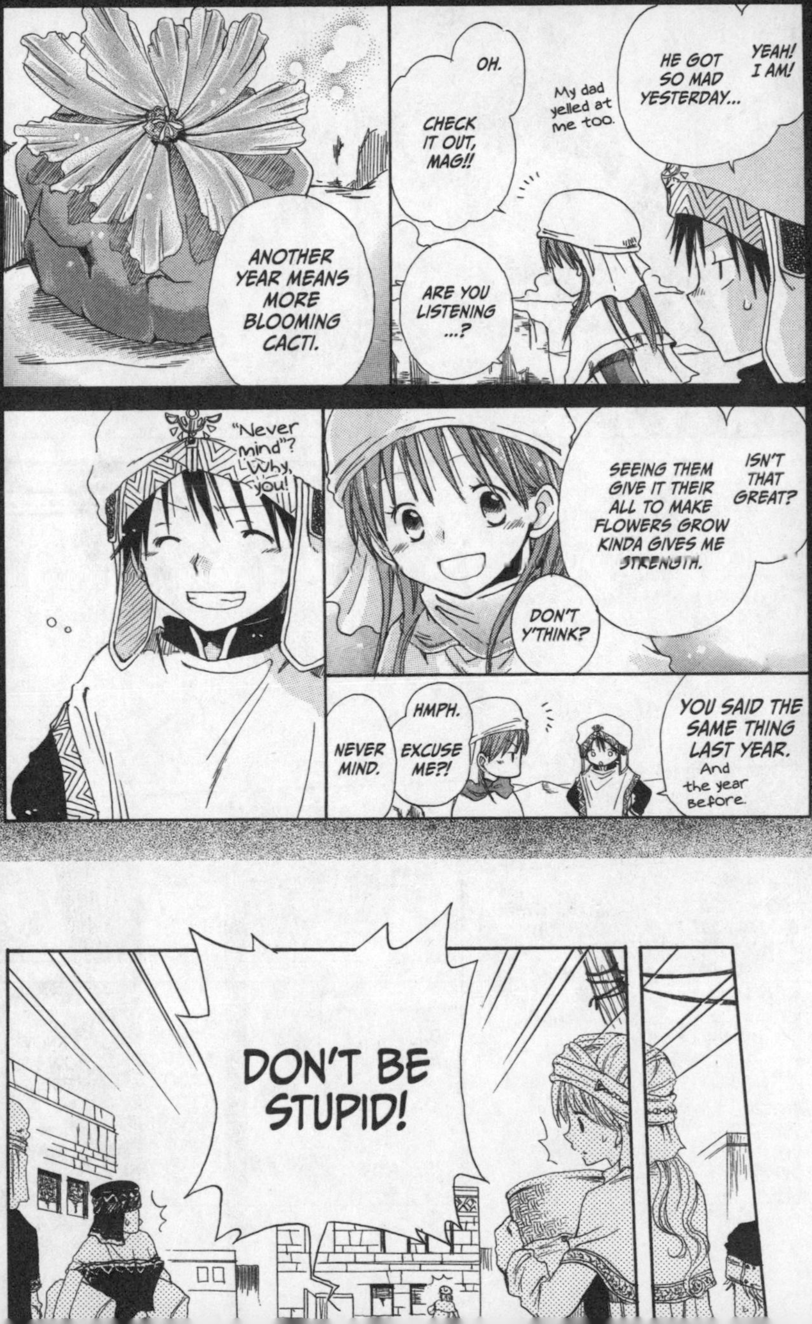
YEAH! I AM!
HE GOT SO MAD YESTERDAY...
My dad yelled at me too.
OH.
CHECK IT OUT, MAG!!
ARE YOU LISTENING ...?
ANOTHER YEAR MEANS MORE BLOOMING CACTI.
ISN'T THAT GREAT?
SEEING THEM GIVE IT THEIR ALL TO MAKE FLOWERS GROW KINDA GIVES ME STRENGTH.
DON'T Y'THINK?
YOU SAID THE SAME THING LAST YEAR.
And the year before.
HMPH.
EXCUSE ME?!
NEVER MIND.
"Never mind"? Why, you!
DON'T BE STUPID!

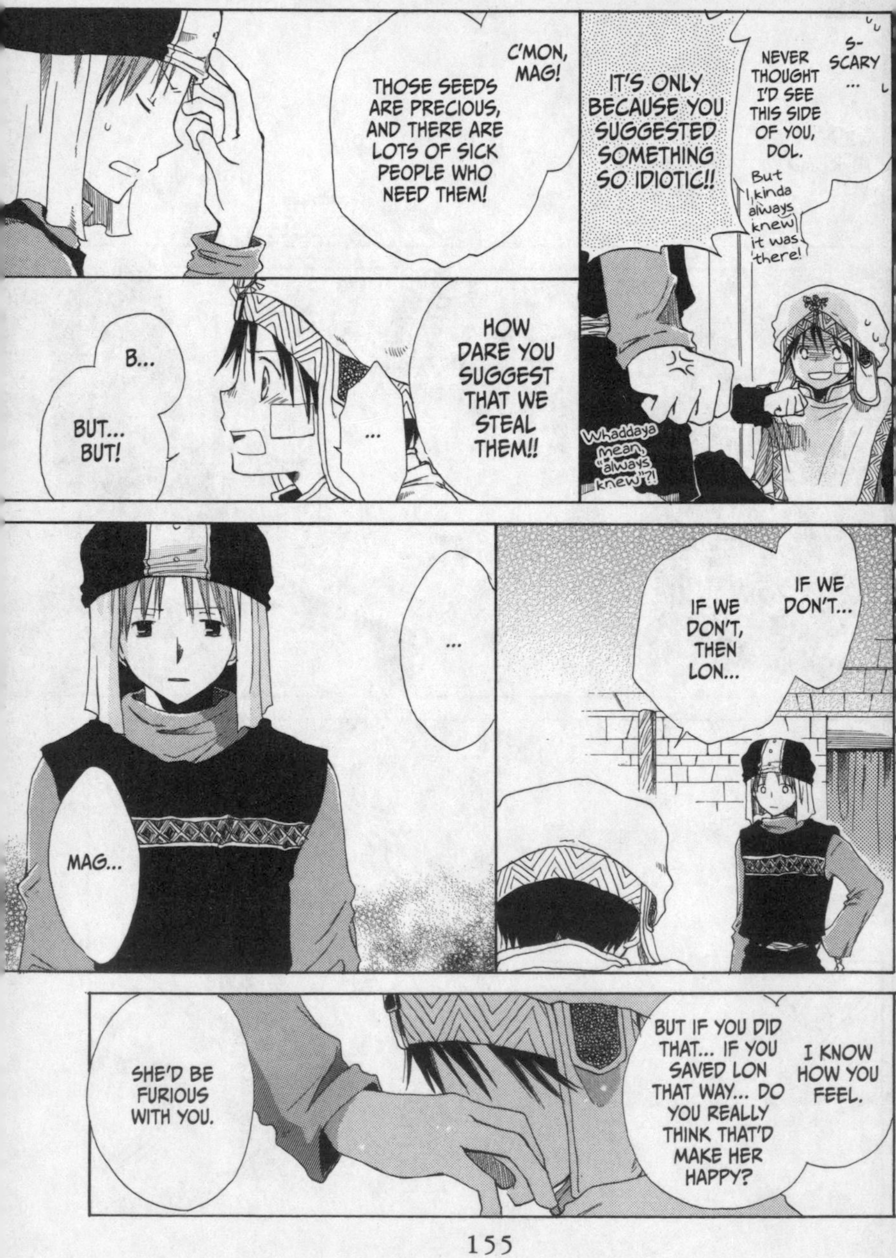
IT'S ONLY BECAUSE YOU SUGGESTED SOMETHING SO IDIOTIC!!
NEVER THOUGHT I'D SEE THIS SIDE OF YOU, DOL.
S-SCARY...
But I kinda always knew it was there!
Whaddaya mean, "always knew"?!
C'MON, MAG!
THOSE SEEDS ARE PRECIOUS, AND THERE ARE LOTS OF SICK PEOPLE WHO NEED THEM!
HOW DARE YOU SUGGEST THAT WE STEAL THEM!!
...
B...
BUT... BUT!
IF WE DON'T...
IF WE DON'T, THEN LON...
...
MAG...
I KNOW HOW YOU FEEL.
BUT IF YOU DID THAT... IF YOU SAVED LON THAT WAY... DO YOU REALLY THINK THAT'D MAKE HER HAPPY?
SHE'D BE FURIOUS WITH YOU.

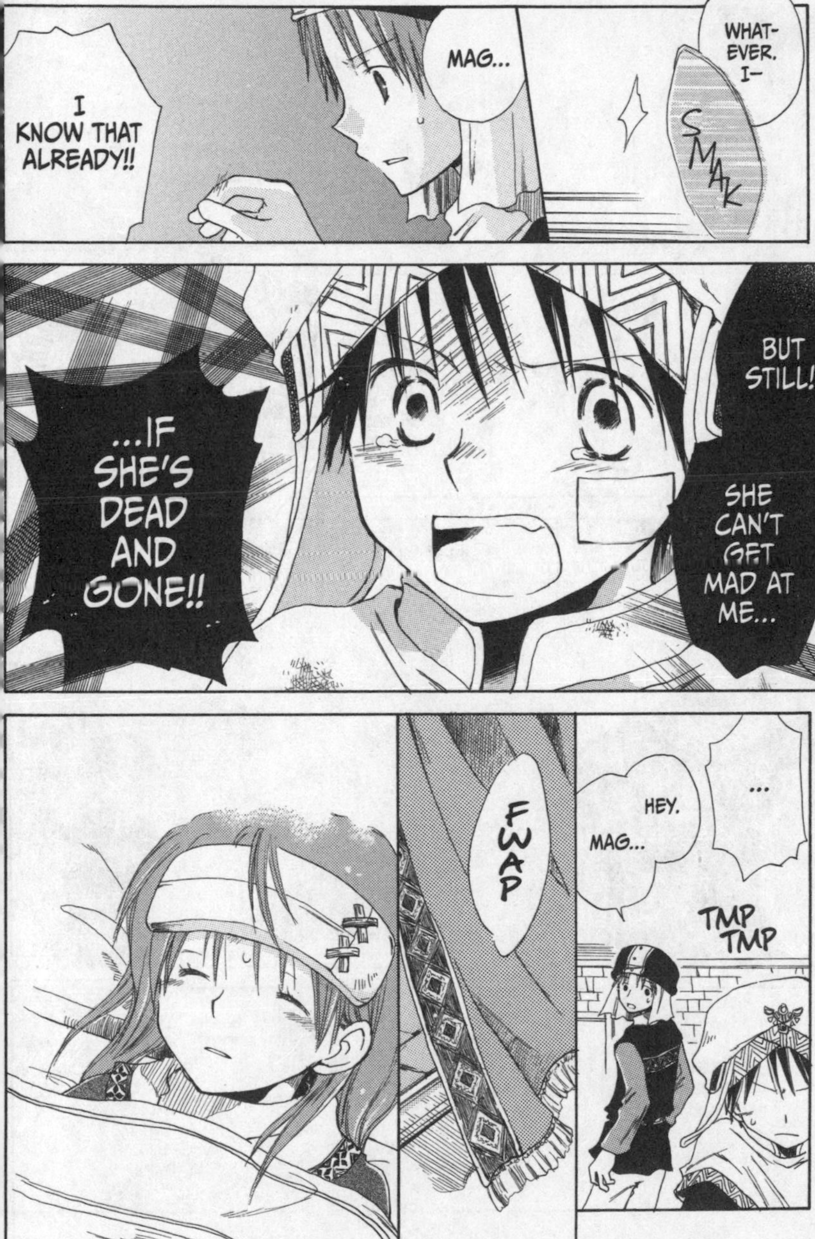
WHAT-EVER. I—
SMAK
MAG...
I KNOW THAT ALREADY!!
BUT STILL!!
SHE CAN'T GET MAD AT ME...
...IF SHE'S DEAD AND GONE!!
...
HEY. MAG...
TMP TMP
FWAP

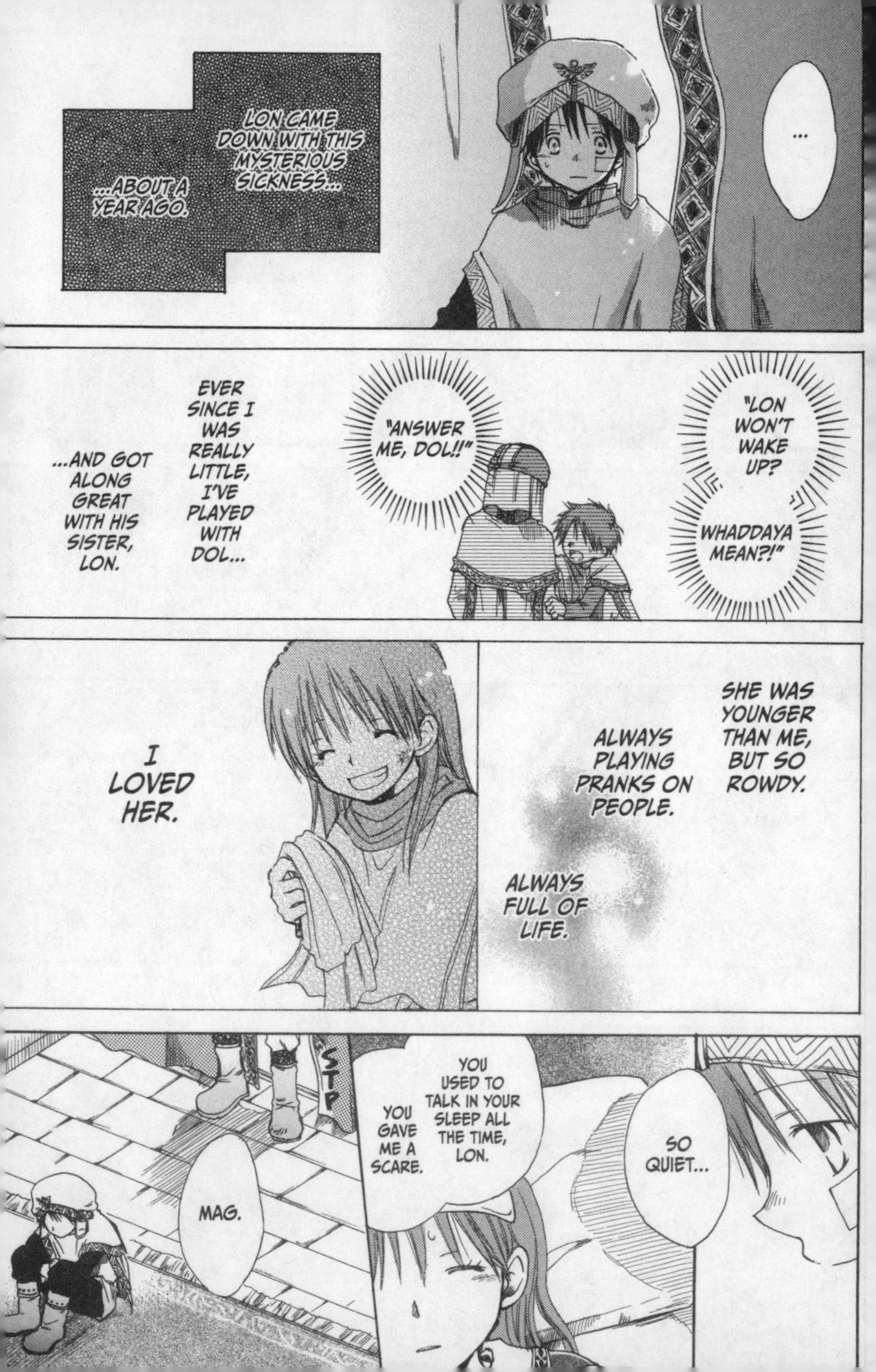
...
LON CAME DOWN WITH THIS MYSTERIOUS SICKNESS...
...ABOUT A YEAR AGO.
"LON WON'T WAKE UP?
WHADDAYA MEAN?!"
"ANSWER ME, DOL!!"
EVER SINCE I WAS REALLY LITTLE, I'VE PLAYED WITH DOL...
...AND GOT ALONG GREAT WITH HIS SISTER, LON.
SHE WAS YOUNGER THAN ME, BUT SO ROWDY.
ALWAYS PLAYING PRANKS ON PEOPLE.
ALWAYS FULL OF LIFE.
I LOVED HER.
SO QUIET...
YOU USED TO TALK IN YOUR SLEEP ALL THE TIME, LON.
YOU GAVE ME A SCARE.
STP
MAG.

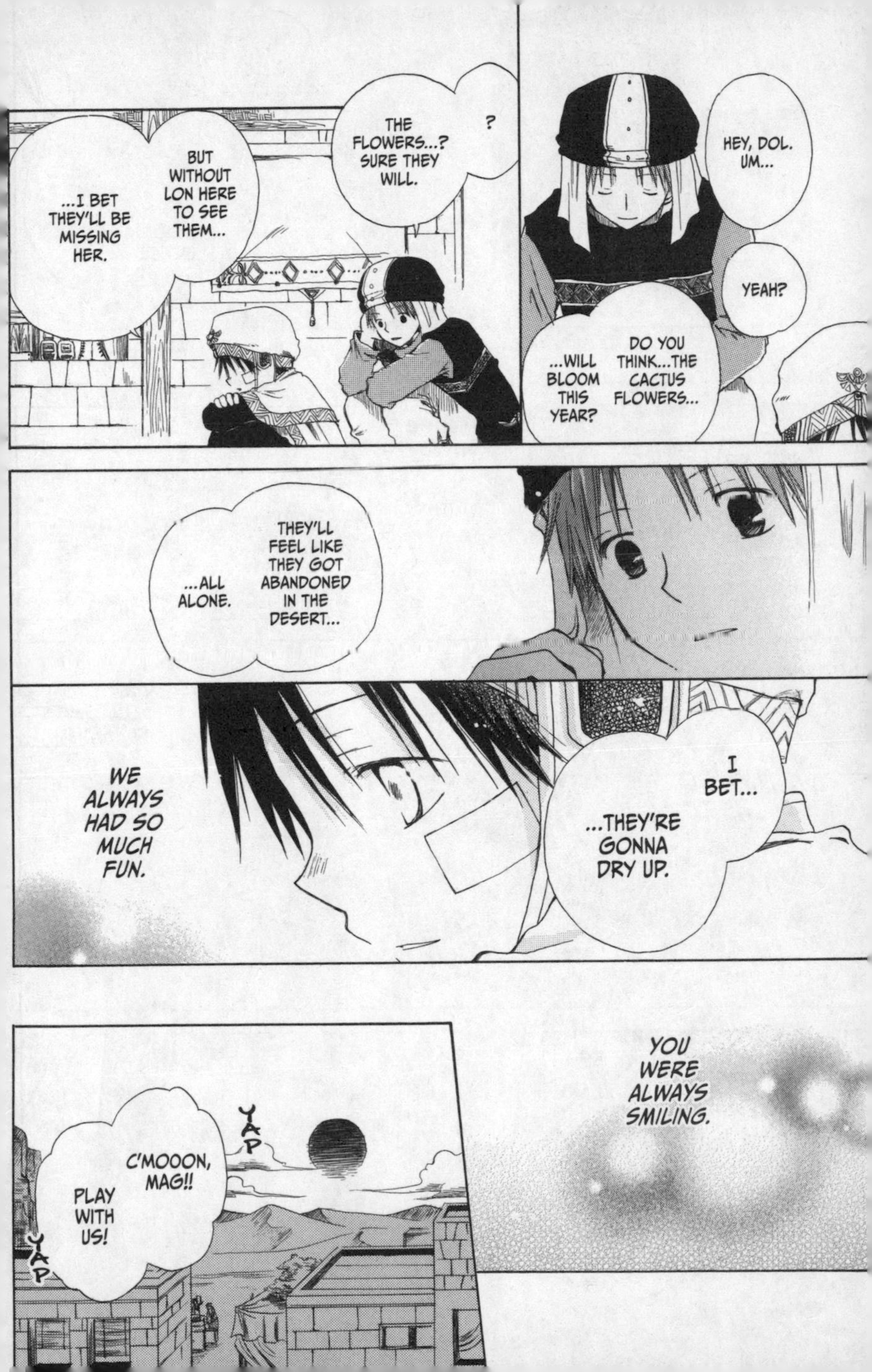
HEY, DOL. UM...
YEAH?
DO YOU THINK...THE CACTUS FLOWERS...
...WILL BLOOM THIS YEAR?
?
THE FLOWERS...? SURE THEY WILL.
BUT WITHOUT LON HERE TO SEE THEM...
...I BET THEY'LL BE MISSING HER.
THEY'LL FEEL LIKE THEY GOT ABANDONED IN THE DESERT...
...ALL ALONE.
I BET...
...THEY'RE GONNA DRY UP.
WE ALWAYS HAD SO MUCH FUN.
YOU WERE ALWAYS SMILING.
YAP
C'MOOON, MAG!!
PLAY WITH US!
YAP

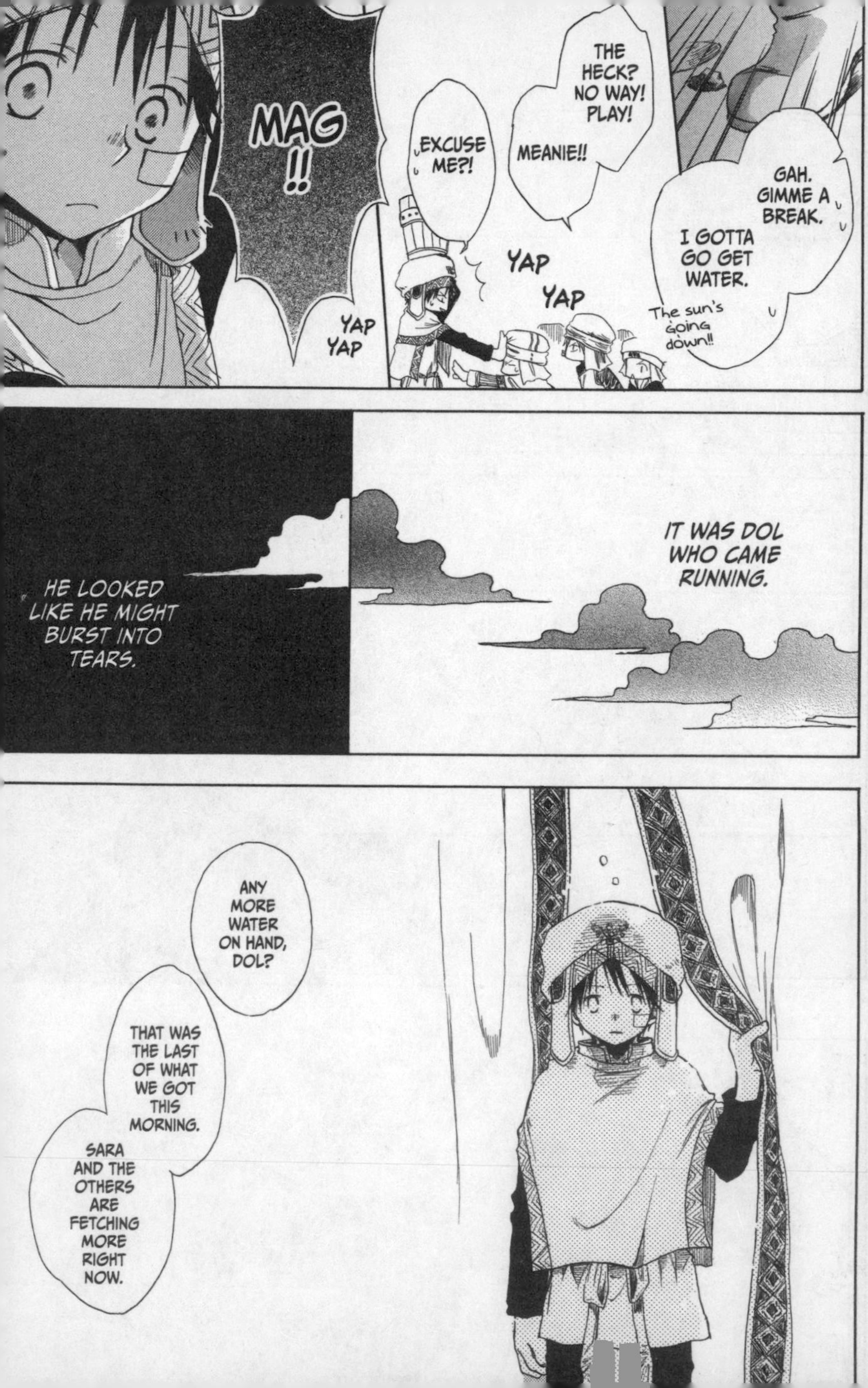
GAH. GIMME A BREAK.
I GOTTA GO GET WATER.
The sun's going down!!
THE HECK? NO WAY! PLAY!
MEANIE!!
EXCUSE ME?!
YAP
YAP
YAP YAP
MAG!!
IT WAS DOL WHO CAME RUNNING.
HE LOOKED LIKE HE MIGHT BURST INTO TEARS.
ANY MORE WATER ON HAND, DOL?
THAT WAS THE LAST OF WHAT WE GOT THIS MORNING.
SARA AND THE OTHERS ARE FETCHING MORE RIGHT NOW.

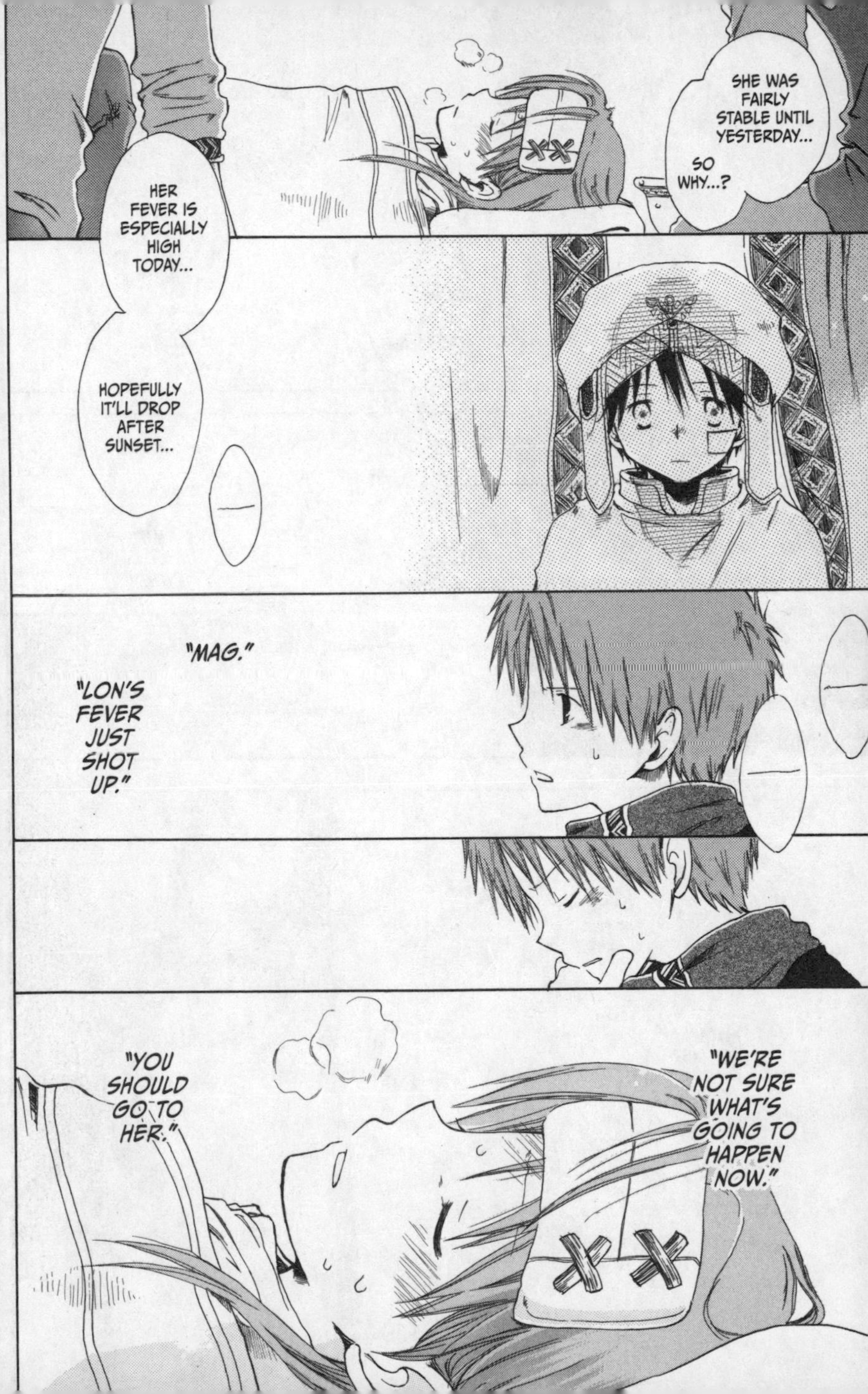
SHE WAS FAIRLY STABLE UNTIL YESTERDAY...
SO WHY...?
HER FEVER IS ESPECIALLY HIGH TODAY...
HOPEFULLY IT'LL DROP AFTER SUNSET...
—
—
"MAG."
"LON'S FEVER JUST SHOT UP."
"WE'RE NOT SURE WHAT'S GOING TO HAPPEN NOW."
"YOU SHOULD GO TO HER."

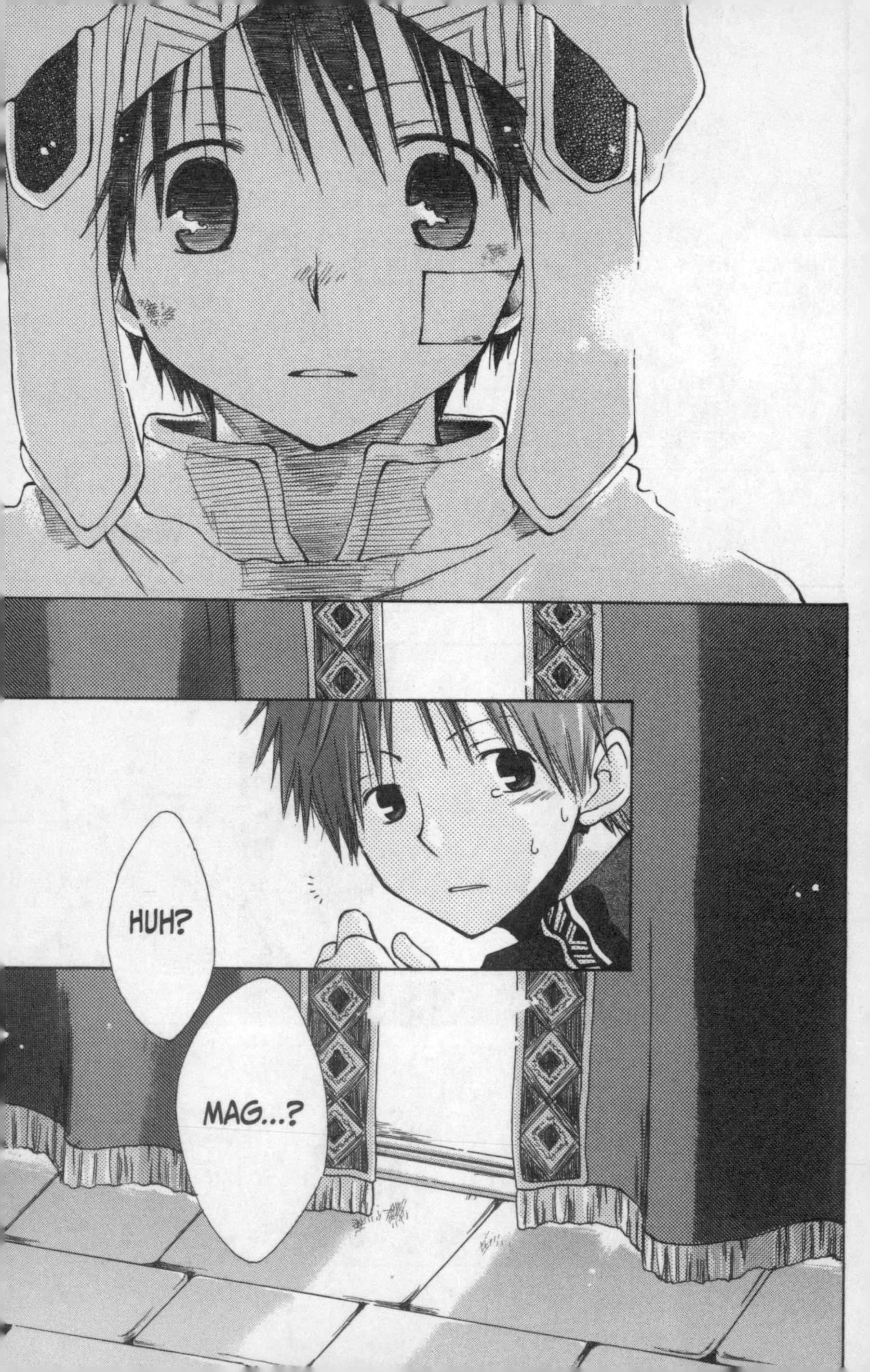
HUH?
MAG...?

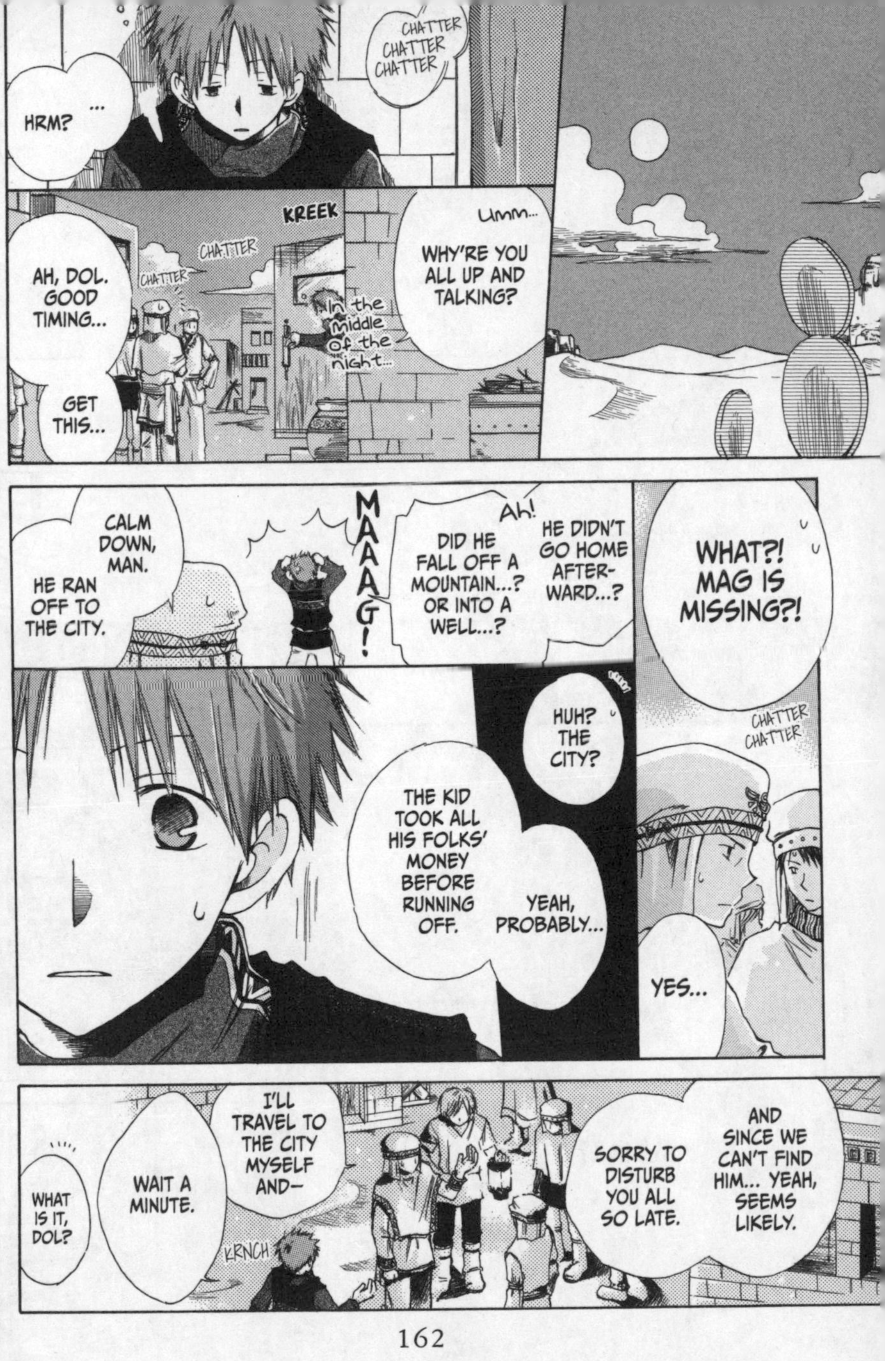
CHATTER CHATTER CHATTER
...
HRM?
Umm...
WHY'RE YOU ALL UP AND TALKING?
In the middle of the night...
KREEK
CHATTER
CHATTER
AH, DOL. GOOD TIMING...
GET THIS...
WHAT?! MAG IS MISSING?!
HE DIDN'T GO HOME AFTER-WARD...?
Ah!
DID HE FALL OFF A MOUNTAIN...? OR INTO A WELL...?
MAAAG!
CALM DOWN, MAN.
HE RAN OFF TO THE CITY.
CHATTER CHATTER
YES...
HUH? THE CITY?
YEAH, PROBABLY...
THE KID TOOK ALL HIS FOLKS' MONEY BEFORE RUNNING OFF.
AND SINCE WE CAN'T FIND HIM... YEAH, SEEMS LIKELY.
SORRY TO DISTURB YOU ALL SO LATE.
I'LL TRAVEL TO THE CITY MYSELF AND—
WAIT A MINUTE.
KRNCH
WHAT IS IT, DOL?

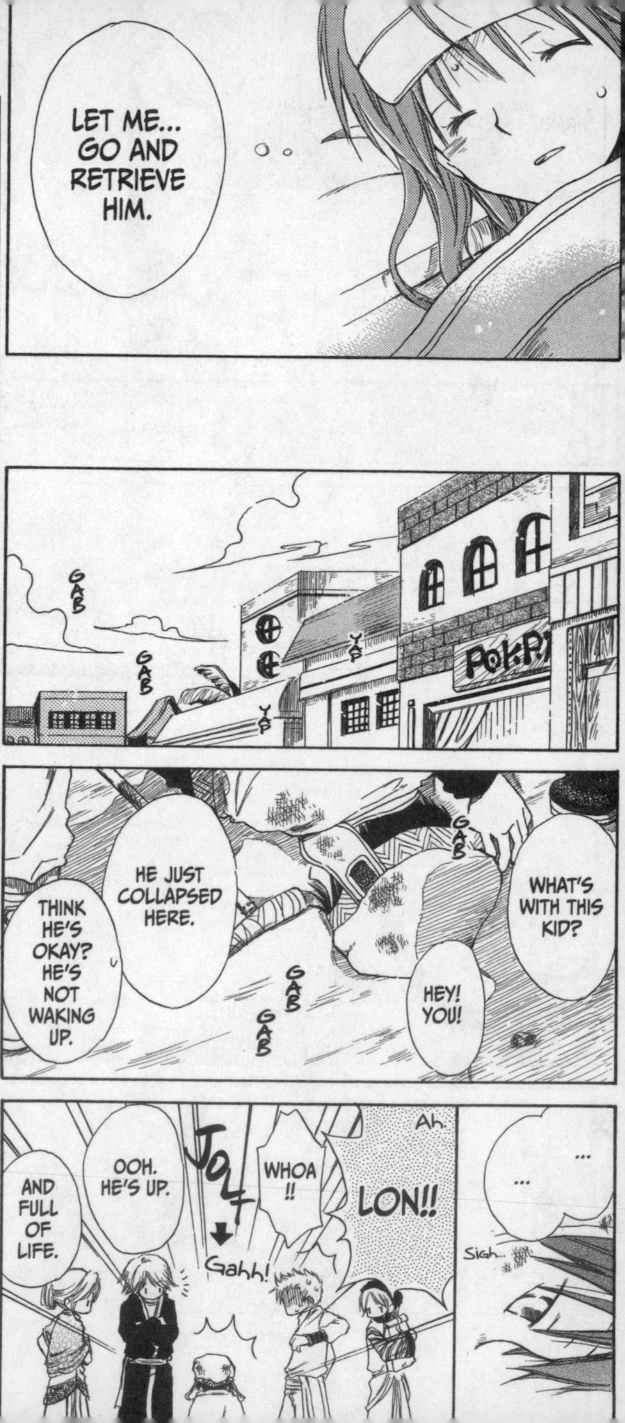
LET ME...
GO AND
RETRIEVE
HIM.
GAB
YAP
GAB
YAP
Po.k.P.
WHAT'S WITH THIS KID?
HEY! YOU!
GAB
GAB
GAB
HE JUST COLLAPSED HERE.
THINK HE'S OKAY? HE'S NOT WAKING UP.
...
...
Sigh...
Ah.
LON!!
WHOA !!
JOLT
Gahh!
OOH. HE'S UP.
AND FULL OF LIFE.

"BEYOND THE DROPS"

This is...
the first...one-shot
story in a while.

This was my third piece ever, I think. How many years ago was it? I can't even count!

It's got my youngest protagonist ever. I'd love to write another story with a young boy as the lead. Even just a few pages would be great! If you've got a boy! And a girl! There's a story just waiting to happen!

...happen!
...happen!

This one's particularly nostalgic for me. I remember having a blast drawing the boy at the booze shop. He's such a helpful character.

Anyway, see you next volume!

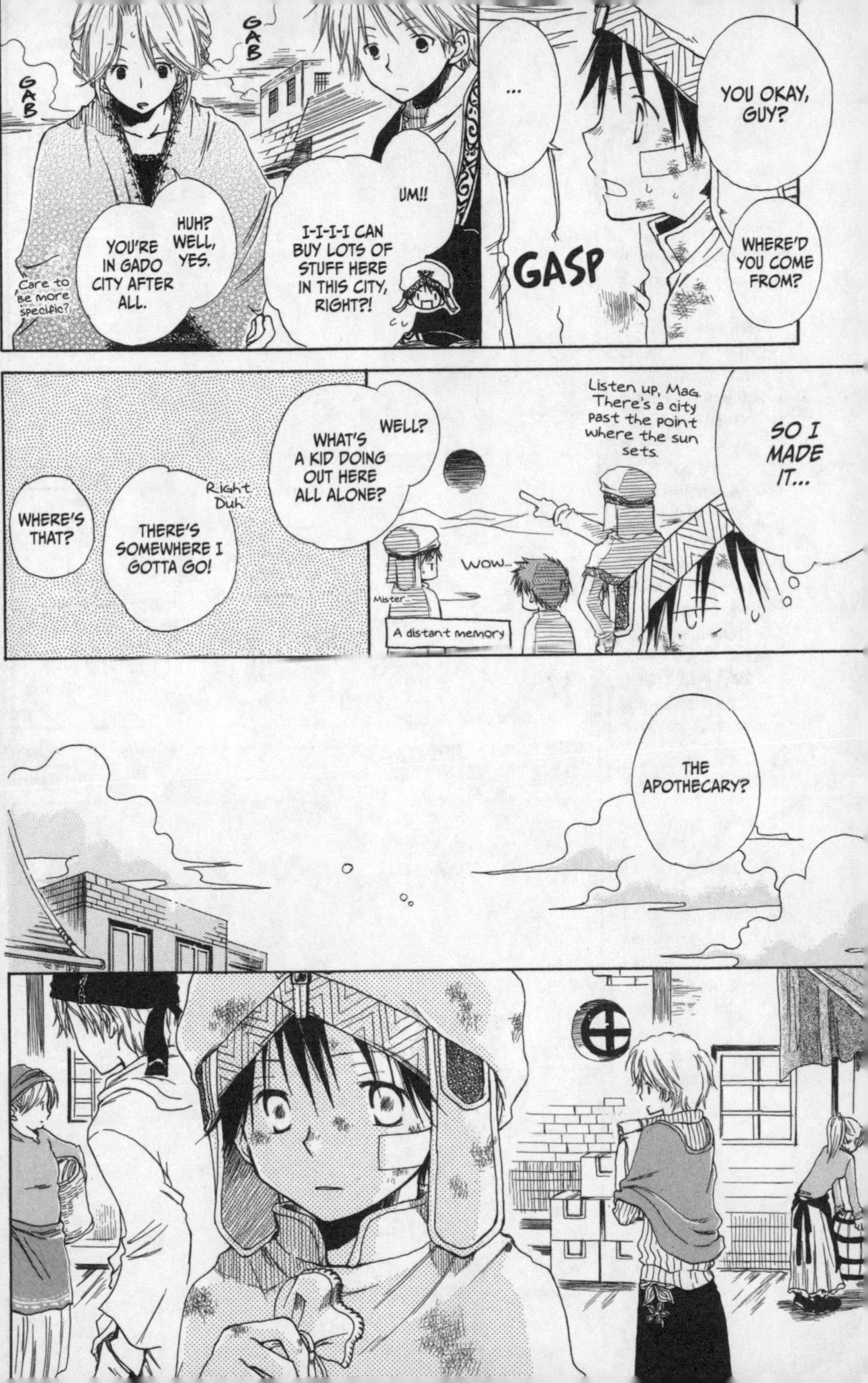
YOU OKAY, GUY?
WHERE'D YOU COME FROM?
GASP
...
UM!!
I-I-I-I CAN BUY LOTS OF STUFF HERE IN THIS CITY, RIGHT?!
GAB
GAB
HUH? WELL, YES.
YOU'RE IN GADO CITY AFTER ALL.
Care to be more specific?
SO I MADE IT...
Listen up, Mag. There's a city past the point where the sun sets.
WOW...
Mister...
A distant memory
WELL?
WHAT'S A KID DOING OUT HERE ALL ALONE?
Right. Duh.
THERE'S SOMEWHERE I GOTTA GO!
WHERE'S THAT?
THE APOTHECARY?

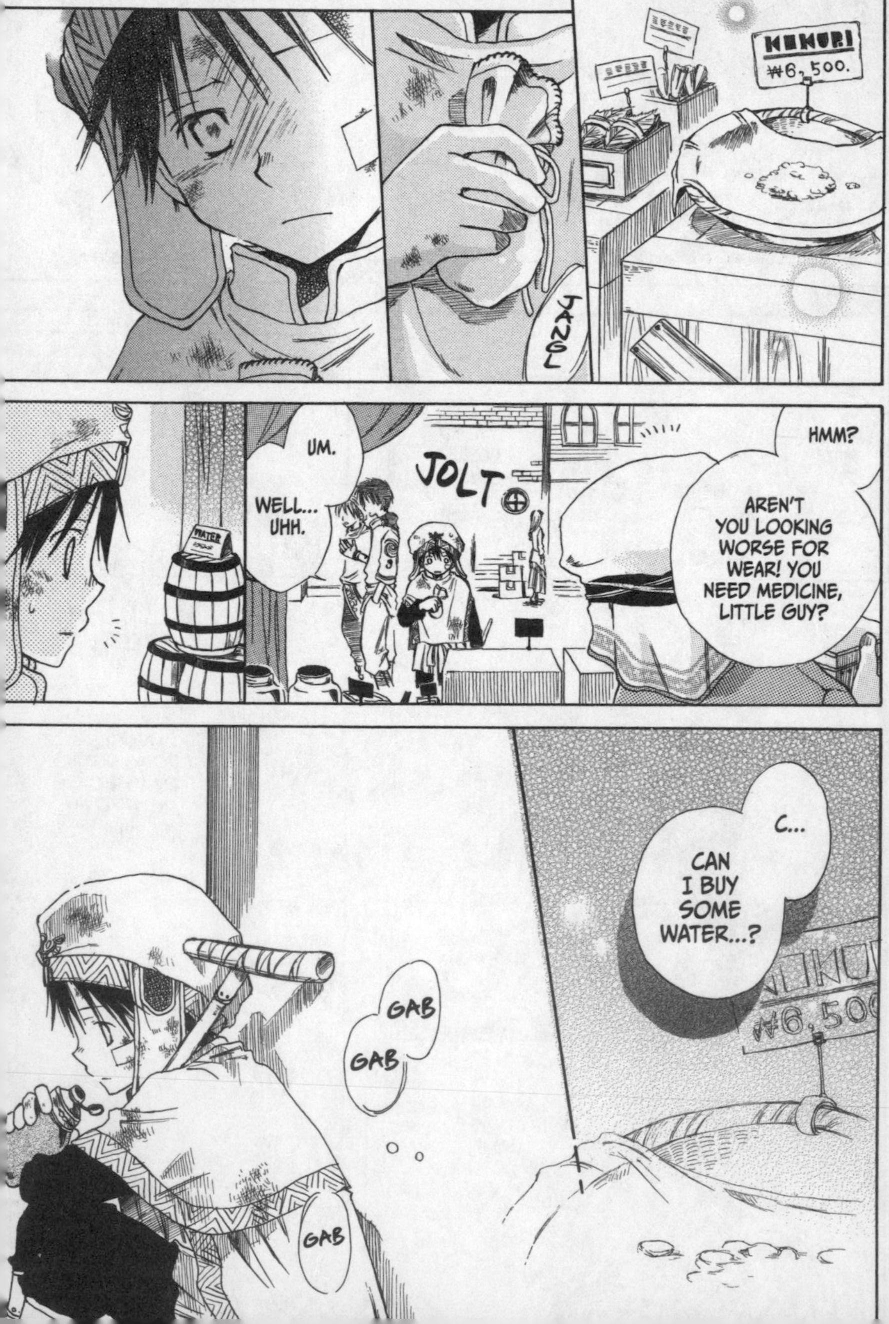
HOMURI
₩6,500.
JANGL
HMM?
AREN'T YOU LOOKING WORSE FOR WEAR! YOU NEED MEDICINE, LITTLE GUY?
JOLT
UM.
WELL... UHH.
WATER
C...
CAN I BUY SOME WATER...?
₩6,500
GAB
GAB
GAB

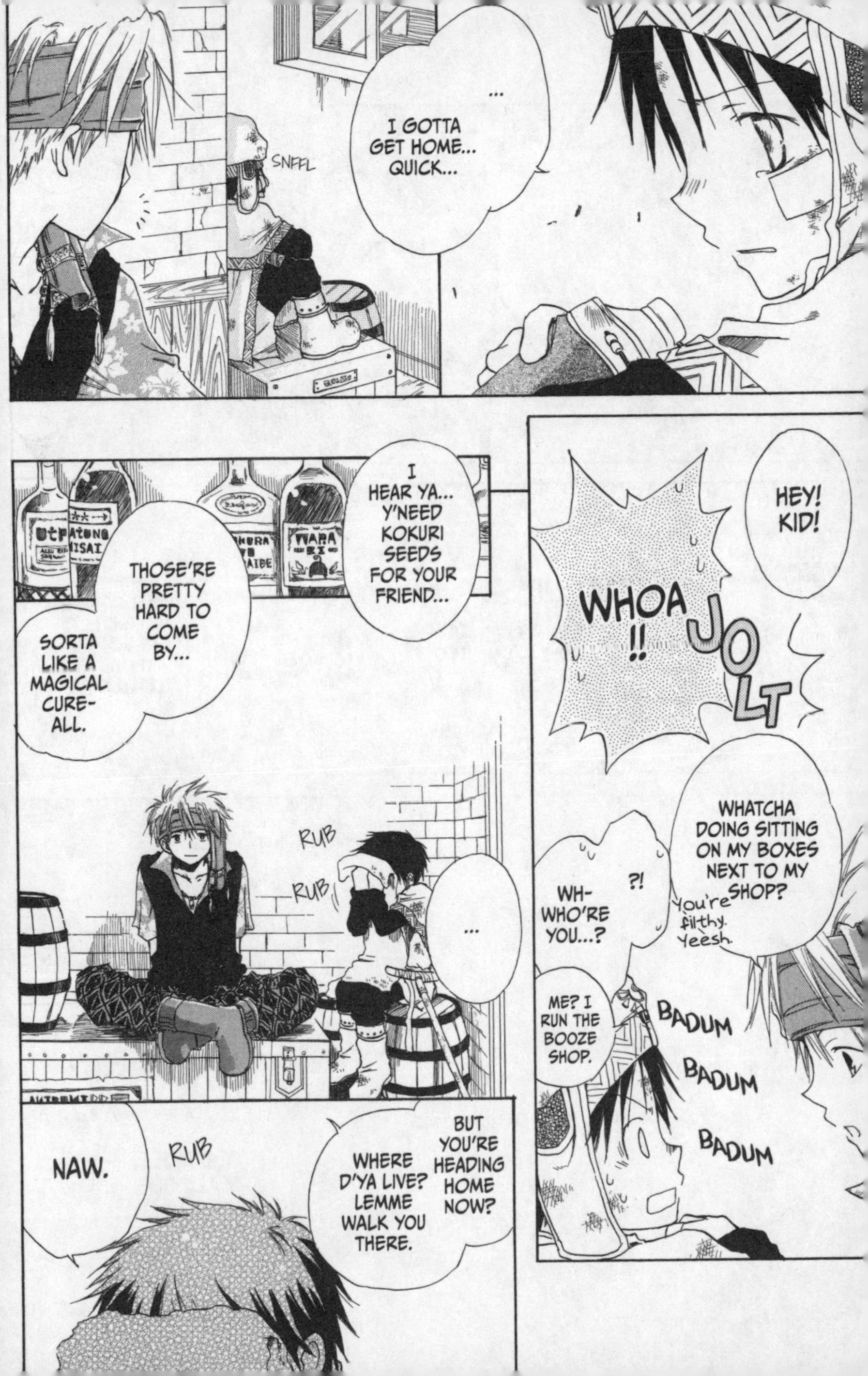
...
I GOTTA GET HOME... QUICK...
SNFFL
HEY! KID!
WHOA !!
JOLT
WHATCHA DOING SITTING ON MY BOXES NEXT TO MY SHOP?
You're filthy. Yeesh.
?!
WH- WHO'RE YOU...?
ME? I RUN THE BOOZE SHOP.
BADUM
BADUM
BADUM
I HEAR YA... Y'NEED KOKURI SEEDS FOR YOUR FRIEND...
THOSE'RE PRETTY HARD TO COME BY...
SORTA LIKE A MAGICAL CURE-ALL.
RUB
RUB
...
BUT YOU'RE HEADING HOME NOW?
WHERE D'YA LIVE? LEMME WALK YOU THERE.
RUB
NAW.

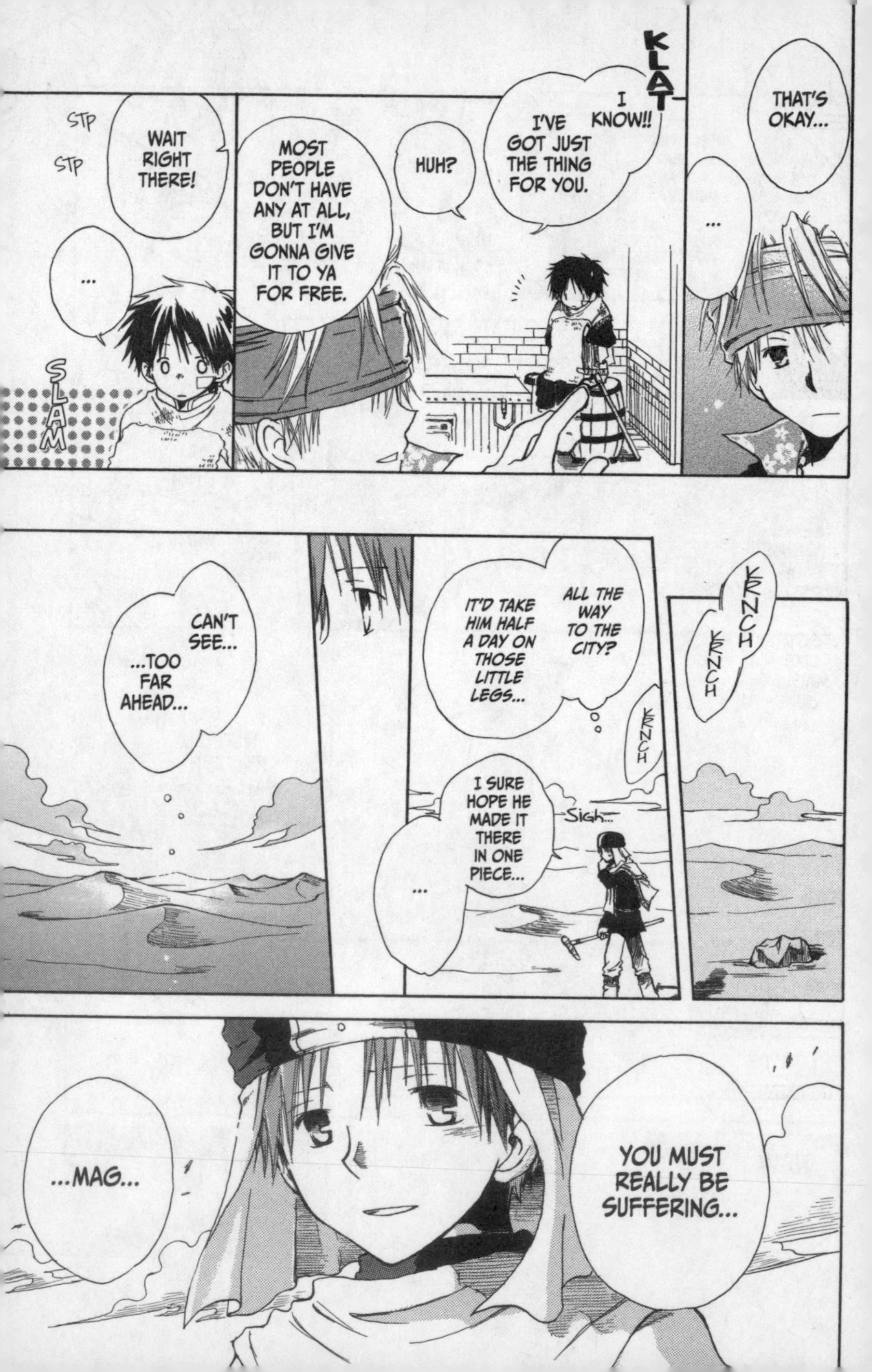
THAT'S OKAY...
...
KLAT
I KNOW!!
I'VE GOT JUST THE THING FOR YOU.
HUH?
MOST PEOPLE DON'T HAVE ANY AT ALL, BUT I'M GONNA GIVE IT TO YA FOR FREE.
WAIT RIGHT THERE!
STP
STP
...
SLAM
KRNCH
KRNCH
KRNCH
ALL THE WAY TO THE CITY?
IT'D TAKE HIM HALF A DAY ON THOSE LITTLE LEGS...
Sigh...
I SURE HOPE HE MADE IT THERE IN ONE PIECE...
...
CAN'T SEE...
...TOO FAR AHEAD...
YOU MUST REALLY BE SUFFERING...
...MAG...

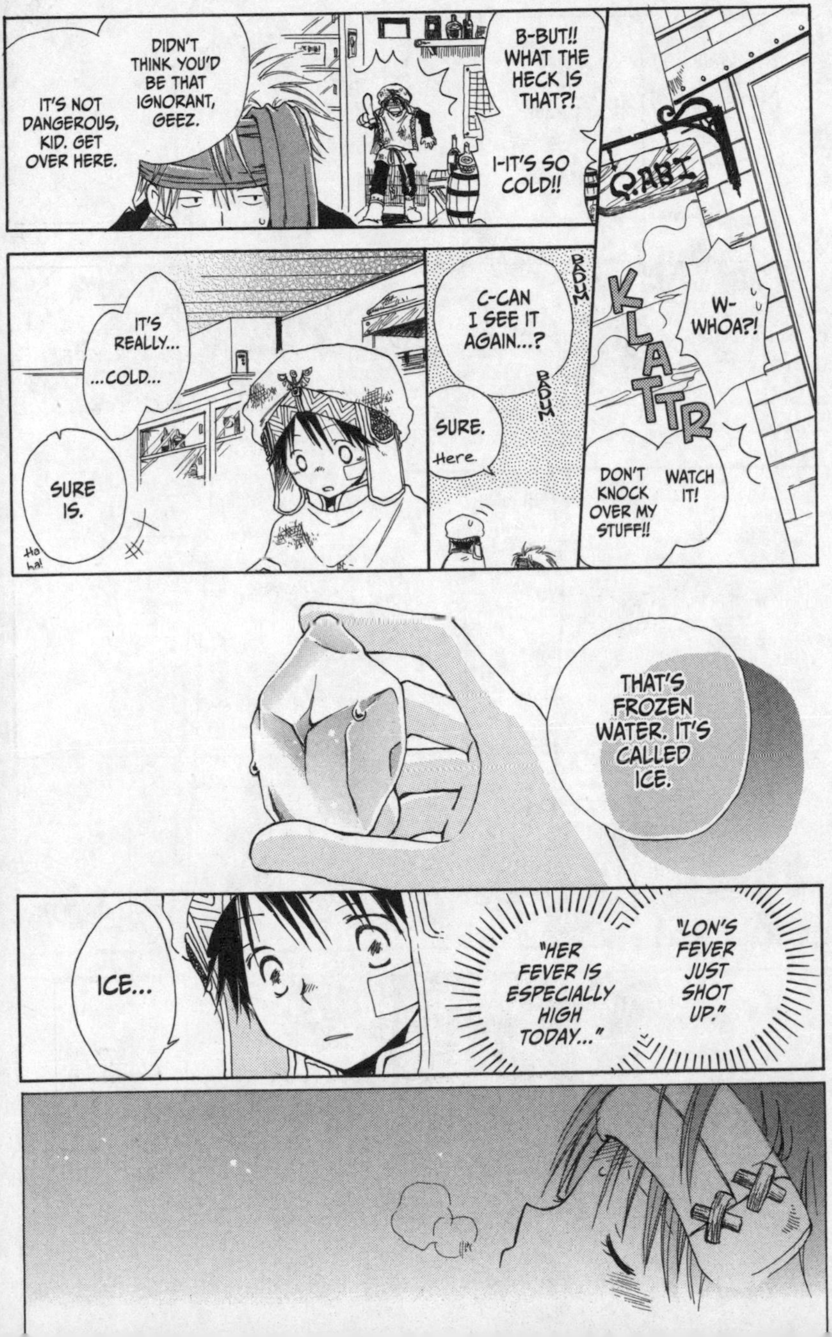
W-WHOA?!
KLATTR
WATCH IT!
DON'T KNOCK OVER MY STUFF!!
B-BUT!! WHAT THE HECK IS THAT?!
I-IT'S SO COLD!!
DIDN'T THINK YOU'D BE THAT IGNORANT, GEEZ.
IT'S NOT DANGEROUS, KID. GET OVER HERE.
BADUM
C-CAN I SEE IT AGAIN...?
BADUM
SURE.
Here.
IT'S REALLY...
...COLD...
SURE IS.
Ha ha!
THAT'S FROZEN WATER. IT'S CALLED ICE.
"LON'S FEVER JUST SHOT UP."
"HER FEVER IS ESPECIALLY HIGH TODAY..."
ICE...

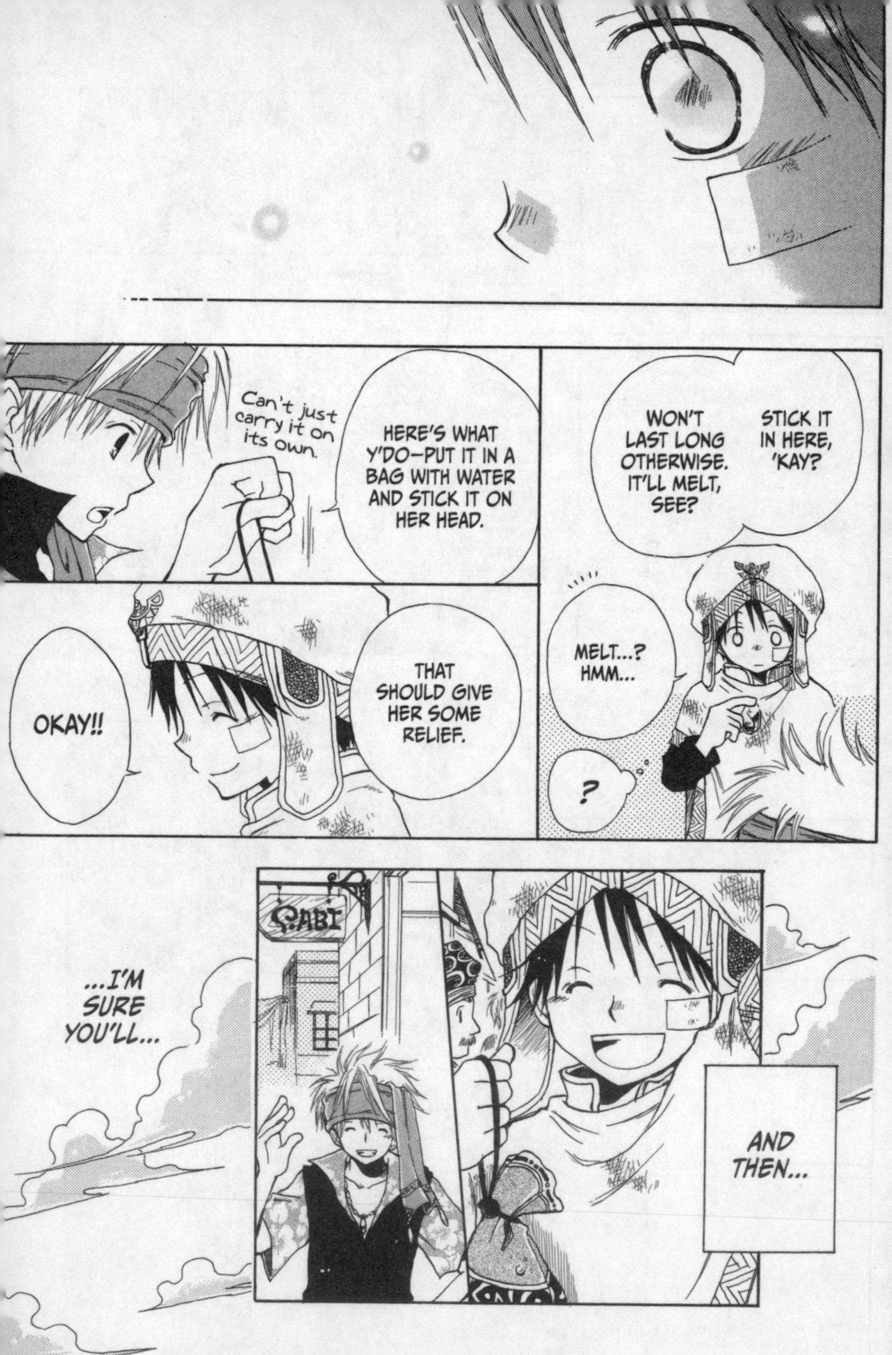
STICK IT IN HERE, 'KAY?
WON'T LAST LONG OTHERWISE. IT'LL MELT, SEE?
MELT...? HMM...
?
HERE'S WHAT Y'DO—PUT IT IN A BAG WITH WATER AND STICK IT ON HER HEAD.
Can't just carry it on its own.
THAT SHOULD GIVE HER SOME RELIEF.
OKAY!!
AND THEN...
...I'M SURE YOU'LL...

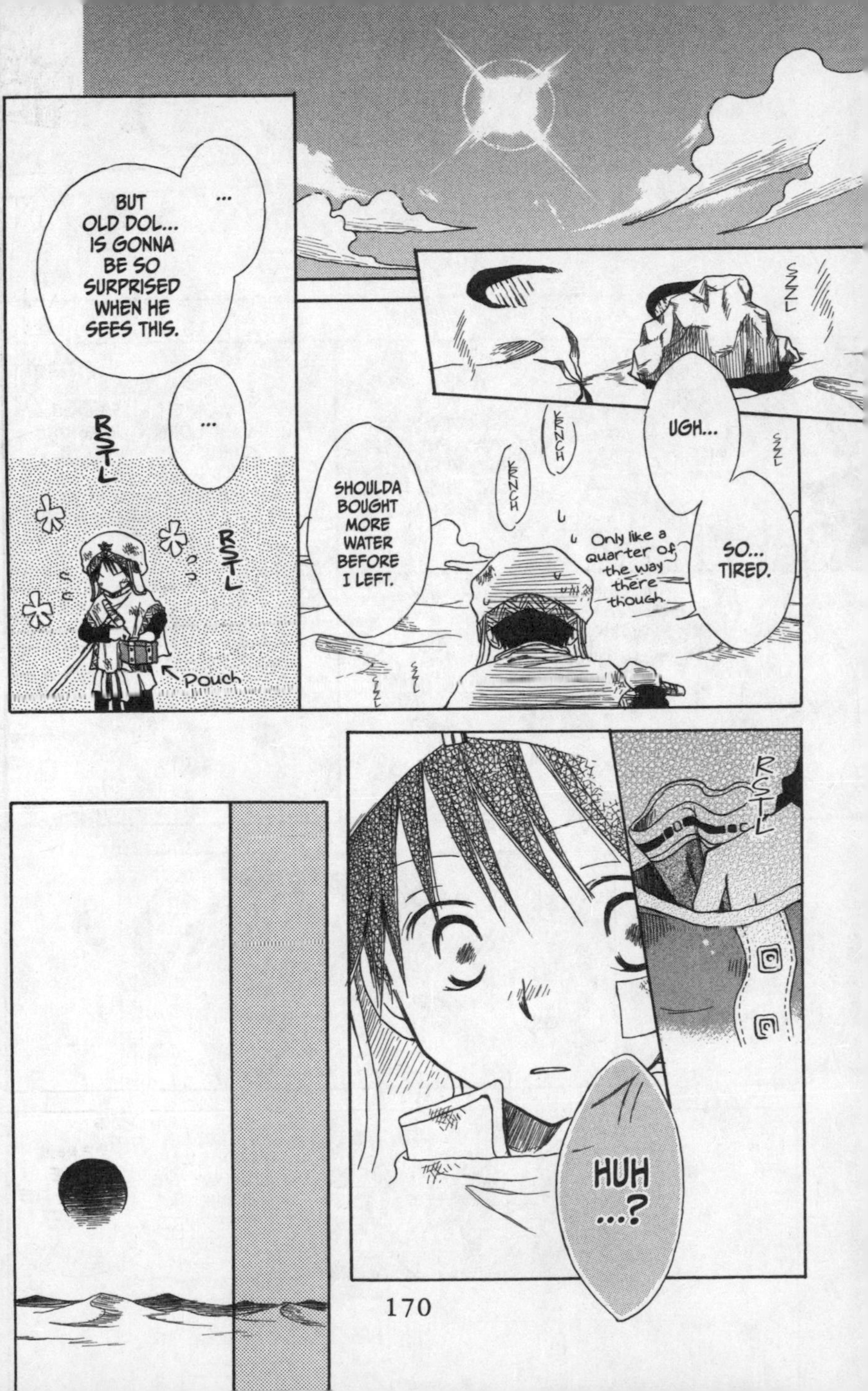
SZZL
UGH...
SZZL
SO... TIRED.
Only like a quarter of the way there though.
KRNCH
KRNCH
SHOULDA BOUGHT MORE WATER BEFORE I LEFT.
SZZL
SZZL
...
BUT OLD DOL... IS GONNA BE SO SURPRISED WHEN HE SEES THIS.
...
RSTL
RSTL
Pouch
RSTL
HUH ...?

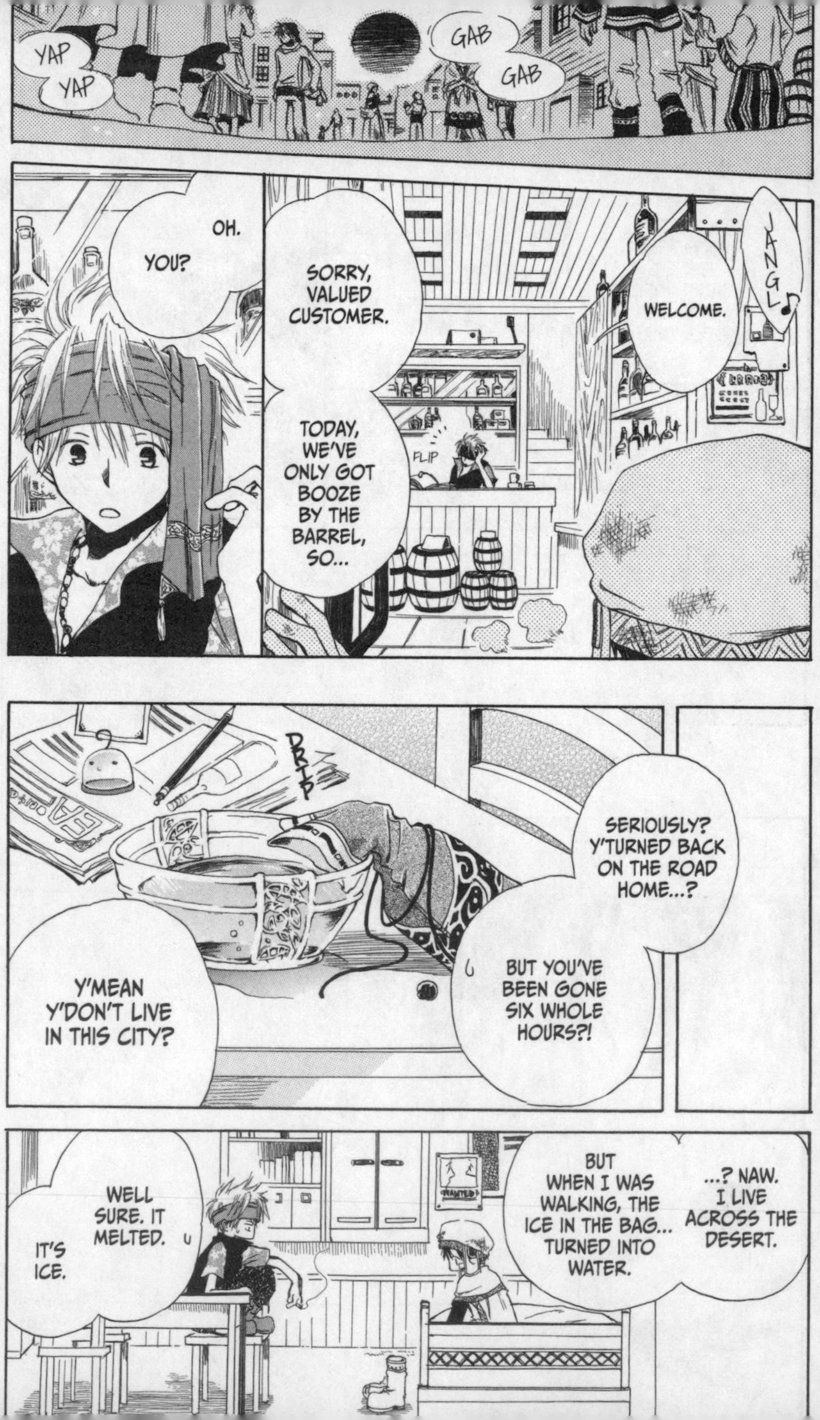
GAB
GAB
YAP
YAP
JANGL♪
WELCOME.
SORRY, VALUED CUSTOMER.
TODAY, WE'VE ONLY GOT BOOZE BY THE BARREL, SO...
FLIP
OH.
YOU?
DRIP
SERIOUSLY? Y'TURNED BACK ON THE ROAD HOME...?
BUT YOU'VE BEEN GONE SIX WHOLE HOURS?!
Y'MEAN Y'DON'T LIVE IN THIS CITY?
...? NAW. I LIVE ACROSS THE DESERT.
BUT WHEN I WAS WALKING, THE ICE IN THE BAG... TURNED INTO WATER.
WELL SURE. IT MELTED.
IT'S ICE.

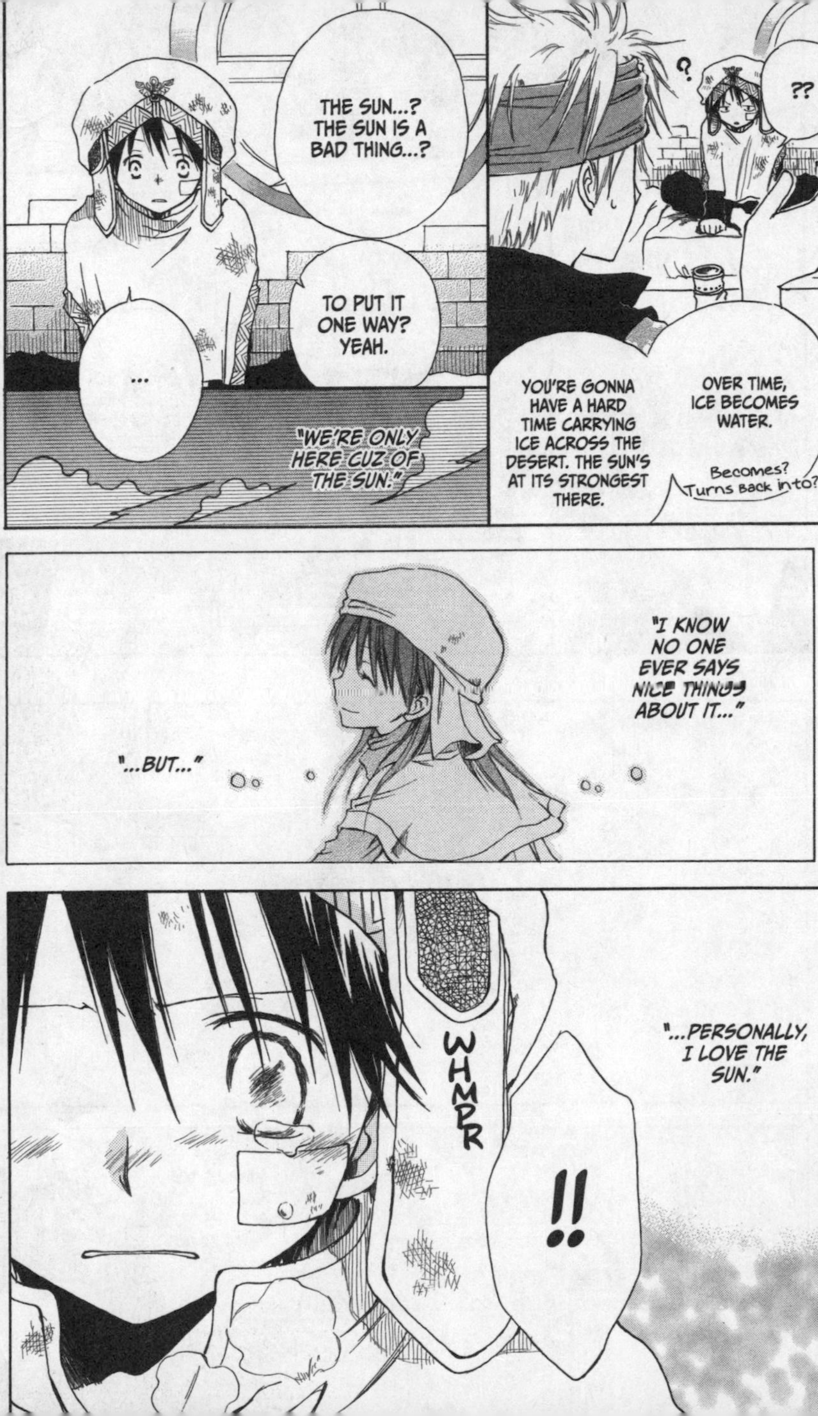
??
?
Over time, ice becomes water.
Erm...
Becomes? Turns back into?
You're gonna have a hard time carrying ice across the desert. The sun's at its strongest there.
The sun...? The sun is a bad thing...?
To put it one way? Yeah.
...
"We're only here cuz of the sun."
"I know no one ever says nice things about it..."
"...But..."
"...Personally, I love the sun."
WHMPR
!!

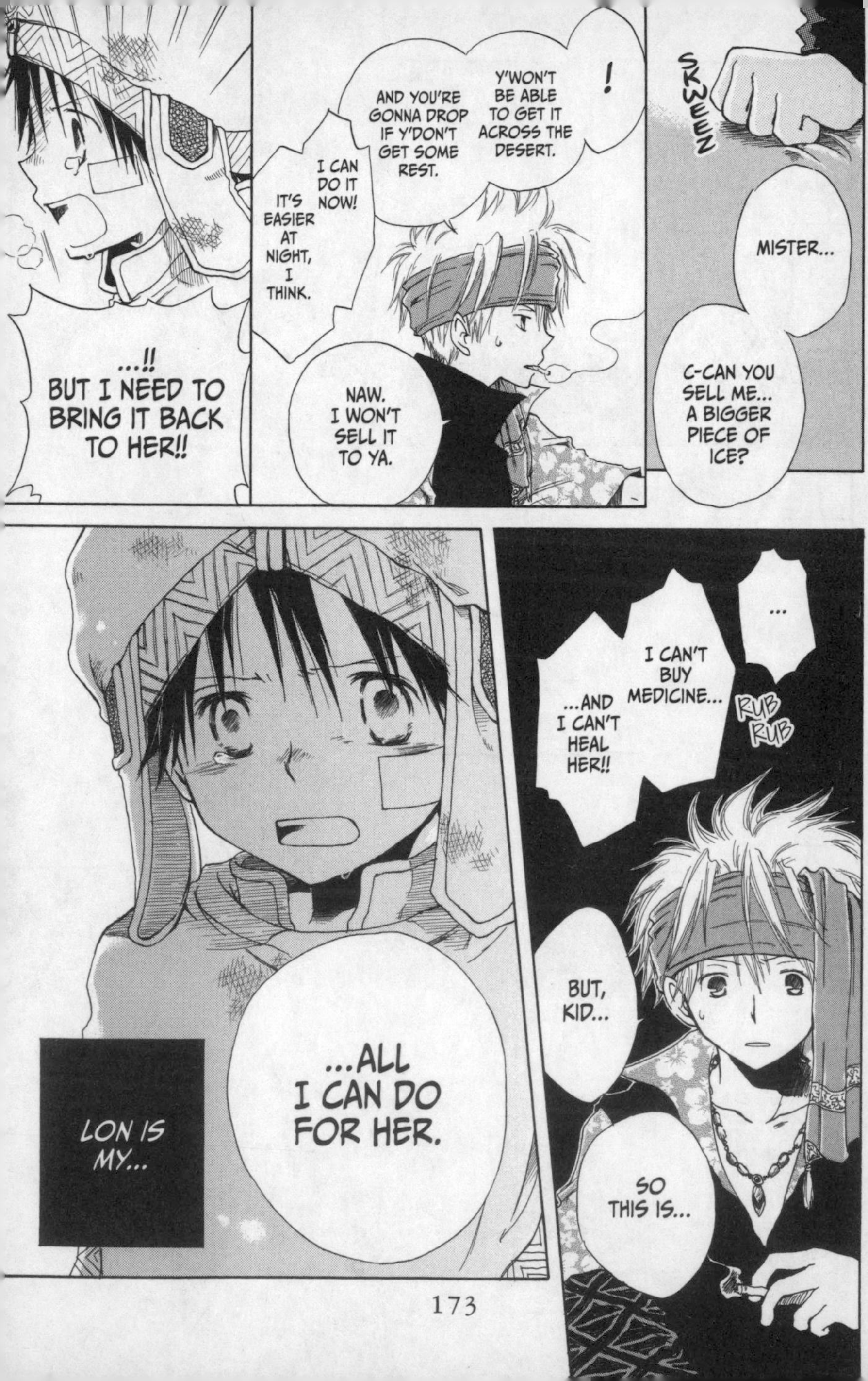

MISTER...
C-CAN YOU SELL ME... A BIGGER PIECE OF ICE?
SKWEEZ
NAW. I WON'T SELL IT TO YA.
!
Y'WON'T BE ABLE TO GET IT ACROSS THE DESERT.
AND YOU'RE GONNA DROP IF Y'DON'T GET SOME REST.
I CAN DO IT NOW!
IT'S EASIER AT NIGHT, I THINK.
...!! BUT I NEED TO BRING IT BACK TO HER!!
...
I CAN'T BUY MEDICINE...
...AND I CAN'T HEAL HER!!
RUB RUB
BUT, KID...
SO THIS IS...
...ALL I CAN DO FOR HER.
LON IS MY...

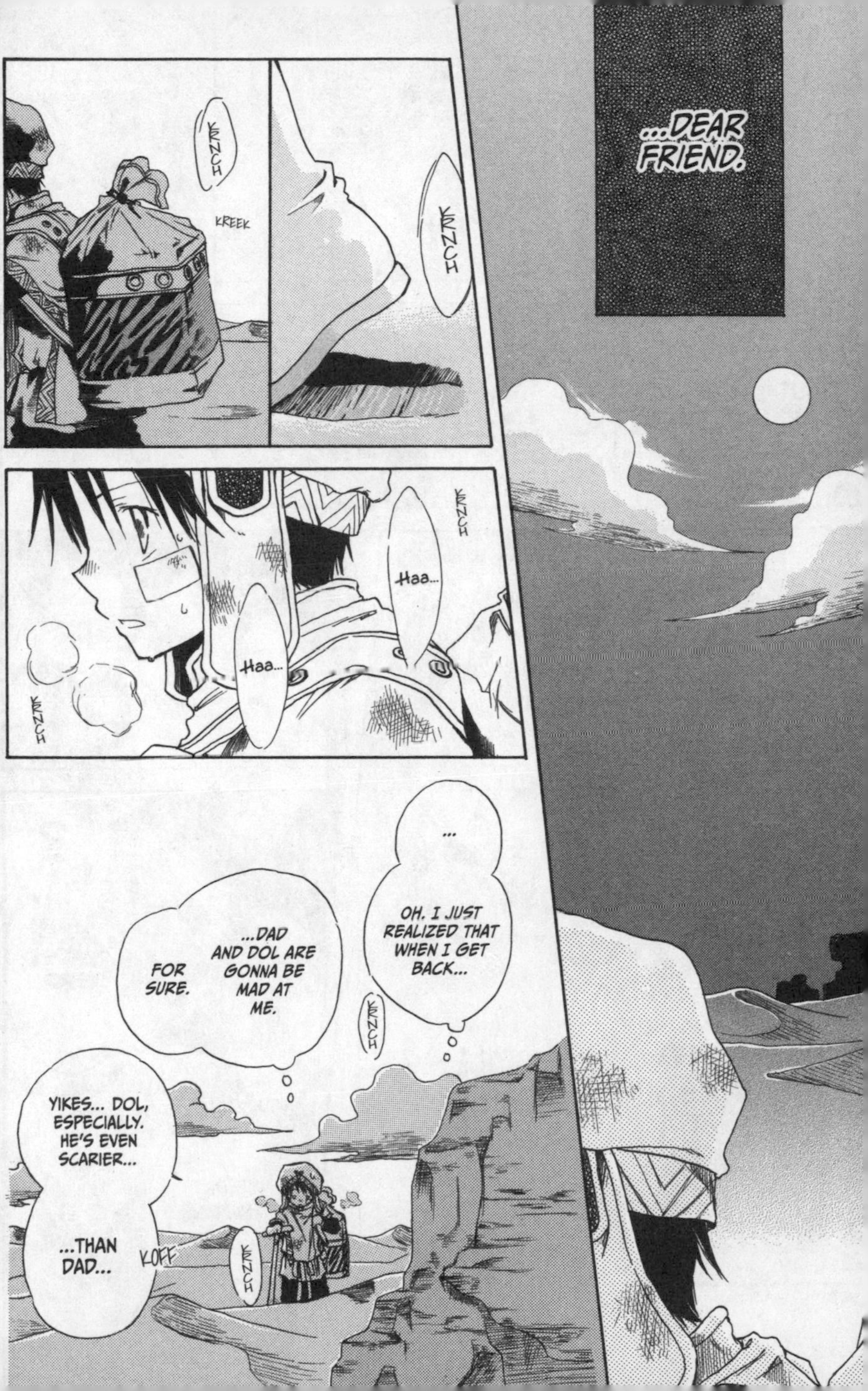
...DEAR FRIEND.
KRENCH
KRENCH
KREEK
Haa...
KRENCH
Haa...
KRENCH
...
OH. I JUST REALIZED THAT WHEN I GET BACK...
KRENCH
...DAD AND DOL ARE GONNA BE MAD AT ME.
FOR SURE.
YIKES... DOL, ESPECIALLY. HE'S EVEN SCARIER...
...THAN DAD...
KOFF
KRENCH

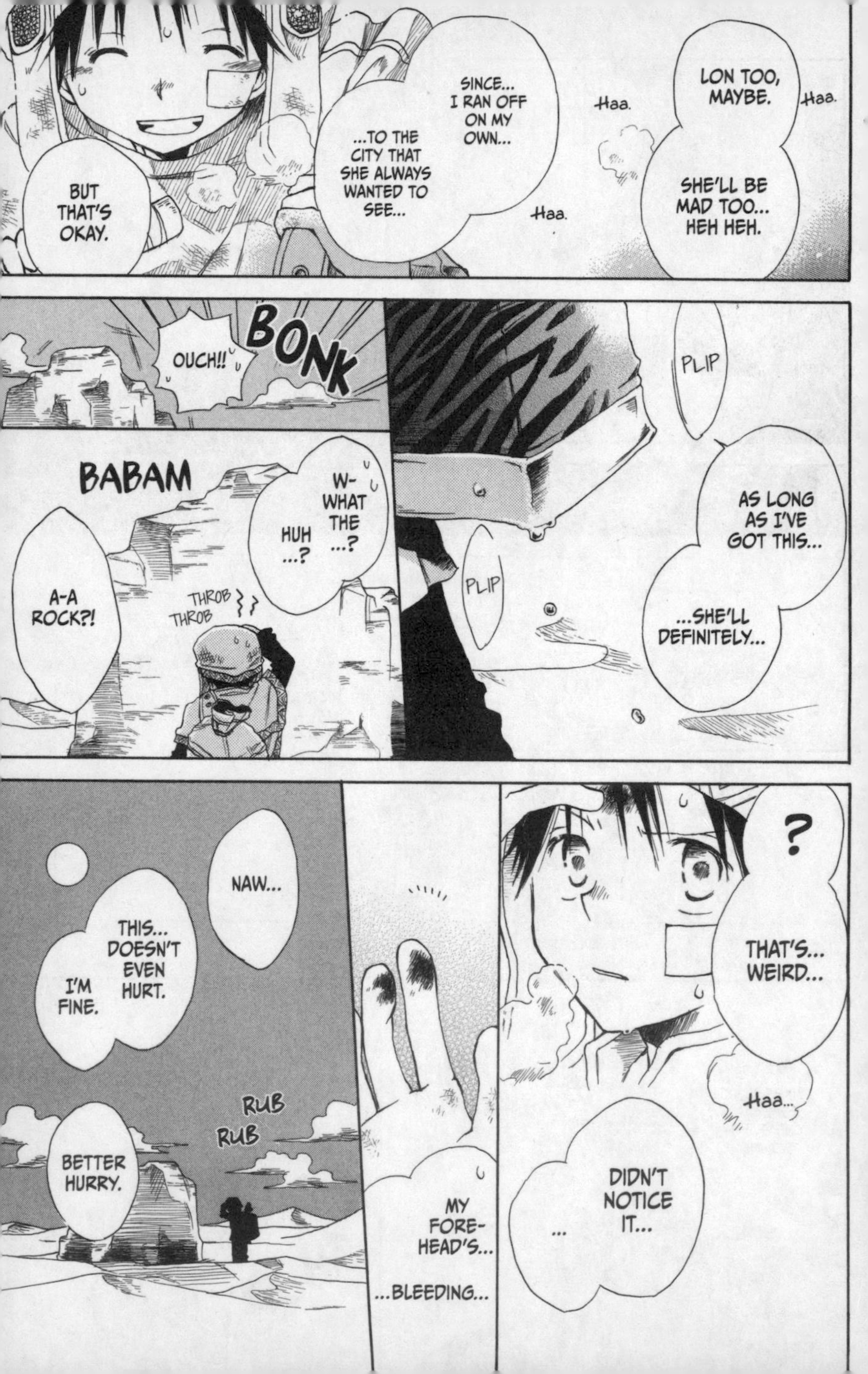
LON TOO, MAYBE.
Haa.
SHE'LL BE MAD TOO... HEH HEH.
Haa.
SINCE... I RAN OFF ON MY OWN...
...TO THE CITY THAT SHE ALWAYS WANTED TO SEE...
Haa.
BUT THAT'S OKAY.
PLIP
AS LONG AS I'VE GOT THIS...
...SHE'LL DEFINITELY...
PLIP
BONK
OUCH!!
BABAM
W-WHAT THE ...?
HUH ...?
THROB THROB
A-A ROCK?!
?
THAT'S... WEIRD...
Haa...
DIDN'T NOTICE IT...
...
MY FOREHEAD'S...
...BLEEDING...
NAW...
THIS... DOESN'T EVEN HURT.
I'M FINE.
RUB RUB
BETTER HURRY.

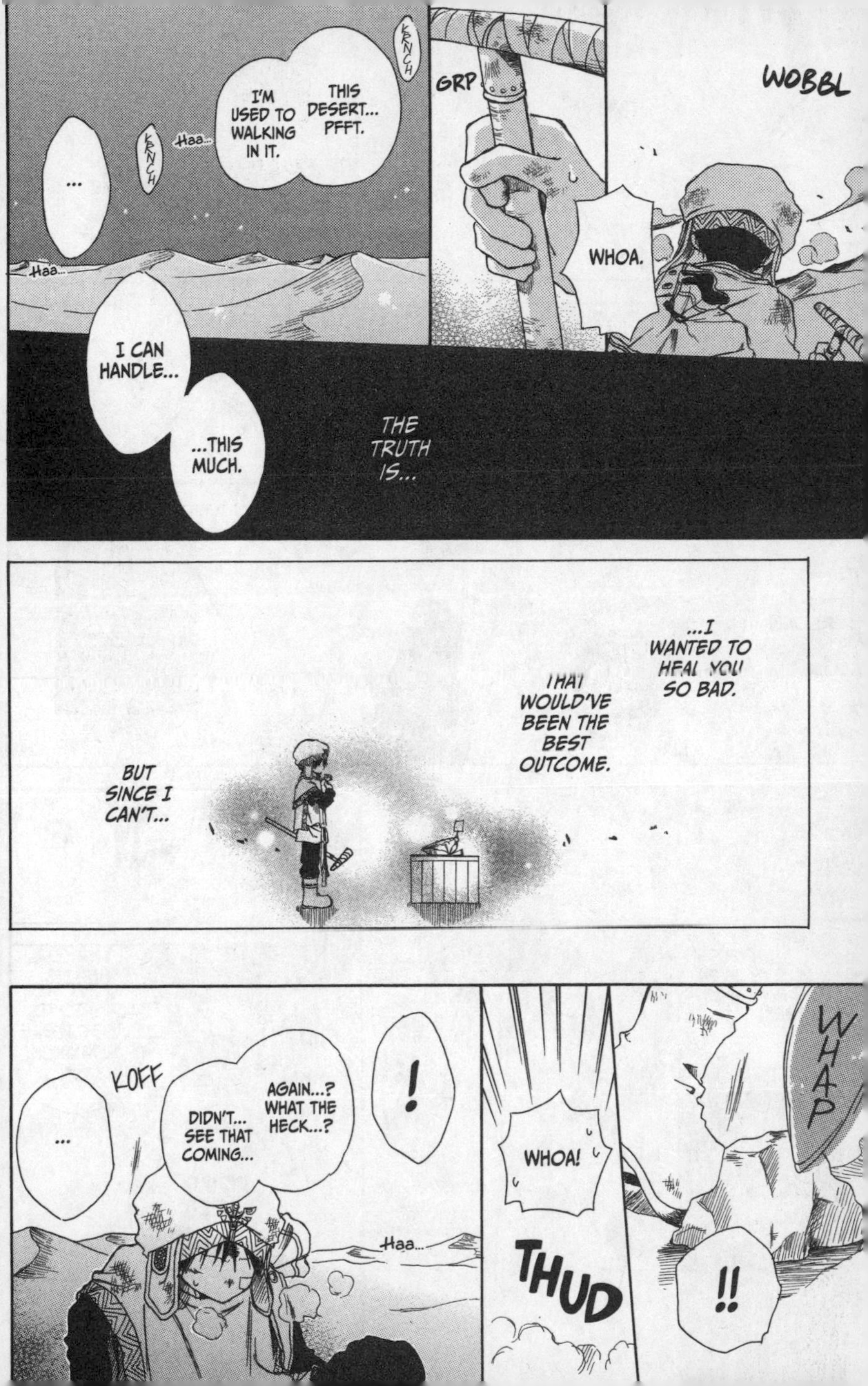
WOBBL
WHOA.
GRP
KRNCH
THIS DESERT... PFFT.
I'M USED TO WALKING IN IT.
Haa...
KRNCH
...
Haa...
I CAN HANDLE...
...THIS MUCH.
THE TRUTH IS...
...I WANTED TO HEAL YOU SO BAD.
THAT WOULD'VE BEEN THE BEST OUTCOME.
BUT SINCE I CAN'T...
WHAP
!!
WHOA!
THUD
!
AGAIN...? WHAT THE HECK...?
DIDN'T... SEE THAT COMING...
KOFF
...
Haa...

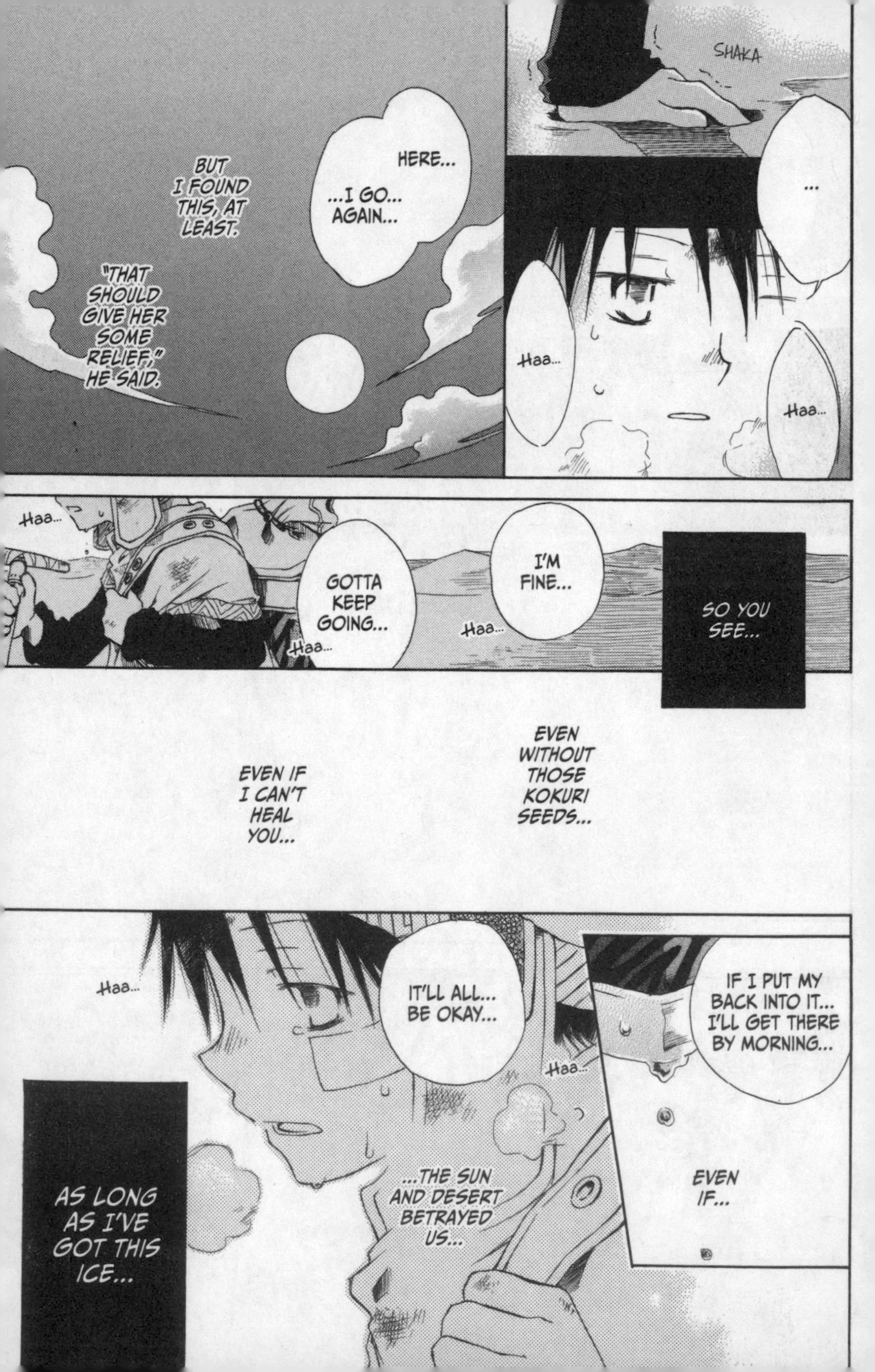
SHAKA
...
Haa...
Haa...
HERE...
...I GO... AGAIN...
BUT I FOUND THIS, AT LEAST.
"THAT SHOULD GIVE HER SOME RELIEF," HE SAID.
SO YOU SEE...
I'M FINE...
Haa...
GOTTA KEEP GOING...
Haa...
Haa...
EVEN WITHOUT THOSE KOKURI SEEDS...
EVEN IF I CAN'T HEAL YOU...
IF I PUT MY BACK INTO IT... I'LL GET THERE BY MORNING...
EVEN IF...
IT'LL ALL... BE OKAY...
Haa...
Haa...
...THE SUN AND DESERT BETRAYED US...
AS LONG AS I'VE GOT THIS ICE...

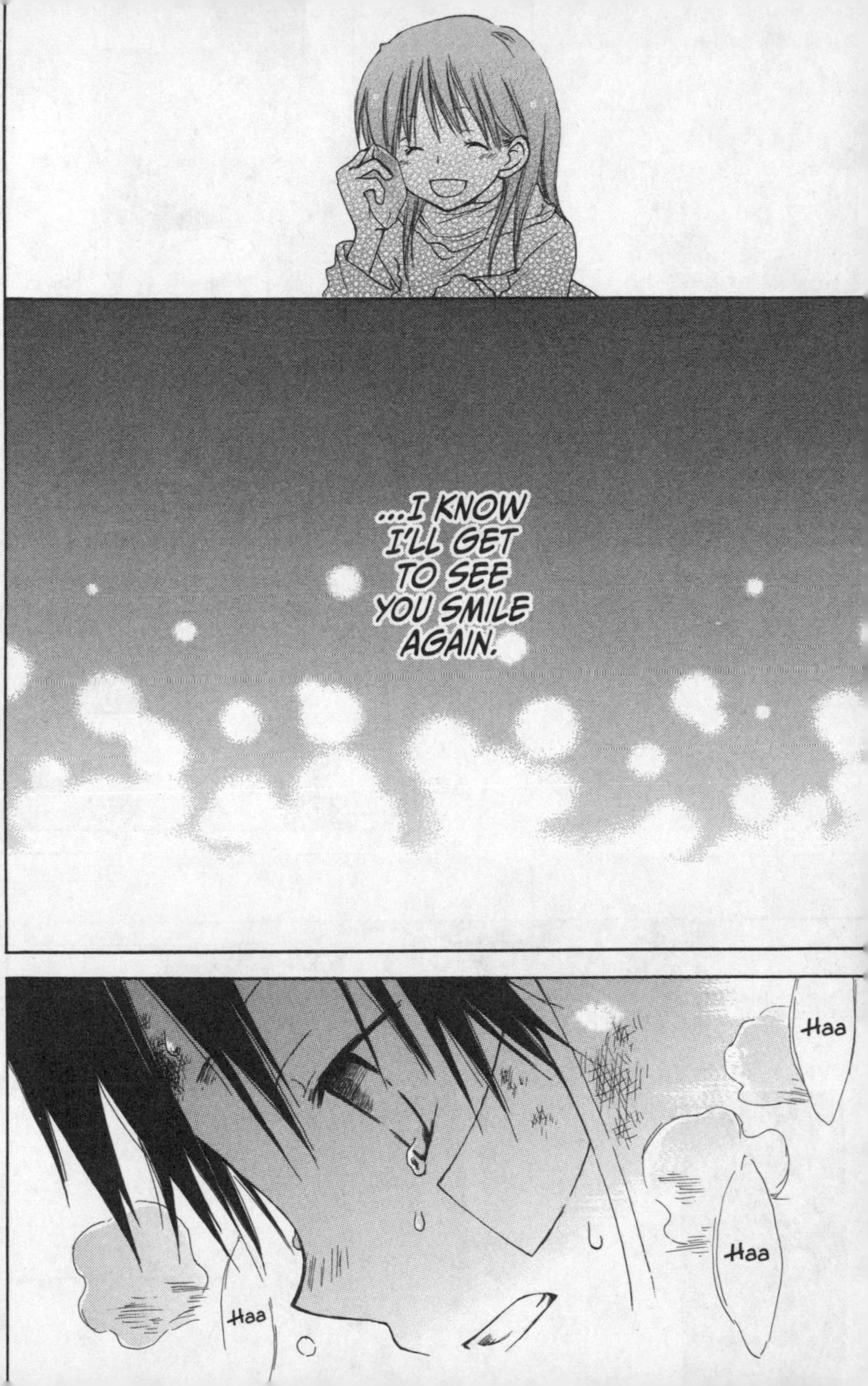
...I KNOW I'LL GET TO SEE YOU SMILE AGAIN.
Haa
Haa
Haa

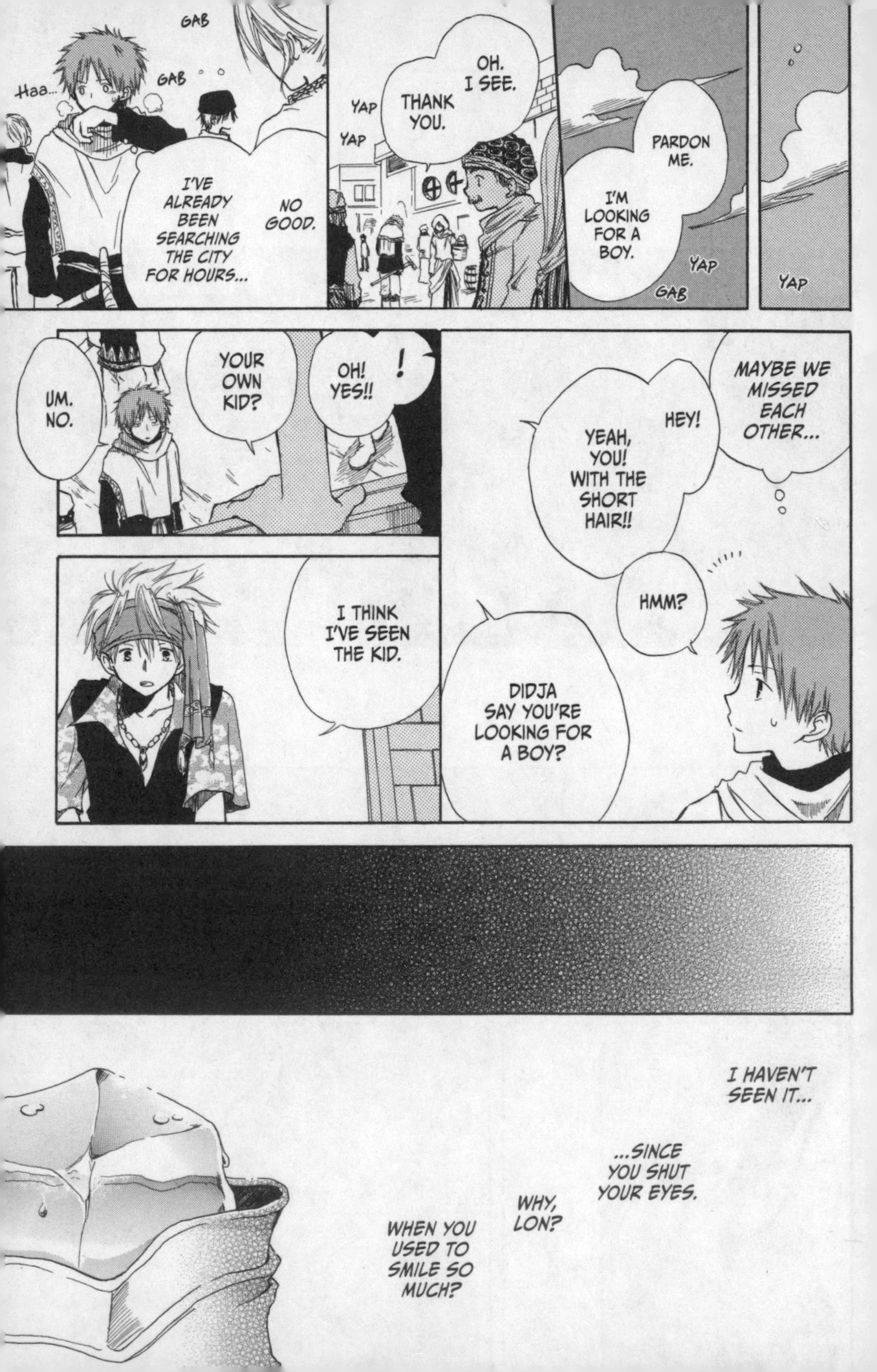
YAP
PARDON ME.
I'M LOOKING FOR A BOY.
YAP
GAB
OH. I SEE.
THANK YOU.
YAP
YAP
GAB
GAB
Haa...
I'VE ALREADY BEEN SEARCHING THE CITY FOR HOURS...
NO GOOD.
MAYBE WE MISSED EACH OTHER...
HEY!
YEAH, YOU! WITH THE SHORT HAIR!!
HMM?
!
OH! YES!!
YOUR OWN KID?
UM. NO.
DIDJA SAY YOU'RE LOOKING FOR A BOY?
I THINK I'VE SEEN THE KID.
I HAVEN'T SEEN IT...
...SINCE YOU SHUT YOUR EYES.
WHY, LON?
WHEN YOU USED TO SMILE SO MUCH?

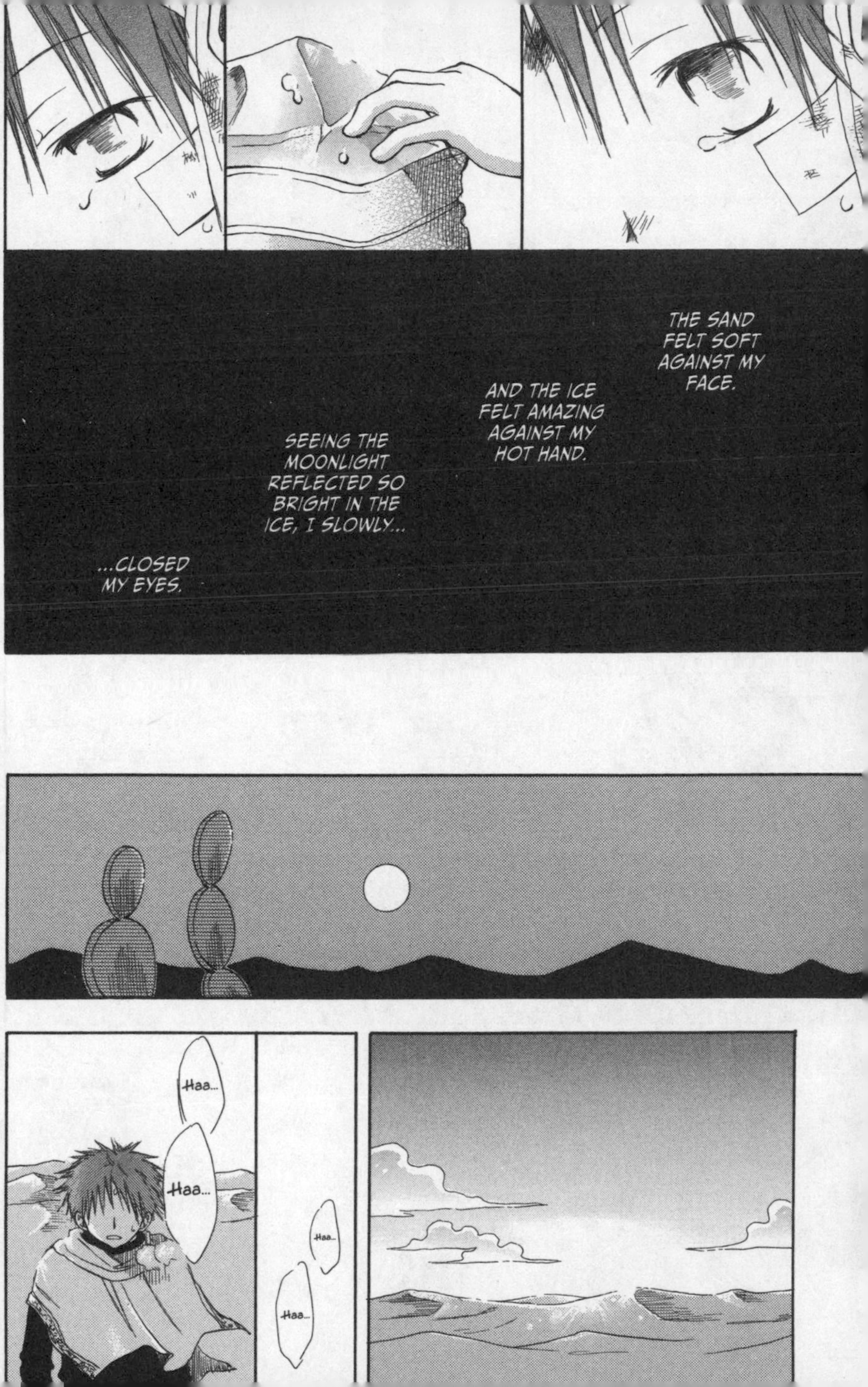
THE SAND FELT SOFT AGAINST MY FACE.
AND THE ICE FELT AMAZING AGAINST MY HOT HAND.
SEEING THE MOONLIGHT REFLECTED SO BRIGHT IN THE ICE, I SLOWLY...
...CLOSED MY EYES.
Haa...
Haa...
Haa...
Haa...

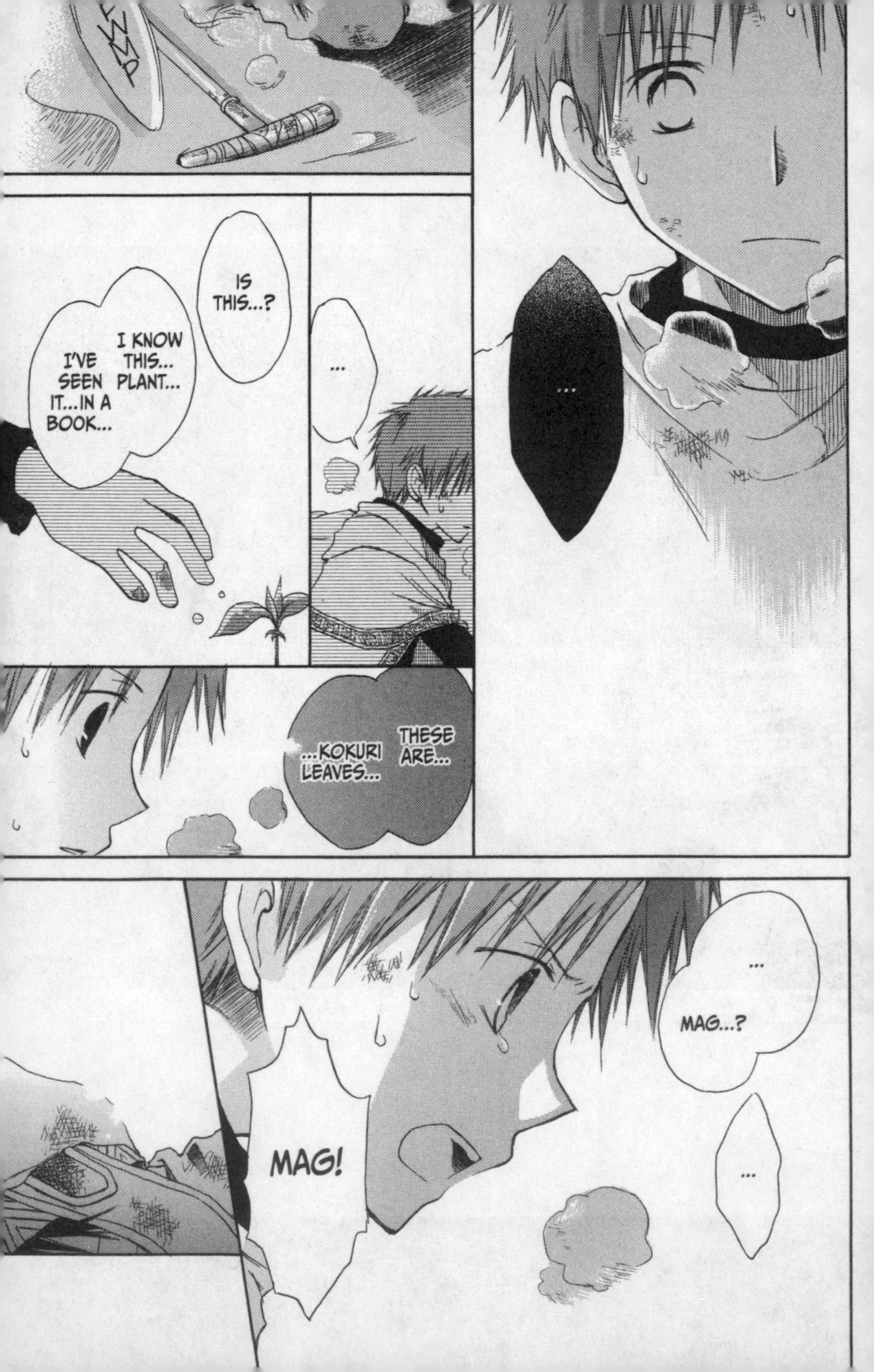
...
...
IS THIS...?
I KNOW THIS... PLANT... I'VE SEEN IT...IN A BOOK...
THESE ARE... ...KOKURI LEAVES...
... MAG...?
...
MAG!

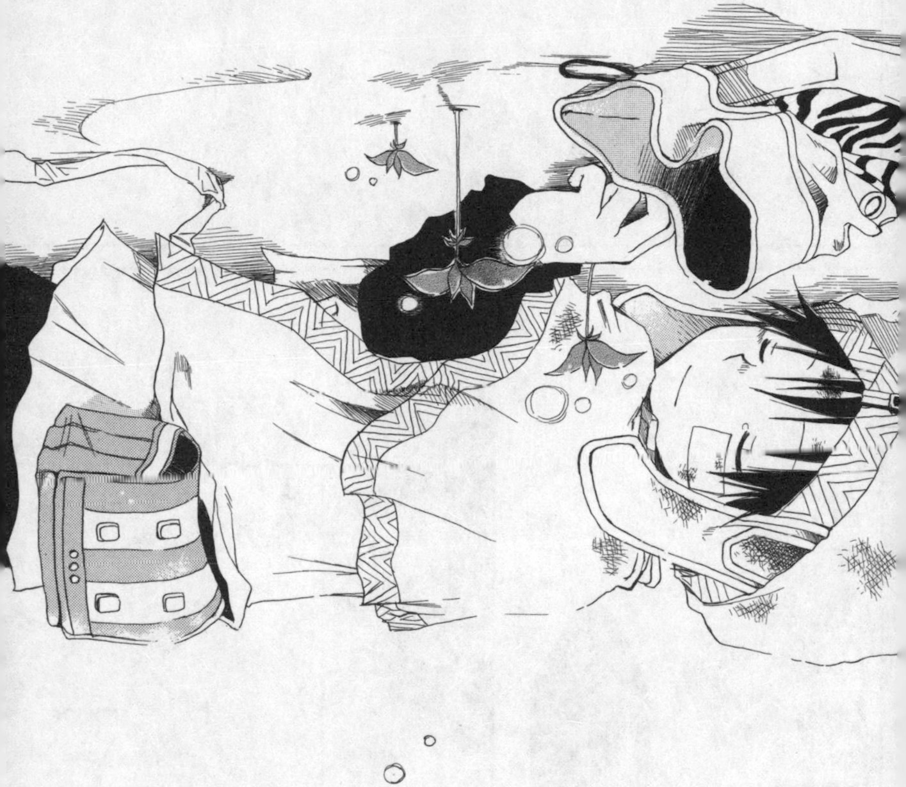

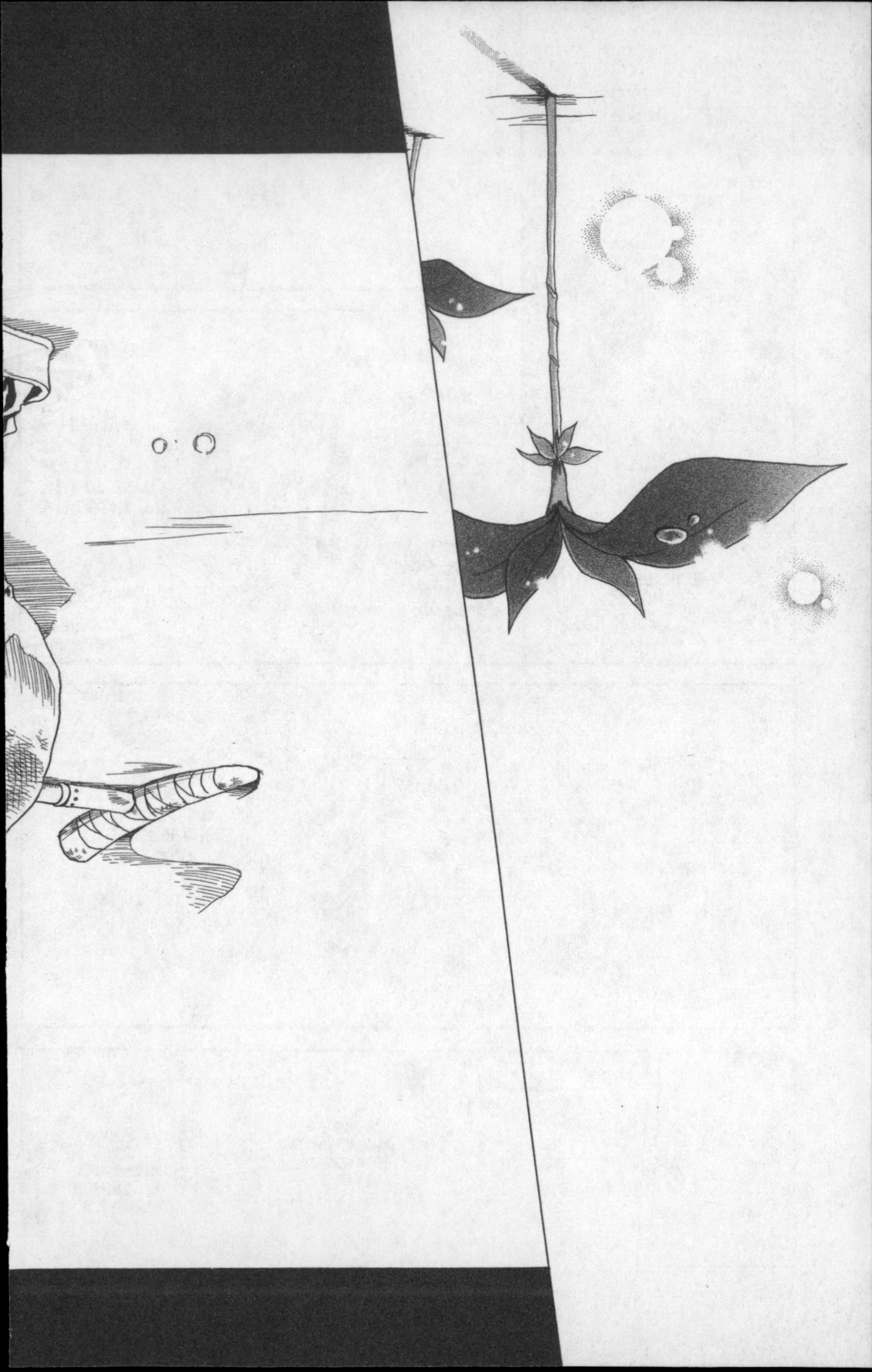

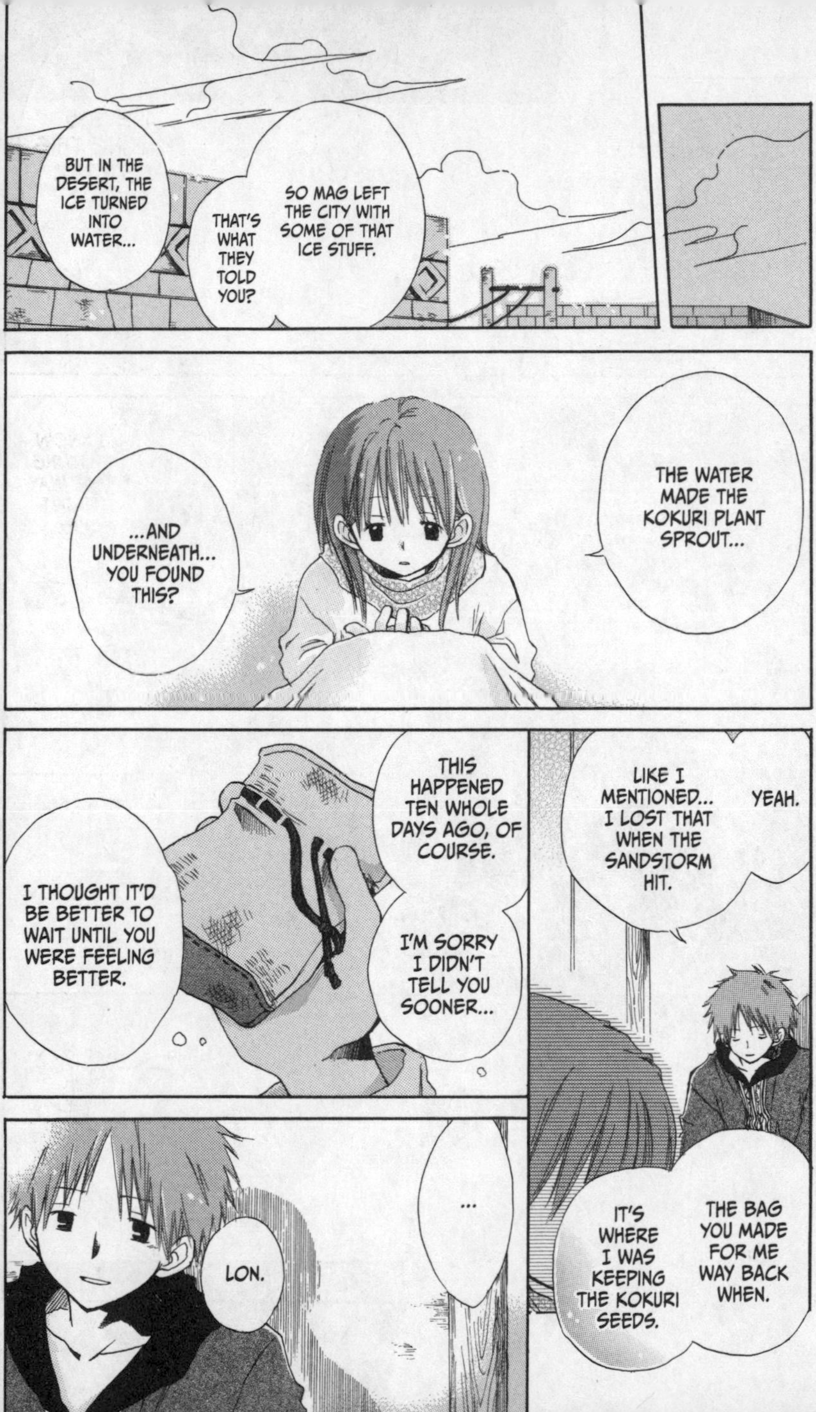
SO MAG LEFT THE CITY WITH SOME OF THAT ICE STUFF.
THAT'S WHAT THEY TOLD YOU?
BUT IN THE DESERT, THE ICE TURNED INTO WATER...
THE WATER MADE THE KOKURI PLANT SPROUT...
...AND UNDERNEATH... YOU FOUND THIS?
YEAH.
LIKE I MENTIONED... I LOST THAT WHEN THE SANDSTORM HIT.
THE BAG YOU MADE FOR ME WAY BACK WHEN.
IT'S WHERE I WAS KEEPING THE KOKURI SEEDS.
THIS HAPPENED TEN WHOLE DAYS AGO, OF COURSE.
I'M SORRY I DIDN'T TELL YOU SOONER...
I THOUGHT IT'D BE BETTER TO WAIT UNTIL YOU WERE FEELING BETTER.
...
LON.

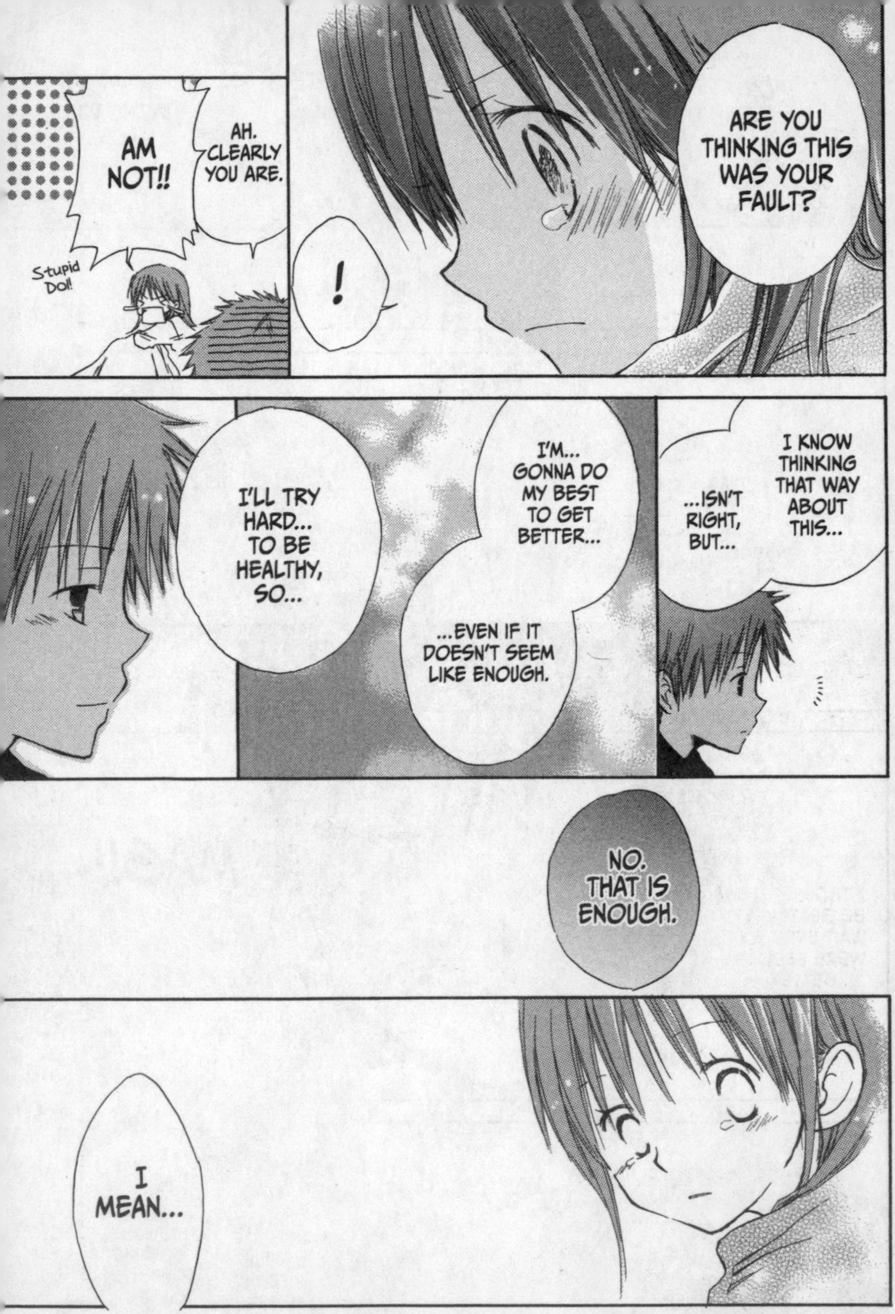
ARE YOU THINKING THIS WAS YOUR FAULT?
!
AH. CLEARLY YOU ARE.
AM NOT!!
Stupid Doll!
I KNOW THINKING THAT WAY ABOUT THIS...
...ISN'T RIGHT, BUT...
I'M... GONNA DO MY BEST TO GET BETTER...
...EVEN IF IT DOESN'T SEEM LIKE ENOUGH.
I'LL TRY HARD... TO BE HEALTHY, SO...
NO. THAT IS ENOUGH.
I MEAN...

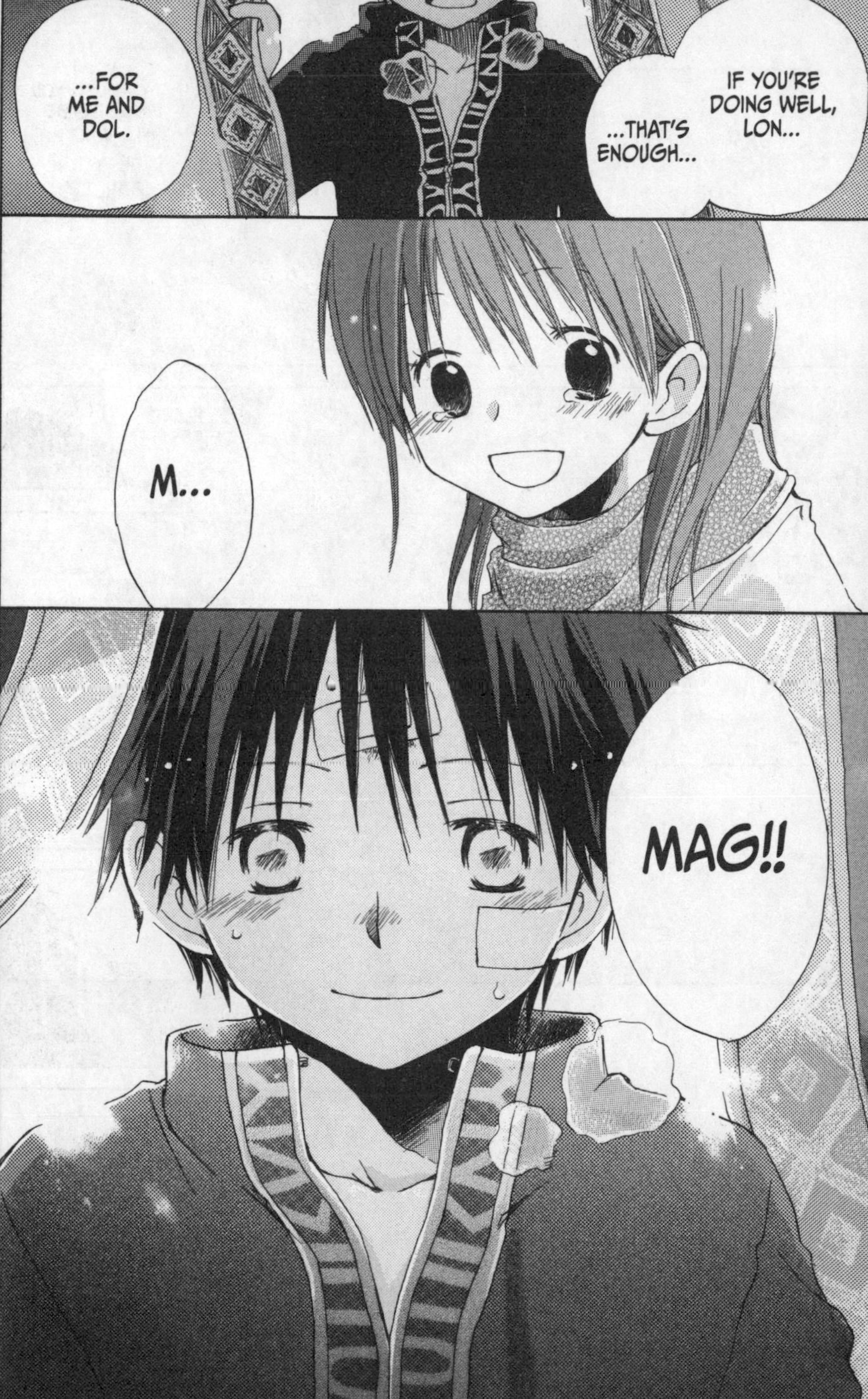
IF YOU'RE DOING WELL, LON...
...THAT'S ENOUGH...
...FOR ME AND DOL.
M...
MAG!!

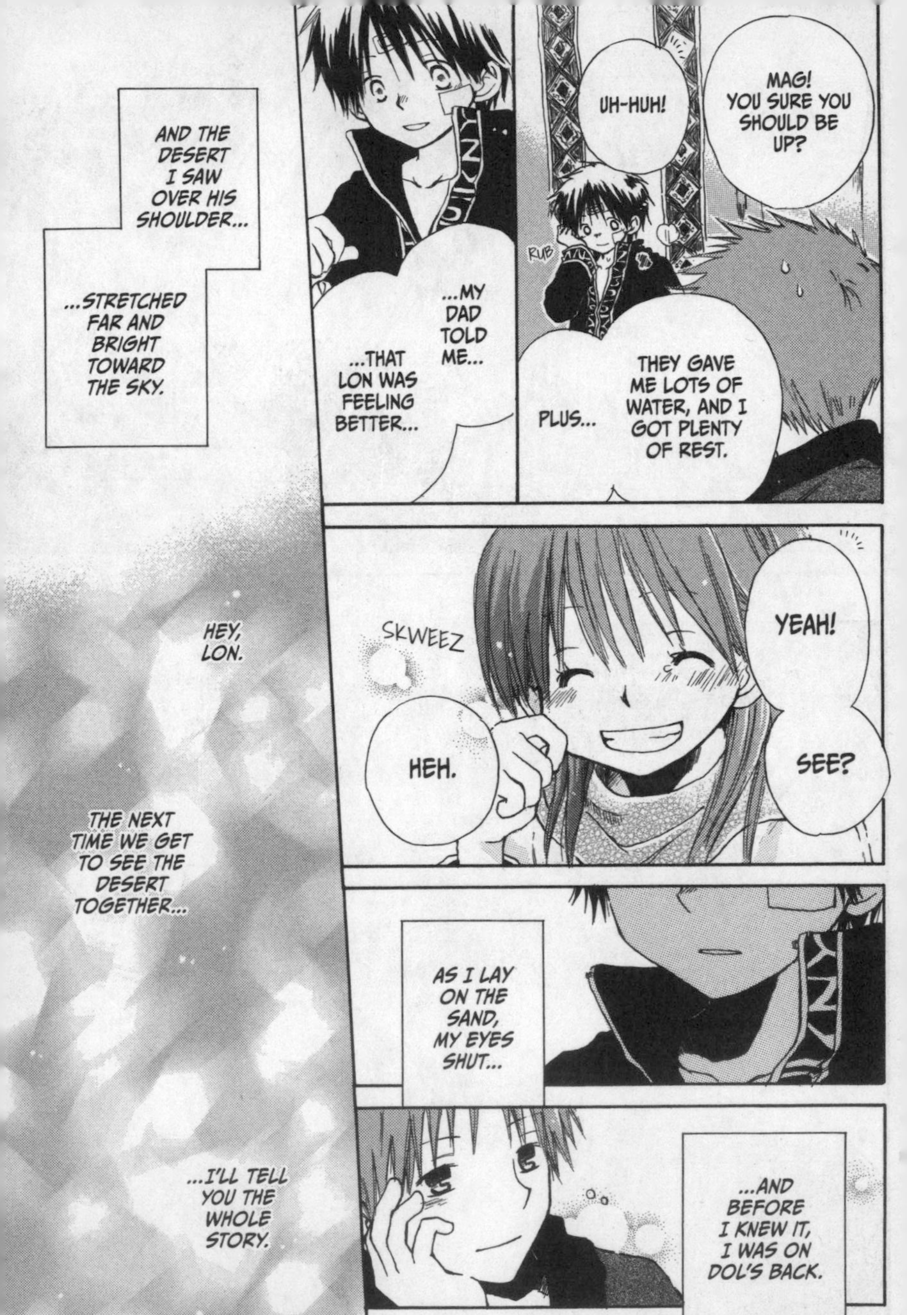
MAG! YOU SURE YOU SHOULD BE UP?
UH-HUH!
RUB
THEY GAVE ME LOTS OF WATER, AND I GOT PLENTY OF REST.
PLUS...
...MY DAD TOLD ME...
...THAT LON WAS FEELING BETTER...
YEAH!
SEE?
SKWEEZ
HEH.
AS I LAY ON THE SAND, MY EYES SHUT...
...AND BEFORE I KNEW IT, I WAS ON DOL'S BACK.
AND THE DESERT I SAW OVER HIS SHOULDER...
...STRETCHED FAR AND BRIGHT TOWARD THE SKY.
HEY, LON.
THE NEXT TIME WE GET TO SEE THE DESERT TOGETHER...
...I'LL TELL YOU THE WHOLE STORY.

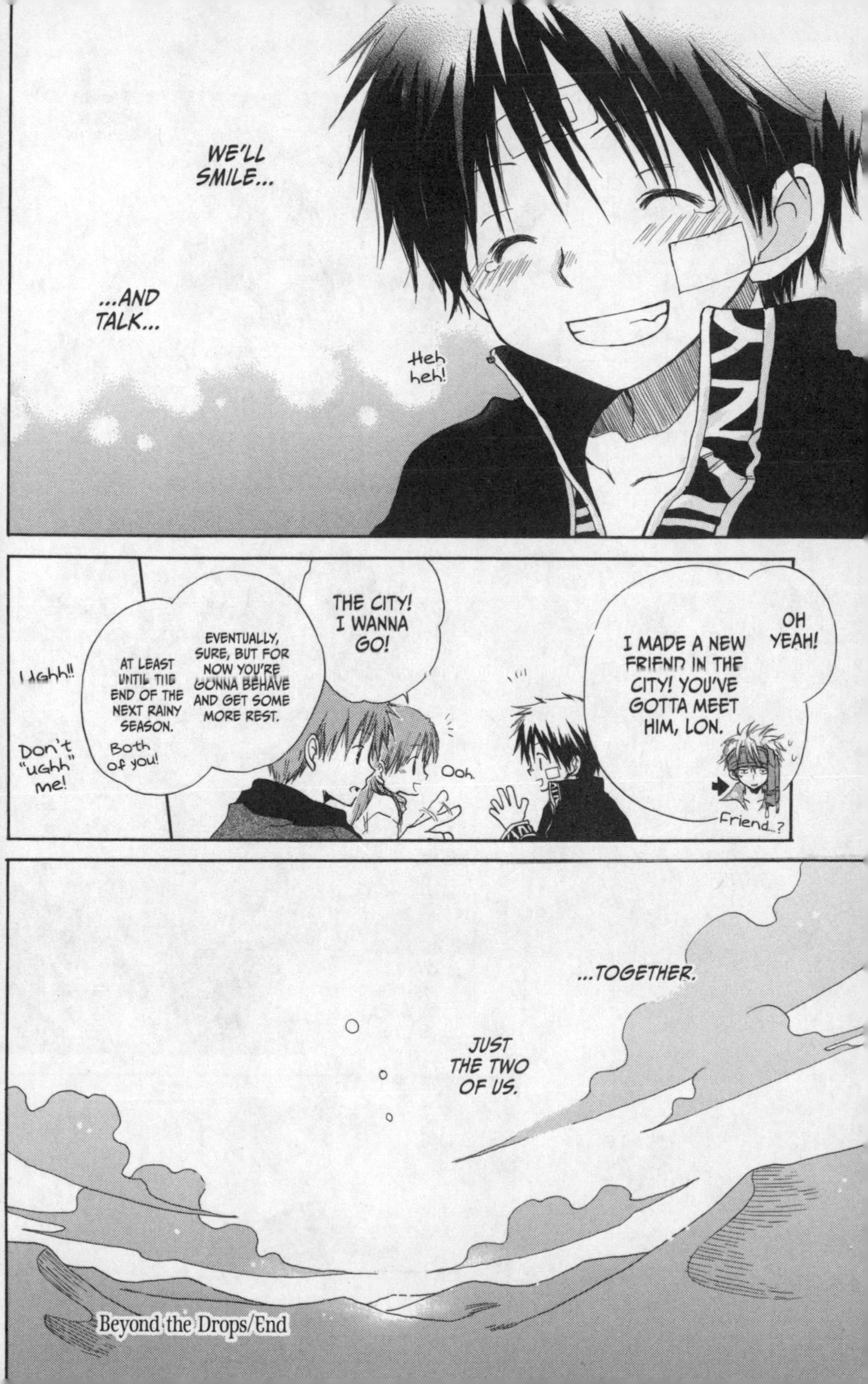
WE'LL SMILE...
...AND TALK...
Heh heh!
OH YEAH!
I MADE A NEW FRIEND IN THE CITY! YOU'VE GOTTA MEET HIM, LON.
Friend...?
Ooh.
THE CITY! I WANNA GO!
EVENTUALLY, SURE, BUT FOR NOW YOU'RE GONNA BEHAVE AND GET SOME MORE REST.
AT LEAST UNTIL THE END OF THE NEXT RAINY SEASON.
Both of you!
Ughh!!
Don't "ughh" me!
...TOGETHER.
JUST THE TWO OF US.
Beyond the Drops/End

Royal Palace Records

Hey, Obi. Why do you call Kiki "Princess Kiki"?
Why was it again?
Dunno. You just always have.
So do you never wanna talk about that ever again?
GAB
GAB
It honestly doesn't matter at this point.
Thought you'd say that.
Oh.
Kiki and Obi?
There they are.
I've got some free time this afternoon. If you're going out, can I tag along?
Well, Kiki?
Ah.
Sure.

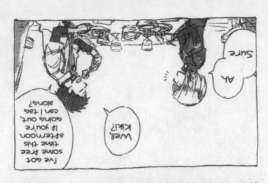

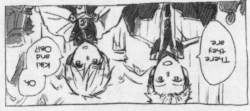

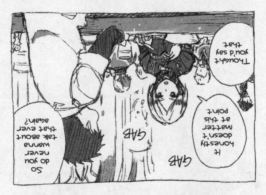

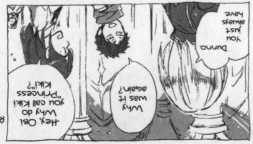

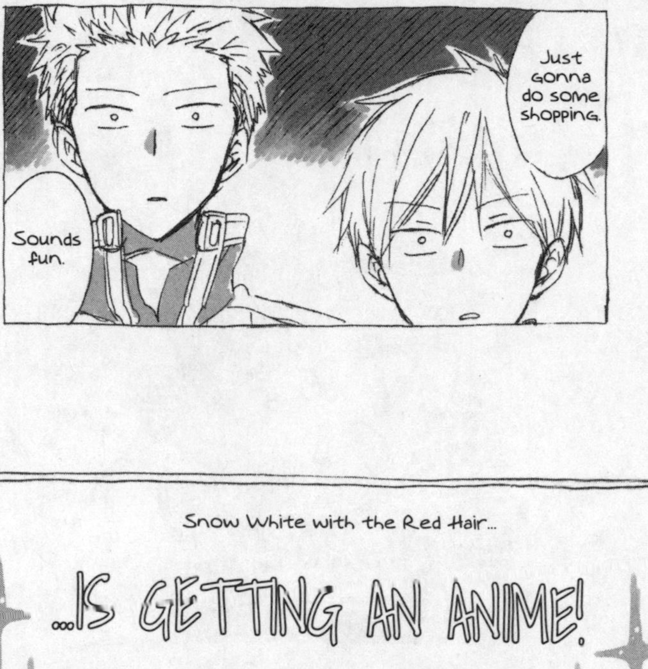
Just gonna do some shopping.
Sounds fun.

Snow White with the Red Hair...

...IS GETTING AN ANIME!

Thank you!

Starting Summer 2015!

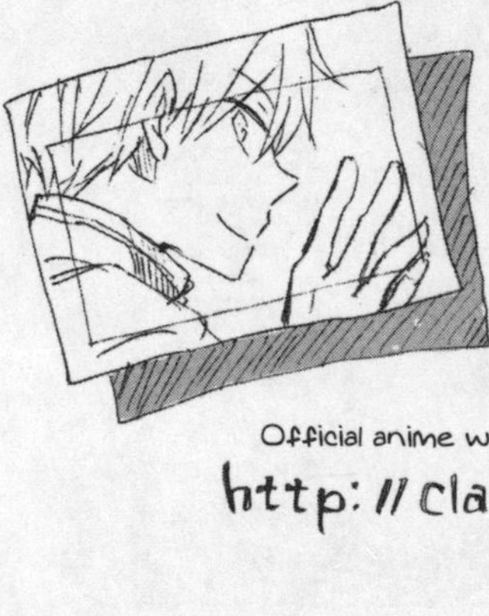

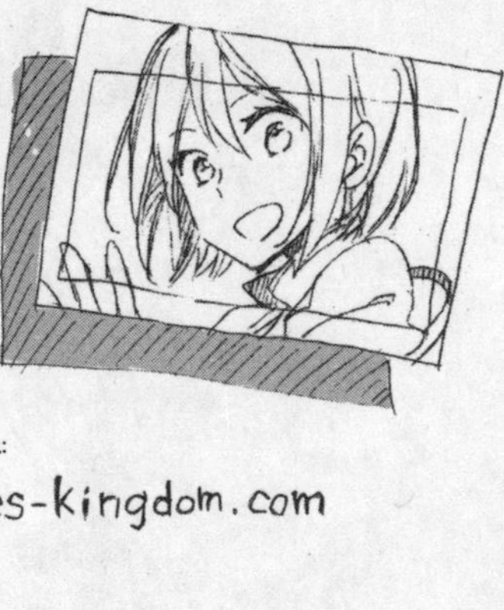

Official anime website:

http://clarines-kingdom.com

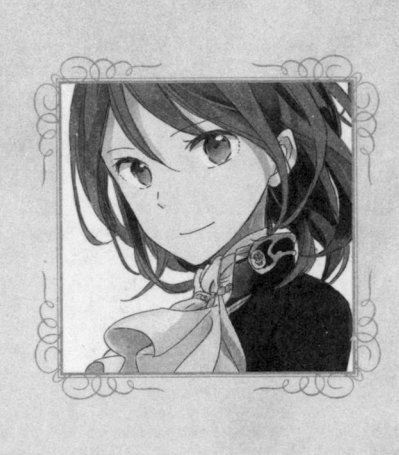

Sorata Akiduki was born on March 21 and is an accomplished shojo manga author. She made her debut in January 2002 with a one-shot titled "Utopia." Her previous works include *Vahlia no Hanamuko* (Vahlia's Bridegroom), *Seishun Kouryakubon* (Youth Strategy Guide) and *Natsu Yasumi Zero Zero Nichime* (00 Days of Summer Vacation). *Snow White with the Red Hair* began serialization in August 2006 in *LaLa DX* in Japan and has since moved to *LaLa*.

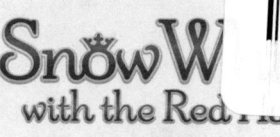

Snow White
with the Red Hair

13

SHOJO BEAT EDITION

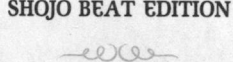

STORY AND ART BY
Sorata Akiduki

TRANSLATION **Caleb Cook**
TOUCH-UP ART & LETTERING **Brandon Bovia**
DESIGN **Alice Lewis**
EDITOR **Karla Clark**

Akagami no Shirayukihime by Sorata Akiduki
© Sorata Akiduki 2015
All rights reserved.
First published in Japan in 2015 by HAKUSENSHA, Inc., Tokyo.
English language translation rights arranged with HAKUSENSHA, Inc., Tokyo.

Printed in Canada

Published by VIZ Media, LLC
P.O. Box 77010
San Francisco, CA 94107

10 9 8 7 6 5 4 3 2 1
First printing, May 2021

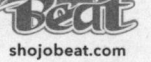

VIZ MEDIA
viz.com

Shojo Beat
shojobeat.com